THE FABRIC OF GENDER

HELEN HARDEN CHENUT

THE FABRIC OF GENDER

WORKING-CLASS
CULTURE
IN
THIRD REPUBLIC
FRANCE

THE PENNSYLVANIA STATE UNIVERSITY PRESS
UNIVERSITY PARK, PENNSYLVANIA

Library of Congress Cataloging-in-Publication Data

Chenut, Helen Harden, 1939–
The fabric of gender : working-class culture in Third Republic France /
Helen Harden Chenut.
p.   cm.
Includes bibliographical references and index.
ISBN 0-271-02520-4 (alk. paper)
1. Textile industry—France—Troyes—History—Third Republic, 1870–1940.
2. Working class—France—Troyes—History—Third Republic, 1870–1940.
3. Industrial relations—France—Troyes—History—Third Republic, 1870–1940.
4. Women textile workers—France—Troyes—History—Third Republic, 1870–1940.
5. Sexual division of labor—France—History—Third Republic, 1870–1940.
I. Title: Working-class culture in Third Republic France.
II. Title.

HD8039 .T42 F818 2005
331.7′677′00944331—dc22
2004015329

CONTENTS

ACKNOWLEDGMENTS

In the course of my research and in writing this book I have incurred many debts among friends and colleagues, here and in France, and it is a pleasure to acknowledge their contributions. With their generous help, advice, expertise, and often shelter over the years I have been able to complete this project. In the early stages in France, I had the privilege of being part of a research team, one of the first at the Centre National de la Recherche Scientifique to focus on gender and work, the Groupe d'études sur les rapports sociaux et sexuels du travail, or GEDISST, in Paris. Discussions and lively debates in research seminars with Danièle Kergoat, Helena Hirata, Danièle Senotier, Chantal Rogerat, and Danièle Chabaud, among others, enriched my analysis of women's industrial work. In the early years of conceptualizing and striving to obtain recognition for gender and women's history in France, I enjoyed the intellectual friendship, collaboration, and complicity of feminist historians Eleni Varikas, Michèle Riot-Sarcey, Florence Rochefort, Christine Bard, Marie-Hélène Zylberberg-Hocquard, and Sian Reynolds. In Troyes, the staff of the Archives départmentales de l'Aube were helpful, resourceful, and engaging as my project and my needs developed from a dissertation into a book, and I wish to thank Xavier Delaselle, director; Claire Pigné (who always found "the carton" I was looking for); Rose Charpentier; Veronique Kientzy; and Philippe Cornette. I also wish to thank Jean Lejeune and Bernard Blée, at the Archives municipales de Troyes, and Thierry Delcourt, Marie Claude Babeau-Wagnon, and Hervé Georget, at the Bibliothèque municipale de Troyes, for their professional help and support. I am deeply grateful to Jacqueline Viard for making me feel a "Troyenne" by adoption over many years of friendship and shelter in Sainte Savine. It is impossible to thank the many other Troyens who shared their knowledge with me, but Jean Darbot, Jeannette and Hugue Petitjean, Daniel Poulet, André Boisseau, and Jean-Louis Humbert deserve special mention. I also acknowledge with gratitude many of the photographs for this book that were loaned by Claude Bérisé from his personal collection.

Finally, Mme Detret in Chateau-Thierry helped me to trace the final years of the Laborieuse in the archives of the Coopérateurs de Champagne.

This study owes much of its initial inspiration to the work of Michelle Perrot. Her multifaceted study of strike movements as a lens for examining working-class culture provided a model of scholarship. I feel enormously privileged to have benefited from her generous and unflagging support, from her many forms of kindness that encouraged and sustained my work. Her energetic defense of women's history in France has allowed many of us, her doctoral students, to find some measure of support for it today. I extend my special thanks also to textile historian Serge Chassagne, whose intellectual friendship, dating from when we met during my oral defense, has developed over the years into collaboration; and to my dear friend and cousin Mary Kergall, for her research and her child-care support.

Several friends here in the United States have contributed to making this study a better book by reading portions of the manuscript. My thanks to Laura Frader, Donald Reid, Judy Coffin, Theresa McBride, Jeff Horn, and Lenard Berlanstein. The work of Lynn Hunt and Colin Heywood on the revolutionary period and the nineteenth century in Troyes also provided me with a valuable fresh rethinking of political, economic, and social questions on the Champagne region, and the possibility of friendly exchange and debate. Several of the chapters also profited from discussions in collective settings: at the Bunting Institute of Radcliffe College (1993–94), at the Social History Seminar at the University of Massachusetts at Amherst, with colleagues at the Labor Studies Research Group at UCI, and finally, at the French History colloquium at the National Humanities Center in North Carolina.

I gratefully acknowledge the financial support of the American Council of Learned Societies, which made it possible for me to take precious time from teaching to write. I also wish to thank the Labor Studies Research Program and the Humanities Center at the University of California at Irvine for generously providing publications subsidies for this book. Among the colleagues in the history department who have lent a special hand to this project, I would like to thank Marc Kanda for drawing the maps.

Finally, my special affection for France has been shared and nurtured with loving support from Maria Chenut, Nicolas Tackett, and especially Timothy Tackett, all of whom have believed in me and in this project. This book is dedicated to them.

Portions of Chapter 4 have been previously published in a somewhat different version in "The Gendering of Skill as Historical Process: The Case of French Knitters in Industrial Troyes, 1880–1939," in *Gender and Class in Modern Europe*, edited by Laura Frader and Sonya Rose, 1996. Copyright 1996 by Cornell University Press.

LIST OF ILLUSTRATIONS

LIST OF ABBREVIATIONS

ADA   Archives départementales de l'Aube

AMT   Archives municipales de l'Aube

AN   Archives nationales

BCS   Bourse des coopératives socialistes

BHVP   Bibliothèque historique de la Ville de Paris

BMD   Bibliothèque Marguerite Durand

BMT   Bibliothèque municipale de Troyes

CFTC   Confédération française des travailleurs chrétiens

CGT   Confédération générale du travail

CGTU   Confédération générale du travail unifié

FNCC   Fédération nationale des coopératives de consommation

PCF   Parti communiste français

POF   Parti ouvrier français

SFIO   Section française de l'internationale ouvrière

UC   Union coopérative

UFSF   Union française pour le suffrage des femmes

INTRODUCTION

"The fear of famine, which was so obsessive in the early days of the revolution, had dissipated," wrote Emile Pouget and Emile Pataud in their 1909 novel, which imagined a revolutionary utopian society.[1] "The drive to produce had been so intense that abundance swelled like a flood—and with it grew enchantment. A joy for life [*joie de vivre*] flowed and extended everywhere, and we laughed at yesterday's worries. . . . Theoreticians of exploitation had repeatedly argued that compulsion was indispensable in harnessing men to work, because without the incentive of hunger, without the lure of profit, man would become lazy." But as the authors described it, a capitalist society destabilized by crises of overproduction and maintained only by government repression could be suddenly transformed by a revolutionary general strike into a more equitable one, as workers took charge of society and their future. As in all utopian writings, the authors mixed fiction with historical reality, and

---

1. Pouget and Pataud 1995, 138–39. This 1909 novel, which could have been subtitled *A Novel of Social Anticipation,* was a misunderstood and ignored work, according to René Mouriaux. His presentation in the recent reprint highlights the way history could be reappropriated to reflect on the future of contemporary society. The two authors were revolutionary syndicalists and militants in the Confédération générale du travail at a moment when the general strike as a strategy was heatedly debated. Jaurès treated the text as an anarchist manifesto that demonstrated once again an "unrealistic" strategy, and ultimately the weakness of syndicalism. Victor Griffuelhes of the CGT responded to Jaurès's criticism by insisting that the book was just a novel and that its authors had not intended it as a manual for revolution. An English translation appeared in 1913, titled *How We Shall Bring About the Revolution: Syndicalism and the Cooperative Commonwealth* (reprint, London: Pluto Press, 1990).

in this case they depicted a future society as envisioned by revolutionary syndicalists who then dominated the Confédération générale du travail (CGT). Pouget and Pataud's vision that workers could manage the production and distribution of material goods, and do a more equitable job than industrial and commercial capitalists, inscribed the aspirations for transforming social relations that were felt by many of their working-class contemporaries. Embedded in the revolutionary appeal of the general strike was the notion that workers could defeat capitalism by their own collective action. The instruments of this transformation would be labor unions and cooperatives, not political parties or the state. The cooperative ideals that underpinned part of this revolutionary project, often promoted as "socialism in everyday life," formed a key element in the socialist imaginary during this period.[2] As workers imagined such alternatives to the liberal republican social order that they identified as the source of their oppression, they sought to liberate themselves. This rare account of a workers' utopia highlights the aspirations for an equality of material well-being and for substantive social and economic rights that form one of the themes of this book.

While France has a past rich in utopian moments, and a historiographical tradition that has sustained its vitality, labor historians have moved away from the exploration of such seemingly subjective worlds.[3] Indeed, in recent years European labor history as a field appears to have lost a sense of direction. The assumptions of the previous generation of labor historians informed by Marxism have been seriously challenged by both political events and the epistemological questioning taking place within history and its related disciplines. The political reasons for this disarray are rooted in the breakdown of European socialisms over the past decade. At present the growth of democracy in Europe remains largely unfinished, and class-centered labor movements, weakened by the economic difficulties of the 1980s recession, have been forced to confront changes outside their national borders. Given this fragile conjuncture, labor historians have turned to rethinking, not their concerns for understanding social movements, but some of the fundamental concepts inherited from Marxism that have largely governed the field. In open forums and recent collective works, labor historians have been engaged in intense historiographical

2. The most pertinent analyses of revolutionary syndicalism are Julliard 1988 and Friedman 1997. For a more pessimistic assessment, see Stearns 1971.

3. The exceptions are Johnson (1974); Rancière (1981), with a different emphasis but equally utopian; and recently, Riot-Sarcey (1998).

debates, many of which have centered on the notion of class.[4] Poststructural-
ism and feminist theory have forced a reexamination of long-accepted premises
about how the history of class politics and society should be written. Feminist
historians in particular have challenged the gendered conventions in which
class analysis has been framed, conventions based almost exclusively on a male
paradigm. In the reworking of such an analysis, some historians have moved
away from studying the historical conditions of industrial capitalism and the
dialectical way in which it shaped working-class culture. In this shift, class has
become, in one recent reformulation, an "imagined community."[5] As a result,
in my view, the nature of social relations remains insufficiently problematized.

Despite these challenges, the questions that labor historians have traditionally raised remain compelling and fundamental to our understanding of past
and present history. How does working-class formation take place in relation
to capitalism, and what is the role of politics in this process? What was the
long-term impact of industrial capitalism on working-class culture? How did
it affect women and the family differently from how it affected men? What
tensions existed between gender and class interests within workers' organizations? How did men and women workers assess their position in society, and
how did they imagine their future? In the French Third Republic, supposedly
committed to liberal democracy, why were workers' demands for greater
social, economic, and gender equality thwarted for so long? All these questions found a significant place in the rich social histories of the 1970s and
1980s, before the class-centered politics of European socialism started to come
apart, but they now need to be reexamined and reconceptualized. Moreover,
new and different questions are emerging that, as we shall see, challenge the
field from several different directions.

The present study provides no simple solution to the analytical dilemmas
in the field. Rather, it seeks to present a multifaceted exploration of working-
class culture during a period of intense social and industrial transformation.

4. For a discussion of past failures and new directions, see Katznelson and Zolberg 1986;
Berlanstein 1993; Frader and Rose 1996. For a overview of the controversy on the concept of class,
see the special issue of *ILWCH* (2000); and the lead essay by Geoff Eley and Keith Nield (2000).

5. The generalized use of this term "imagined community" to describe social class was
borrowed and extrapolated from Benedict Anderson's *Imagined Communities: Reflections on the
Origins and Spread of Nationalism* (1983). For a discussion of the postmodern implications of
class analysis in terms of "imagined community" concerning Troyes in particular, see Heywood
1998, 172–75. Heywood himself reasserts a social history position, proposing an interpretation
of class that places greater weight on social factors that, he feels, have been neglected by recent
labor historians.

It focuses on a microcosm of labor and community during the long Third Republic, centered on the textile town of Troyes, just east of Paris, in the province of Champagne.[6] However, this study has wider social significance, since it raises questions concerning the nature of French industrialization, working-class formation, and the interaction of family and industrial capitalism. Integral to this analysis is the interrelation of socialism, class, and gender as it operates in workplace production and in everyday consumption. Recounted in the book is the evolution of worker's lives, including their struggles for incremental changes, which reveal a problematic social progression marked notably by three major strikes, two lockouts, and many more conflicts involving walkouts or work stoppages as signs of discontent. During this period millworkers were, in fact, locked in an adversarial relationship with millowners, whose monopoly over the labor market in a monoindustrial town largely determined the workers' future. While a shared culture of textile production provided significant social cohesion, the dynamic of bourgeois industrial capitalism predominated, structuring workers' lives. In the process, textile workers created an autonomous counterculture that interacted with the dominant culture. They founded formal institutions such as labor unions, consumer cooperatives, and socialist parties that would direct their struggles.

From the moment I arrived in Troyes, it seemed to me that the notion of a distinctive working-class culture was imprinted on the landscape of that nineteenth-century mill town, with its sheds and chimneys. The departmental archives were even housed in a reconverted knitted goods factory at the time. This historic residual culture of textile production came alive as I interviewed men and women workers, local historians, and archivists and as I came to reflect on the complex and overlapping meanings of culture. My reflections were aided by the work of Raymond Williams, whose Marxist framework for thinking about culture provides materialist methods for analyzing social and cultural change.[7] Williams understands culture "as a whole social process," one in which individuals define and shape their whole lives in a process that he links to Gramsci's notion of hegemony. Hegemony, Williams argues, "is a lived system of meanings and values—constitutive and constituting—which as they are experienced as practices appear as reciprocally confirming. It thus

6. Troyes is a major textile manufacturing and commercial center located administratively in the department of the Aube.

7. Raymond Williams 1977, esp. chaps. 6–9. See also Hall 1994; and in relation to gender, Rose 1992, 13–14.

constitutes a sense of reality for most people in society."[8] He identifies various forms in which the layers of dominant, residual, and emergent cultures operate in this hegemonic process and help to explain "the lived dominance and subordination of particular classes," but also their continued resistance to it. This conceptual framework, with its extensive view of culture, seemed pertinent to my efforts to discover the working-class culture in Troyes that had emerged in opposition to bourgeois industrial capitalism. It also shed light on the gendered practices of a male-dominated labor movement that was itself constitutive of this political culture of opposition.

More recently, William Sewell's reflections on the historical evolution of French working-class culture, and his more extended general analysis of the notions of culture that are used in the expanding field of cultural history, have also been an important influence.[9] In some respects, Sewell reworks and refines William's framework by lending greater autonomy to culture in relation to politics, economics, and other aspects of social life. Sewell is primarily concerned with the dialectical interaction between "a culture as system and a culture as practice," between "culture as an abstract category of social life, and cultures in the more concrete and pluralized sense." As he reminds us, culture as a system belongs to the "semiotic dimension of human social practice,"[10] and as such informs our understanding of recognized social codes, meanings, and values. It represents the ways people attempt to order their experiences and, ultimately, their world. Sewell argues that, contrary to the classical anthropological model stressing the coherence of culture, current approaches demonstrate that "culture is a sphere of practical activity that [is] shot through by willful action, power relations, struggle, contradiction, and change."[11] In my view, French working-class culture over the period examined here exhibits just such a set of multiple variables in the process of constant redefinition and search for coherence. French socialism, in and of itself, has always been a work in progress, handicapped by factions within and long-standing rivalries between its component groups. At the turn of the century labor unions competed to some extent with political parties, offering different strategies for empowering men and women workers to liberate themselves. Contradictions,

---

8. Raymond Williams 1977, 110.

9. Sewell 1999, 35–61. His earlier study (1980) on the evolution of trade corporations from the eighteenth century through the revolution of 1848 has been equally important.

10. Sewell 1999, 48.

11. Ibid., 44.

however, are never more apparent than in socialism's failures in practice to effect sufficient changes for women.

Gender differences have also been central to the conceptualization of worker identity, class formation, and the making of a distinctive counterculture that forms the basis of this study. Over the past two decades, feminist historians have stressed the importance of conceptualizing gender differences in the process of industrialization and the formation of working-class culture. These studies have helped to both critique and renew many of the analytical categories that formed the basis of European working-class history. In the search for new ways to theorize class, feminist historians have radically put into question the paradigm of the "universal" male worker as producer.[12] The result has been the destabilizing of class as an analytical category and, as Kathleen Canning has proposed, the opening up of "class as a postulated identity or ideology that is always embedded in specific historical settings."[13] This new conceptualization has been useful in two ways: first, by favoring the possibility of multisited or overlapping identities, including gendered ones, among both male and female workers; and second, by exploring the heterogeneity of the working class in ways that embrace diversity, contested meanings, and conflictual practices.

While the concept of gender itself has come to be used more broadly, becoming almost synonymous with women, it has also been beset by questions that dispute its initial formulation. In many ways the distinctions between sex and gender that were postulated at the outset have become obscured as the concept of gender became more generalized. This very fact has led Joan Scott to argue recently that the notion of gender had "lost its critical edge" in feminist scholarship, and to provoke a judicious reassessment of current assumptions with regard to what she cites as its "generally accepted usage."[14] She rightly urges feminist historians to accept the premise that both sexual and gender identities are not fixed and stable, and for this reason, there is a necessity to historicize those categories of analysis that identify and secure sexual difference. This shift or evolution in the usage of *gender* in the United States represents to some extent its popular recognition and adoption in scholarship and the academy.

12. See Frader and Rose 1996, Rose 1997. See also the more pessimistic assessment of the status of gender and its impact within labor history in Frader 2003.
13. Canning 1992, 767.
14. Scott 1999, xii. The first edition appeared in 1988, and many of the essays on gender and working-class history had a strong influence on my critical thinking and treatment of women textile workers in Chenut 1988.

The situation in France is, however, very different. The concept of gender, premised as it is on conflictual relations of power between the sexes, has so far failed to secure legitimacy in scholarship and the university. Moreover, there has been strong cultural opposition to any debate on why this situation is particularly problematic. Perceived by its critics as an Anglo-American import, the concept of gender remained entrenched in English by the French refusal to translate and adopt it into the language of social science and historical research. The reasons behind this resistance are eminently political.[15] They have to do with the status of history in France, a largely male-dominated discipline whose prestige is linked to its role in defining the nation and the foundational myths of the Republic itself. French feminist historians have recently carried their struggle to the practice of politics in a campaign to challenge the historic defense of universal human rights through a law demanding "parity" with men as candidates nominated for election to political office.[16] The controversy highlights the historical perception of politics as a male sphere in France, and the effective domination of political practice by men. But the struggle over parity also has raised deep-seated questions about the absence of a political language that recognizes women as individual subjects, and, as Eleni Varikas has so eloquently argued, about the apparent historical antinomy between French universalism and the acceptance of differences.[17] Sexual differences in particular, but also racial, religious, and other differences, she contends, have given rise to hierarchical categories of exclusion, produced by this universalist logic. And in the process, "the problematics of sexual difference, together with the notions and theoretical tools to analyze it, . . . have been developed out of political struggles, forged in the complex dynamic of confrontation and in symbiosis with the intellectual traditions and philosophical and political strands in each country."[18] In France, then, the turn to gender has met particular resistance from within the political culture.

However, the debate over the introduction of the term *gender* intervened in France after feminist researchers and scholars had already begun employing other terms derived from Simone de Beauvoir's *Second Sex* and from Marxism.[19]

---

15. Fassin 1999; Fraisse 1996; Thébaud 1998, III–61; Frader 2003, 21–31.
16. A short list would include Mossuz-Lavau 1998, Amar 1999.
17. Varikas 2005.
18. Ibid., 40.
19. Ibid., 41. Eleni Varikas clearly retraces the intellectual controversies over the usage of terms to express the conflictual nature of gender relations among leading feminist scholars of this period of the late 1970s and 1980s.

Several of these scholars adapted Marxist terminology in creative ways to ana-lyze power relations at work in the practices of housework, the sexual division of labor, the gendering of technology, reproduction and motherhood, power relations that stressed the subordination of women.[20] Working in France at the time and writing an earlier version of this study in French, I employed the term "rapports sociaux de sexes," a distinctive Marxian formulation, to signify the inherently conflictual relations of power between the sexes.[21] Using the American term *gender* would have restricted my audience within a Paris uni-versity setting, and it would have been incomprehensible outside it. In the post–May 1968 climate, socialist feminists encountered suspicion and hostility from Marxists, whose paradigms were already under criticism from other directions.[22] Despite these difficulties, feminist historians working from the margins have succeeded in establishing women's history as a field, while strug-gling to integrate it into the university curriculum. It is only more recently that the term *genre* has come to be more widely adopted by feminist histori-ans and social scientists, as their scholarship has focused more directly on theorizing the notion of "difference."

My work draws on this excellent scholarship and its feminist inspiration, and shares the goal to rewrite a more complex and gender-inclusive history. In no way does this study discard the notion of class. On the contrary, it seeks to expand the notion in order to apprehend the multiple sites of worker identity, and thus to understand the ideological diversity within class itself. I will argue that working-class identity was not only a product of collective action and labor militancy at a historical moment, or of a particular relation-ship to the means of production. It was also rooted in social origins, family education, and social networks; it was embedded in local culture and associa-tions that were formed in opposition to the dominant bourgeoisie. Class marked the clothes workers wore and was experienced daily at the factory gate. Ultimately, it determined their life expectancy in many cases. And finally, class-conscious identity also drove an individual desire for social mobility and for escaping from the estate of industrial waged labor. By returning to the

20. Socialist feminists in France, but also in other countries of Europe, were attracted to Marxist terminology for expressing women's oppression. The following titles represent a small selection from a much larger body of work in French: Kergoat 1982, 1984b; Tabet 1979; Guillaumin 1992.

21. Chenut 1988. The analytic deconstructive use of gender to understand the production of social meanings was rendered by the terms *masculin* and *féminin*.

22. Varikas 2004, 42–51, and M. Perrot 1998, viii.

material culture of everyday life, and by reconstructing the multiple sites of worker identity, we gain a greater understanding of workers' capacity for solidarity and resistance in Troyes.

From the beginning I have adopted a number of research strategies for exploring these issues. The first has been to examine "la longue durée." Most studies of working-class culture in France have focused on the "long" nineteenth century, ending with World War I, a period that includes early industrialization and the emergence of an organized labor movement. A small number of authors have looked at the interwar years, often represented by labor historians as a period of decline in labor militancy and union membership.[23] Such periodization tends to overlook the crucial continuities between the nineteenth and twentieth centuries, including a number of unsettled conflicts over workers' aspirations for leisure, shorter hours, and higher wages.[24] The account presented here deliberately spans the entire Third Republic, from the 1870s to 1940. The longer time frame highlights the interconnections between workers' prewar demands and those of the 1920s and 1930s. While postponed by the war, these demands reemerged in the 1920s with an urgency that helps to explain the "social explosion" of the Popular Front and the very slow emergence of a modern, more unified consumer society. Finally, following working-class culture over some sixty years provides a greater understanding of the evolution of industrial and commercial capitalism and underscores the striking discontinuities that mark the history of gender and social equality in France. In fact, the failures of the longest republic in French history with regard to women and workers appear with great salience.

A second strategy has been to use the microcosm of the local study. Admittedly, there are various limitations to such an approach, limitations embedded in the peculiarities and distinctive character of the chosen locality. I would argue, however, that a local study provides the most appropriate setting for an in-depth, comprehensive treatment of the emergence of a working-class culture and identity. Whenever possible I have endeavored to make comparisons with other regions of textile production in France, so that the bigger picture might be viewed within the microcosm. The choice of Troyes was determined by several important factors. As the capital of the French knitted goods industry since the mid-nineteenth century, Troyes has a rich residual culture of textile production and a long-standing practice of commerce. The

23. Noiriel 1986, 156–58.
24. Cross 1999, 2–17.

early predominance of women in this production was crucial to my study, particularly since the subsequent dramatic increase in their numbers during the twentieth century had gone largely unexplained. Both these factors confirmed the existence of rich archival resources and a limited number of local and regional studies that treated the economic history of the industry. But studying the twentieth century has allowed the possibility of interviewing men and women workers who had been active in the interwar years. There are, in fact, many "unknown" and ordinary men and women workers who make brief appearances in this book. Their presence in the archival sources, and among those who were willing to share their working lives with me and my tape recorder, enrich these pages.

Facilitating my third strategy, the use of visual evidence as texts to be analyzed and interpreted emerged in the course of my research as a means of understanding the advent of important twentieth-century changes in material culture, industrial technology, and workers' changing perceptions regarding the world around them. The role of advertising, photography, and finally the cinema played an increasingly significant part in their lives. Vanessa Schwartz has recently argued eloquently for historians to reexamine Walter Benjamin's insightful reflections on the relation between art, technology, and mass culture and thus to explore the world of twentieth-century popular culture from visual sources.[25]

Finally, I have attempted in this study to approach a "total history." The work of Michelle Perrot was fundamental in broadening my analysis of workers' culture outside the workplace, and in tracing working women in the "silences of history."[26] In enlarging the focus from the mill workshop and the home to the cooperative store, the street, community festivals, and new forms of urban leisure, the purpose is to provide a comprehensive, more coherent depiction of workers' lives. This may be said to be a difficult, and ultimately unattainable, goal, but it led me to expand my inquiry in new directions and to integrate particular components, several of which are not typically treated in a single study of working-class culture. My own interests and the nature of my sources led me to privilege certain of these: gender and class, production and consumption, industrialization and industrial homework, political culture and utopia. All these components are relational and intersect to some

25. Schwartz 2001. See also Enstad 1999 on women garment workers and on the role of fashion, dime fiction, and film in creating political subjectivities.
26. M. Perrot 1974 and the essays in M. Perrot 1998.

extent with one another to form a particular configuration within the pur-
view of this book.

GENDER AND CLASS

One of the main purposes of this study is to highlight the gendered nature
of social and political change—the differential impact of such change on men
and women textile workers over the long term. In this regard, several different problematics have been explored. The first concerns the question of how
gender distinctions inside and outside the workplace were constructed and
maintained. Gender distinctions permeated textile production from its inception in the Champagne region. In Troyes, women workers could claim to
have a *métier*, meaning a skilled occupation within the craft tradition, and a
gendered work identity that overlapped to some extent with that of men's.
Bonnetier and *bonnetière* were generic and gendered terms for workers in the
knitted goods industry, recognized by the town and industrial community.
The question then becomes, why were women's work skills devalued over
time in relation to those of men? How did the increasing feminization of
the labor force take place, and what impact did it have on this pattern of
deskilling? Written sources were generally silent on the question of the feminization of the trade, and local historians simply attributed it to the "customary" sexual division of labor. Life history interviews were especially important
for questioning assumptions about the nature of women's work. In large part
this testimony formed the basis for reconstructing women's tasks in the labor
process, and lead to greater understanding of the evolution of their garment-
making skills. Generations of women millworkers in Troyes had taken pride in
their work and the economic livelihood it afforded.[27] For this reason, workingwomen's perceptions of their trade often contradicted the increasingly
pejorative image of the "factory girl," found, for example, in the postwar press.
Their testimony provided fundamental insights into gender and class differences that were often obscured in written records.

The second angle of inquiry explores the ways in which women were marginalized from decision-making and leadership responsibilities within workers'

---

27. In a monoindustrial mill town such as Troyes, women workers identified themselves
with their trade. Carolyn Steedman (1987) remarks on a similar sense of pride among the
weavers in her mother's hometown of Burnley (117).

organizations, even when their professional and family interests were at stake. New sites of labor militancy appear, enlarging our notion of the political, when women's activism outside the workplace is taken into account. We need to ask, What exactly do traditional politics include, and why do they not include women? And when labor organizations did promote women as leaders, how were they perceived? Privileged testimony from a woman leader of the Confédération générale du travail unitaire (CGTU) in Troyes revealed exemplary ways in which politics was defined as male and even conferred masculinity.[28] In fact, women militants both could and did exercise formal political responsibility within the union and transform it to significant ends in moments of collective action. For example, during the strike of 1921, CGTU militant Suzanne Gallois dispersed an angry, vengeful crowd of striking workers by putting a sequestered millowner to work at the humiliating female task of peeling potatoes, thus probably saving his life. She deliberately linked gender-role reversal from the private sphere to public political protest. Her timely action defused the risk of violence and led to renewed negotiations to end the strike. Politics must be construed in ways that include women, whether or not sharing power is explicitly or implicitly recognized.

Finally, I examine the contradictory strategies with which male political leaders experimented in their attempts to organize women textile workers. Clearly, many socialists, including the followers of Jules Guesde, acknowledged women's formal equality with men and women's right to work and earn equal wages. But in practice, these socialists refused to share power with women, whose political rights were never a priority. Political rivalries and infighting among socialist factions alienated workingwomen from joining parties and unions that did not address their interests. The Section française de l'internationale ouvrière (SFIO), the revolutionary syndicalists, and to a lesser extent the French Communist Party made essentially the same mistakes as the Guesdists. Gender differences were maintained in discriminatory practices against women workers that persisted during the long Third Republic. For these reasons, women textile workers found it difficult to identify themselves with male-dominated political parties and labor unions. As a result their membership fluctuated sharply, or dropped significantly in relation to men's. How and why this happened is one of the themes explored in the pages that follow.

28. On this question of sexed subject identities, see Scott 1999, 70; Chenut 1998.

PRODUCTION AND CONSUMPTION

The study of material culture demonstrates the profound connection between production and consumption, an association that many nineteenth-century workers felt instinctively, and at times even acutely, as they struggled to earn a living wage. The consumption of goods is an essential part of economic life, but it has rarely been given the attention it deserves.[29] Labor historians have tended to treat consumption as a source of worker alienation from serious politics, especially when the goals of consumer cooperatives appeared to contradict those of socialist politics. Many nineteenth-century socialist militants associated cooperation with the "reformist" wing of the socialist movement. Workers' consumer cooperatives, they argued, did not have sufficiently revolutionary goals. They helped to manage, and to some extent collaborate with, the capitalist economic and social order. To be sure, some strands of the cooperative movement were decidedly defensive or mutualist in nature. But, in fact, worker consumer cooperatives often provided a tangible economic basis for worker autonomy and solidarity, and they engaged commercial capitalism in a very direct way. As Ellen Furlough has argued, "[I]t was precisely the interweaving of political socialism, trade unionism, and cooperation that accounted for the strength of the labor movement before World War I."[30] In their revolutionary utopia, Pouget and Pataud envisaged an important role for the unions in socializing production and in ensuring an equitable distribution of goods, a role that strongly resembled the one historically exercised by the workers' producer and consumer cooperatives before and during World War I.

Social scientists in nineteenth-century France studied working-class consumption through the lens of political economy and social reform, with the aim of measuring the extent of social inequalities. By contrast, most of the current work on the history of consumer society in France has relied on a wide variety of approaches, revealing to some extent a lack of consensus about how to study this history.[31] Almost all this work has focused exclusively on the Paris market and the bourgeois consumer. As a result, our knowledge of

29. See Joyce Appleby, "Consumption in Early Modern Thought," in *Consumption and the World of Goods,* ed. John Brewer and Roy Porter (New York: Routledge, 1993); and Stearns's (1997) excellent historiographical overview.

30. Furlough 1991, 9.

31. See the studies by Auslander (1996), Tiersten (2001), and Rosalind Williams (1982).

what the industrial proletariat in the provinces owned and consumed has been neglected.[32] Given French elitist cultural attitudes and a manufacturing tradition of producing luxury, quality goods, it is not surprising that most of the current research has ignored more marginal consumers. However, much of the twentieth-century scholarship on consumer society raises the fundamental question of when more democratic access to goods or mass consumption emerged in Europe.[33] Certainly the periodization and stages of market development are different from those in the United States.[34] French workers as consumers lagged noticeably behind their American counterparts in the interwar years.

In this study I explore working-class consumption as it intersects with production, gender, and class, focusing on the men and women who produced mainly luxury knitted goods for an elite and export market. How did workers conceive of their own needs and desires? How was consumer behavior related to demands for leisure and higher wages? In Troyes, a large workers' consumer cooperative of socialist inspiration, the Laborieuse, was founded in 1886 at the same time as the knitters' union, revealing the importance attached by men and women workers to defending their right to work and their right to consume. We explore this cooperative, which was conceived as a socialist alternative to commercial capitalism and which provided solidarity and cohesion for working-class culture over a period of nearly fifty years. But the records of the cooperative store could not reveal all aspects of consumer behavior. Other sources, such as inventories after death, worker budgets, advertising, and store catalogs, suggested a wider variety of worker consumer practices driven by necessity and thrift but also by a desire for pleasure and social mobility.

The social meaning of clothing, and its distinctive status as an object of consumption, occupies a central place in our analysis of consumer behavior in relation to class and gender. What clothing did workers actually own during this period? What meanings did they attach to the clothes they wore? These are difficult questions to answer, because many workers accumulated few possessions of value in life. Period photographs help us to identify workers as a distinct social group, for they were often clearly differentiated by their

32. Several authors do address workers as consumers, notably Auslander (1996b), Coffin (1996a, 1996b), and D. Roche (1994).

33. The most pertinent work on this question has been done by Victoria de Grazia with Ellen Furlough (1996).

34. See, notably, Stearns 1997; Cohen 1999, 2003.

dress from others throughout most of the period covered by this study. Yet egalitarian aspirations for greater social mobility through dress were evident in consumer behavior in the shops and in the street. Visual evidence allows us to follow the ways in which collective identity was affirmed, for example, by male workers through their caps, and the manner in which female workers explored personal identity in clothing, which they refashioned using their own skills. Workingwomen were typically disciplined by thrift in the purchase of clothing and other consumer items. But only gradually and unevenly did workers' consumer patterns change over this long period. The tensions between individual needs and those that were more socially defined through fashion, between family budget constraints and egalitarian desires, all add to the complexities of defining worker consumer behavior.

INDUSTRIALIZATION AND INDUSTRIAL HOMEWORK

Recent reinterpretations of industrialization have underscored the importance of alternative paths to industrial development, both regional and national, paths that are different from the advanced British model, traditionally presented as the master narrative.[35] By contrast, the French pattern of industrialization has always been considered a special and perplexing case because of its relatively slow pace, diverse regional structures, craft tradition, and the small scale of industry throughout most of the nineteenth century. The notion of a linear process of industrial development passing through clearly defined sequential stages contradicts the reality of many national histories, not just the French one. In rewriting the history of industrialization, economic historians are now uncovering a wide diversity of paths. In Troyes, the persistence of small-scale firms and traditional forms of outworking, existing alongside the more modern factory system that emerged in the late nineteenth century, confirms that industrialization did not follow a single logic and dynamic. Moreover, late industrialization of the type that existed in Troyes did not necessarily depend on one strategy of mechanization. It is thus recognized that work organization was subject to social and political struggles and imperatives, as well as economic and technical ones. This study clearly establishes the link between labor conflicts, lack of modernization, and the shifting of production

35. Sabel and Zeitlin 1985, 1997; concerning the garment industry itself, see Green 1997.

in search of a cheaper, more compliant workforce. Millowners in Troyes de-centralized production to artisans and small workshops in the surrounding countryside as a way to circumvent labor law restrictions and union militancy. Clearly, this "flexible" use of capital and labor, and the adversarial relationship between manufacturers in Troyes and a highly combative labor force, helped to shape the particular pattern of small-scale production that predominated in the urban mills.

From this perspective, the industrial system in Troyes invites an interesting comparison with systems in other textile regions of France. Millowners in Troyes integrated machine construction, spinning, and dyeing with knitted-textile and garment manufacturing. As in most traditional French textile regions, bourgeois entrepreneurs who founded family firms dominated the landscape. Some of these men rose from the ranks of artisan metalworkers or knitters, bringing with them their mechanical skills and a passion for invention. But the majority originated from merchant families whose well-developed commercial sense and solid family assets led them to search for ways to expand their markets overseas. As millowners shifted production from basic hosiery to luxury knitted goods, they came to depend more and more on female labor and specialized garment-making skills. This dependence was publicly acknowl-edged by one local manufacturer, who characterized the woman worker and her economic importance to the local industry with the superb metaphor of "the goose that lays the golden egg."[36] If this was indeed the case, we are led to ask, to what extent did manufacturers conceive of technological change in the term of the feminization of the labor force?

Feminist historians have, in fact, brought new approaches to the study of industrialization, first of all, by questioning inequalities in the sexual division of labor; second, by analyzing the gendering of tools and technology; and third, by deconstructing the division between the public and private spheres. This presumption of a public/private dichotomy, inherited uncritically from nineteenth-century social reformers and historians, became incorporated into the narrative of European industrialization. In their counternarrative, feminist historians have demonstrated how women continued to be employed in "flex-ible" structures of industrial homework, which bore a strong resemblance to the sweatshops of the late nineteenth century. Judith Coffin and Nancy Green,

36. This characterization of women's work was offered by millowner Léon Vitoux to the Parliamentary Commission of Inquiry on the Textile Industry in 1904. See Chapter 2.

in particular, have shown how the garment industry never really separated home and work. The findings of the present study confirm the persistence of industrial homework in Troyes in several different forms, as manufacturers widely practiced the distribution of work to married women who were at home with children. But not all homeworkers were women: the artisan dream of numerous male millworkers was to provide a livelihood for their wives and children in a family-run workshop. Industrial homework intersected with this artisan dream of relative autonomy from the harsh discipline and the immorality that was perceived to exist in the modern mill.

POLITICAL CULTURE AND UTOPIA

How were workers drawn to politics in the Champagne region? And more important, why did various forms of socialism survive there throughout the Third Republic? This book covers a long time frame, running from the beginnings of socialism in the 1870s to the exercise of political power by the Left under the Popular Front in the 1930s. The followers of Jules Guesde organized in Troyes, as well as in the northern textile towns of Lille, Roubaix, and Tourcoing, as described by Patricia Hilden.[37] There were, however, significant differences between the two working-class constituencies that made the Guesdists task of organizing in Troyes more challenging. Millworkers in Troyes were drawn from rural homeworkers, many of whom were semi-independent, highly combative, and resistant to the form of paternalism that was practiced by Catholic manufacturers to the north. In fact, the virtual absence of paternalism (with a few notable exceptions) opened the political field to the influence of several socialist sects, together with the Radical Party, which was well established in the Aube. Such ideological diversity forced Guesdists into polemics with their rivals on the left. While several exceptional Guesdist militants were able to discipline and train a core of committed local leaders, the majority of textile workers were more loosely organized and refractory to the ideological stance of the Parti ouvrier français (POF). By narrowing their focus to electoral socialism and campaign politics, thus targeting a male worker constituency, the POF lost many opportunities to engage disenfranchised workingwomen and rebellious young workers. In Troyes, these younger men, together

37. Hilden 1986.

with other dissidents inspired by the Paris Commune, later joined forces with revolutionary syndicalism and the CGT. Direct action syndicalism, as it has been called, was an effort to empower workers in ways not offered by socialist party electoral politics. Workers turned to creating their own institutions, which became islands of autonomy and solidarity within the dominant capitalist society.[38]

As noted earlier, however, it was the Guesdists' attitude toward women workers that led to their biggest losses. In theory, the Guesdists defended women's right to work, since logically waged work would give women some form of economic independence, and would enlist them in the ranks of socialist militancy. But in practice, the Guesdist policies toward women workers were both confusing and contradictory, thus alienating many working women, particularly within the Guesdist-dominated national textile union. The problematic relationship between women textile workers and late nineteenth-century socialism and syndicalism raises questions about the nature of politics itself and the male domination of labor organizations. How were women workers recruited, and how were their issues addressed? Why did so few women accede to assuming political responsibilities within parties and unions? Did the labor movement deliberately cultivate a masculine self-image?[39] From this perspective, the present study follows the long march for women's rights—the right to work, to vote, to exercise political responsibilities—interwoven with the expansion of democracy and the history of socialism. Ultimately, French socialists, in the best Marxist tradition, made women's emancipation subordinate to the success of a socialist revolution.[40] Even as a dramatic feminization of the labor force during this period increased women workers' numerical strength, their wages stagnated and their political and social rights lagged behind those of men.

Yet in the long run, socialist politics in Troyes injected a utopian dimension into working-class culture that strengthened the counterculture of opposition. This utopian thread, woven into egalitarian discourse and practice, helped to sustain socialist militancy, at least among a minority. While much of the Guesdist rhetoric presented a negative goal—the destruction of capitalism— many workers in fact invested their energies in the positive tasks of constructing a socialist library, a cooperative store, and other associations through which

38. Julliard 1988, 37.
39. Frader 2003, 24–25.
40. On Guesdism and women workers, see Hilden 1986 and 1987. See also Stuart 1992, 1997a, 1997b.

they sought to offset the inequalities of birth and class. Certainly, the utopian inspiration within revolutionary syndicalism mobilized workers to challenge the industrial order in Troyes through direct strike action and union demands for greater worker autonomy. Their incentive was also behind the founding of the workers' consumer cooperative the Laborieuse, which provided a long-standing material basis for solidarity and community. Utopian aspirations also fostered the popular mobilization against fascism—identified locally with capitalism—a mobilization that defended the strong Popular Front movement in Troyes.

OVERVIEW

The opening chapter introduces the world of textile culture through the general strike of 1900 and the lockout that ensued for two long months. This dramatic event, presented here from multiple viewpoints, introduces also the protagonists of our study: the men and women textile workers, the strike committee, millowners, local officials, journalists, political candidates, and even national political figures who were briefly drawn into the struggle. The strike was transformed by local and national politics as opposing forces sought support from the Radical government in nearby Paris. In fact, in this chapter many of the themes treated in the book are set forth through the microcosm of the strike. I pose the problem of workers' discontent with "social democracy" as practiced in the Third Republic, and suggest their alternative vision of a social republic. Ultimately, the strike failed after Guesdist leaders sought to channel worker resistance toward promoting the POF's own local electoral objectives. Thereafter, a significant minority of the working class regrouped behind a revolutionary syndicalist strategy of direct action, promoted by the newly founded industrial union the Confédération générale du travail (CGT). Local workers' institutions of solidarity then became the basis of a strong counterculture that sustained socialism until the mid-twentieth century.

In the following three chapters we turn back to follow broad economic and social developments in the region from the mid-nineteenth century on. Chapter 2 examines the origins of the hosiery industry, or as it is now called, knitted goods industry, in the Aube department of Champagne. It describes the distinctive path toward industrialization that enabled Troyes to emerge by 1900 as the leading producer of knitted textiles in France. The focus of

Chapter 3 is the socialist movement, introduced by the followers of Jules Guesde, as it developed within the region from 1880 to 1914. Several strands of French socialism, in fact, vied for workers' allegiance, but in Troyes the Guesdists predominated; through propaganda and political networks, they were able to organize effectively among the knitters, metalworkers, and railroad employees. This study is an attempt to explain why the Guesdists ultimately failed to garner sufficient votes among textile workers and why revolutionary syndicalism found favor for subsequent collective action in Champagne.

The organizing theme of Chapter 4 is the distinctive culture of textile production in Troyes in the late nineteenth century. The knitters' trade was handed down not only from father to son, but also from mother to daughter. It was the *métier obligé*—the requisite trade—beginning in the family workshop. In the transition to the factory system, many of the customary assumptions concerning the gendered nature of work were transferred to the particular mode of industrial capitalism in Troyes. Gender-structured practices ranged from the sexual division of labor to the separation of workspaces and from the apprenticeship ladder to the organization of the local work festival, the Fête de la Bonneterie. In fact, the evolution of the festival itself highlights the transformation of Troyes from an industrial society to a more modern commercial and consumer one.

For analytical purposes, the theme of working-class consumption is treated by period in two separate chapters in which the emphasis is on the incremental nature of change for workers as consumers. An overview of the entire period of the Third Republic is revealing of how workers were only very slowly integrated into an expanded consumer market by the end of the 1930s. Chapter 5 begins with early socialist demands for shorter working hours and higher wages and with the creation and development of the workers' consumer cooperative the Laborieuse, from 1886 to 1914. Chapter 7 follows the cooperative's expansion in the interwar years, as it faced competition from the new merchandising techniques of commercial capitalism and struggled to preserve the store's working-class character in accord with socialist principles. Both these chapters are united by the overarching question of when more democratic access to goods enabled workers to become consumers of the clothing they helped to produce. Why did socially stratified markets for goods persist? The analysis is an attempt to take into account gendered consumer practices, social strategies, and individual desires, all of which to some extent governed consumer behavior.

The political culture of the interwar years is treated in Chapters 6 and 8, in which I describe events in Troyes that were directly influenced by national ones. Chapter 6 covers the period encompassing the irreversible feminization of the labor force, changes in the work process that intensified work discipline, and a mass strike in 1921. The strike was followed by the decentralization of production to the countryside. The depression and the Popular Front form the subject of Chapter 8. Wage cuts, unemployment, and short-time work contributed to the growing antagonism between textile workers and millowners during the 1930s, culminating in the massive strikes of June 1936 and in the ultimate victory of the Popular Front both locally and nationally. One of the significant features of the Popular Front movement in Troyes was the divisive nature of the alliance among left-wing parties and the renewed hostility between employers and unions during and after negotiations to establish a historic collective bargaining agreement for the industry.

The Popular Front formed one of those utopian moments in French working-class history; the first factory occupations in 1936 offered workers the hope that dialogue and negotiation would not only transform social relations with employers in the workplace but would also alter interactions beyond the factory, in society at large. It was in some sense the brief and partial realization of Pouget and Pataud's revolutionary general strike—but only after the Left had won a parliamentary victory, and thus legitimately controlled the state. While that 1909 novel in no way anticipated the events of 1936, the utopian aspirations of working-class culture that it expressed surfaced once again, alive and resilient.

THE GREAT STRIKE

Les travailleurs de l'usine
De l'atelier, du bureau
Ont des salaires de famine
Sont réduit au pain à l'eau

C'est 8 heures, 8 heures
8 heures,
C'est 8 heures qu'il nous faut
oh! oh! oh! oh!

La faim force nos compagnes
A laisser seuls nos marmots
Pour aller 12 heures au bagne
Enrichir les aristots.

C'est 8 heures . . .

—ETIENNE PÉDRON, "CHANT DU 1ER MAI"
LE REVEIL DES TRAVAILLEURS DE L'AUBE,
APRIL 24, 1897

On Friday, February 16, 1900, more than one hundred young male workers suddenly walked off their jobs in the Mauchauffée textile mill in Troyes, without having formulated a set of demands. With no prior warning they left their workshops and marched up the narrow cobblestoned street, the rue Belgand, in the shadow of the town's largest mill, near the train station. Then they headed in the direction of the Halle de la Bonneterie, the former textile merchants' marketplace in the center of Troyes, now occupied by the labor unions, where they gathered to formulate and discuss their grievances.

Their sudden walkout was not inspired by socialist leader Etienne Pédron's revolutionary May Day song in defense of the eight-hour day, although many local observers feared his influence and imagined that he was the ringleader behind the revolt. Millowners remained convinced throughout the strike that

it was politically motivated.[1] The young workers' walkout sparked a spontaneous defensive movement, based on latent discontent over wages and working
conditions, that spread through the town in a matter of days. The resulting
great strike, of more than twelve thousand men and women workers of all
ages, was to last for a bitter two months. It opposed loosely organized textile
workers against an intransigent coalition of millowners, who were divided
among themselves by their religious and political convictions but united in
their fear of socialism. The timing of the strike corresponded with growing
socialist electoral strength in the Aube department in anticipation of partial
legislative elections that very same weekend following the initial walkout. For
this reason Louis Mony, the Radical mayor of Troyes, was seriously troubled.
Potential political unrest at this time might tip the election either to the anti-
republican Right or to the revolutionary members of the Marxist Parti ouvrier
français (POF), who opposed collaboration with bourgeois republicans. The
strike was thus quickly transformed by both local and national politics. The
workplace conflict first mobilized the entire milltown community, then soon
widened into a political struggle that eventually led striking workers from
Troyes to nearby Paris to seek government support.

Troyes is roughly 150 kilometers east of Paris. In 1900 the town counted
some fifty thousand inhabitants and a prosperous knitted goods industry that
had dominated the local economy since the mid-nineteenth century. During
this period rural outworkers with a long experience of the trade had migrated
to Troyes, swelling the numbers of urban textile workers employed in the
mills. The majority of these were employed in small urban workshops of some
20 to 250 workers who resided in the nearby suburbs. In contrast, the
Mauchauffée mill on the rue Belgand, where the strike began, represented the
largest employer, with more than 1,300 workers, and was the very image of
modern capitalist concentration of labor. Maurice Mauchauffée had been a
pioneer of integrated textile production from 1875, when he established a
metalworking factory, to manufacture machines for his knitted goods mill,
and a dyeworks adjacent to the rue Belgand. By 1900 he commanded a large
workforce in Troyes and in the nearby countryside, as well as a network of
sales representatives in Paris, the Far East, and Madagascar and along the

---

1. This explanation was cited by the millowners association, la Chambre syndicale patronale
de la bonneterie, in their deposition before the parliamentary commission of inquiry that visited
Troyes in 1904 (AN C 7318).

African coasts.[2] Mauchauffée had sufficient reserves of capital and stocks of knitted goods to wait out a strike.

The walkout that precipitated the strike was ostensibly motivated by wage demands. The young apprentice knitters, or *rebrousseurs,* felt passed over by concessions granted by Mauchauffée to the skilled knitters, and, knowing that their walkout would effectively disrupt production, they walked out without submitting their grievances.[3] A 15 percent wage increase was what they subsequently demanded. The following day, they took their case to the justice of the peace for arbitration, as stipulated by law, but millowners refused to acknowledge this official procedure. On Sunday morning, February 18, some eight hundred young men gathered in the Halle de la Bonneterie to discuss their demands. By this time, young rebrousseurs from other mills had joined the movement to claim not only a wage increase but also a change in the pay procedure.[4] They demanded to be paid directly by the millowner, not by the knitters, as was still the practice in many mills. The young men engaged in this occupation, who were age fourteen to twenty, were rebelling against being treated as unskilled workers, in a relation of disguised apprenticeship to the skilled knitters who subcontracted the work. This dependent relationship and the method of payment it generated were fraught with social tensions. The rebrousseurs were joined by the *commis-bonnetiers,* who were also apprentice knitters, and together, on Monday, February 19, they voted to initiate a general strike if their demands were not met. The meeting closed with cries of "Vive la grève générale!"

Millowners met at the offices of the Chambre syndicale patronale (the employers' organization) to consider the situation and decided in a show of solidarity to resist this youthful revolt. But the very absence of the young workers, who occupied a key position, effectively halted production in several mills. The work stoppage released latent wage dissatisfaction among many men and women textile workers. As a result the numbers of strikers swelled.

2. Bergeron 1978, 93–94.
3. The rebrousseurs could effectively block production. Fully fashioned stockings, shaped to the leg, were knit in two stages on separate machines. The rebrousseur's task was to slip the stitches of stockings onto a metal plate between the two stages of the knitting process. The work was subcontracted and consequently bound them to piece rates paid directly by the knitters.
4. ADA SC 417.

"VIVE LA GRÈVE GÉNÉRAL"

By Tuesday, February 20, the strike had spread to ten additional mills and had touched off demands for wage increases by male and female workers in other occupations. Strikers met at the Halle de la Bonneterie to elect delegates who would constitute a permanent strike committee and present the workers' written demands to the government's local administrator, the prefect. Delegates assembled workers according to workshop and craft occupation, to draw up a list of their grievances. Women delegates organized strikers in their own mill workshops, since they worked separately from men. Striking workers filled the bars, cafés, and meeting rooms of the town. From their headquarters in a town hall meeting room, the strike committee first sent a delegation down the street to inform the prefect of their intentions: the declaration of a general strike. Given the electoral campaign in progress, the workers' threat of a general strike raised the possibility that their revolt might move toward more ambitious revolutionary goals. In the spirit of the moment, this strategy could appeal across craft and political divisions to ignite a wider conflict.

The equivocal nature of the notion itself served strike leaders' objectives of forging worker solidarity.[5] Arguably, a general strike was a problematic means of revolt. But revolutionary syndicalist sympathizers within the textile unions were convinced that it could effectively mobilize workers to take direct action on their own behalf across craft lines.[6] For the young rebrousseurs who were inspired by revolutionary ideals, a work stoppage could effectively spark a general strike, the radicalizing effects of which might provoke other workers to "flex their muscles" and take over the mills.[7] In their view, this strike would strengthen workers' resolve to act for themselves, rather than turning to politicians and political parties for solutions. However, both socialist leader Jules Guesde, head of the POF, and local leader Etienne Pédron had previously voiced their objections to the notion of a general strike. Both leaders had argued that it would divide the working class if the moment were badly

5. For a discussion of the evolution in the meanings attached to the term *general strike*, see M. Perrot 1974, chap. 4. See also Riot-Sarcey et al. 2002, s.v. "grève générale," 104–5.

6. See Stuart 1992, 217–21. Stuart's excellent analysis of the opposition between Guesdist strategies as a political party and anarchosyndicalist ideas of mobilization and direct action provide a real sense of alternative visions of socialist practice in France.

7. Emile Pouget's definition of the general strike in *Le Père Peinard* (September 4–11, 1892) evokes this image of strikers "flexing their muscles" to show the difference between an ordinary strike, in which workers were idled, and a general strike that would, once workers had taken control of the mills, put them back to work.

chosen.[8] Guesdist militants in Troyes had yet another strategy. Over the past decade, they had been organizing among textile workers to carry socialist ideals outside the workplace and into the local political arena. Operating within a disciplined POF group committed to the republican system of parliamentary democracy, they were dedicated to promoting class revolution by the ballot. By contrast, the strike committee seemed to defy these very disciplined channels of action and to generate a structure of its own, one with an alternative vision of worker solidarity. Ultimately, the strike committee's purpose was defined in the heat of the action and transformed under the guidance of the POF militants.

In the meantime, partial legislative elections for deputy to the National Assembly were taking place in Troyes on Sunday, February 19. Pédron was the POF candidate, and he made a strong showing, carrying 38 percent of the vote and running second to the Radical candidate, Gaston Arbouin, who was editor in chief of the local paper with the largest circulation, Le Petit Troyen.[9] Pédron's success forced a runoff election, held two weeks later. As a militant organizer and propagandist for the POF in the Aube, Pédron had mobilized workers in Troyes for the first May Day celebration in 1890 with his song in favor of the eight-hour day. Through songs and plays depicting the struggles of working-class life, Pédron appealed to the political imagination of a broad spectrum of workers. His reputation as a fiery orator and committed socialist brought him back and forth to Troyes as a choice candidate for the POF. But the Radicals feared that Pédron's popularity among the knitters would further divide the vote, allowing the right-wing nationalist and clerical candidate to win. Mayor Louis Mony, for one, was deeply troubled by the strong show of socialist strength in Sunday's legislative election and by the workers' vote in favor of a general strike. But his attitude also reflected the contradictions within his own party in power since 1899.[10] How far left could he lean in

8. Guesdist socialists insisted on strategic reflection before a strike to determine if the moment was favorable for collective action. Pédron voted with the Guesdist minority at the Congress of Nantes against the general strike: "means that can only be detrimental to the working class by dividing workers into partisans or nonpartisans of the strike, and that will consequently disorganize existing syndicalist forces to the advantage of the capitalist class" (Le Socialiste, 27 Octobre 1894, as quoted in Bedin 1977, 111).

9. Results for the first round of the partial legislative elections were as follows: Arbouin, 45 percent; Pédron, 38.5 percent; Brissot, 16 percent. Pédron's major support came from voters in Troyes. It is interesting to note an overall abstention of about 22 percent. See Le Petit Troyen, February 20,1900; Baroin 1970, 166.

10. Many local Guesdists had contested the tactical alliance in Paris that had brought POF member Alexandre Millerand as minister of commerce into the left-wing coalition government

support of a labor movement imbued with socialist ideals without losing support from his own partisans? POF members in Troyes had strongly rejected class collaboration with the local Radicals as an electoral strategy. So, despite Etienne Pédron's success in the partial legislative elections, the POF agreed to withdraw his candidacy in the runoff election on March 4 in favor of the Radical candidate, Gaston Arbouin, who was finally elected by a significant majority. The press hailed the victory as a true affirmation of republican and democratic principles on the part of the electorate. Nevertheless, Guesdist socialists were predicting that, after municipal elections in May, "the red flag of the proletariat will float victorious over the town hall."[11] Given this uneasy political climate, Mony hurried to Paris on February 21 to consult with the Waldeck government.

Once the general strike had been called, those workers still occupied in the mills were forced into idleness and congregated anxiously at the mill gates. Many crowded in the square in front of the town hall to follow events. Work had all but stopped in the mills. At 4:00 P.M. on the twenty-second, more than three thousand workers, men and women, thronged the Halle de la Bonneterie at one end of town, while an equal number filled the meeting room in the town hall at the other. Both meetings voted for the general strike and broke up with cries of "Vive la grève générale! Vive l'union ouvrière!"

Earlier strikes on a smaller scale had raised similar wage demands that, in fact, masked other workplace grievances. The factory and workshop system in Troyes had spawned diverse forms of production that in turn generated different and competing wage rates. The diversity of articles manufactured in urban mills and rural workshops and the differences in knitting-machine gauges, together with the wage deductions practiced by certain manufacturers, all represented so many ways to divide workers among themselves. What some striking knitters demanded was unified piece rates for all the Troyes mills. They wanted to reduce the disparities in wages between different mills, but also to fight competition from rural workers, whose lower wages undercut theirs. "Unified piece rates" was a grievance that appealed to unity and to trade solidarity. It was a grievance with a political future, since the Fédération nationale de l'industrie textile took it up as an objective in their national

---

of moderate premier Waldeck-Rousseau. The members of the POF in Troyes had only grudgingly accepted "Millerandisme."

11. *Le Socialiste,* February 25, 1900.

program several years later.[12] But when millowners categorically refused to discuss wages in these terms, workers shifted to demanding a concrete 15 percent increase over the current rates.

Women workers were a strong component of the movement from the outset. They numbered nearly half the adult labor force in the Troyes mills in 1900. Male skilled workers operated the knitting machines, while women prepared the raw materials (spinning) and seamed and finished the articles produced. Like the men, their demands were presented by their mill, workshop, and occupational groups. Consider the case of a group of seamers who wrote to the prefect: "We women workers at the Raguet mills, having made known our grievances to the owners, who refused to accept them, we declare ourselves on strike."[13] There followed a list of demands, among them the abolition of deductions for thread, needles, and lighting and an end to paying "pour comptes" and to seaming camisoles without first basting them. At issue was the employers' practice of sanctioning what they saw as poorly executed work by peremptory wage deductions known as *pour comptes*. This practice was bitterly resented by all pieceworkers, who claimed the right to quality control over their own production. For male knitters and other machine operatives, the grievances involved charges for lighting and the replacement of machine needles broken during production, all charges that they asserted that millowners deducted from their pay at higher than cost.[14] For workers in all knitting trades this practice of wage deductions of various sorts carried with it the employers' arbitrary power to link pay procedures to the smooth operation of the work process and to the quality of the product, rather than to the worker's skill and the time and effort spent in production.[15] Such practices added to the extreme variability of wages and the sense of job insecurity that textile workers felt about conditions in the mills.

Strikers multiplied their efforts to bring their co-workers into the movement. The Radical newspaper, *Le Petit Troyen*, carried urgent summons to strike meetings on February 23: "The women seamers of the Delostal mills convoke their comrades to a 10 o'clock meeting today at Monsieur Pierrard's

---

12. AMT F 689.
13. ADA SC 417.
14. *Le Reveil des Travailleurs de l'Aube*, April 7–14, 1900.
15. For the nineteenth-century workplace assumptions about wages and deductions that still governed the textile trade during the first half of the century, see Reddy 1984, 209–13 and 294–95. See also Sewell 1986a, esp. 67–70.

wine bar, Faubourg Croncels, urgent."[16] Even workers from the St.-Julien dyeworks, usually the last to come out on strike, convened with their co-workers
to discuss the general strike. By multiplying the number of small groups of
organized strikers, the strike committee reached out to include growing numbers in their offensive action. Even the *chambres syndicales* (craft unions), which
had attempted to organize the skilled male knitters into embryonic unions
by trade during the 1890s, seized the moment to recruit new members into
their associations. But the real momentum behind the strike came from the
permanent strike committee and its 158 elected delegates, highly representative
of those who had initiated and led the action.[17] They became the real voices of
the movement, the motor of protest until the very end.

The debate over wages and piece rates rapidly developed into a battle
between two fixed versions of reality. Public positional language became an
important means of gaining townspeople's support. On February 26 the
millowners' association, the Chambre syndicale patronale des fabricants de
bonneterie, wrote to the prefect submitting the average daily wages for male
and female operatives in their mills. The employers affirmed that these figures
had been established "from the pay registers of each of the undersigned mills"
and were "rigorously exact."[18] The millowners' letter was published in several
local newspapers the next day. Many observers wondered why these average
daily wages were made public. It was certainly not common practice in this age
of industrial liberalism, committed to secrecy.[19] Beyond the actual numbers,
the millowners' action suggested their desire to maintain absolute control over
pay procedures, and in this way forestall workers' pretensions to contest the
issue further. By bringing the wage debate out into the open, before the
public eye, they could exert pressure on the strikers and confirm their good
faith by agreeing in advance to submit their pay registers to a committee of
inspection. However, the fact that several big millowners closed their factories
on Saturday, February 24, made such claims to honest dealing highly suspicious. So when a general lockout was declared on Tuesday, February 27, it
aroused great public suspicion and anger.

The strike committee then set about unmasking the millowners' game. On
March 2 the committee wrote to the prefect that, given the average wages

16. *Le Petit Troyen,* February 23, 1900.
17. AMT 2J 47.
18. ADA SC 417.
19. According to *Le Petit Troyen,* the average wages appeared higher than in reality. See
Bedin 1977, 150.

published in the press, they would accept "purely and simply the wages that *Messieurs les patrons* had thus offered them."[20] In this way they disputed the validity of the millowners' figures and, in sum, called their bluff. Moreover, they contended that a unified system of piece rates was necessary to determine any average daily wage for the three hundred days that workers claimed constituted the work year. This was the logic behind the strikers' position. The committee repeated the young rebrousseurs' demand for a 15 percent increase in wages, insisting that many of these workers were married and heads of households.

However, this time the millowners responded harshly, confirming their intention not to change piece rates currently in place in their mills: "[T]he infinite diversity of work procedures carried out in our factories necessitates special conditions rarely applicable to one craft occupation in each mill, and even less so to an ensemble of all mills in Troyes," they argued. Moreover, they refused to discuss the issue with the strike committee and treated their demands as "incoherent."[21] To buttress their argument, the Chambre syndicale patronale asserted that wages in Troyes were higher than those offered in other centers for knitted goods in France, and that local wages had to be kept competitive. These same arguments concerning competitors' wages would regularly serve to block wage protests in the future.

From this very moment, the strike entered a more political phase and became embedded in local, even national, politics. For some contemporary observers the strike had appeared to be politically motivated from the outset, driven by Guesdist electoralism. Both POF leader Jules Guesde and socialist deputy Jean Jaurès had come to Troyes on February 11, several days before the strike erupted, to attend a mass meeting of some three thousand people to support Pédron's candidacy for deputy. Consequently, the police were quick to call attention to the political potential of the strike as it developed. After strikers addressed their first calls for support to socialist leaders Jean Jaurès, Jules Guesde, and Paul Lafargue, the police commissioner wrote to the prefect, on February 22, "In this strike the workers demands are subordinate, it is the political question which dominates everything. Whatever the cost, the socialists intend to come to power and obtain a majority in the town council

20. Letter from the Comité permanent de la grève générale to the préfet de l'Aube, March 2, 1900, ADA SC 417.
21. Letter from the Chambre syndicale patronale to the prefect, March 9, 1900, ADA SC 417.

in the May elections."[22] Police reports sought to credit the theory that instructions and strike funds arrived daily from POF leaders in Paris seeking to prolong the strike.[23]

However, the sudden walkout by the young rebrousseurs that had precipitated the strike, and their insistence on the autonomy of their movement, belie this explanation. The latent discontent of both men and women workers who quickly joined the movement suggests that the strike originated as a spontaneous, defensive action. Emile Pouget's correspondent in Troyes noted with satisfaction that the strike had generalized in three days.[24] Such discontent was then galvanized by class interests that Guesdist socialists then strategically defined in their propaganda. The POF was not at the origin of the strike, but once the movement started, the local Guesdists gave the strikers full support. The POF and the state were only two of the many actors in this conflict that implicated class interests in Troyes and the state's local representatives on several levels.

THE ACTORS IN AN EVOLVING EVENT

Who were the strikers? The sudden mobilization of the Troyes working class was a powerful expression of workplace discontent. Their action was structured by several organized groups: the strike committee, assembled at the town hall; the *chambres syndicales* and other unions, far too weak to lead a mass movement but eager to seize the opportunity for collective action; the leaders of the POF, with headquarters at the Maison du Peuple near the town hall; and finally the delegates, both men and women workers, designated by striking co-workers to represent their trade and workshop.

At the outset the strike committee styled itself in written communications to the press and the prefect as "the permanent committee of the general strike." It was composed of 158 delegates from different mill workshops: sixty-four male workers, fifty-four female workers, and forty young rebrousseurs.[25] This

22. Letter from the Direction de la Sûreté to the prefect, February 22, 1900, ADA SC 417.
23. Ibid.
24. Emile Pouget ran a weekly newspaper called *Le Père Peinard,* which carried revolutionary syndicalist propaganda but also regular columns on workplace conflicts. His correspondent in Troyes wrote well-informed articles on the strike in Troyes, signing his column as "Freedom," in English. See *Le Père Peinard,* March 5–12, 1900, for coverage of the strike's evolution.
25. *Le Petit Troyen,* February 23, 1900.

loosely integrated group became the executive organ for worker mobilization and for the negotiation of decisions taken by the general assembly of strikers. However, the Chambre syndicale patronale denied the strike committee's role as spokesman for workers' demands, refused all dialogue with the committee, and never recognized it as in any way representative of "their" workers. Some delegates, but certainly not all, were trained socialist militants, and some were drawn from categories of experienced millworkers.[26] At its core the committee relied on POF militants organized by Etienne Pédron, among them knitters such as Céléstin Philbois, who much later became SFIO deputy from Troyes. Philbois presided over daily strike meetings at the Maison du Peuple. The committee thus maintained effective control over the strike as it spread in the early days and gained support among millworkers.

Gender, class, and age solidarity operated within a loosely structured executive that derived its collective authority from the various assemblies of strikers. Women workers, for example, were early recognized as active in number and solidarity. More than twelve hundred women millworkers had gathered in the town hall on February 22 and voted to join the strike movement. *Le Petit Troyen* reported that these same women vowed in the heat of the moment to join the union.[27] When rumors circulated later that if the knitters and rebrousseurs obtained satisfaction of their demands they would return to work and abandon the women, the strike committee hastened to emphasize that "no, we workers will not abandon women workers who have made common cause with our movement."[28] Militants on the strike committee channeled effective action through daily, multiple meetings in the cafés and wine bars of the town, but they also sent delegations of strikers into the countryside to seek the solidarity of rural outworkers.

The involvement of unions in the strike organization was minimal, and their membership was divided. The largest union, the Association syndicale des ouvriers et ouvrières de toutes les professions se rattachant à la bonneterie, was composed of workers from across several craft occupations who were employed in the trade.[29] Despite the effort to regroup diverse categories of workers and to recruit women into their numbers, membership was modest.

26. For a partial list of the strike committee members, see the committee's letter to the prefect, March 2, 1900, ADA SC 417.
27. *Le Petit Troyen,* February 22, 1900.
28. *La Dépêche Troyenne,* March 7, 1900.
29. Founded in May 1886.

Once the strike had been declared, unions sought to exploit the political moment to recruit new members. The *chambres syndicales* were more traditional craft organizations, their membership more exclusionary in terms of skill and their action more conservative concerning strikes.[30] The *chambres syndicales,* like the unions, called their members to meetings, but they also reminded them to pay their membership dues and restricted aid to those who did. Divisions between workers' organizations along these craft lines were a source of conflict, and ultimately of weakness, in the movement.

While local leaders of the POF were not the instigators of the strike, they threw their wholehearted support behind it. By 1900, Etienne Pédron had officially left Troyes for other party functions in the suburbs of Paris, and his lieutenant, Hébert Corgéron, a knitter's son from Estissac, had taken his place.[31] The party headquarters at the Maison du Peuple housed several workers' associations and a consumer cooperative. When the strike was declared, these organizations opened their doors to strikers. Guesdist groups set up solidarity committees to defend the strike, to seek credit and donations from local shopkeepers, and to pressure town councils to vote for aid for strikers. Without such structures behind the movement—the fruit of ten years of Guesdist militancy in Troyes and the Aube—the strike would have collapsed. Yet the POF party newspaper, *Le Reveil des Travailleurs de l'Aube,* which served as a forum for strike support, never gave directives to strikers on which course of action to take. Jules Guesde had never been a systematic partisan of strikes. The ultimate battle for Guesde and his disciples was an electoral one, for socialist control of the town hall.

Women workers played an active role in the strike. They patterned their action on the male craft tradition, with which they identified, organizing by occupation and workshop to discuss and formulate their demands. While some women ran soup kitchens or networked with women homeworkers to bring them out on strike, still others became delegates to the strike committee. Such women assumed political roles for themselves in order to defend their jobs and class concerns. Several women on the strike committee took responsibility for organizing co-workers and for presenting their grievances.

30. A *chambre syndicale* of knitters called the Chambre syndicale des ouvriers circulaires, tailbouis et tubulaires, created in 1894, admitted new members only through introduction by old members in the craft tradition and sought to control access to jobs (ADA M 2345).

31. Corgéron exercised his trade as a coiffeur, which, like tending a neighborhood bar, offered him a livelihood that politics could not.

This was the case of Lecolle Carabin, mandated by the seamers of the Raguet mill to be delegate to the strike committee. She had probably drafted, as well as signed, the strike declaration on February 20. Her name reappeared in the delegation sent by the strike committee on March 2 to inform the prefect of the committee's position regarding the average wages published by the millowners. More important, she was noted as the only female member of the worker delegation to Paris that presented strikers' demands to Premier René Waldeck-Rousseau on April 5. She was an activist who left only an ephemeral trace in history. We know only that she was born in Nancy and became the wife of an unskilled hosiery worker, then the mother of a young rebrousseur who had begun work in the mills by 1906.[32] Lecolle Carabin stayed out on strike until the bitter end.

While the strike spread to the smaller mills, the dyeworks, and the knitting-machine factories, it did not have the unanimous support of textile workers in Troyes. In the early days of mobilization, "strikers, both men and women, wore the red *cocarde* pinned to the left of their chest" to distinguish themselves from workers who were simply unemployed or idle.[33] But the strike movement gained momentum when the millowners countered with a lockout on February 27. By mid-March the press estimated that there were some twelve thousand strikers and unemployed, a figure significant for the very fact that it represented one-quarter of the town's population.[34] The exact number of strikers is difficult to corroborate, but by all accounts strikers greatly outnumbered nonstrikers. One of the strike leaders' major concerns was to gain the solidarity of rural outworkers. They feared that the Troyes manufacturers would contract with women homeworkers or small family workshops to circumvent the strike. Their fears were to some extent justified. In April, when the mills reopened, some strikers could not resume work, because their machines had been displaced to the countryside during the strike. The movement, however, did spread to the outlying suburbs of Troyes during the first week. A sympathizer, who cautiously signed his letter to *Le Petit Troyen* as "Jean du Peuple," wrote to denounce the number of rural artisans who were accommodating the millowners by accepting orders during the strike.[35] A

32. Prior to 1906, no gender distinctions were made in the occupational breakdown of census reports. See Scott 1988. I traced Lecolle Carabin in the 1901 and 1906 census reports after finding her address through her husband's name on the voting list.
33. *Le Petit Républicain*, February 23, 1900.
34. *La Dépêche Troyenne*, March 13, 1900.
35. *Le Petit Troyen*, February 23, 1900.

delegation of strikers arrived on February 24 in nearby Romilly-sur-Seine, the second industrial center in the Aube, to bring the knitters out in support of their movement. But work continued there until the lockout in Troyes. From that moment, the strike gained momentum, spreading to other nearby centers such as the Pays d'Othe, to the southwest of Troyes.

Millowners in Troyes had been surprised by the outbreak of the strike and by its rapid extension. They feared the influence of the POF militants who had been recruited among the textile workers and whom they designated as "collectivistes," because the party advocated the collectivization of the means of production. From the millowners' perspective, the possibility of electoral success by Guesdist candidates in the Aube represented a potential danger to bourgeois property and to the liberal industrial order. Even after the strike ended in April, Léon Poron publicly threatened to close down his mill if the socialists were victorious in the May municipal elections.[36] But millowners were also concerned by Radical republican politics at the national level. Hence their distrust of the Radical mayor of Troyes and the government in Paris. The left-wing coalition government headed by Waldeck-Rousseau had created uncertainty about its policy toward industry by naming socialist Alexandre Millerand as minister of commerce. Troyes millowners had for years been fending off what they identified as government interference in labor relations: the new protective legislation of 1892 and 1900 had set limits to employers' authority by shortening working hours and banning night work for women and children in factories.[37] Auguste Mortier, one of Troyes's leading manufacturers and a member of the international jury for the Paris World's Fair, spoke for the employers' association in 1904, reproaching the government for "interference in the world of work." He exhorted the government to devise a "national policy and not a policy expressing class or political party interests."[38] Troyes millowners argued that social-reform legislation tended to separate citizens into two political camps, employers and workers. It was this very "political" aspect of the strike to which employers objected. To retain their power and authority, they refused to negotiate with the strike committee and stubbornly insisted on receiving only delegations from their own mills. The millowners' attitude toward the strike presumed a consensus on the issue of

36. Bedin 1977, 171.
37. The most recent law at the time restricting working hours in factories, voted in 1900, revised an earlier hour law of 1892 banning night labor for women and children.
38. Rapport de la Chambre de commerce de Troyes (1904), AN C 7318.

piece rates. But it was only in concert and through negotiation that they reached a publicized agreement on the average daily wages paid in the mills. Once this question had been settled to their satisfaction, they formed a united front and closed their factories, to maintain that unity.

However, divisions appeared little by little in what strikers termed "the bosses' coalition." There were, in fact, important differences between and among them, beginning with the most obvious religious and political ones: Pierre Valton and Paul Raguet were Catholic supporters of the clerical cause, Frédéric Lange and Maurice Mauchauffée adhered to the liberal laissez-faire principles of the Opportunists, while Charles Boisson and Louis Bonbon espoused Radical Party politics.[39] The larger mills were in the process of restructuring their capital, which meant that millowners with a fortune behind them, such as Mauchauffée and Léon Poron, were in a position to resist and to wait out a long strike.[40] It was in fact Mauchauffée and Poron who insisted on making no concessions to workers' demands.[41] Poron accepted a personal polemical role in the press against the Guesdist leaders, but he refused to negotiate. In the end the millowners' intransigence, manifested against proposals from all three actors (the mayor of Troyes, the prefect, and the strikers), turned public opinion against them. Even if the strike leaders had lost some support as the conflict dragged on, the reopening of the mills and the resumption of work did not take place in the way the millowners anticipated.

But it also became increasingly difficult to maintain the lockout because townspeople and shopkeepers openly expressed general indignation in the local press. Public opinion in Troyes clearly supported the strikers, evidenced by the many small shopkeepers who simply extended credit to strikers for the duration of the conflict or donated free bread, wine, and other staples. *Le Petit Troyen* published a daily list of small donations, collections, and direct aid offered by townspeople after the lockout began.[42] Administrators at the

39. See the analysis of these positions in *Le Reveil des Travailleurs de l'Aube,* March 17–24, 1900.

40. Bergeron 1978, 92–94. The restructuring of their capital allowed several manufacturers, including Mauchauffée and Lange, to set up sales agencies in the French colonies. Mauchauffée was the director of the largest mill in Troyes (thirteen hundred employees) and owned branches in the Aube countryside, the Côte d'Or and the Vosges. Lange was president of the Chambre syndicale patronale and used his position to establish a market for Troyes's knitted goods at the Colonial Exhibit in Hanoi in 1902.

41. Report by the commissaire de police to the prefect, February 20, 1900. ADA SC 417.

42. See the lists published in *Le Petit Troyen* from the lockout, February 27, to the end of the strike.

public housing project the Cité Meunier aux Charmilles suspended rent payments. Measures to generate support emerged from other local sources. Soup kitchens and fund-raising public balls—demonstrating the organizational skills of the strike committee—promoted public goodwill.

Notable support also came from the workers' consumer cooperative in Troyes, the Laborieuse, a socialist-inspired wing of the labor movement. By 1900, the Laborieuse grouped more than 2,245 families in a cooperative store that offered goods and services. Shareholders voted in favor of 1,000 francs in direct aid to the strike committee and distributed some 1,246 francs to cooperative members who were on strike or unemployed. In principle the cooperative did not extend credit—purchases were on a cash-only basis—but this principle was obviously bent to fit the circumstances. As an institution of working-class solidarity whose motto was "Tous pour chacun, chacun pour tous," the Laborieuse fulfilled its mission by coming immediately to workers' aid. More important, it established a relief fund to meet future eventualities of the kind it was now facing.[43]

Mayor Louis Mony reacted to the lockout by requesting the town council fund a series of measures in aid of "needy families" affected by the strike. The council voted for five thousand francs in aid on February 27, in a measure that created some awkward exchanges between Mony and the Radical minister of the interior in Paris, who tried to pressure Mony to cancel the vote.[44] On the local level, millowners did not welcome the mayor's efforts to mediate with the strikers. As the conflict deepened and widened, Mony sought to conciliate both sides, thus appearing to not support the strike. Despite the order and calm in which the strike continued to evolve, Mony decided that he could no longer tolerate the processions and brass bands in the streets that invariably accompanied visitors arriving from the railroad station to the Maison du Peuple. So he attempted to ban them. At this point Louis Casabona, editor in chief of *La Dépêche Troyenne,* published an editorial in which he sided with the music makers in the strike: "Yes, [strikers] demonstrate in the streets of Troyes behind the tricolor flag [not the red flag] and the brass band, they sing the *chanson de la grève* and the workers' "Internationale." . . . It appears that someone wants to keep the strikers from singing. Such measures would be a

43. Rapport du Conseil d'administration de la Laborieuse, AG, August 18, 1900, ADA M 2352. See Chapter 5 for a longer development on the Laborieuse.
44. The Radical government had, in fact, the authority to annul the town's appropriation of aid to strikes if it so wished.

provocation."[45] Mony had overreacted and had to back down. In fact, the strike had not provoked any violence that would have attracted the national press or additional government troops to the scene. Only the political pressure exercised by local elections, by Millerand's presence in the left-wing coalition government, and by the efforts of socialist factions to forge unity at the national level raised the political stakes in what was to become a much wider social and political conflict.

THE STRIKE SPREADS

At the very outset of the conflict, strikers launched appeals for aid to national socialist leaders and to workers' associations all over France. Aid arrived in various forms, but only very slowly, which meant that both strikers and the local Guesdist militants held out for three weeks before any apparent outside help arrived. The POF and other socialist solidarity groups sent speakers, including deputies, militants, journalists, and two feminists. The only nationally recognized socialist leader to appear on the scene during the strike was Jean Allemane, a skilled worker who had founded a splinter party, the Parti ouvrier socialiste révolutionnaire. Unlike Guesde, he was a proponent of the general strike as a proletarian political weapon. Allemane spent several days in Troyes toward the end of the strike. All these speakers arrived by train, often just for the day, and were accompanied from the station by a procession of strikers and militants, together with the Sainte-Savine brass band, to the Halle de la Bonneterie, where meetings took place. The visits provided an occasion to fill the streets with festive crowds, who in an orderly way demonstrated in support of the strike.

The visits by two socialist feminists contrasted singularly with the passage of male political personalities through the town. Police reports referred to them as *citoyennes* (female citizens) using the republican form of address. No mention was made of their feminist or other political affiliations. Marie Bonnevial was a militant syndicalist who wrote a regular column on women's work for the well-known French feminist daily newspaper, *La Fronde*. She arrived to speak to a strike fund-raising meeting on March 22, bringing with her a donation of 220 francs on behalf of feminist Marguerite Durand and the

45. *La Dépêche Troyenne,* March 16, 1900.

staff of the paper.[46] Her talk was directed primarily at women workers, whom she urged to establish an independent and separate labor union from those of men and to continue the struggle. The police reports dismissed Bonnevial's talk as "totally insignificant," and the local press hardly mentioned it at all. We are led to believe that, despite her former ties with Jules Guesde, Marie Bonnevial's ideas on single-sex syndicalism did not draw an interested audience from among striking women workers. By contrast, the press commented in greater detail on the arrival of Mme Sorgue, the nom de guerre of Antoinette Cauvin, who was widely known in feminist and socialist circles. She came to play an effective role, together with other members of the socialist group, in negotiations toward ending the strike.[47]

In the following weeks, every speaker tried to harden the workers' resolve. "Hold out to the bitter end" became the slogan, commonly understood as "until they obtained satisfaction of their demands." Speakers praised the workers' calm and urged them to join the unions. They brought promises of aid; among them was Maxence Roldes, the first speaker to arrive in Troyes on March 9, on behalf of his newspaper *La Petite République*. Other speakers came to promote worker solidarity with other regions of France, including Plastre, deputy from the Gard, where knitters were also on strike. Such promises of aid encouraged strikers to hold out for satisfaction of their demands. During the first few weeks, the material problems of the strike had been resolved by credit from shopkeepers in town and by a daily distribution of goods at the town hall. But expectations of outside aid dragged on without results. How was it possible to hold out after three long weeks of strike?

On March 10, nonstrikers established a "Committee of Unemployed," headed by a leader of the employer-dominated Cercle catholique d'ouvriers.

46. *La Fronde* published some information on the strike in Troyes from February 28 on, but it is interesting to note that their reporting did not mention the presence of women workers among the strikers until March 21, on the eve of Mme Bonnevial's visit to Troyes. Bonnevial has an interesting personal itinerary for her support of many causes. Her experience in both syndicalism and socialism took her into feminism. As a primary school teacher, she was one of the founders, together with Aline Valette, of the Syndicat de l'enseignement. In 1904 she became president of the Ligue française pour le droit des femmes, a women's suffrage association. For more biographical information, see Sowerwine 1982; Corradin 1999, 150–51.

47. Mme Sorgue appeared in Lille during the general strike of 1903–4 in the Nord, where striking workers delegated her to carry their demands to Paris. Sorgue declared at the SFIO congress in Nancy in 1907: "I don't believe that women will emancipate themselves through the ballot. I believe . . . that the proletarian woman will only emancipate herself through union struggles, that is, through the struggle for economic equality" (Sowerwine 1982, 116–17; Hilden 1986, 160; Zylberberg-Hocquard 1981, 122).

They contended that they, too, were out of work and that they had been refused relief by the strike committee. While it was generally recognized that aid should be distributed only to those on strike, this quarrel over relief reflected obvious religious and political divisions among textile workers. Moreover, these divisions mirrored individual differences among the millowners, some of whom acted paternalistically to draw their workers back to the job. So relief donations to the unemployed poured in from various sources, some identified in the columns of *Le Petit Troyen* by a decidedly public political statement, revealing that the strike had stirred up mixed emotions from some townspeople. The strike committee sought to counter this campaign by defying the millowners to reopen their workshops and see who was willing to return to work. Their defiance sought to prove once and for all that the committee was not maintaining the strike through undue pressure. A peaceful demonstration of some eight thousand strikers on March 13 represented a show of strength.[48] But by March 17 the Committee of Unemployed had succeeded in pressuring millowners to establish lists of the unemployed who wanted to return to work.

Hoping to turn the tide, the strike committee published in *Le Reveil des Travailleurs* a symbolic appeal for solidarity, on March 18, historic anniversary of the proclamation of the Paris Commune. It was addressed to "la France ouvrière," to workers' cooperatives, to the republican and socialist press, from the twelve thousand striking workers of Troyes: "For more than three weeks we have been on strike to obtain a change in an unfair work contract. . . . During these three weeks we have valiantly upheld the workers' flag against the millowners, and we have not sought relief or assistance. . . . Today, since employers have refused all concessions, our situation has become difficult; the struggle may last much longer, we know how to accept sacrifices. But should our companions, our children, be made to feel the sufferings of hunger because we wanted to better our lot? . . . We appeal to la France ouvrière and to all those who respect justice and solidarity." This exalted appeal to fraternal solidarity for goods, donations, and relief funds carried with it the claim to a material share in the Republic. That same day, Emile Clévy and Ernest Lozach, two knitters and POF militants, had organized a meeting at the Halle de la Bonneterie to commemorate the Paris Commune. Ever the propagandist and orator, Lozach invoked the revolutionary memory of the Commune in

48. *La Dépêche Troyenne,* March 13, 1900.

terms that legitimated urban revolt, proclaiming, "The Commune alone saved the Republic against the bourgeois schemes of Thiers and others."[49] The message for the present was not lost to his listeners: history was not over, and it could be remade through continued worker resistance.

The perspective of prolonged resistance divided the strike movement at a time when, on March 20, millowners began to put registers in the workshops, encouraging a return to work. In the following days those speakers to arrive in Troyes all attempted to counter these overtures to end the strike. The reopening of most mills on Tuesday, March 27, placed strikers in an even more difficult situation. While the millowners had decided to reopen their factories, they had made no concessions. Only 2,900 workers out of 7,910 reported for work, according to police reports. The strike committee reacted by calling for demonstrations outside the factory gates, and a procession of about 1,800 strikers marched through the streets, singing the "Drapeau rouge" and "La chanson de la grève." Some unemployed workers and a few strikers went to look for work, but since there were not enough workers for a full shift, they were sent home. An editorial in the Radical *La Dépêche Troyenne* ironized that workers' resistance had taught the millowners a lesson: to get workers to return to work, it was not enough just to reopen the factory gates.[50] As the week wore on and the strikers' situation became more difficult, strike delegates turned to the mayor to relay to the Chambre syndicale patronale their willingness to make concessions. By March 31, the strike committee had decided on a more aggressive course of action. They would post a broadside in town in response to the millowners, and they would send a worker delegation to Paris to speak with Premier Waldeck-Rousseau and request his arbitration.

On April 2, a small delegation composed of four male knitters and one woman seamer, Lecolle Carabin from the Raguet mills, set out for Paris by train.[51] They were received by the head of the socialist group in the Chamber of Deputies with a promise of support. The following day, Mayor Louis Mony and Gaston Arbouin, the newly elected Radical deputy, accompanied the worker delegation to a meeting with Premier Waldeck-Rousseau. The government's response was to offer a restatement of the liberal republican position on the "social question," one that favored the manufacturer as the

49. ADA W 750.
50. *La Dépêche Troyenne,* March 28, 1900.
51. For the identity of these workers, see letter from the Direction de la Sûreté to the prefect, ADA SC 417.

source of economic growth and social stability. In explicit terms, the premier claimed that he was "powerless to intervene" in this type of conflict, except to instruct the prefect to urge both sides to use the arbitration procedures provided under the law. Implied in this statement was the protection and respect of private property, and "la liberté du travail." Waldeck-Rousseau left worker delegates to return to Troyes empty-handed.[52]

Several socialist speakers had in the meantime arrived in town in an effort to block the movement to return to work without obtaining some concessions. At a public meeting on April 4, Albert Walter, socialist deputy from St. Denis, together with Mme Sorgue newly arrived from Paris, encouraged the striking workers to continue their action. But a strike committee spokesman announced that they were seeking through the prefect a meeting with mill-owners, and he intimated that if the strikers were willing to make concessions, the employers would be too. The debate split the meeting, with the knitters opposed to further resistance, and the rebrousseurs determined to hold out until the bitter end. Faced with the failure of the workers' delegation to Paris to obtain any positive government support, as reported that evening, strikers were inevitably divided over what course to take.

At a meeting with the prefect the following day, Walter and Mme Sorgue entered into negotiations with a representative of the Chambre syndicale patronale and obtained some satisfaction of workers' secondary demands. Mill-owners agreed to eliminate most wage deductions, which workers felt unjustly penalized their daily production. However, the owners refused discussion of an increase in piece rates. Reporting back to the assembly of strikers, Mme Sorgue advised workers to return to their jobs, given the millowners' concessions. But strikers remained divided: such meager concessions after so many sacrifices! As no clear line of action emerged from the assembly, it was proposed that strike delegates carry out a vote by secret ballot, workshop by workshop. By April 7, this consultation process had led to a majority vote in favor of continuing the strike, which a general assembly of strikers then voted to confirm. Nevertheless there was considerable grumbling against the invited speakers, who, despite promises of aid, had left town without ultimately delivering the goods. Strikers were feeling more and more isolated.

On April 10, Jean Allemane arrived in Troyes. He was the most important socialist leader of working-class origin to lend his personal support to the

52. ADA SC 417.

strikers. Allemane commanded respect for his political experience as a recognized leader of the Parti ouvrier socialiste révolutionnaire, artisan typographer and union militant.[53] To those textile workers drawn to revolutionary syndicalism, Allemane represented a current of French socialism that appealed to direct action within the union movement. By the time he arrived, support was dwindling for the strike. Six of the largest mills were working full shifts. At a public meeting, Allemane urged the assembled 450 strikers to resist and to unite behind the union. The present crisis, he argued, was brought about by the big millowners, who were starving their workers and seeking to ruin the smaller manufacturers. Allemane cautioned workers not to accept verbal promises from their employers, because only written agreements on concessions would be binding. The strike movement gained new momentum as he promised to lead a delegation to each factory gate to encourage worker support. So by the following day strike delegates were handing out leaflets for a general assembly that evening, at which Allemane was to report on his discussions with the mayor.

A crowd of some fifteen hundred workers filled the hall at the Maison du Peuple to hear Allemane speak. He called on workers to continue their resistance, insisting that "this strike must end in favor of workers' demands." Allemane reported that he and the mayor had obtained the millowners' agreement to rehire all the striking workers. Once he had given these assurances, Allemane proposed his vision of how a future socialist society would operate. He favored abolishing money, for he felt the present bourgeois state was corrupt (the state was a *faux monnayeur* [counterfeiter]), and that money should be replaced with work coupons that could be exchanged for goods at municipal trading centers. Above all, workers should unionize and educate themselves by creating socialist libraries where women and children could also learn. In this case he was preaching to the converted, since two such libraries already existed in town.[54] Then Allemane addressed the young rebrousseurs who had sparked the strike, and invited them to continue their struggle.[55] When Allemane left the following day, support for the strike quickly dissolved and the rebrousseurs were left to negotiate a settlement on their own.

53. See Reynolds 1984.
54. Radical journalist Gaston Arbouin had helped to found a lending library, the Bibliothèque démocratique et populaire, in 1878, and the Maison du Peuple contained a small library of socialist publications.
55. Letter from Direction de la Sureté to the préfet, April 11, 1900. ADA SC 417.

By April 15, most of the mills announced that all their workers had returned to the job. Those who had decided to stay out on strike did not find work. The prefect finally declared the strike officially ended, on April 18, since all the mills were operating fully staffed. Strikers without work demanded official intervention to return to their former jobs. They called themselves "strike victims," and, in fact, there were numerous socialist militants among them. According to the police list, employers had indeed taken advantage of the strike to weed out workers whom they considered undesirable.[56] In some cases workers found that their knitting machines had been sent to rural outworkers or to the World's Fair exhibition halls in Paris. Under these conditions, in the aftermath of the strike, divisions among workers resurfaced rapidly. Inevitable disputes broke out between those workers who had resumed work before the others and those who had held out longer in solidarity.

The prefect put pressure on the millowners to rehire all strikers, by reminding them of their agreement. However, the president of the Chambre syndicale patronale replied that they had agreed to rehire "enough workers to operate the existing machines, and that was what they had done." He admitted that many employers had sent machines to rural outworkers or had replaced strikers with new workers "to encourage the return to work." The concession to rehire strikers, he argued, was made in the interest of facilitating their return, but workers had not seized the opportunity very effectively.[57] Millowners thus marked the end of this bitter strike by forcing the last strikers to look elsewhere for work, thereby reasserting employer control over the workplace.

CONSEQUENCES OF THE STRIKE

The conclusion of the long two-month strike left all the actors in Troyes reassessing their situation. Millowners in Troyes had evidently won the strike by refusing to redress major worker grievances concerning wages. While the long interruption in production had caused them some financial prejudice at a time when orders for the spring collection were running high, they had in fact strengthened their position of authority. They had granted only

56. Letter from commissaire to prefect, April 20, 1900, ADA SC 417.
57. Letter from the Chambre syndicale patronale to the prefect, April 24, 1900. ADA SC 417.

minimal concessions and forced strikers back to work. More important, they had succeeded in neither recognizing nor legitimizing the strike committee and the unions. Thus when the mills reopened, each employer felt legitimated to rehire whomever he wished from the pool of former employees and to eliminate troublemakers. In this sense they had reconstituted what millowner Léon Poron referred to as "the big industrial family." In a highly polemical letter published in *Le Petit Troyen* on March 29, Poron attacked the socialists' notion of class struggle in these terms: "Bosses are not cut from a different cloth from that of their workers; they make up one big family with them, one body in which no member can suffer without that suffering being shared by all other members of that body which constitutes the industrial family. In this family each brings his labor and each receives a share of the product. . . . Equality in the sharing of the product of this labor presupposes equality in the effort and the service rendered."[58] Poron's representation here of family capitalism in Troyes as "an industrial body" evoked a type of late nineteenth-century paternalism, in which the employer as self-styled patriarch sought to legitimize his authority and bind workers to factory jobs.[59] More explicitly, Poron's paternalistic language attempted to counter the class-solidarity appeal of socialism. The family metaphor concealed the issue of domination, that is, the millowners' monopoly over the labor market, a monopoly that they had so ruthlessly used in the lockout. Poron's image of French family capitalism could hardly have found acceptance among the many knitters who had formerly worked as artisans, directing their own family workshop in a world of semi-autonomy that the factory system had undermined and supplanted.

Troyes millowners had succeeded in adopting and maintaining a common front, thanks in part to the lockout. Pressure from the large manufacturers must have weighed heavily in the decision to use such a method, so rarely employed in France.[60] Surprised by the sudden outbreak of the conflict and its rapid development, millowners seized on the lockout as a way of regaining control and imposing employer solidarity at a moment when, in fact, there were important divergences among them and an unfavorable political context. When

58. Poron was in fact replying to Guesdist leader Henri Corgéron's letter in the press explaining the need to collectivize the means of production.

59. See Donald Reid's (1992) analysis of such paternal metaphors.

60. Lockouts were used in only 3.1 percent of conflicts studied by Michelle Perrot during the period 1871–90. It was a tactic used essentially by "small family manufacturers with modest workshops." See M. Perrot 1974, 2:683–87.

all this is said, millowners must have measured the lockout's effectiveness as a weapon by their decisive victory over the strike. For this reason, they would have recourse to it again in the next big strike, in 1921. In revenge, public opinion in Troyes never accepted the monthlong lockout, which deprived a major part of the town population of a livelihood.[61]

The strike's failure had unfortunate consequences for the Troyes working class. Despite their calm, dignified attitude and the absence of violence, strike leaders never succeeded in obtaining recognition from millowners or government representatives that their cause was just. Strikers had counted on a favorable political context, and they had followed the newly established grievance procedures to affirm their rights as workers against the millowners' authority. An editorial in the *Reveil des Travailleurs de l'Aube* titled "Autorité patronale" accused those who had fomented antisocialist sentiment of avoiding debate on the real issue raised by the strike, that is, the legitimacy of the right of workers to defend their interests.

> We are defending workers' interests and rights. What are these rights? The right to a livelihood assured by the proper organization of work; the right to develop one's intelligence and knowledge and to taste intellectual pleasures; the right to debate working conditions that should respond to production needs but also spare a worker's health and safeguard his dignity; the right to own property guaranteed to everyone by the suppression of capitalist privileges (profits on wages, on savings, monopolies, etc.). It is clear that such demands are very general and that they have nothing to do with the hatred inspired by one boss or another. . . . Our demands for restrictions on employers' authority have been countered by an outdated notion of property rights.[62]

Defined in these terms, workers' substantive rights indeed went unrecognized in a bourgeois Third Republic that had an unimpressive record of social reform and a liberal respect for private property. The author reminded his readers of what was at stake in these workers' demands: "When popular sovereignty asserted politically by the ballot becomes economically affirmed by

61. See *La Dépêche Troyenne,* March 13, 1900, and the strike report sent to the minister of commerce, ADA SC 417.

62. Editorial in *Le Reveil des Travailleurs de l'Aube,* March 18, 1900.

the right to own property and the right to work, our bourgeois Republic will have become a socialist Republic."[63] These words echoed those of workers in February 1848 who had claimed economic equality through property in their labor and a guaranteed right to work. But by the century's end, liberal industrialists persisted in denying workers' rights to organize defensively, while the left-wing coalition of Radicals, socialists, and moderates in power in Paris sought to preserve the republican regime through limited concessions to the social agenda.

Millowners had violated the right to work. Their successful imposition of a lockout only emphasized the basic inequality between members of the "industrial body" so graphically represented by Léon Poron.[64] The workers' movement felt totally impotent against the lockout, which revealed the entrenched structure of millowners' power. These feelings were expressed by the leader of the knitters union of nearby Romilly during the congress of the Fédération nationale de l'industrie textile held in Troyes in August 1908. The lockout, he argued, magnified the workers' sense of class struggle, but what means were there to contain and contravene such practices carried out by employers?[65] It is obvious that syndicalism had no weapon to match the lockout during this early period in its history.

The strike movement also failed to create lasting solidarity among textile workers of different occupations. While this was especially true of the young rebrousseurs, who formed the most volatile part of the labor force, their revolt had challenged just such divisions. Above and beyond the more "political" demand for unified piece rates, in which a strategy was proposed for combating the existing competition among workers, the strike had proved the failure of forging collective interests based on craft identities. Militant strike leaders had retreated before the problems of achieving this objective and scaled back their demand to a 15 percent increase in wages. However, the question of unified piece rates remained important to the Fédération nationale de l'industrie

63. Ibid.

64. In *La Dépêche Troyenne,* Louis Casabona refuted Poron's arguments by taking up the same image of the "industrial body": "[O]ne of the (body's) organs—Monsieur Poron—absorbs everything to the detriment of the others. Monsieur Poron absorbs and gets richer, his workers produce and expend their strength without any appreciable gain for them. There is, therefore, no equality" (March 29, 1900).

65. *L'Ouvrier Textile,* September 1, 1908. The question of the lockout embarrassed textile federation president Victor Renard, who argued that the only way to combat a lockout was to build a strong union.

textile and its leader, Victor Renard, who saw it as a means "to bring more rational and, above all, more just pay procedures to the textile workforce."[66]

The rebrousseurs were the only category of workers to distance themselves from the strike movement. They initiated and led the strike at the outset, and then they held out to the bitter end, without obtaining satisfaction of their demands. One of the unresolved issues of the strike was the question of their wages and the practice of subcontracting their work. Their permanent discontent resulted in periodic strikes for ostensibly the same motives from 1904 through 1913. In fact, in a show of autonomy they established their own separate union, the Syndicat des rebrousseurs de Troyes, and attended textile federation congresses alongside members of the knitters' union. But many of these young men were hostile to union discipline and preferred direct strike action or walkouts when conflicts arose.[67]

Syndicalism appeared to be the most obvious victim of the strike. However, low union membership, internal factions, and separate unions founded on craft interests were all factors that had weakened the Troyes labor movement going into the strike. At the national level the textile federation had long recognized that hosiery workers were difficult to organize because many of them were homeworkers or had previously been independent artisans. Beyond the specific structural problems of organizing the Troyes textile workers, it was evident that a vast majority of them had rejected the hierarchical political framework proposed by POF leaders, who had consistently subordinated syndicalism to party directives and political goals.[68] Both the Guesdist newspaper, *Le Reveil des Travailleurs,* and the Radical *Le Petit Troyen* laid the failure of the strike to the weakness of the unions. The immediate effect of the great strike was to split the knitters' union from the Guesdist-dominated federation of unions in the Aube; local knitters led their small following to join the Confédération générale du travail (CGT), a national federation of industrial

66. For this question and the ensuing debates at the Congresses in Troyes (1908) and Fourmies (1912), see *L'Ouvrier Textile,* November 1, 1909.

67. In October 1913 several young rebrousseurs from the Mauchauffée mills were fired as ringleaders of a strike movement. They organized a procession of a thousand workers to accompany the young mill director to his home. This incident provoked a lockout at the mill and the intervention of the union to negotiate a settlement. See *L'Ouvrier Textile,* December 1, 1913.

68. Gerard Noiriel suggests that, during this intense period of socialist organizing at the national level, syndicalism and socialist parties were appealing to the same constituency, which might explain the difficulties of creating a unified labor movement, and the absence of a workers' collective identity. See Noiriel 1986, 118–19.

unions that had been founded in 1895. Proponents of revolutionary syndicalism dominated the new CGT, appealing above factious socialist politics to direct practical action and to the unifying force of the general strike. In the following years the number of wage disputes and small conflicts that broke out in Troyes demonstrates that supporters of revolutionary syndicalism's strategy of direct action came to dominate the local labor movement.

Women textile workers, who had sworn to join the union in the heat of the strike, found their place within the cohesive strike movement and its expression of class solidarity. Their specific grievances were an expression of a sense of collective trade identity, or *métier,* very similar to that felt by their male co-workers. But women's strike participation exceeded their willingness to join the union, and neither local union leader Emile Clévy nor national textile federation leader Renard made any direct appeal at this critical moment to unionize women workers. Male domination of the textile unions ensured that the question of women's work and its relation to syndicalism would remain a problematic issue largely defined in patriarchal terms. Thus several years later at the textile federation congress held in Troyes in 1908, Renard reaffirmed the male right to work in terms that stressed women's domestic duties. Renard claimed that "women were competing more and more with men who were often forced to stay home to care for the kids and the *pot-au-feu,* while their wives were obliged to extend their working day, after long hours in the factory or spinning mill, so as to finish up the chores at home; this constitutes an area of hardship and privation of all kinds."[69] For Renard, women were not primarily workers; they were housewives and mothers. For that reason their place was at home making the family *pot-au-feu.* Renard's attitude toward women in the textile union betrayed a shift in Guesdist efforts, from recruiting women into unions to supporting protective legislation that would restrict women and children's labor, a shift reflected in union newspapers.[70] Male militants no longer framed the struggle in terms of class solidarity, which might draw women into the unions.

With the failure of the strike, political tensions remained high in Troyes in anticipation of municipal elections in May. Militants from the POF attempted to mobilize their constituency in support of their candidates and a municipal social welfare program that would put into practice reforms concerning

69. *L'Ouvrier Textile,* October 1, 1908.
70. For an analysis of this shift as it concerns women textile workers in the Nord, see Hilden 1986, chap. 4.

wages, hours and workers' families.[71] At the same time, Guesdist militants appealed to defeated workers to get out and vote for their party: "[Y]ou are the social equal of your boss; you even represent more than he does because you outnumber him." Guesdists even sought to incite an act of revenge against the lockout. One editorialist in *Le Reveil des Travailleurs* extended the lockout metaphor into electoral politics: "The bourgeoisie believes that elected mandates belong to them, and they will lose no opportunity to organize a veritable lockout against us if we compete against them inside their fortress. . . . If workers, out of timidity or fear, refuse to react . . . the resulting rout will be more dangerous than struggle! Frightened soldiers are the first to be killed."[72] Indeed, one of the principal reasons that the great strike had failed was that the millowners' lockout had proved stronger than a divided working class.

In the first round, on May 6, the POF candidate, Hébert Corgeron, finished ahead of the Radicals and two splinter socialist factions,[73] but second behind the Right, a list of self-styled independent republicans. The label for the latter was clearly misleading, because the list included conservatives and supporters of clericalism. For *Le Petit Troyen* the choice for republican voters was clearly to support the POF, since "the collectivistes are republicans; the clericals, whatever label they choose to wear, are the irreconcilable enemies of the Republic."[74] The other left-wing parties withdrew their candidates in favor of the POF. But in the runoff election on May 13, the right-wing list carried the day by a small majority of some 280 votes, thereby ending for a number of years the socialist bid for control of the town hall in Troyes.[75] The newly elected mayor was Charles Lemblin-Armant, who came from a conservative wine-grower family. Short-term support for the Right undoubtedly came from

71. *Le Reveil des Travailleurs de l'Aube,* April 21–28, 1900. The POF municipal welfare program strongly resembled the successful experiences of Guesdists in Roubaix, including the school lunches instituted by women workers. See Hilden 1986, 203–5.

72. *Le Reveil des Travailleurs de l'Aube,* April 21–28, 1900.

73. This politically mixed group was made up of a minority faction within the POF from the *quartier bas,* or workers' quarter, in Troyes, and some former municipal councilors, who as workers had been elected on the Radical ticket.

74. *Le Petit Troyen,* May 7, 1900.

75. In the first round the POF obtained 23.9 percent, the independent socialists 4.92 percent, the Radicals 15.79 percent and the Right 27.61 percent; and in the second round the Right obtained 4,764 votes, against 4,482 for the POF. See *Le Petit Troyen,* May 7 and May 14, 1900; Bedin 1977, 176. Political parties were often badly structured during this period and splintered into factions, which was particularly true among socialists. The creation of the SFIO in 1905 would finally bring unity and provide the basis for parliamentary electoral mandates. The SFIO finally won power in Troyes when Emile Clévy was elected mayor in 1919.

those Radical voters who typically identified social order and stability with small producers and family-based entrepreneurs. But these runoff elections in May 1900 raise important questions concerning workers' confidence in electoral socialism: were the Guesdists held responsible for the strike's failure? And how do we account for the fact that one out of every five registered voters abstained?[76]

While the POF did lose the elections in Troyes, its electoral success extended to the town hall in nearby Romilly and to forty newly elected officials in five communes in the Aube. At the turn of the century, the Guesdist party could claim strong support for candidates in local and parliamentary elections in the Aube, the Seine, and the Nord. But the institutions that they had fostered to buttress their political action—the knitters' union and the workers' consumer cooperative the Sociale—foundered or were taken over by other socialist groups within the working class. The strike marked both the culmination of Guesdist fervor and militancy among the millworkers as well as a new beginning, as the labor movement was impelled by the failure of the strike to regroup their defenses behind the CGT and revolutionary syndicalism. Workers faced an arrogant coalition of millowners, confidently consolidating their gains in a social and political context that would prove less favorable to workplace conflict.

The failure of the great strike of 1900 pinpoints many of the issues of intense social and economic transformation in French working-class culture that are the subject of this book. The great strike posed the problem of power at every level: in the mills, the municipality and the state. It gave expression to worker grievances against arbitrary millowner practices with relation to wages and working conditions, grievances that implicated the Third Republic's failures to curb employer authority, protect workers' rights, and legislate reform. Interwoven into the conflict were significant threads of working-class culture, the fabric of gender and class solidarity in the face of the lockout, and the socialist-inspired mobilization and resistance that, while not immediately successful, proved its resilience ultimately into the mid-twentieth century. In this sense,

76. Overall, 20 percent of registered voters abstained in the runoff election. It is possible that abstentions represented a significant number of embittered workers. There is a markedly even distribution of abstentions in all neighborhoods of the city. See the detailed election results in *Le Petit Troyen*, May 14, 1900. See also the comments of Heywood (1998, 177–78). Pouget's weekly, *Le Père Peinard*, contained a regular notice from Troyes calling for workers to join an "abstentionist group" in the *quartier bas* to create propaganda for the electoral campaign period.

the strike did make a difference to both millowners and workers. Their worlds would never be the same again. Workers' identities and struggles for control within the workplace were transformed by the conflict. Capitalist millowners consolidated production within a factory system that increasingly eroded worker autonomy. What did endure was the culture of textile production and commerce, already deeply rooted in the history of the Champagne region.

Millowners in Troyes had hitherto upheld their authority in labor and industrial affairs relatively unhampered by politics and the state. The kind of family capitalism they so ardently practiced in the past, which is treated in the following chapter, was based on a shared experience in merchant manufacturing. While the authority of employers emerged strengthened by their strike victory in the short run, their prerogatives had been sufficiently contested for them to seek some form of long-term social peace with their workers. The government in Paris had not intervened in Troyes. But just four years later, Jean Jaurès would condemn the refusal of textile employers to arbitrate a textile workers' strike in Armentières, another Guesdist stronghold in the Nord. By engaging "each other in disastrous competition that always ends in the cutting of wages," Jaurès argued, they maintained a level of anarchy in the trade.[77] His attack in the Chamber of Deputies provoked a vote to establish a parliamentary commission of inquiry to examine working conditions in textile mills throughout France. The Troyes mills were not spared the commission's scrutiny in 1904. To ensure their future, millowners had to address the social costs of more concentrated, centralized production. With their goods already protected by a high-tariff policy, the entrepreneurs of Troyes set out to create more efficient, dynamic companies and to transform their town into a showcase of French knitted goods production.

Divisions among workers and within the labor movement were the inevitable result of the strike's failure to obtain substantive changes. Outside the workplace, the setback to Guesdist socialist goals that had been experienced in Troyes merely complicated the confusion and tension between revolutionary and reformist factions within French socialism as a whole. At that very moment in 1900, Jean Jaurès was striving to forge a unified party. By the time unity came in April 1905 with the creation of the SFIO, the controversial Alexandre Millerand had been expelled from the party, and Jules Guesde had

77. Quoted in Goldberg 1962, 314–15. See Reddy's (1984) detailed account and analysis of the 1903 strike in Armentières (309–23).

reluctantly accepted Jaurès's unitary strategy. Guesde did so, however, only after seeking support from the Socialist International to ensure that the SFIO would maintain its revolutionary goals as a party of class struggle.[78] Guesde brought his party into the SFIO in the interests of socialist unity, but refused to compromise on the question of class collaboration and reformism. Jaurès tried to steer a middle course, to keep the revolutionary elements of his party as republicans within an uneasy coalition. To many Guesdist militants and revolutionary syndicalists, however, Jaurès's vision of parliamentary socialism was suspect. Emile Clévy wrote to Guesde from Troyes on May 22, 1906: "I find Jaurès is no more of a socialist than he was yesterday or rather that he is so for himself, but little so for the party."[79] Jaurès inspired distrust in Clévy. The former's personal motives and parliamentary tactics seemed to offer a slim hope for radical social change.

A parallel evolution within the labor movement had taken place in 1895 when the craft unions merged with the industrial unions to form the Confédération générale du travail (CGT). In 1906 the CGT voted at its congress in Amiens to operate independently of organized political parties. The Troyes knitters' union had by this time left the Guesdist camp and adhered to this unitary strategy by joining the CGT. But the revolt of the rebrousseurs, combined with craft separatism and political factionalism, kept local union membership small. This numerical weakness reflected the situation of organized labor in France as a whole.

Many townspeople, industrialists, and administrative officials had readily imagined that a socialist spark had ignited the conflict, yet the relative absence of disorder and violence among workers disarmed those political observers on the right who had called for repression. On the left, revolutionary syndicalists explained the workers' relatively calm behavior during the strike by accusing socialist leaders of having preached passive resistance.[80] In fact, the revolutionary ethos of the general strike quickly faded, and wage claims and working conditions reemerged as the crucial issues. The strike had revealed what

78. See Willard's (1991) treatment of the struggle between Jaurès and Guesde at the 1904 Amsterdam conference of the International (88 ff.). See also Goldberg's (1962) description of the same duel (322 ff.).

79. Willard 1991, 95.

80. In his account of the strike in *Le Père Peinard,* the local correspondent accused the socialist leaders of being "des endormeurs" by urging workers to remain calm even when confronted with provocations. Such advice was motivated by electoralism, in his view: "I know Troyes workers well enough to know that under ordinary circumstances, no one would let an insult go by without responding" (April 1–7, 1900).

was primarily at stake: the claim by many workers that their low wages did not give them a fair share in the benefits of French economic growth. Workers argued that the right to work—and to produce the luxury knitted goods sent for display at the Paris World's Fair in 1900—should also ensure the right to consume according to one's needs.[81] Thus many workers, both within and outside organized labor, expressed material concerns for family and community in the changing work environment of technological advances and increased productivity.

Millowners' fear of working-class unity and socialism was very real. At best, certain millowners accepted debating or exchanging ideas with individual workers, perhaps because of the very absence of organized paternalist policies. The case of industrialist Léon Poron was, however, unusual. In 1901, a year after the great strike, Poron covered the walls of the town center with green posters that carried a series of polemical messages concerning his own particular reading of socialism. His campaign continued in letters to the local newspapers. Poron claimed that mechanization under capitalism had not only benefited millowners, but also the working class, who lived, he argued, in greater comfort than that of thirty years ago. An editor of the socialist *Reveil des Travailleurs* refuted Poron's claims, using well-known Marxist principles: the advent of industrial capitalism had caused the artisans' loss of the tools of their trade, he argued, together with their means of livelihood and their property in labor. He called on Poron to come live at their homes and share their "comfort." In conclusion, he claimed that "the knitter in the mill is no longer a man, from the moment he responds to the mill whistle: he is an individual with labor power, but lacking freedom or will. It is the capitalist millowner who has stolen his freedom."[82]

There are several layers of argument in this millworker's reaction to the existing social order. Most evident are the socialist principles he used to express his loss of freedom as a waged worker under capitalism. But he also affirmed a collective awareness that there was little material comfort in exchange for that symbolic wage, despite Poron's claims. Social differentiation through material comforts and life expectancy was an experience of everyday life in this small mill town. The notion of a living wage underpinned worker consciousness of not only the material present, but also the survival of one's

81. This is the subject of Chapter 5.
82. *Le Reveil des Travailleurs de l'Aube*, March 1–8, 1901. The article is signed by Georges Maillet, the secretary of the mairie de Romilly.

family in the future. Finally, this millworker identified himself in gendered terms, as a man who felt less of a man through his labor. His claim for wage justice as a manly breadwinner forced him to defend his very job against the millowner's threat of a lockout. As workers attempted to give meaning to their working lives, they voiced all these concerns. Class as a language of opposition was one of these concerns.

As I hope will emerge from this book, striking textile workers in Troyes expressed a healthy distrust of parliamentary socialism, politicians, and the state. In their view, the government's tolerance of the lockout and its policy of nonintervention had only confirmed the workers' own preference for direct action, their reluctance to join unions, and their desire for equity. Socialist militants critical of the Third Republic referred to the parliamentary regime metaphorically as the "Assiette au Beurre," in other words, a system that nurtured politicians on fat sinecures. At the POF congress in Bar-sur-Seine on April 15, 1900, Etienne Pédron attacked the Waldeck-Rousseau government's program: "We don't live in a republic, because if we did, there would be no fear of anticlericalism, or nationalism, or any other [doctrine]; but those who govern . . . are only ambitious men who work in their own interest [*qui tiennent l'assiette au beurre*]. . . . We therefore demand the end of this preciously conservative republic and the founding of a social republic."[83]

83. Report of the police commissioner, April 16, 1900, ADA W 62. Pédron employed the popular expression "tiennent l'assiette au beurre" in reference to those politicians of the Third Republic whom he regarded as defending their own bourgeois privileges and interests. The phrase was also the title of a satirical weekly that caricatured the political world from the viewpoint and in defense of the worker and the underdog. See Dixmier and Dixmier 1974.

THE WORLD OF TEXTILE WORK:
CONTINUITY AND CHANGE

Our story begins with the land and the people of the Champagne region in the late eighteenth century. In fact, if we were to trace the residual culture of textile commerce and industry to its roots in the region, the story would begin much earlier.[1] The focus of this chapter is the regional pattern of industrialization—developing out of the land, the capital, and the labor—seen in its distinctiveness and in relation to other textile regions of France. I will trace the evolution of the hosiery industry from its origins and through its development from domestic manufacture to an urban industrial factory system, during which time new structures and technology laid the basis for the industrial world of the great strike. This long slow process of industrialization consisted of advances and retreats, commercial successes but also failures, and the transformation of handloom textile workers into machine operators, and eventually minders. For many reasons this was not a linear process, as I will show, but one that entailed a move from the rural dispersion of production to urban concentration, then back to decentralization, shifts that reveal the persistence

---

1. The term "residual" comes from Claude Fohlen's study of the textile industry under the Second Empire, the first work to provide a national overview of textile production during this important period of economic and technological change. He proposed a typology of three regional patterns of textile production: residual, polyvalent, and implanted. He characterized the Champagne region as "residual" because the textile industry was able to maintain itself after the availability of local raw materials, such as flax and wool, declined (Fohlen 1956, 162–63, 175–81; Ricommard 1934; P. Roberts 1996; Colomès 1943; Darbot 1980a. See also the comparative perspective on French industrialization in Horn, forthcoming).

of an outwork system that was the outgrowth of domestic manufacture. Capital investment in new technology and the difficulties of fully mechanizing knitted goods production form another part of this story of continuity and change. And finally, I examine the historical actors, the millowners and millworkers, whose lives were interwoven in a dialectical relationship over this long period of the Third Republic.

As in many other regions of France, the towns and the countryside of the Aube developed in a symbiotic relationship. Jules Michelet offers a striking panorama of the topography and culture of the Champagne region in his *Tableau de la France,* published in 1833. Michelet characterized the barren soil and treeless landscape surrounding Troyes in these grim terms: "It is disappointing to descend from the sunny hillsides of Burgundy to the low chalky plains of Champagne. Even if we were to ignore the desert of lower Champagne, the countryside is generally flat, pallid and of a dreary prosaicness. The animals are frail looking; there is little variety in mineral and plant life. Cheerless rivers flow between two rows of young poplar trees. . . . Châlons is scarcely any more cheerful than the surrounding plains. Troyes is almost as ugly as it is industrious." Michelet's bleak, unappealing description of Troyes and the surrounding countryside intimated how difficult it was to earn a livelihood on such barren chalky soil. Both local industry and commerce were born from this prime exigency of not being able to live sufficiently off the land. Michelet explained how the custom of partible inheritance (ownership divided among all children) had emptied the pockets of the landed nobility in Champagne, turning them toward commerce. The form of commerce they elected, however, was not the heroic, adventurous, luxury trade of other regions of Europe. Rather, the commerce and industry of Champagne was profoundly plebeian, as Michelet demonstrated: "At the fairs of Troyes, where traders came from all over Europe, thread, yard goods, cotton caps or bonnets, leather ware were sold. . . . These cheap goods, so necessary to everyone, made the country rich. The nobles sat down graciously at their counters and treated the peasants with civility."[2]

The land itself, then, the vast chalky, treeless plain that extended northward from Troyes, commonly known as la Champagne *pouilleuse* (dry Champagne)—in contrast to the more varied landscape of la Champagne *humide* further south and east—provided few natural resources for the population.

2. Michelet 1987, 112–13.

The inhabitants needed to supplement traditional agriculture with rural industry. Handloom weaving and textile manufacturing, implanted since the fifteenth century in those areas of lower Champagne with poor soil, provided a subsistence to peasants, especially during the winter months. The Barrois, or la Champagne *humide,* provided some natural resources that could sustain cereal, vineyards, and livestock production. The three major industrial towns of the region, Troyes, Romilly, and Arcis, were located along the river valleys of the Seine and the Aube. Thus it was primarily in the villages and small towns around these centers that the widespread ownership of small plots of land, combined with poor soil, created the conditions for rural textile industry. Troyes itself was the ancient capital of the *comté* of Champagne. Already in 1570 it had been an industrious, commercial textile town with a population estimated at thirty thousand, of which "nearly a quarter . . . were employed in the textile industry as weavers, carders, drapers, dyers and shearers."[3] In the eighteenth century it remained an important textile trading center for French wool and for silk from Lyon. In 1790 it became the administrative capital of the newly created department of the Aube. Badly affected by both the political and industrial crises of the Revolution, it had rebounded by the mid-nineteenth century and had become a hosiery town of national commercial importance, with a population of thirty-one thousand.[4] Approximately sixty hosiery merchants established in Troyes dominated a vital rural "putting-out" industry of knitting frames organized around a central marketplace in the town.[5]

RURAL INDUSTRY: FROM WOVEN TO KNITTED TEXTILES

The principal characteristics of the nineteenth-century French textile industry were its dispersion in the countryside and its extreme diversity. For rural industry to thrive it needed both raw materials cultivated locally and a ready source of labor among the peasantry.[6] This was the case in the region surrounding Troyes, where local supplies of wool were traditionally woven into a coarse, heavy serge. Although woolen fabric of this kind gradually fell out of

---

3. P. Roberts 1996, 11–12. Roberts's population figures are based on a study of the tax rolls.

4. Babeau 1874, 29. The textile industry had been paralysed by a commercial treaty signed with England in 1787 that favored the importation of English cottons.

5. The following section on the development of domestic manufacture of hosiery in the Aube is drawn from Heywood 1976, 90–111, and Ricommard 1934.

6. On the development of the rural textile industry in the region of Cholet, see Liu 1994.

fashion in the early nineteenth century, the cultivation of flax and hemp in the damp region of Champagne, supported the continuation of a linen industry.[7] However, it was above all cotton that became the motor of the nineteenth-century textile industry in the Aube, as in most of France. By midcentury cheap raw cotton, largely imported from the United States, had stimulated a major shift from wool and linen to cotton in the region of Troyes.[8] The new preference was partially driven by popular demand for cotton clothing across social classes. Troyes's reputation for textile production thus became linked to quality production of a particular weave of linen and cotton cloth.

Other sectors of the textile industry also existed in the Aube, such as spinning mills, and, in the Seine valley near Troyes, bleaching and dyeing works that specialized in the treatment and finishing of cloth. Sources for the period indicate the importance of both hand and mechanical cotton spinning to supply the yarn for weavers and knitters. According to one estimate, in 1784 the number of handspinners had risen to more than fifteen thousand, to keep pace with the increased demand for yarn.[9] The early introduction of the spinning jenny in the 1780s, at an experimental stage of mechanization, seems to have spread in the region of Troyes, creating what one observer called competition with agriculture for labor.[10] But the grievance lists of 1789, written by journeymen knitters in Troyes, complained of the poor quality of yarn produced by these machines, and women handspinners revolted against their use in 1791.[11] Other sources suggest not only that rural textile production in the Aube was widespread at the time of the Revolution, but also that a considerable number of peasant-workers depended on it for their livelihood. The minister of the interior, Jean-Marie Roland, addressed a special request to the legislative assembly for aid on behalf of the manufacturers in Troyes to offset the high price of cotton. Administrators of the department feared that "the twenty thousand inhabitants of Troyes and those of the one hundred surrounding bourgs and villages . . . would soon be lacking a resource [cotton],

7. The decline in the production of coarse woolen cloth came from the local industry's inability to convert to the more expensive lighter woolens and production of these became the speciality of Reims. See Clause 1987, 9–27.

8. Fohlen (1956) cites the growing predominance of French cotton imports from the United States up until the Civil War: 55 percent in 1820, 70 percent in 1833, 78 percent in 1850, and 93 percent by 1860 (128–29).

9. See Heywood 1981, 557. Heywood cites "Mémoire de Bruyard sur les fabriques de la Champagne et de la Picardie," December 14, 1784.

10. Charles Ballot (1923) details some 160 jennies working in the region of Troyes (47–48).

11. Vernier 1909, 192.

the deprivation of which was considered a scourge as frightful as famine of food."[12] While the minister's comparison between a grain and a cotton famine might appear alarmist, an industrial recession in reaction to a commercial treaty signed with England in 1786 had already forced a temporary shift to wool and linen production within the local woven-textile industry. By the early nineteenth century, the region of Troyes had maintained its reputation for the mastery of the whole process of textile production (spinning, weaving, knitting, bleaching, and finishing cloth). Handloom weaving still predominated in the Aube, but hosiery production represented the second most important industry, with fifteen hundred knitting frames reported.[13] According to all reports, there were solid structures for the industrialization of hosiery that would continue to be important to the city's economy.

Knitted fabric, formed by interlacing a single thread in a series of connected loops, can be distinguished from woven cloth, which is produced by interweaving two threads, the warp and the weft. Knitted fabric has an elastic quality that makes it more comfortable than woven cloth to wear close to the body, but also more difficult to handle when working. Hosiery production took longer to mechanize than did spinning or weaving because it was a much more complex process. Like handloom weaving, knitting on the hand frame (*métier à bras*) first became implanted in France in residual textile areas where a local supply of raw materials and ready rural labor prevailed. Besides Troyes and the Aube, such manufacturing was concentrated in only two other major French centers, each specializing in a particular product: the region of Roanne, which produced woolen shawls, capes, and scarves from the mid-nineteenth century; and the areas around Vigan and Ganges (Gard and Hérault), where luxury silk stockings became the speciality from the eighteenth century.[14]

Mechanized Knitting in the Aube

The knitting frame had been introduced in France in 1654 by Jean-Baptiste Colbert, who established protective regulations for its use, limiting the

12. April 26, 1792, as quoted in Tarlé 1910, 22–23.

13. As late as 1810, there was still a substantially greater number of weavers (an estimated two thousand) than of knitters (twelve hundred) in Troyes itself. See "Situation de la fabrique au mois de mai 1810," Archives du Conseil des prud'hommes de Troyes. Document communicated by Alain Cottereau.

14. For Roanne, see Poisat 1982a; for Vigan and Ganges, see Cosson 1987, 39–73. Limited small-scale and noncommercial production was scattered in Normandy.

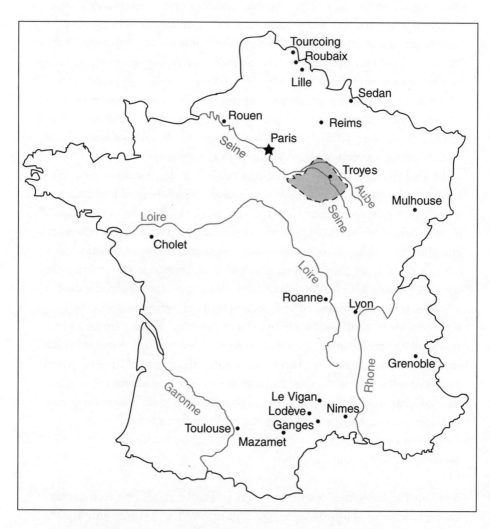

Figure 1   Map of France showing principal cities and major textile centers at mid-nineteenth century. The shaded area represents the department of the Aube.

privilege to certain towns. The royal ordinance of March 30, 1700, that authorized eighteen towns to employ the hand-frame knitter did not include Troyes. As the result of a special petition by Pierre Grassin, a seigneur from Arcis-sur-Aube, who wanted to found a new industry for local weavers after a fire had destroyed the town, the knitting frame was introduced there in 1733. It was not until 1746 that the frame was first established in Troyes at the Hôpital de la Trinité, an orphanage and charitable institution for the poor.[15] By 1771 there were more than sixty knitting frames operating in this institution, some of which served to train apprentice knitters in the town.

Early opposition to the use of the frame came from some thirty hand knitters in the Corporation des Bonnetiers in Troyes. From the late Middle Ages, hand knitters in the town had produced the *bonnets* (nightcaps) that gave the French hosiery industry its name, *la bonneterie,* together with a more limited luxury production of cotton and silk stockings. The corporation of hand knitters sought to prevent growing competition to their trade from the Hôpital de la Trinité, which soon began employing urban knitters who were neither indigent nor orphaned. The corporation demanded authorization for its own members to use the frame and the suppression of privileges once granted to the charity knitting workshop at the *hôpital.* The dispute was sent to the lieutenant general of police in Troyes, then to the Parlement of Paris, and on to the Conseil d'Etat, before a settlement was reached, which declared the *hôpital* free to employ anyone it wished. This settlement also paved the way for the rapid spread of the knitting frame to the countryside.[16] The Hôpital de la Trinité closed its doors in 1794 in the midst of the revolutionary turmoil and the high price of raw materials.[17]

The rural hosiery industry developed rapidly during the early part of the nineteenth century. It spread to the countryside from two urban centers: first from Arcis to the region of Romilly, located northwest of Troyes along the Seine River valley; then from Troyes, to the northeast (Fontaine-les-Grès) and the southeast (the Pays d'Othe). The number of active knitting frames in these areas of the Aube attested to the vitality of rural hosiery production. In 1819, manufacturer and statesman Jean Antoine Chaptal ranked the Aube as the

---

15. Ricommard 1934, 21. Textile historian S. D. Chapman (2003) notes that "hand knitting was a required occupation in England in work houses, hospitals, orphanages, prisons and even barracks," 830.

16. For the details of this dispute, see Ricommard 1934, 7–11 and 24–29; Heywood 1976, 107.

17. Darbot 1980b.

leading center for hosiery production, with 4,200 knitting frames, well ahead of the southern Gard region, with only 1,100.[18] We have a concrete picture of the industry at midcentury thanks to Gréau Aîné, president of the chamber of commerce in Troyes, who compiled an industrial statistical survey in 1846. If we can believe his figures, there were no fewer than 10,812 knitting frames in the Aube, of which 3,510 were found in the arrondissement of Troyes and 867 in the town proper.[19] This inventory covered not only the technical potential of hand-knitting frames for the hosiery industry, but also the other branches of textile production in the Aube.

Cotton hosiery, or *bonneterie* as it was known in France, came to dominate the economic activity of the Aube to such an extent that it was soon the principal motor of local nineteenth-century industrial development. This dominance was even accentuated after the transition to the factory system, when new mass-production technology and the search for market outlets would lead millowners into more diversified production, especially in the period of great national prosperity during the Belle Epoque. The progression over the course of the nineteenth century is striking: production in the Aube represented "23.5 percent of French cotton hosiery in 1806, 33 percent in 1846, and 57 percent in 1913."[20]

Why did this new industry prosper in the countryside and develop so rapidly during the first half of the nineteenth century? Historians have offered different explanations. In one theory, the hosiery industry grew out of the very structures that had served the woven-textile industry: "the same raw materials, spun the same way, a similar work process and the same commercial structures."[21] While this interpretation serves to underscore residual organizational structures in Troyes, it does not explain the rapid development of production in the countryside. Between 1750 and 1850, knitting frames in the town represented only one quarter of those in the area as a whole.[22] Commercial capitalism, which at this stage dominated the organization of the industry through the putting-out system, did not control production until the mid-nineteenth

18. Chaptal 1819, 15–151, cited in Fohlen 1956, 179.
19. Gréau 1850. Gréau's report was prefaced by appeals for tariff protection and was strongly motivated by local textile merchants' efforts to oppose the introduction of free trade with England. Gréau was a leading hosiery manufacturer in Troyes, committed to protectionism. See English historian William Felkin's (1867) comments on this report some twenty years later (545–48).
20. Chapman 2003, 2:824–25.
21. Darbot 1980a, 2.
22. Heywood 1976, 95.

century. In fact, small rural workshops predominated in the production of hosiery. Local metalworkers rapidly undertook the construction and adaptation of wooden knitting frames, while peasants in the Aube found a supplementary source of income in framework knitting, which could be profitably combined with working the land. Initially, the start-up costs of owning a knitting frame at home were relatively cheap and a market was ensured for finished products. But above all, approximately 40 percent of the rural population of the Aube owned the land on which they lived, and although the majority of landholdings were small, less than five hectares, the peasants had little motivation to migrate in search of better wages.[23]

Thus, an abundant supply of cheap rural labor already trained in the textile trade and the widespread ownership of land remain the most important factors in the steady growth of the hosiery industry. Other factors equally crucial to local industrial development were those described by Michelet: the lack of natural resources in this barren region of Champagne; the small divisions of cultivable land; and subsistence farming, which forced peasants to seek supplementary work to survive. The hosiery industry spread most rapidly in precisely those regions where the soil was least productive: to the villages north and west of Troyes in the Seine River valley and in the Pays d'Othe. Colin Heywood has argued that the existence of rural industry was responsible for the slow, sustained population growth up until 1850 in the hosiery-producing villages of the Aube.[24] While the population of France as a whole was distinguished by a long-term decline in both birthrates and death rates over the course of the nineteenth century, the population of the Aube increased until 1850 because, arguably, it could be sustained by small-scale hosiery production.[25] But however valuable such dual activity was to the peasant-knitter, it afforded only a bare subsistence and did not provide sufficient security in times of economic crisis. The poverty and low wages of the domestic system made the knitter's life an unenviable one throughout the nineteenth century.

23. Ibid., 99–101. Heywood calculates this land holding pattern from the assessments for the land tax in the Aube in 1842.
24. Ibid., 101–5.
25. Ibid. Heywood gives the following figures from the census: 1801: 231,455 inhabitants, 1821: 230,688 (-0.3 percent), 1831: 246,361 (+6.7 percent), 1841: 258,180 (+4.8 percent), 1851: 265,247 (+2.7 percent), then a decline to some 246,000 inhabitants in 1901. Immigration as well as natural increases accounted for increased population density in this overwhelmingly rural department.

The Putting-Out System

Domestic manufacture for home and commercial consumption has been abundantly described for various regions of France, from Rouen and Lille to Cholet, Lyon, and Mazamet.[26] The artisan family workshop had a protean character that would seem adaptable to many different circumstances. In fact, the term *domestic,* or *putting-out, system* masks very diverse social relations of production that link the producer to the capitalist merchant (*négociant*). Marx speaks of a process in which the worker is progressively dispossessed of the means of production. He understood this process as one of several stages in the development of industrial capitalism and in the formation of an industrial proletariat. Recent scholarship has more closely examined the complexity of social relations in the organization of both textile production and marketing at this early stage. Historians William Reddy and Tessie Liu emphasize the fluidity of roles between producer, consumer, and possible intermediaries in this complex system. They argue, in fact, that the division of labor between the producer of cloth and the merchant who markets the finished product— regardless of who buys the raw materials and who owns the loom—will vary according to labor-market conditions, historical period, and regional patterns of economic development.[27] Liu's analysis of small-scale linen production in the western region of Cholet demonstrates that eighteenth-century small producers had some control over the production process and therefore, she maintains, should not be viewed as "proletarians," but rather as "entrepreneurs." By 1850, the resistance of weaving households had successfully defeated attempts to mechanize and develop larger-scale textile manufacturing. However, these same artisans were subsequently forced to compromise and share the market with industrial capitalists.[28] The system in the Aube was different. Evidence clearly shows that merchants were in control of two key factors: they alone had the capital to purchase the necessary raw materials, primarily imported American cotton; and they controlled the markets for finished goods through the retailing networks of Paris.[29] As a consequence, the peasant-knitters in the Aube found themselves tightly linked to the merchant hosiers (*fabricants*).

26. Chassagne 1991; 1979, 97–114; Chaplain 1984; Gullickson 1986; Liu 1994; Cazals 1983; Reddy 1984.
27. See the very clear discussion in "The Putting-Out Wilderness," chap. 3 of Liu 1994; see also Reddy 1984.
28. Reddy 1984, 10; Liu 1994, 57–69.
29. Tarlé (1910) cites four distinct types of organization of the putting-out system: (1) direct

To be sure, the peasant-knitter who worked at home could count on the help of his family. If he had the means to buy his own yarn, he could have it spun by his wife and children, then produce the goods himself on his knitting frame and sell them to a merchant. This semi-independent form of domestic manufacture existed in the region thanks in part to the purchasing center (*comptoir d'escompte*) established in 1820 by Jean-Baptiste Doré in the village of Fontaine-les-Grès, located halfway between Romilly and Troyes. Doré served not only as a supplier of raw materials but also as a banker (*escompteur*), advancing the necessary capital for individuals to start up production at home. In 1859 there were five such *escompteurs* listed in the *Annuaire de l'Aube*.[30] But by 1870 these banking intermediaries had disappeared from the scene, and commercial capitalists and merchant bankers in Troyes who had invested in the factory system increasingly dominated local manufacturing.

Even at midcentury, however, most of the peasant-knitters of the region were employed directly by a merchant hosier (*donneur d'ordres*). In his novel *Le député d'Arcis,* first published in 1843, Balzac vividly portrayed the relations between such worker-peasants and the merchants, or *fabricants,* whom he described as "bankers in goods" (*banquiers de marchandises*): "Almost all of the considerable French hosiery industry is located around Troyes. For a distance of about thirty miles around this town the countryside abounds with knitters, whose stocking frames can be seen through the open doors as one passes by the villages. These knitters produce for an agent who in turn works for a speculator known as a manufacturer [fabricant]. This manufacturer deals with a firm in Paris or often with an ordinary hosiery retailer, both of whom have a sign advertising "Hosiery Manufacturer," but neither of them produces a single stocking, cap or sock."[31] Philéas Beauvisage, the *fabricant* created by Balzac in this novel, made his fortune by speculating on the price of cotton in 1814.

The system described by Balzac was defined later in the nineteenth century by the sociologist and social reformer Frédéric Le Play as the "fabrique collective." Even though Balzac might have exaggerated to some extent the social

relations between producer and consumer; (2) an intermediary acting between the producer, who supplies his own raw materials, and the consumer or the market; (3) merchant providing the raw materials to the producer; and finally (4) merchant providing both the raw materials and the tools. Tarlé includes the social relations of production in Troyes in the third type, with supporting evidence from an inspector reporting in 1782 ("Visite des fabriques de toiles et de toileries de la généralité de Chalons, Troyes, année 1782," AN F12 650), 50.

30. Fohlen 1956, 118. *Comptoirs d'escompte* existed in many parts of France.

31. Balzac 1966, 582–83.

relations of production in Arcis in order to create his character, he neverthe-less revealed the power structure underlying this system of manufacturing in the Aube. On the one hand, there were isolated worker-peasants, captives in their home workshops, subject to seasonal unemployment; and on the other, the merchants who controlled commercial capital. The merchant advanced the raw materials to the worker-peasant, leased him the knitting frame, commis-sioned the goods, and undertook to sell them when finished. To be sure, the knitter was able to maintain mastery over the work process and to retain the knowledge and *savoir-faire* that constituted the tools of his trade.[32] He could incorporate his family members in this system of production, organize their work so as to deliver the finished goods at a fixed schedule and price, and pick up the raw materials for the following week's work. However, within this system the peasant-knitter no longer had control over certain conditions of production; more important, over the price of the finished product; and ulti-mately, over the price of his labor.[33]

To understand the "invisible threads," as Marx called them, that bound the peasant-knitter to his merchant hosier, we need to analyze the social and eco-nomic consequences of such a system in the Aube during the first half of the nineteenth century.[34] Knitters were recognized during this period as the poor-est members of the village because of their low wages, undernourishment, and the lack of a steady means of gaining a livelihood. An official inquiry in 1834 reported a considerable difference between the wages paid in the towns of the Aube (1.5 francs a day) and those much lower in the countryside (1 franc per day).[35] In 1837 the subprefect of Arcis noted: "All the individuals employed full time in this type of work are of a generally weak and vicious disposition. Many of them suffer from scrofula, a condition that they pass on to their children. This disease is attributed to their way of life and above all to the filth and

32. The phrase in French translates roughly as "know-how" and is construed to include both the intellectual and manual skills that constitute the sense of craft.

33. See Darbot 1980a for a slightly idealized vision of the domestic production system; and Poisat 1982a for a Marxist analysis of the relation between domestic manufacture and the process of deskilling. Liu (1994) argues that the term *fabricant* is ambiguous, that it could refer to "celui qui fabrique" as well as "celui qui fait fabriquer" (57).

34. Marx wrote: "Besides the factory operatives, the manufacturing workmen and handi-craftsmen whom it concentrates in large masses at one spot, and directly commands, capital also sets in motion, by means of invisible threads, another army: that of workers in domestic indus-tries who dwell in large towns and are also scattered over the face of the country" (1974, 434).

35. Ministry of Commerce, Enquête relative à divers prohibitions établies à l'entrée des produits étrangers commencé le 8 Octobre 1834 (1835), vol. 3, cited in Heywood 1976, 96.

insalubrity of their homes."[36] In these circumstances it is not surprising that the severe economic crisis of 1847–48 left many workers and their families unprotected and hungry. Gréau, himself a hosiery manufacturer, commented on the town's relief efforts: "[T]hanks to this complementarity of industrial and agricultural work in the Aube, 34,000 workers out of 40,000 were able during the terrible crisis . . . to turn to resources that were not available in the towns. Out of 14,000 working people in the Troyes district, only 6,000 received assistance, of whom 1,500 were heads of families, working primarily in the spinning and knitting mills, and this aid taxed the municipal administration."[37] If this author stressed the relative advantages of the rural over the urban labor forces for surviving the crisis, an 1848 governmental "Inquiry on Labor" revealed a more complex picture.[38] Even in periods of relative prosperity, peasant-knitters were said to remain vulnerable to wage reductions. Merchant hosiers could, in fact, exploit the seasonal nature of hosiery work as a part-time trade for most peasant families. Commercial capitalism in Troyes continued to dominate the organization of the hosiery industry, the purchase of imported cotton, and the sale of the finished products to relatively distant domestic markets, until the factory system shifted production to the towns.

The social relations of production were thus a consequence of the domestic putting-out system. It could be argued, as Gerard Noiriel and other historians have done, that the association of rural industry and agricultural activity, based on widespread peasant ownership of land in France, created a working class that viewed "industrial work primarily as one variety of rural employment."[39] Dual activity of this kind represented a constant characteristic of French industrialization until mechanization improved later in the century. However, such was the precariousness of existence for many unskilled workers, including textile workers, that multiple employment, sometimes combined with seasonal migration, became a strategy for survival. Several nineteenth-century worker autobiographies have documented experiences of this kind.[40]

36. See the letter from the subprefect of Arcis to the prefect, October 8,1837, ADA M 2331, cited in Heywood 1976, 96.

37. Report by M. Gréau Aîné, July 21, 1848, cited in Ricommard 1934, 53–54.

38. Colin Heywood (1976) calculates from the figures given in the inquiry that a family with two children, living in a rural village outside of Troyes, needed a minimum of 650 francs a year to live, and that a knitter working with his wife and one child could earn 645 francs, assuming that he was able to work a full year (96).

39. Noiriel 1986, chap. 2.

40. See esp. Truquin 1977. Truquin describes working conditions in a wool spinning mill near Amiens in 1846, one of his many jobs, and compares them to the domestic system in

For the knitters of Troyes and the Aube, relations between the town and the countryside entailed the coexistence of two modes of industrial production: a domestic mode dispersed in rural workshops, and a more industrial one based in the two large towns. While the existence of cheap rural labor contributed to overall industrial growth in the Aube, such a static, captive labor force discouraged technological innovation and, ultimately, social and economic change. Change of this kind could only take place in urban industrial workshops after the transition to the factory system toward the last quarter of the nineteenth century. Yet the practice of putting out work to rural knitters persisted in various forms as a production strategy well into the twentieth century. The slow transition to the factory system in the Aube was no doubt partly a result of the resilience of rural industry. But, as we shall see, once mills became concentrated in Troyes, millowners sometimes found important *social* reasons to decentralize production—to counter growing worker resistance and strikes.

At the same time as the first technical improvements made to William Lee's knitting frame had begun to transform the industry, a new form of production developed in Troyes. The urban artisan (*façonnier*) appeared, working in close collaboration with the merchant hosiers for the filling of regular orders and the marketing of finished goods. Urban knitters of this kind worked on finer cotton yarn to produce higher-quality goods than those of their rural counterparts. Gréau calculated that a knitter working on the hand frame could produce in one week either one dozen fully fashioned women's stockings, or one and a half dozen fully fashioned gloves, or nine dozen *mitaines* (mittens).[41] The introduction, in about 1840, of circular frames that produced a continuously knit fabric for cut-and-sew goods led to a second division of labor. Experiments were conducted with new forms of energy as means to operate this circular frame. The greater productivity of such machines, combined with the difficulties of the 1848 industrial recession, provoked a "Luddite" revolt in Romilly. In their anger against their unemployment and poverty, hand-frame knitters destroyed all the circular frames in the town. In Troyes, the Republican Committee warned the workers against this type of excessive behavior and exhorted them to respect the machines.[42] While the

---

Reims. He concludes that work in the mill is more tolerable than that in the confined space of a domestic workshop (50).

41. Gréau 1851, 12–13.

42. Colomes 1943, 104–5.

technical predominance of Troyes and Romilly had not yet fully modified the organization of production, it did serve to strengthen merchant capitalism in the two towns. As the most important commercial center in the Aube, Troyes established a hosiery market, the Halle de la Bonneterie, in 1837. The major part of hosiery production remained, however, in the countryside. During the years of industrial recession in the 1840s, knitters in Troyes who lacked work complained about merchant hosiers who put out work to rural women.[43] A gendered dimension to the competition for work in difficult times cannot be excluded, because women were customarily paid lower wages. This raises the question of the sexual division of labor within the domestic manufacture.

Men's Work, Women's Work

Historians of textile work have generally paid more attention to the social than to the sexual division of labor.[44] They have emphasized a linear process of development stretching from the guilds and the first collective industrial structures, such as the Manufacture de la Trinité in Troyes, to rural artisan production under the putting-out system and finally to the factory system. A common point of reference for describing the sexual division of labor in the hosiery industry is the image in Diderot and d'Alembert's *Encyclopédie*: the male head of household working on the knitting frame, his wife spinning and winding yarn on the *bobinoir* (Fig. 2). Such a representation of domestic textile production appears fixed for eternity, reproducing an essentialist and abstract notion of the complementarity of men's and women's work in ancien régime society. The very static nature of the image inhibits any sense of sequence or hierarchy in the tasks. The two individuals are portrayed in economic partnership as a self-sufficient household. A closer look reveals a social, as well as an economic, logic to the sexual division of labor represented here: the male head of household, working on the most productive tool of the trade, the knitting frame, is acknowledged as the producer. Women and children, subordinate in fact to the husband and father, carried out secondary or auxiliary tasks, such as spinning.[45]

43. Peudon 1962.
44. It is important to cite here the exceptions: Hufton (1975, 1–22), Liu (1994), Horn (forthcoming), and Hafter (1995).
45. See Sewell 1986b. Sewell argues that the images are designed to convey the "primacy of science over human skill" and that the generic figures and discrete tools "argue for a cultural construction of the capitalist mode of production well in advance of its practical realization."

Figure 2   The sexual division of labor in domestic knitting manufacture as represented in the *Encyclopédie* of Diderot and d'Alembert, c. 1765. Musée de la Bonneterie.

Attention to questions of gender exposes the hierarchy of tasks and tools in the hosiery trade. According to the earliest statutes of the knitters' guild of Arcis-sur-Aube, "women and young girls cannot operate the knitting frame."[46] In theory, at least, the all-male members of the guild reserved for themselves exclusive use of the most productive tool, the one conferring the greatest economic power. Such restrictions on women's work were designed to protect the *savoir-faire,* the secrets of the trade, and thus limit access to the profession. In reality, however, such restrictions were poorly enforced in Troyes and most likely did not even apply in the countryside, particularly with the spread of hosiery as a rural industry in the early nineteenth century. The peasant-knitter was obliged to organize the production process to include the entire family, and even work the knitting frame during the agricultural season. It is likely that both women and older children relieved the father at the frame when work was required in the fields. Gréau, writing in 1848, gives us the following description: "Knitting frames are found in the smallest hamlets; often there

Diderot's fascination with new techniques and tools was nowhere so evident as with the knitting frame—it has one of the longest entries in the entire *Encyclopédie.*

46. Cited by Ricommard 1934, 22.

is only one per household. The peasant-knitter [*fabricant-agriculteur*] owes the crop in his field to his knitting frame. It never rests idle, but is constantly operated either by the father, the mother, the son, or even the young daughter, so that when one family member stops knitting, it is to go work in the fields or on some other household task."[47]

The urban hosiery workshop operated somewhat differently. But here too there was considerable ambiguity regarding women's tasks. According to nineteenth-century social reformer Jules Simon in his classic text on women's work, *L'ouvrière* (1861), "Both men and women work in the hosiery industry, but the fact that women are in the majority can be explained by the nature of the work, which is not tiring and can easily be done intermittently. Apprenticeship is not long, two months' time or half of one's wages on fifty kilos of knitted fabric produced. A woman working on the circular frame rarely earns more than 1.5 francs a day, and the seaming is paid 5 centimes an hour at most. Women are also assigned to . . . unwinding the yarn for very minimal wages."[48] Simon's description is interesting because it provides evidence that women worked on the circular knitting frame, introduced around 1840. The descriptions of the work as relatively "not tiring," "intermittent," and requiring a short apprenticeship correspond to the characterizations of work traditionally reserved for women.

Other sources suggest rather different roles for women during this stage of the putting-out system. Julien Ricommard reported in his history of the industry that under the Communauté des bonnetiers d'Arcis, "women sorted, old men carded, old women spun, young women sewed."[49] These auxiliary tasks of preparation of raw materials were assigned according to sex and age as each family member's contribution to the household economy. Such work did not have a fixed price, but when calculated into the family budget, it was an essential service to the family enterprise at a historical period when marriage represented an economic partnership. The rural family operated as a basic unit of textile production. Women's tasks—spinning and sewing—were compatible with other household responsibilities, including child care, and varied according to family size and structure. Women living in towns obviously had access to more varied work. Some could find piecework, as many poor women did, according to the archives of the Hôpital de la Trinité in

47. Gréau 1851, 13.
48. Simon 1861, 204–5.
49. Ricommard 1934, 23. His source for this quote is unclear.

Troyes: "[M]any poor orphaned young women or those whose parents were unable to help them were housed and fed at the hospital; they were employed in buying, spinning, winding, and sorting the cotton yarn used by the factory, in sewing, folding, finishing, and putting into packages the stockings produced."[50] Often the factory would have the stockings sewn by children and old women of the orphanage, but it also put out the same work to urban women.

This brief examination of the preindustrial stage of hosiery production, organized around essentially rural households linked to the towns by a commercial network of putters-out (*fabricants*) and merchant capitalists (*négociants*), corresponds roughly to the situation described by Balzac in the 1840s. The relatively slow transition from small-scale dispersed production to a more centralized, mechanized, and capitalist form of production took place distinctly later in Troyes by comparison with other textile centers. In fact, the transformative impact of the new technologies would not have a major effect until the period 1860–90. While many of the structures of rural industry persist during these later years, local merchant capitalists would now invest their fortunes, borrow, or lend capital to develop and mechanize the Troyes hosiery industry for large-scale production.

FROM MERCHANT TO INDUSTRIAL CAPITALISM

The transition to the factory system was facilitated by technological progress in mechanizing knitting, using new forms of energy, and the availability of sufficient local capital to launch such enterprises. This phase in the economic and social transformation of the industry saw the consolidation of family capitalism in an industrial bourgeoisie centered in Troyes. The history of this period, and particularly of those industrialists, merchants, bankers, and inventors of knitting machines who contributed to the growth of the industry, is less well known. Several short biographical studies exist on the early entrepreneurs and inventors, but very few millowners have written their own family history.[51]

50. Quoted in Darbot 1980b, 19. The document quoted dates from 1754. Period documents provide evidence of the tariffs paid by the Manufacture: "[A worker] produced two to three stockings a day, depending on the gauge and the size, and an average worker earned in 1777 around 5 livres a week . . . while a spinner or a seamer earned scarcely 3 livres" (27).

51. The intensely private family capitalism in Troyes has not produced a historian and, more important, has not made available to historians many of the records of their lives and their

For our purposes, a study of the millowners is essential to understanding the history of the working class and the culture of textile production and consumption in the region. To grasp the distinctiveness of the path to industrialization chosen by those entrepreneurs in Troyes, we need to analyze the particular characteristics of family capitalism in the town. How did one become a millowner in mid-nineteenth-century Troyes? What strategies did millowners devise to develop their industry, and how did they perceive the workers? To draw the rural knitters into the factory system and create a stable, loyal labor force, millowners generally relied on some form of paternalism, providing social welfare benefits to meet their workers' needs and create better relations.

Millowners: From Family Capitalism to Industrial Capitalism

The industrial milieu in Troyes had its roots in two distinct social groups: on the one hand, the merchants (*négociants*) and manufacturers (*fabricants*) who controlled the putting-out system in the Aube, and on the other, the technicians, artisans, and mechanics, some of them of rather modest social origins, who were trained in textile work in the family workshop. The first group clearly accumulated and possessed the capital necessary to invest in the industry; the second group consisted of "self-made" men whose upward social mobility into the ranks of the industrial bourgeoisie was the result of technical knowledge, hard work, personal good fortune, and opportune marriage into wealthy families.

Among the first group we find the merchant manufacturers, those "bankers in goods" (*banquiers de marchandises*) identified by Balzac; merchant bankers; and wholesalers (*revendeurs en gros*), whose important capital assets allowed them to engage in related commercial activities.[52] Many of these men belonged to the business milieu constituted around the Halle de la Bonneterie, the

---

mills. The exception to this general silence on the history of industrial families in Troyes is the Valton family, who published monographs on each of the three generations to run the family firm: *Antoine Quincarlet* (1985); *Pierre Valton et ses fils* (1986); and *Les fils de Valton* (1987). On Emmanuel Buxtorf, engineer, banker and mayor of Troyes, see Margaret Dubuisson, "Emmanuel Buxtorf," *La Vie en Champagne,* October 1979 and Claverie-Rospide 1995; on inventors relatively unknown such as Joseph-Julien Jacquin, artisan clockmaker and inventor of the automatic mechanism for casting off stitches for fully fashioned goods, see Darbot 1989; also 1984, 47–54.

52. See the excellent preliminary study of this social group by Nivelle (1975), who worked from business bankruptcy records.

merchant marketplace founded in 1837. Gréau details some sixty commercial houses operating in hosiery production in 1846. By the mid-nineteenth century, Troyes had not yet become the center of hosiery production, but the town's merchants dominated the marketing of the knitted goods produced in the region through a commercial network for both domestic and international sales. Local investment capital came from several sources. Millers such as Clement Marot used their capital to support rural spinning mills. The Herbin, Poron, and Doré families were merchant manufacturers who accumulated enough capital from the outwork system to concentrate production gradually in their own urban mills. There is some disagreement over how far the commercial bourgeoisie actually went in their financial support for long-term industrial growth in the cotton hosiery industry at midcentury.[53] Inventor and manufacturer Joseph-Julien Jacquin, who held several patents for his improvements to knitting machines, had to go into exile for his republican opinions in 1852.[54] Other local manufacturers supported more moderate men of order and were thus able to weather the political uncertainties, problems of unemployment, and food shortages that sharpened class and labor relations during the revolution of 1848 in Troyes.[55]

The second social group, consisting of artisans, mechanics, and technicians, had more diverse social and geographical origins. The dissemination of hand-knitting frames in the countryside favored a diffusion of knowledge among peasant knitting families. Knitters organized production in such a way as to supply the labor and skills necessary to transform the yarn into stockings for a "prix de façon." To maintain their productivity and earn their livelihood, they had to keep their frames in good repair. Many of the inventors of improvements to knitting machinery came from this artisan milieu of knitters, mechanics, and metalworkers, who circulated in the countryside to set up and repair frames. It was a breeding ground for technical innovation, beginning with Jean-Auguste Delarothière, who made five important contributions to the circular knitter from 1828 to 1847.[56] Both Hippolyte Degageux and Linard Hubert worked in knitting-machine-construction firms and made several patented improvements before attempting to set up their own firms. Auguste

53. Heywood 1994, 167–84.
54. Darbot 1984.
55. Heywood 1990, 108–20.
56. Jean-Auguste Delarothière (1783–1854), born in Amiens to a humble family, became a knitter and came to Troyes, where he was able to commercialize several of his patented improvements to the circular knitter. See Darbot 1989, 11–13.

Mortier reports in his 1891 history of knitting technology that 612 patents were registered between 1878 and 1888 in the town of Troyes itself.[57] Not all these patents could be exploited by the inventors themselves. However, the success of several entrepreneurs in perfecting or constructing new models of knitting machinery from their own patents is undeniable, and it encouraged the search for continued technical innovation in machine workshops. Other technicians and engineers, such as Emmanuel Buxtorf, hired inventors in their construction workshops. Still others, among them Léon Poron, kept abreast of the latest English inventions in order to buy patents, improve them, and incorporate them into his own metalworking factory. In this way several generations of hosiery manufacturers became trained as technicians and integrated the construction of knitting machinery into their mills.

The commercial bourgeoisie of the town apparently provided financial backing for innovations in textile technology during the 1860s spurt in technical development. The Chamber of Commerce and Industry, founded in 1817, formed a pressure group to seek state aid to commercialize certain inventions, notably those of Delarothière. However, the group's primary interest and motivation was to lobby the government in defense of local economic interests during the debate on the Anglo-French trade treaty of 1860. Troyes industrialists were hostile to free trade and consistently demanded high tariffs on imported hosiery, knitted goods, and cloth to protect their industry. Protection, notably against the British textile industry, was virtually a dogma among French textile manufacturers, who considered it the state's obligation to aid industrial entrepreneurs.[58]

Banking capital also poured into industrial development thanks to the Buxtorf family, a group of merchant hosiers from Switzerland who came to Troyes around 1806 and developed banking activity closely linked to the putting-out industry. This family belonged to the worlds of both industry and banking. Emmanuel Buxtorf's three sons continued the tradition: Bernard took over his father's cotton import business and in 1848 subsequently became the director of the Comptoir national d'escompte, an institution in Troyes that advanced capital at interest to local industrialists; Adolphe succeeded his elder brother at the head of the cotton trade; and Emanuel, the best known of the family, was an engineer who went on to found a firm for knitting-machine

57. Mortier 1891, 55.
58. Fohlen 1956, 91.

construction in 1853. He developed thirty-nine patented inventions during the course of his career as a technician. The Buxtorf family's support and personal vision of the local hosiery industry's development corresponded to a period of economic and technological transformation that laid the basis for a solid capitalist infrastructure. Emmanuel Buxtorf became mayor of Troyes in the difficult period of 1871, and he founded the Ecole française de bonneterie in 1888 to train skilled foremen for the local industry. Emanuel also continued the family banking business in association with the Koechlin machine works in Mulhouse, founding Buxtorf-Koechlin, Weiss et Cie in 1882, which later became the Comptoir d'escompte de l'Aube. This Protestant Alsacian institution poured capital into the Troyes textile industries after 1871, particularly in spinning and hosiery.[59] Another local banking institution, E. Vignes et Cie, a branch of the Crédit Agricole, lent money at interest to textile entrepreneurs. Vignes was an important hosiery manufacturer associated with the firm Raguet fils et R. Vignes in Troyes.[60] While millowners appeared to find capital and credit locally from banks, *escompteurs* (lenders), notaries, and family alliances during this period, it is only in the last quarter of the nineteenth century that industrialists began to dominate commercial and financial interests in the knitted goods industry. The foundation in 1883 of the Chambre Syndicale des Fabricants de Bonneterie, the hosiery millowners union, marked this shift from commercial to industrial capitalism.

Among millowners of more modest social origins, there were seemingly few barriers to upward mobility during this particular period. This translates into more fluid social groups and less obvious class divisions at the level of technicians and small manufacturers. Throughout the knitted goods industry there was a powerful professional motivation to innovate, to patent inventions, and to found small hosiery firms for independent or even subcontracted production, a motivation that formed the spirit of these times. In fact, it is during this period of the 1880s and 1890s that a man named Pierre Valton, with roots as a technician, began to construct his own enterprise through hard work and marriage into a hosiery manufacturing family. Valton represents just one case we will examine in exploring the founding of several such

59. Claverie-Rospide 1995, 25–32; Humbert 1995, 8–9; Nivelle 1975; see also Burns 1992, chap. 2.

60. On the bank's governing board sat the president of the Chamber of Commerce of Troyes and Edmé-Auguste Hoppenot, who owned one of the largest local spinning mills, the Filature de Schappe. See Humbert 1995, 9.

dynasties of Troyes knitwear manufacturing families, which extend over three generations.

Enterprising Family Capitalism

The principal characteristics of family capitalism in Troyes can only be roughly sketched here, through summary portraits of several leading hosiery millowners. Our study focuses on the major entrepreneur in each family firm at around 1900, at the height of social and technological development in the industry. Overall, the overlapping histories of the families and their firms reveal a concerted strategy by Troyes industrialists to ensure their firm's future through professional training and marriages into other textile manufacturing families. Certain family reconstructions demonstrate their longevity, beyond the rule of three generations that is usually evidenced in France, well into the twentieth century.[61] Moreover, from a historical perspective these family firms emerge relatively late in the process of industrialization. Their stories have not yet found a historian.

From 1860, intense social, economic, and technological changes in the textile industry compelled millowners to restructure their firms and reorganize production processes to a considerable extent. These structural transformations meant new forms of family capitalism. The individual millowner with limited capital had to seek out alliances with other sources of capital and knowledge by creating *sociétés à nom collectif* (general partnerships). At this stage, investment in factory work also required new forms of energy—necessary for the more complex and expensive knitting machinery—first water, and then steam power, which had become widespread by 1880. The new knitting frames provided more automatic functions, which increased the speed and productivity of the machines, now capable of knitting in series. Two knitting frames in particular created an added dynamic to production: first, the improved circular frame, capable of producing such articles as vests and underwear; and second, the Cotton patent frame, which was invented in England in 1862, displayed at the World's Fair in Paris in 1867, and made in Troyes by the Couturat Company from 1878. The Cotton frame became the archetypal mass-production knitter, symbol of the modern factory. The economic logic of these technical changes meant a greater concentration of the labor force in large-scale urban factories.

61. Lévy-Leboyer 1985, 3–7.

For many independent artisans and peasant-knitters, this forward march of the factory system signaled the slow loss of many forms of autonomy.

The family capitalism practiced by this first generation of Troyes industrialists can be characterized by its spirit of hard work and private management and by a strategy of alliances within the industrial bourgeoisie. Family capitalism entailed both financial and human capital. This generation's children were trained early in their lives to carry on the family business, and they married into other families connected to the knitting trade.[62] The Valton family is an exemplary case of this process in Troyes. Pierre Valton, son of a small knitting manufacturer in the suburbs of Troyes, joined the firm of Antoine Quinquarlet as a *commis* in 1850 under an apprenticeship contract. His assiduous work caught his employer's attention, but also that of his employer's daughter, Noemie Quinquarlet, who worked in the family business. Pierre married Noemie in 1859, only after Antoine Quinquarlet had sufficiently tested his future son-in-law's capacities to accept responsibilities in the business. Noemie's dowry was a share in the family firm that accrued 5 percent interest for Pierre each year, a powerful bond to the family enterprise.[63] André, the son of Noemie and Pierre, while young entered the business as his grandfather's secretary, trained by him to oversee the mill's production of knitted goods.

The legal transition around 1880 from personal family firm to limited partnership took place with some personal friction between the two families. The same difficulty appeared when Antoine Quinquarlet wanted to retire some five years later. According to the family history, "Antoine Quinquarlet, as the founder and head of the family, had to ensure the future of his enterprise by choosing among his successors according to merit, loyalty to the business, competence, and, understandably, family ties. The decision therefore to reject the leadership of certain members invariably aroused resentment and jealousies that would surface later."[64] At issue was the family name, together with the capacities of individual family members to manage the family capital. The collaboration between Pierre and his son André, on the one hand, and with Henri Quinquarlet, Antoine's son, on the other, quickly turned to hostility,

62. Fohlen (1956) re-creates the "mentalité patronale" of the Second Empire from the memoirs of several authors whose families were textile millowners in the Catholic north and the Protestant east of France (83–91).

63. Boucraut and Boucraut 1985, 1986. See also my analysis of this form of family capitalism in "Famille, capital, travail textile" (1991), 131–46. Women did not have control over their inheritance at this time, and Noemie's dowry became community property managed by her husband, Pierre.

64. Boucraut and Boucraut 1985, 35.

which led to the dissolution of the firm in 1891 and the founding by Pierre and André of their own firm, Valton and Sons, in 1894.

To ensure the future of this firm, Pierre, the father of eleven children, early on brought four of his sons into the business to learn the day-to-day management of textile production. The young third generation was also sent abroad for specialized technical training. In England, Pierre's sons learned the mechanics of knitting machines and in Switzerland, the techniques of dyeing, finishing, and textile management. This innovation in training underscores the need by 1900 for millowners to develop new technical skills in the organization of textile production in order that a family enterprise such as Valton and Sons could survive. The sons learned the lessons they would need to become partners in their father's enterprise.

Other millowning families in Troyes adopted similar strategies of family alliances to find such new skills and knowledge. Hosiery manufacturer Léon Vitoux formed a partnership with his son-in-law, Léon Poron, engineer and manufacturer of knitting machines; in 1876 Armand and Charles Poron associated their sons, Léon, Henri, and Jules, together with their nephew Auguste Mortier, polytechnician, in a limited partnership (*société à nom collectif*) in a firm called Poron Brothers, Sons and Mortier. Such marriages between families of manufacturers served to consolidate links between the hosiery industry and related ones such as dyeing and spinning. Thus Marcel Vitoux, Léon's son, married Madeleine Dupont, the daughter of an important cotton-spinning-mill owner. Many such examples can be found in Troyes in which economic interests were contracted through marriage into other bourgeois industrial families.

Family capitalism of this kind, based on personal fortune and intermarriage within the same trade, could guarantee solid structures for continuity in the family firm. But it could also be a source of potential weakness, as one historian has noted: "The knitwear industry of Troyes and the Aube was confined for a long time within structures that provided both solidity and fragility. The solidity resulted from the nature of this type of employer, whose business ethos was marked by a spirit of frugality, competent management, a well-ordered business administration, . . . and an emphasis on craftsmanship, but a certain weakness came from the lack of initiative, the manufacturers' individualism, from the limited nature of relations between millowners, and consequently from insufficient capital resources available."[65] As we have seen

65. Lazzarotti 1971, 7.

in the case of the Valton family, jealousies between family members, suspicion toward "outsiders," even personal vanity over continuation of the family name, could weaken the family partnership.

The first generation of knitwear manufacturers in Troyes was well known for hard work and a certain commercial and technical dynamism. Several of them, including Buxtorf and Mortier, were convinced that the industry's future depended on founding a professional school in Troyes for training young business and technical managers, made to measure for their needs. On their initiative, the Ecole française de bonneterie was founded in 1888, offering both theoretical and practical courses in the knitwear trade. This venture proved successful, and it survives today in a modified form to meet the industry's technical research needs.

By 1900 millowners had restructured their firms to meet the rising costs of hiring more workers, purchasing new machines, and accumulating the necessary capital for reinvestment in large-scale production. At this time most of the large firms were restructured as limited companies (*sociétés anonymes*). But the concomitant development of large urban workshops with increasing numbers of workers assembled in the same physical space helped foster major new difficulties for the capitalist owners. Conflicts over hours, working conditions, pay procedures, and wages all came to the fore, notably in the great strike of 1900. When confronted with the problems of a large industrial workforce, millowners in many textile regions turned to paternalist policies of various inspiration, above all in the form of social welfare programs for their workers.

The Meanings of Paternalism

As hosiery work in the Aube became more and more dissociated from agriculture, many rural knitters migrated to the town and its environs, looking for more steady work. By 1850, Troyes had already become the primary center for hosiery production in the Aube. In a monoindustrial town such as Troyes, relations between workers and millowners necessarily developed into a relationship of mutual dependence. Alain Cottereau has characterized this system as "urban clientelism," operating according to a "tacit compromise between employer and worker controls." Within such a system, "employers secure from stable workers a certain degree of allegiance, whereby they are willing to ignore frontiers between place of work, family life and urban life; the counterpart of this is that the authority of employers is contained within strict limits."[66] Thus employers' authority in Troyes was consolidated around their virtual monopoly over the labor market, itself an outgrowth and development of the rural putting-out system.

Recent scholarship on the permanence of paternalism has emphasized the diversity of forms of labor management and social relations underlying this phenomenon, forms that include a gendered dimension.[67] In fact, different regional or local models operated between employers and workers, depending primarily on historical conditions, the type of industry, and the nature of industrial relations. In the discussion of paternalism that follows, we will explore the meaning of paternalism in Troyes in this context and examine the distinctive features of the system as it operated in the hosiery industry.[68]

In many respects, paternalism as a practice in the mills of Troyes was similar to practices followed in other French textile towns such as Roubaix-Tourcoing, Lille, and Mulhouse.[69] The authority of employers was determined primarily by their virtual monopoly over the labor market. But another important ingredient was their technical expertise, a highly recognized competence among millowners, whose social roots in some cases went back to the independent artisan milieu. Yves Schwartz has underscored this technical dimension of paternalism among millowners in Mulhouse, which promoted in its wake a technical culture.[70] Troyes millowners showed a similar concern for technical skills developed in the recruitment and training of millworkers. However, for those workers whose technical skills had been honed in the relative autonomy of the family workshop, the experience of factory work provoked resistance to discipline and control. In Troyes, further autonomy was derived from family and community networks in this town that proved fertile ground for the seeds of socialism.

The rare sources culled from millowners' archives point to the virtual absence of social welfare programs for workers around 1900. Millowners defended their weak record in this respect before the Parliamentary Commission of Inquiry on the Textile Industry in 1904. The commission's purpose was to determine whether further state intervention in favor of workers was

66. Cottereau 1986, 130.
67. Debouzy 1988. For the mining industry, see Reid 1992, Accampo 1989.
68. Limited and fragmented sources from millowners have hampered efforts to provide a consistent record in this respect. I worked from certain archival documents and from oral testimony from men and women workers active in the 1920s and 1930s.
69. Y. Schwartz 1979, 9–77. See also Burns 1992, chap. 2; Hilden 1986, chap. 3.
70. Y. Schwartz 1979.

necessary, and employers in Troyes attempted to provide evidence that it was not. In their statement the owners placed particular emphasis on worker job mobility, a common strategy used by individuals faced with unemployment or the arbitrary lowering of piece rates. Employers argued: "Worker mobility has always constituted an obstacle to establishing any provident aid society in each mill. Therefore none exists in the hosiery mills, neither retirement plans, nor unemployment insurance, nor the creation of cheap worker housing; money collected from fines constitutes a fund for workers in case of illness, and such money is therefore returned to them in some form or other."[71] Thus the fines collected to enforce mill discipline, they contended, served in the long run to relieve worker hardship.

But if the absence of paternalist policies to consolidate the workforce was the rule, not all Troyes industrialists followed such a laissez-faire logic in relation to their workers. We can distinguish two currents of social action engaged in by local employers seeking the solicitude of their labor force in order to better control it. The first current had its roots in social Catholicism. The employer, acting in a role modeled on that of the father in the Christian family, founded an association to promote the social welfare of his millworkers. This form of patronage developed around practices that were later formulated in the papal encyclical Rerum Novarum of 1891. The second current of paternalism could be characterized as humanist or progressive. Following this vision, millwork was organized according to principles of social progress that the millowner believed to be in the workers' interests. Here, employers felt themselves invested with a social mission to protect their employees and thus ensure social stability and the proper functioning of their firm. Paternalist policies of this kind were informed by a certain concept of social order prevalent under the Third Republic.

The Valton and Hoppenot families in Troyes and André Doré in Fontaine-les-Grès each exemplified the Catholic current of paternalism, which they practiced in what was known as the "Christian factory." According to the Valton family history, "social work" had been "severely neglected" in Troyes during the nineteenth century, and it was the pioneering policies of Léon Harmel in the Marne that "inspired the founders of the family firm." From the firm's founding in 1892, the Valton family managers had committed 10 percent of their profits to a social welfare fund that would operate until

71. "Rapport de la Chambre de commerce de Troyes, procès-verbaux" (1906), 72.

1950.[72] The spirit of social Catholicism that imbued this industrial dynasty penetrated the life of their mill, which was dedicated to Saint Joseph. The aim of the project was to bring workers into the Catholic way of life through employer-run collaborative groups called Cercles catholiques d'ouvriers. Their stated objective was to ensure "the alliance . . . between employers and workers in the same trade . . . on the common grounds of their moral and material interests."[73] Such an alliance, according to the association's statutes, rested not only on the recognition of reciprocal duties in the management of the workers' fund (*caisse du travail*), but also on the personal example of Christian life set by the employer as the father figure. In addition, the family carried out charitable work in favor of workers' households under this patronage system. Initially, this overtly religious system functioned until passage of the 1884 law that legalized unions. Catholic employers subsequently founded mixed unions, composed of both workers and employers, though they were prohibited by law from mixing religious or political activities with purely economic and professional interests.

However, given the fundamental inequality between employers and workers, a system of patronage as Christian duty, following the patriarchal-family model, could create narrow relations of dependence. Patronage of this kind represented an additional means of control over knitters, who were totally dependent on their wages, as the following letter addressed to André Valton suggests: "Monsieur André, it is my sad duty to advise you that for the moment I can no longer pay my contributions to the *caisse du travail* because I have not had enough work over the past two months. It is with great sorrow that I tell you that for the first time I will be obliged to use my bonus to pay my rent; however, your workshop is not lacking in profitable knitting frames for those who are in good standing."[74] This knitter, who had obviously sat idled, because his frame was in disrepair or because of low orders for the article he produced, ended his letter with a respectful request to be assigned to a more productive knitting machine so that he could earn his livelihood. Such demands for paternalist protection were typical within the small family firm.

72. Boucraut and Boucraut 1986, 59. Léon Harmel, an industrialist at Val-des-Bois in the nearby department of Marne, was active in the social Catholicism movement and had founded social welfare projects in his factories in the late nineteenth century.

73. Les statuts de Cercles ouvriers catholiques, Archives of the Musée de la bonneterie. See Hilden's (1986) account of Cercles catholiques among Catholic employers in the Lille-Roubaix-Tourcoing region, 113–22.

74. Manuscript letter from Victor Baudart, Archives of the Musée de la bonneterie.

Between the lines, letters of this kind revealed the inherent contradictions of a *caisse du travail* that imposed contributions, based on work over which the employees no longer had any control. To obtain benefits, they needed to continue working.[75]

Another form of Catholic paternalism was practiced by Henri Hoppenot, owner of the silk-spinning mill la Filature de Schappe, in Troyes. Hoppenot came from an industrial family linked by marriage to textile industrialists in Lyon. His spinning mill was modeled on the Catholic convent factory system, practiced in the Lyon region for silk textiles.[76] Women workers were recruited from the surrounding countryside and given lodging alongside the mill in boardinghouse dormitories staffed by nuns who also served as supervisors and disciplinarians in the mill.[77] Meals were provided at a refectory or canteen.[78] This specific form of discipline, reserved for young women workers, combined moral education with training in textile work, following a pattern similar to that practiced by other Catholic institutions.

Still another system was operated by André Doré in Fontaine-les-Grès, a village situated halfway between Romilly and Troyes on the country's main route to Paris. This family firm originated in a purchasing and putting-out center that had been established by Jean-Baptiste Doré in 1819. Since 1862, the firm had specialized in solid, classic, quality socks and stockings, marketed under the brand name DD. By maintaining a constantly evolving outwork system to small village workshops, the firm provided rural workers with an alternative to migration. In 1918, it finally became more profitable to centralize production in mills and fetch workers by bus from the countryside. André Doré, the grandson of Jean-Baptiste, created special social welfare programs for his workers when he took over the firm in 1908. He established an apprentice training center, a Catholic church, worker housing, a boardinghouse for women workers, a company store, a canteen, a sports stadium, and a recreation center (*salle des fêtes*). Under his leadership, production expanded to some 180,000 dozens of socks annually, and management organized the

75. See Reid's (1992) discussion of Bonnemort's pension situation in *Germinal* (989–90).
76. Accounts of the *couvents soyeux* (industrial convents) can be found in Lucie Baud, "Le témoignage de Lucie Baud, ouvrière en soie," *Le Mouvement Social* 105 (October 1978): 139–46; and Auzias and Houel 1982.
77. Testimony from Mme Enault, interview, 1986. She worked in a spinning mill from age thirteen. For similar disciplinary practices targeting women millworkers in the Nord, see Hilden 1986.
78. "Société Anonyme de Filatures de Schappe," *Illustration Economique et Financière*, 1924, 32.

busing of workers from the neighboring countryside.[79] Workers could lease their knitting machines, buy their homes on credit, and have their children professionally trained in the trade, arrangements that invariably produced strong ties that bound workers to the firm for life. Entrepreneurship was often combined with political leadership, as the head of the firm served as elected mayor of the town.[80] The company town created by Doré was not unlike those in many industrialized countries, notably in the chocolate industry (Hershey, Pennsylvania, and Meunier in France are obvious examples).

The second current of paternalism described earlier, based on humanist or progressive principles, was certainly less common in Troyes. It was practiced above all by a few industrialists who seemed primarily concerned with maintaining good relations between workers and employers in order to make the factory system more productive. Social protection for their employees seemed to operate in the best interests of both workers and millowners. In 1904, Léon Vitoux-Derrey, a prominent hosiery manufacturer in Troyes, wrote to the president of the Parliamentary Commission of Inquiry on the Textile Industry, expressing his self-styled paternalist philosophy in these terms: "Over the past fourteen years, since my mill was founded in 1890, I have been concerned with developing the material well-being of the working class by paying wages unknown until then on the Troyes labor market. This profitable example has certainly had a favorable influence, for firms stimulated by these results have been obliged to follow suit in the interest of material progress."[81] While Vitoux bragged about emulation, there is little evidence to support his claim that he had disciples regarding wages.

Léon Vitoux affirmed his support for worker retirement funds and the creation of a mutual-aid fund for his personnel. He also announced that he was experimenting with a crèche at his mill for working mothers with young children. He explained to the commission how it was intended to work: "I am experiencing some difficulties in the beginning, but I feel certain to overcome them and to succeed. The biggest objection is the following: mothers fear that their children will catch cold. I will have them fetched at home. This represents a little sacrifice on my part, it's true, but should one stop on the path of progress when it is a matter of improving the worker's lot and when

79. Musée de la publicité 1988 (Bibliothèque Forney).
80. Prévot 1931.
81. Manuscript document submitted to the parliamentary commission of inquiry, AN C 7318.

her contribution is indispensable to me? If it is a woman's right to nourish her child, it is my duty to give her the means to do it."[82] A declaration of intentions of this kind serves as a reminder that one should not confuse discourse with practice in the realm of paternalist policies. In fact, as S. Kott notes, "what [employer] discourse conveys is less a reality than their desires and aspirations. The realization, the concrete fulfillment of such policies often comes up against a conflicting logic on the ground."[83] Our sources do not confirm that workers' children were actually fetched at home, and that Vitoux's crèche actually operated very long. Moreover, women workers' resistance to the crèche project suggests that there were real limits to support for such sex-specific paternalist measures, since they often held hidden agendas.[84] At this time, there were few child-care alternatives to those provided by the extended family at home. Only the outwork system allowed mothers to combine productive and reproductive work. In any case, at the time of the commission's inquiry, Vitoux's was the only crèche program reported by a millowner in the questionnaire returned by the Chambre de commerce de Troyes.

The social policies of Vitoux, and his particular solicitude toward working mothers, constitute an important reminder of paternalism's selective nature and of the sex-specific forms of many welfare policies in targeting working-class women.[85] Vitoux was also concerned to provide the inquiry commission with his thoughts on how factory life could be made compatible with family life. Doubtless he had in mind changes to the laws of 1892 and 1900 concerning the reduction of women's working hours that Troyes millowners had opposed. Vitoux's paternalist project included a particular vision of the working-class family that was crucial to maintaining the social order and essential to ensuring women workers' labor in the mills, by now indispensable to factory production in Troyes.

82. Ibid.

83. S. Kott, "La Haute Alsace: Une région modèle en matière d'habitat ouvrier (1853–1914)," *Revue de l'Economie Sociale,* January 1988, as quoted in Debouzy 1988, 15 n. 31.

84. Employer-sponsored crèches often imposed on working-class women rules of hygiene, food, and clothing based on principles of bourgeois morality. Women workers at the Courtauld's silk factory in Halstead, England, refused to bring their children to the factory crèche, which was subsequently forced to close after only three years. See Lown 1988, 64–68. For the textile mills of northern France, Hilden (1986) underscores the indifference of the millowners to reform and discusses the lack of crèches to help working mothers in Lille-Roubaix-Tourcoing (81–82).

85. See Stewart 1989, and the essays in Accampo et al. 1995.

THE TRANSITION TO THE FACTORY SYSTEM

The second half of the nineteenth century saw a significant movement of population in the Aube: the progressive migration of knitters from the countryside to the industrial towns, linked to their increased specialization in hosiery production in a variety of forms.[86] The overall population of the department peaked in the mid-nineteenth century and then began a slow and steady decline into the mid-twentieth century. Thus between 1851 and 1901, the number of inhabitants decreased by 7 percent, passing from about 265,000 to about 246,000.[87] Yet such figures mask a significant redistribution of population between town and country, as rural inhabitants severed contact with the land and moved to the two major industrial towns of the department. In the second half of the nineteenth century, the population of Troyes nearly doubled, from 31,027 in 1851 to 53,146 in 1901, while that of Romilly increased by 40 percent during the same period, creating a second center for hosiery production.[88] The rural exodus slowed between 1901 and 1954, but the population of Troyes continued to grow. Moreover, much of the population expansion throughout this period took place outside the old walls surrounding the town's historic center, with the movement of growing numbers of the working class into the industrial suburbs.

Of course, even in the early nineteenth century the peasant-knitters maintained important links with the towns. But while formerly rural knitters went to the towns for an apprenticeship and then returned home to the countryside, the transformation of knitting technology in the later nineteenth century was compelling permanent migration. By the 1860s the growing complexity of knitting machines forced knitters to specialize on one type of frame. The introduction of new forms of energy, harnessed to these more productive frames, made the hand frames of rural knitters less competitive in relation to those operating in urban mills. One obvious conclusion that can be drawn from this migration pattern is that well into the twentieth century, much of Troyes's working class had been shaped by the experience of rural society and possessed skills largely inherited from textile outwork. Such common professional and geographic origins marked the labor force that filled the urban workshops of Troyes and Romilly.

86. See Lazzarotti 1971, 7; and Favier 1963, 18 and 170–72.
87. Favier 1963, 18.
88. Ibid., 34. The growth of population in Romilly was probably caused in part by the creation in 1875 of a metalworking and repair center for the regional railroad line.

Millworkers: From Peasants and Homeworkers to an Urban Proletariat

While the great majority of the worker population of these two towns came from the Aube itself, there was also some migration from Alsace and Lorraine after the Franco-Prussian War. Between 1876 and 1881 there was an annual in-migration of 900 inhabitants into the department, and from 1881 to 1886 the figure rose to more than 970.[89] Many of these new arrivals were textile work-ers who had fled Prussian occupation. Among the workers born between 1893 and 1911 who were interviewed for this study, a substantial number had parents who arrived in this wave of migration from eastern France. Since their arrival corresponded with a period of development and expansion of the hosiery industry, they readily found work in the spinning mills and dyeworks of Troyes, or in the regional railroad company.

Two other features of the demographic situation in the Aube and among the working class need to be underlined. In the first place, the birthrate in the department was one of the lowest in France. In the Aube, Hubert Favier com-mented, "the birthrate was notably inferior to the general average in France throughout the entire nineteenth century." Indeed through the beginning of World War I, "the population of the Aube was older than the French popu-lation in general."[90] The reasons for this low reproductive rate are uncertain. A local primary school teacher, writing in 1917, was convinced that it was linked to "voluntary abstention: no one has children, because they don't want chil-dren. . . . Living is expensive, and as no one wants to deprive themselves, the husband works on the one hand, and the wife on the other, the family work-shop bringing the promise of good wages."[91] Other contemporary observers, who expressed growing anxiety over the French population decline that accompanied the end of World War I, were quick to put the onus on women and on women's involvement in industrial work.

The prospect of an aging and dwindling labor force was also a major con-cern for millowner Léon Vitoux. In his deposition before the parliamentary commission of inquiry in 1904, he placed France's problem of depopulation in direct relation to the reproductive behavior of his women workers. To support his contention, he cited the following figures concerning the workingwomen in his own mill: "[I]n one female workshop consisting of 125 women and young girls . . . there are 49 married or widowed women, 49 children, and

89. Ibid., 26–27.
90. Ibid., 22.
91. Lagoguey 1918, 259.

19 unmarried young women. . . . Among these, 16 couples have no children, 15 have one child, 8 have two children, 1 has three, one widow has two, 3 widows have three; the 19 unmarried women are 25 to 40 years old." What conclusions did he draw from these figures? "Women should return to their family role, in the private sphere" to ensure the survival and dignity of the working-class family. Through the reduction of working hours to nine hours a day for women in factories, working mothers could more readily combine factory work with household tasks and reproduce the labor force. Vitoux's findings were evoked in support of the working-class family, but he must also have had the long-term interests of his factory in mind.[92]

But if the low fertility of women industrial workers was related in part to the probable practice of voluntary birth control, it was also linked to a second feature of working-class demography, a stark reality that many historians have overlooked: exceptionally high gender-specific mortality. In fact, there was a huge discrepancy in life expectancy for women textile workers in Troyes in comparison with that of the general population of the town. An analysis of a sample from the Table des successions, a register maintained for appraising estate taxes at the time of death, reveals a pattern of unusually high mortality among women textile workers that persisted over a relatively long period. From 1878 to 1880, for example, such women died 12 years younger than other Troyes women. Fully one-third died before the age of 30, most of them as single women. A similar pattern held true for the later period, 1896–99: on the eve of the twentieth century, half of women textile workers in Troyes were dying by the age of 36. Indeed, as late as 1924–27, the mean age at death for women textile workers was still only 41.9, while the corresponding age for all women in Troyes was twenty years greater.[93] Many of these working women died at the Hôtel Dieu, where the cause of death was almost always noted to be tuberculosis.

To be sure, over the same periods, male textile workers also tended to die younger than the general population, though they consistently fared better than women. For the period 1878–80, the average age at death for male

92. Enquête parlementaire (1904), AN C 7318.
93. These figures are drawn from a systematic sample of deaths listed under names beginning with the letters B, C, and M for the years 1878–80, 1896–99, 1909–11, and 1924–27. For all those years, n = 264 for women textile workers, and n = 223 for men textile workers. Analysis of the Table des successions (ADA 3Q, Table des successions, 8218, 8226, 14367, 14378) for these periods suggests that, young or old, almost none had possessions of any value at the time of their death. For the earliest period, many textile workers were given certificates of "indigence" and died at the Hôtel Dieu.

textile workers was about 51, compared with 55 for the general male population in Troyes. For reasons that are not entirely clear, the average age at death
dropped to 47.2 during the years 1896–99. However, by the mid-1920s life
expectancy for male workers had rebounded to 52.2 years, still more than ten
years longer than for their female counterparts.

However stunning these figures may seem, other studies of mortality among
textile workers for this period reveal similar findings. Thus, Patricia Hilden
concluded that women workers in the textile mills of Lille died "in their
mid-thirties" in the late nineteenth century.[94] Many contemporary studies, by
doctors, journalists, or union militants, such as the Bonneff brothers, also
took note of this phenomenon in the years before World War I. Journalist
Marcelle Capy, writing for the union newspaper *La Bataille Syndicaliste* during
the war, reported that women working in the linen and wool mills of Lille
suffered from exposure at an early age to dust, heat, and humidity. The lack
of hygiene, long working hours, and low wages were responsible, she argued,
for the fact that male workers hardly lived beyond the age of 40 and women
beyond the age of 35.[95] Such studies concerned both the spinning and woven-
textile industries in the Nord, where working conditions were noticeably
dirtier and more unhealthy than in hosiery. Single women working in less-
skilled jobs were probably most vulnerable, dying young from malnutrition
and tuberculosis. But married women, who were compelled to combine child-
bearing with continued millwork, also found their lives measurably shortened,
a trend that persisted well into the twentieth century.

Such gender-specific demographic patterns are all the more significant
because of another original feature of textile work in Troyes and the Aube:
the high level of participation of women in the labor force.[96] The two main
economic activities of the department over a very long period were agriculture and textiles. But unfortunately, nineteenth-century census reports do not
present gender breakdowns for categories such as *ouvriers* (manual workers)

94. See Hilden 1986, 33–34.
95. Marcelle Capy, "Drames du travail," *La Bataille Syndicaliste,* April 17, 1914. She refers to
an official study of hygiene among textile workers by Dr. Verhaeghe, but she also visits several
mills during March and April 1914 to report on working conditions. Her observations are tinted
with a despair bordering on paternalism, with the result that she condemns both the desperate
working and living conditions and most workers, regarding them as submissive or resigned to
their fate. See her article on living conditions, "Mal logés, mal nourris," *La Bataille Syndicaliste,*
April 18, 1914. See also Bonneff and Bonneff 1914.
96. The figures were culled from the *Statistiques du recensement générale de la population* for
1896, 1906, 1911, 1921, 1926, 1931, and 1936.

or *employés* (white-collar workers), and the discrete category *woman worker* appears only in 1906. But according to the data for the first third of the twentieth century, women already represented more than half (52.5 percent) of hosiery workers in the department in 1906, and by 1921 that proportion had risen to more than three-fifths (61.5 percent), a proportion that declined only slightly into the 1930s. Such ratios are even more striking when compared with those of the large textile factory system of Lille-Roubaix-Tourcoing, where women represented only 36 percent of the total labor force in 1896.[97] Moreover, the census categories may very well underrepresent the number of women actually employed in textile work, especially those engaged on a part-time basis. Particularly problematic is the number listed as holding specific employment at home as "outworkers," or *travailleurs isolés*.[98] Indeed, it is very likely that the censuses convey only partial figures for the number of women actually working at home. In 1901 only 2,049 women among the *travailleurs isolés* were said to be working as "stocking seamers." But it is easy to imagine that this type of women's work was underrecorded and that the data given is unreliable. Subcontracting was a common and widespread practice in hosiery production, yet it was invariably difficult to count statistically. The increasing feminization of the hosiery labor force is also a feature that most historians of the industry assumed to be a natural pattern of textile and garment work, little related, in fact, to the expansion of the industry as a whole. We will be reexamining this assumption in the course of this study, with the aim of explaining the complexity of gender and social relations behind such a marked pattern of femininization.

The Family Artisan Workshop: Le Façonnier

Despite the rapid advances of the factory system, hosiery production remained surprisingly dispersed, even at the beginning of the twentieth century, and the large urban mill was still a rarity. As late as 1900, the family workshop represented an appealing alternative, a mode of resistance in some respects to the world of factory work, embedded in the historical experience of men and women workers in Troyes as an idealized way of life.

Indeed, one way for the rural knitter to avoid both migration and the factory system was to establish himself as a *façonnier* (subcontracted artisan),

97. Hilden 1986, 24.
98. Scott 1988, "A Statistical Representation of Work," 113–38.

specializing in the production of certain articles for a designated manufacturer. The latter often provided the necessary knitting machines, on a loan or lease agreement, since the expenses of setting up complex knitting machinery required an important capital investment. The façonnier, on his part, provided the workshop, in which he organized hosiery production among his family members, together with the requisite knowledge and skills. A rural outworker employed in this way generally had a garden-size plot of land, perhaps some fields, and a house, part of which was converted into a workshop. This system of artisan work seemed to provide flexibility for both parties. However, in reality, the social and property relations involved made this type of work relationship far from ideal, and the customary verbal agreements between the façonnier and the manufacturer underscore the former's status as a dependent subcontractor and producer.[99] Façonniers were implicitly forbidden from working for any other manufacturer than the one who leased the knitting machines. For the articles produced, he was paid a prix de façon, which clearly did not correspond to a wage. It represented the cost of the transformation of the raw materials produced by the artisan's labor and skills. The labor of other household members and hired workers was subsumed in the price. No account was taken of working hours, which might easily involve twelve hours a day spent in the family workshop, in contrast to the ten hours commonly practiced in the mills during this period. The prix de façon generally fell below piece rates paid to millworkers operating the same knitting frame.[100] In many ways, then, the artisan's dependence on the manufacturer carried with it an extensive engagement for exclusive service not unlike that involved in the older putting-out system, of which it was certainly an outgrowth.[101]

Even Auguste Mortier, a leading hosiery manufacturer, criticized the exploitation engendered by this system of "travail à façon," a system "in appearance

99. See the observations of rural primary school teacher E. Jamarey (1900), and the deposition of the Association syndicale des ouvriers façonniers de Romilly et de ses environs before the parliamentary commission of inquiry (AN C 7318, p. 105). They also confirm this practice of a verbal contract. Many of the concrete obligations assumed by both parties have been preserved in a rare written contract (1887; Archives of the Conseil des prud'hommes de Troyes). See also Liu 1994, esp. 138–39. Workers in the Cholet region labored under similar agreements.

100. Jamerey (1900) indicates that the daily income of an adult knitter, operating the *métier hollandais,* was Fr 2 for a twelve-hour day, or Fr 1.60 for ten hours. The average piece rate in the Troyes mills for the same knitting frame was Fr 5.76 a day, as quoted by the millowners, and Fr 3.50 to Fr 4 a day, according to workers' testimony.

101. An extreme case of such stability and dependence is cited by Jamerey (1900), who recorded the case of a seventy-three-year-old knitter in his village "working for the same mill, possibly the same millowner, for the past 62 years!"

advantageous [but] in reality detrimental to the hosiery industry." The irregu-
larity of manufacturers' orders led to frequent variations in prices and left the
knitter without a fixed "wage" and "in a state of material difficulties" that
had serious consequences. Mortier went on to characterize this system as a
competitive game that translated into "a continual down-spiraling of wages."
He signaled, for example, the reduction of the prix de façon around 1889 and
the façonniers' difficulties in keeping pace with the new norms of productivity
generated by mechanized knitting in the mills.[102]

Clearly, however, the façonnier played an important role in the apprenticeship and transmission of *savoir-faire* to generations of knitters in Troyes. Male
workers trained in this fashion often moved on to jobs as foremen in the
urban mills. But knitting skills were also passed down through the female
line, as many women assisted their husbands in the artisan workshop, working alongside their children. Jamerey's report on the rural hosiery industry
in Maizières-la-Grande Paroisse at the time of the 1900 Paris World's Fair
provides particularly interesting details of a rural family workshop.[103] His
descriptions of the rural knitter's life stressed the division of labor according
to sex and age: "Until 1870, about half the small knitting frames were operated
manually by men, the other half by women and young men. Since the introduction of the Paget knitter [*métier hollandais*], the knitting frame has been
operated by men because it would be too tiring for women to work it continuously; it is only briefly their task. The role of young people and the elderly
is to unwind yarn, to prepare the transition for the next knitting operation
[rebrousser], for all knitting machines have a special accessory called a *re-
brousseuse* that children can use." Jamerey's description confirms that all family
members were employed in the production of hosiery. Although gender and
technical divisions of labor existed, and women generally operated machines
requiring less physical strength than men, they nevertheless shared the burden
of labor on all machines. The important point is that women and children did
productive labor and that their work was budgeted into the family economy,
even if its monetary value was subsumed in the prix de façon.

102. Mortier 1891, 41–42.
103. Jamerey's (1900) description of the artisan workshop centered on a household that was
composed of "a 52-year-old widow of a knitter, mother, and head of household; her oldest son,
aged 34 and married; the latter's wife, aged 29; and the younger son, aged 16. Production was
shared among family members according to the size of the machines: the two men minded
the large flatbed knitter and the winder [*bobinoir*]; the two women minded the small knitter
and winder, while they cut and seamed the stockings and sorted them into dozens. It was hard
work for the women, who toiled for fourteen hours."

Thus family-based production allowed families to work together and women to continue their domestic chores. There was, however, a price to pay in the endless hours spent at work to earn a livelihood, a fact that Jamerey hardly mentioned. His construction of this family world of work was freighted with the discourse of social reform that underpinned the Le Play family model. But writing as he did in 1900, he could not hide the short-lived nature of the rural artisan world he depicted at the time. By 1895, declining prices for finished goods was creating a difficult situation for many rural artisans of this kind. There were limits to the flexibility of this family system of rural producers, and an idle knitter could no longer survive. Increasingly, at the close of the nineteenth century, the children of such families were choosing to leave the countryside for work in the urban mills.

Yet the outwork system was widespread, especially in rural centers such as Aix-en-Othe, Fontaine-les-Grès, and Arcis-sur-Aube that maintained the system of small-scale production. So the resilience of outwork under various, protean forms, well into the twentieth century, should not be underestimated. In many cases the rural artisan became an urban one, and here the relations of production changed, as we shall see in a later section. By 1900, the expansion of the factory system in proximity to the old urban center of Troyes revitalized industrial faubourgs, among them Sainte-Savine, in which the urban façonnier could establish home and workshop in close association with nearby mills.[104] However, in their response to the parliamentary inquiry of 1904, millowners complained bitterly of "disastrous competition" from these same façonniers and demanded that such family workshops be regulated by the current factory legislation and made to respect the new shortened working hours, just as factories were forced to do. A stricter application of these new laws would allow millowners to combat "those manufacturers without factories who put out all their work to rural knitters."[105] Again Auguste Mortier, in his role as rapporteur at the Paris World's Fair, cited the competition from rural work-shops, whose use of new petrol motors continued to bring prices down. "The rural façonnier has been able to set up at home the large Cotton flatbed

104. The relation between urbanization and industrialization in French towns has been the object of many recent studies. The distinctive residential and industrial pattern of Sainte-Savine and its relation to Troyes has at last found its historian. See the work in progress of Jean-Louis Humbert (1994).

105. See testimony by the Chambre syndicale des fabricants de bonneterie before the par-liamentary commission (1904), p. 82; also the report of the Commission départementale du travail (ADA SC 667).

knitters that until now had remained the prerogative of factories with steam power and big producers; he has brought about a disastrous competition with the big producers over certain articles of mass consumption. Working day and night, with no regard for factory laws and no overhead, using the labor of his wife and children, he has forced prices down over the past two years by 30 percent on those articles he produced."[106] The contradictions of flexible outworking through the façonniers were such that both urban and rural workshops could represent a challenge to large millowners.

THE WORLD OF FACTORY WORK IN 1900

Why did factory production become for the most part a necessity, or at the least a preferred industrial strategy, so relatively late in Troyes? What roles did labor and technology play in these changes? To answer these questions, we need to examine the organization of production around 1900.

During the 1880s and 1890s, the economic recession that developed in France also affected the hosiery industry in Troyes. These difficult years slowed industrial growth until the end of the century. However, sheltered by high protective tariffs, manufacturers in Troyes were able to complete a process of slow concentration toward larger-scale factory production. They introduced more modern high-speed knitting machinery and expanded their markets outside France. This stage of industrialization was accompanied by an influx of workers in Troyes, which abetted social tensions for jobs and housing. Yet the great majority of workers were still employed in relatively small urban workshops. Out of twenty-seven hosiery mills inventoried during the great strike of 1900, there were sixteen that employed between 20 and 250 men and women workers; there was only one large mill, the Mauchauffée firm, employing more than 1,000 workers.[107] Such a large mass-production mill would remain a rarity until after 1920. Hosiery production in Troyes and the nearby suburbs employed roughly eight thousand workers, a labor force in which women textile workers already outnumbered men by 1900.

Technological change, coupled with the growth in demand for luxury knitted goods, encouraged entrepreneurs to increase capital investments in

106. Mortier 1902, 238.
107. ADA SC 417. These figures are compiled from the police inventory of strikers in the mills.

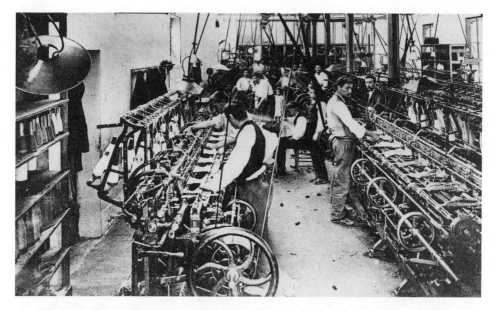

Figure 3   Knitting-machine workshop in a Troyes mill, showing the Cotton patent knitting machines for producing fully fashioned stockings. The seated figure in the center is an older man who is training the young rebrousseur standing next to him, c. 1900. Archives départementales de l'Aube.

mass-production machinery. These new knitting machines greatly increased productivity, but certain stages in the production process were not as efficiently mechanized as was knitting. These "technological gaps," so to speak, were filled to a large extent by women workers.[108] With the demand for ready-to-wear knitwear, made from cut-and-sewn knitted fabric, women seamers were required in greater number than before. Both these factors help to explain why women workers were by 1900 in greater demand in hosiery. Moreover, millowners in Troyes now had sufficient access to capital and credit to purchase new machinery and to fill large orders of knitwear. Thus, the improvement in knitting technology favored a more centralized production system and allowed those enterprising millowners with capital to master the whole series of operations necessary to turn raw cotton into knitwear.[109]

While the concentration of production in more efficient large-scale mills was to become an economic and technical imperative within the coming two

108. The term is Tabet's (1979, 5–62).
109. See Marglin 1973, 43–45.

decades, the transition to the factory system was at this stage relatively slow, and it was hampered by the persistence of small producers and outworkers. A report from the British Board of Trade in 1907 described the network of mills and workshops that continued to dominate the organization of hosiery production in Troyes: "The system of making an article, from first to last, under the same roof is only carried out to a small extent by the hosiery manufacturers of Troyes. More commonly they have none but the mechanical part of the work done in their mills, and give out cutting, mending, embroidery, making up of underclothing and the like to women living in the town, who receive about 25 percent less than would be paid for similar work in the factory."[110] Putting out the unmechanized tasks to local women to finish by hand still seemed a viable economic option. However, the larger hosiery firms faced problems of scaling down their inventory and adapting their production to changes in fashion, problems that small firms could manage with greater flexibility.

Questions of industrial competition among millowners in Troyes and with other textile centers plagued these prewar years. Typically, millowners made the strategic claim that the state was acting against their particular interests. But there are many examples in the parliamentary inquiry of 1904 of millowners' outright hostility toward what they regarded as state intervention in industrial questions. They were particularly opposed to the laws shortening working hours in the factories, strictures they felt were prejudicial to French industry in relation to foreign competitors. Their arguments were essentially the same as in 1884, when they opposed the regulation of women's and children's labor: shortening the working day meant cutting productivity and increasing the cost price of knitted goods; and regulating adult labor meant limiting individual freedom. Faced with the shorter-hours law of 1900, Troyes millowners sought special exemptions for overtime hours when needed, and they reiterated their pleas for more protective duties.

In this atmosphere of intense competition in 1900, hosiery millowners found themselves confronted with their own contradictions. Their industry produced more knitted goods than the country could consume, and any attempt to reduce production entailed a willful struggle to eliminate weaker competitors. They admitted as much themselves, without trying to analyze the factors that had contributed to increased productivity over the past years.[111]

110. AMT 4F 530, p. 356.
111. See the report of the Chambre de commerce de Troyes (1904), 80, AN C 7318.

By far the most important factors were the improvements to knitting machines and the resulting specialization of knitters' work.

Technological Change and Knitters' Work

The technical complexity of knitting machines and the variety of articles produced made knitting an intricate operation. Production in the Troyes mills was labor intensive, and that labor had to be skilled. As a hosiery manufacturer in 1895 explained, "[H]osiery production is not limited to just knitting the raw materials used to feed the knitting frames; it involves making garments, either by cutting the knitted fabric or by fully fashioning them on the frames, seaming and finishing them to make clothing."[112] For these reasons, labor accounted for a half or even two-thirds of the cost price of an article at the end of the nineteenth century.[113] Historically, the work process was divided into several operations, assigned to men, women, and children according to their sex, age, and ability. As we have already seen, men appropriated the knitting frame and the technical knowledge required to repair and adjust the machine. The mechanics of knitting technology were decidedly a masculine preserve, and the technical skills so prized for their prestige and productivity were those that developed out of the craft tradition.

The most important technical transformations during this period concerned the knitters' work. Powered knitting frames now had more automatic functions, and thus produced articles with greater speed and in series. Two of the most productive frames were, first, the Paget, a solid but flexible machine invented in England, and manufactured in Troyes by the Poron company, that served to produce quality articles made in family workshops; and second, the Cotton flatbed knitter, invented in England in 1862, displayed at the Paris World's Fair of 1867, and constructed from 1878 by Couturat manufacturers in Troyes. It was the Cotton frame that would become the mass-production knitter of the modern mill. With multiple heads, it could simultaneously knit several fully fashioned articles. These new knitting frames contributed to diversifying knitted goods production. The Cotton flatbed frame knitted open-worked or embroidered articles; the circular frame made complex Jacquard

112. Jules Herbin, Rapport sur les modifications au règlement sur le travail des filles mineurs et des femmes dans l'industrie à la Chambre de Commerce de Troyes, December 6, 1895, Archives du Musée de la bonneterie.

113. Parliamentary inquiry of 1904, p. 507, AN C 7318. See also Heywood 1994, 174–75.

patterns. It was now possible to produce on the same frame a greater number of different articles, so that a manufacturer could diversify his production and gain in flexibility with response to fashion changes. Overall, the mechanization of hosiery production had different social consequences for the gendered division of labor. For the knitters, improvements made to powered knitting frames required fewer adjustments to regulate them, but, as a result, employers were quick to give knitters more machines to mind.[114] The leap in productivity produced by these high-powered frames provoked worker anxiety that unemployment would follow the decline in wages already evident since 1890. Testimony from worker delegates sent from Troyes to the Paris World's Fair of 1900 evoked similar concerns. One knitter, Amédée Selves, expressed his anxiety in a series of existential questions: "What conclusion can been drawn from all this progress demonstrated at the World's Fair? How can we truly foresee the future miseries that will result from such progress in increased productivity? For everything has been made to produce more. As a consequence of reducing the number of productive workers, what will society do with those who are idled?"[115] But even with the improved knitting frames of the period, it was still not possible to knit the complete stocking without passing through transitional operations that required manual *rebroussage,* poorly paid and subordinate work that was executed primarily by young apprentices, whose revolt had sparked the great strike of 1900.

Women's work was less affected by technical innovation. Customarily, women were employed to prepare the raw materials (spinning or winding), and to seam and finish knitted goods. The tasks assigned to them entailed using simple, manual tools or operating small machines such as seamers. The fact that many of their tasks were only partially mechanized led to a need for increasing numbers of "nimble fingers" to sew and finish goods. Seaming was labor intensive. The first loopers and seamers—types of small sewing machines—together with other accessory machines, became progressively more reliable during this period. Small machines to make buttonholes were introduced; but for the most part, these technical improvements resulted in a greater specialization, and even a rationalization, of women's tasks. At this time, several female-dominated occupations became identified by the machine the women operated, much as was true for their male counterparts. The

114. Government work inspector's report in the parliamentary inquiry of 1904, AN C 7318.
115. Testimony of M. Selves, secretary of the Association syndicale des ouvriers bonnetiers, AMT 2F 47.

increased productivity of the mass-production knitting frames did create additional jobs for women in finishing and sewing, specialized tasks that were both manual and mechanized. Many of these tasks relied on women's aptitudes for, and competences in, sewing, embroidery, mending, and ironing—all skills acquired largely through family education.

The Precariousness of Work and Wages

Workers' testimony during this period reflected two major concerns, the precariousness of work and the extreme variability of wages. For many hosiery workers, new norms of productivity imposed by mass-production machines, and the intensification of work itself, seemed secondary preoccupations. When millowners requested a more flexible application of shorter-hours legislation, allowing them exemptions for overtime work, militant workers in Troyes demanded a reduction in periods of unemployment through establishment of the eight-hour day and a minimum wage.[116]

In his testimony before the parliamentary commission of inquiry, Emile Clévy, representing the Chambre syndicale des ouvriers bonnetiers de Troyes, claimed that knitters did not work more than 225 days a year on average.[117] Seasonal unemployment was a given in the knitted goods industry, which followed the fashion market. But Clévy imputed the blame to the organization of work and to mechanization: "In the knitted goods industry, where mechanization has totally transformed and modernized the tools of the trade every day, unemployment is becoming more and more common. Thus certain knitting machines produce in one day what a worker operating a Paget frame only twenty years ago would have produced in one week."[118] From the worker's viewpoint, there was an obvious contradiction between unemployment that resulted from the increased productivity of the knitting machines, and employers' demands for overtime work at their discretion. In fact, millworkers denounced this forced unemployment and demanded that the state create an unemployment fund, to be financed by fines from millowners who worked their employees more than ten hours a day.[119] Clearly, workers perceived that

116. Ibid.
117. Testimony of Emile Clévy in parliamentary inquiry of 1904, p. 96.
118. Rapport de l'Association syndicale des ouvriers bonnetiers in parliamentary inquiry of 1904, p. 98.
119. Testimony of Emile Clévy, in parliamentary inquiry of 1904, p. 95.

unemployment was not inevitable. Rather, they experienced it as a mishap of mechanization, a consequence of bad work organization under capitalism. In the largest mills, when one knitter was asked to mind several knitting machines and his piece rate was simultaneously reduced by 20 percent, and subsequently several other knitters were laid off, the changes were immediately denounced in the working-class press.[120] Such practices divided workers among themselves and created unemployment. For labor militants, the obvious remedy was the eight-hour day.

Workers also mounted resistance to wage reductions that resulted from idleness imposed by difficulties in executing work or in operating the machines. As Clévy explained: "This originates in the piece-rate system practiced in the knitted goods industry, which has little relation to the actual work done. Knitting machines are precise but fragile; the smallest change in temperature disrupts their operation and always makes it uncertain what the knitter will earn in a day and produces a constant variation in wages. Moreover, when a machine works badly, wages are still notably reduced by the fines for broken needles that the worker must pay. Once again, if the raw materials employed are of bad quality, the worker's daily wages are reduced by paying for broken needles, hooks, or plates that the millowners mark down at higher than cost."[121] Thus workers denounced the piece-rate wage system and the organization of work.

The uncertainty of work and of wages were closely related. Workers' productivity was subject to the risks of badly functioning, unreliable machines and cheap-quality yarn. Wages were further reduced by the employers' policy of wage deductions, practiced for broken needles and *pour comptes*, that were imputed to workers. All these factors—unemployment caused by technical problems, variations in piece rates, wage deductions—contributed to the uncertain calculation of daily wages and added to the precariousness of workers' existence. All these grievances emerged in the great strike of 1900. While women workers actively supported the strike and its demands, they were faced with gender-specific problems with regard to their work and status as women, wives, and mothers. Generally, Troyes millowners had systematically opposed

120. See *Le Reveil des Travailleurs de l'Aube,* September 3–10, 1898. The requirement that one worker mind several Cotton patent knitters began around 1894 in the largest mill in Troyes, the Mauchauffée mill (ADA M 2293).

121. Testimony of Emile Clévy to the parliamentary commission of inquiry of 1904. The extreme variations in piece rates practiced in the Troyes mills also struck the notice of English observers in 1907. See AMT 4F 530, p. 356.

protective legislation for women, shorter hours, and the regulation of their working conditions on the grounds that such measures interfered with "la liberté du travail."

"Pampering the Goose That Lays the Golden Eggs"

During the debates over protective legislation for women working in industry, millowners in Troyes had lobbied against government intervention. After the passage of the law of 1892 that restricted working hours of women and children in factories, millowners sought to have such restrictions temporarily lifted in relation to adult women workers.[122] Such efforts underscore the importance to the knitted goods industry of women's work during this period. Women were in much demand to seam and finish the luxury garments of the Belle Epoque. For this reason, some millowners recognized the need to treat women workers with a particular consideration that would make factory work compatible with women's domestic duties.

Hosiery manufacturer Léon Vitoux was an accommodating, benevolent employer. In a singular deposition before the parliamentary commission of inquiry concerning women's industrial work, he constructed a special case in favor of reducing women's working hours to nine hours a day.[123] Vitoux's text dissolved the boundaries between public and private life. It focused on women workers' needs as if meeting these was a moral imperative for sustaining French motherhood. His primary concern was that married women and mothers should continue to work and to combine factory work with housework and raising children. In his opinion, "it was necessary to create a situation that was compatible with their aptitudes, their role in the household, the family and society in general, that they could be good wives, good mothers, and good housekeepers, while working in the mill workshop." Vitoux addressed women workers' double roles, as industrial producers and mothers of the future labor force. Even so, he readily conceded that their work was indispensable to the Troyes hosiery industry. He did so in these striking terms: "Let us remind the legislator that, when he inscribed in the law eleven hours

122. See *Voeux émis sur le travail des enfants, des filles mineures et des femmes par la Chambre de Commerce de Troyes à sa séance du 6 Décembre 1895,* Archives du Musée de la bonneterie.
123. Speech made before the Chambre syndicale patronale de bonneterie and deposited in the records of the parliamentary inquiry in December 1904 accompanied by a letter of explanation (AN C 7318).

of industrial work for the woman, she must still work five more hours at home; let us remind him that the law, whose purpose is to regulate work, intends at the same time to protect women and girls. This is what I would call, if you allow me, pampering the goose that lays the golden eggs. Let us not ourselves forget that woman is for our industry a question of life and death, and that we must treat her gently." Vitoux's choice of metaphor is certainly not innocent. Women's work was not only a vital part of the industry; more important, it was a source of millowners' profits.[124]

To be sure, Vitoux claimed to pay the best wages on the Troyes labor market.[125] Unlike other Troyes millowners, he contended that shorter hours for women would not slow their productivity. At this time, women worked both in the mills and in their homes as operators of seamers and loopers. Vitoux attempted to show through a time-motion study of these two women's occupations what the women's work actually produced. The fact that such work was mechanized allowed him to control and calculate their productivity more accurately than before. His observations, those of an early Frederick Taylor, show that Vitoux had understood that women workers used the piece-rate system to guarantee themselves steady wages, pacing their productivity accordingly. In Vitoux's mind were two objectives: to maintain women in the mills by assigning them tasks that were compatible with their status as mothers and housekeepers, and to preserve individual economic roles through the best possible organization of work. These issues suggest that worker productivity and discipline would become the overarching goals of the modern factory system.

In this chapter we have traced the pattern of textile industrialization in the Aube along a sinuous, complex path, from its origins as a rural putting-out industry to its development as a more concentrated modern factory system by

124. Vitoux's metaphor was obviously directed at the profit side of women's work. Where in English we use *goose*, in French they use *hen*: "la poule aux oeufs d'or." It is possible to read a pun into Vitoux's metaphor: *poule* can be used as a term of either condescension or endearment. Anthropologist Paola Tabet has another interpretation of the "hen that lays": "In fact, a shift in meaning would seem to occur between the *capacity* and the *fact* of procreating, and the latter meaning, instead of being the end of a process that obviously necessitates two sexes, becomes the essence of women's nature itself. The woman produces by herself not only the ovula, but also the child, in such a way that 'the exchange of fertile women' seems to be an exchange of laying hens. This shift is not however innocent." See Tabet 1985, 65.

125. According to the prefect's findings during the strike of 1900, strikers demanded a uniform wage scale based on the wages paid at Vitoux's mill.

the end of the nineteenth century. This pattern followed to some extent an economic logic, from small-scale domestic manufacture to a mixed factory and outwork system, employing new sources of energy, complex knitting technology, and, in certain cases, vertical integration of the whole production process within the same mill. However, the factory system came to dominate, but never totally eliminate, the artisan network system. The resilience and persistence of outwork in the Aube can be explained by several historical factors. In their experience with the outwork system, manufacturers came to understand the financial advantages it presented in terms of lower fixed-capital costs, thus reducing risks in a fluctuating fashion market. Moreover, as worker resistance to the factory system grew, millowners came to rely on the flexibility of outworkers—especially rural women—notably their relative disinterest in labor movements and their willingness to work long hours. By 1900, the coexistence of these two forms of production, one dominating the other, created a dense urban network of mills and workshops in Troyes and the surrounding suburbs. This was one of the distinctive features of the Troyes mills in relation to those of other textile regions of France.

Over half a century, this pattern of industrialization had created a widespread technical textile culture. During its most creative period in the 1880s, this shared textile culture became the source of inventions for improving knitting technology. Rural industry also provided a skilled labor force, endowed with a residual culture of textile production. Millowners profited from this ready-made labor force, trained in the family workshop, and they created a unique system in which it could be used socially and economically in new ways for the production of quality, fashionable goods. The working-class family was thus an important factor of transmission of this technical culture, as we will see in the following chapters.

By 1900, a number of leading millowners in Troyes had equipped their industry with considerable economic power through mastery of the whole process of knitted goods production. Their mills combined under one roof machine construction, spinning, and dyeworks, together with knitting and garment making. Their ability to take advantage of the economies of scale meant that they were able to outproduce their smaller rivals and to maintain a technological advantage in the trade. As the commercial market for luxury goods peaked in the Belle Epoque, they were able to meet the demand. In historical perspective, these technological changes in the mechanization of textile production came relatively late in the course of industrialization.

The feminization of the textile labor force was another distinctive trait of industrialization in Troyes. Increasing numbers of women workers were necessary as the industry expanded production beyond stockings and socks to fashion knitwear and underwear. The diversification of production to more luxury goods, fashioned from cut-and-sewn knitted fabric, required more women employed as seamers, loopers, and finishers. Women workers' significant place in production strengthened their manifold identity as *bonnetières*—as wives and mothers in increasingly women-centered workshops. Léon Vitoux had acknowledged how vital women's work was for the future of an industry that by 1906 employed 53 percent of women of working age in the Aube. After 1900, women workers increasingly identified with this trade that provided their livelihood and established the reputation of Troyes as the fashion capital of the knitted goods industry.

3

MILLWORKERS, SOCIALISM, AND
THE LABOR MOVEMENT

The town of Troyes in 1900 was surrounded by tree-lined boulevards and public gardens that revealed the boundaries of the old walled medieval city. While the ramparts had been torn down between 1835 and 1842, the visible outline of the old walls remained, giving the town the familiar shape of a champagne cork, the so-called Bouchon de Champagne. Within the center, narrow streets were lined with half-timbered houses, huddled tightly together, their high, gabled facades hiding passages into a dense web of courtyards, stables, and workshops. The town itself was bisected by a canal that brought water and transported goods from the Seine. To the west of the canal was the *quartier haut,* the administrative, commercial, and market section inhabited for the most part by merchants, bourgeois, and notables; while to the east was the *quartier bas* encircled by the Seine and irrigated by a number of smaller canals. Subject to flooding at certain times of the year, the *quartier bas* was considered a damp and particularly unhealthy place to live. Some of its inhabitants—artisans, workers, and day casuals—labored in artisan workshops that used the waters to dye and bleach textiles or tan leather. The canal wound its way back to the Seine through this area, and its waters were frequently polluted by industrial and human waste. A medical study on the eve of the Revolution of 1789 attributed the premature death of weavers' families from typhoid and tuberculosis to the bad quality of the air and water in the *quartier bas*.[1]

---

1. Picard 1873. Dr. Picard painted a particularly grim picture of weavers' lives in Troyes in 1786: "Weavers spend their lives in cellar workshops; they spend their nights in dirty,

Rising sharply above the humble, crowded, predominantly workers' quarter, the cathédrale de Saint-Pierre dominated the landscape on the right bank of the main canal.

The old topography of Troyes had been further reshaped by the town's transition to the factory system. While in 1870 small hosiery workshops were still situated within the center of town, by 1900 rapid industrialization and concentration had forced production outside the former ramparts and the newly traced peripheral boulevards.[2] Three factors contributed to the localization of hosiery mills on the town's periphery: the proximity of water (the rivers Seine and Vienne), access to the railroad lines, and availability of the main connecting roads to Paris. When Troyes was linked by train to the Paris–Mulhouse line in 1858, the railroad station was constructed on the eastern side of the left bank near the main road to Paris. Many of the largest mills were clustered in the faubourg Sainte-Savine within a few blocks of the station. By 1900, Troyes was encircled by an industrial belt of faubourgs, connected by tramways.

Suzanne Gallois, a militant syndicalist who entered the mills just before World War I, described the town in terms that evoked Théophile Steinlen's great gray charcoal drawings of working-class life. It was a town governed by the whistles of the mills. Time was factory time. Gallois related how men and women workers would stop along the way to work to buy a *casse-croute* (snack) and some bread or have a drink. The bakeries opened at 4:00 A.M. and there were cafés on every block.

> I knew Troyes in early 1914–15, an ugly town due to the fact that it
> was damp. It was an old town, and there were uneven cobblestones,
> and obviously the mills—there were many of them—there were tall
> chimney stacks, and every morning you could hear the different whis-
> tles that called their cohorts of workers, and by the sound of their
> horn you could say: "there, that's the Poron mill, there's still five

poorly ventilated rooms in which the whole family eats and sleeps; noxious air penetrates from outside. . . . The violent and repeated movements made by knitters in operating the knitting frame disturb their breathing and cause problems in the circulation of blood." He concluded that the average life expectancy in Troyes was twenty-six years. See also the description of Troyes in Chartier et al. 1998, 423–24.

2. In 1870 there were 87 hosiery fabricants listed in Troyes, with three-quarters of them located within the inner city, or Bouchon de Champagne; in addition, there were 7 dyeworks along the Seine and the Vienne, 7 spinning mills, 4 manufacturers of knitting machines, 13 manufacturers of knitting needles, and 27 textile finishers (*apprêteurs*). See Humbert 1996, 18.

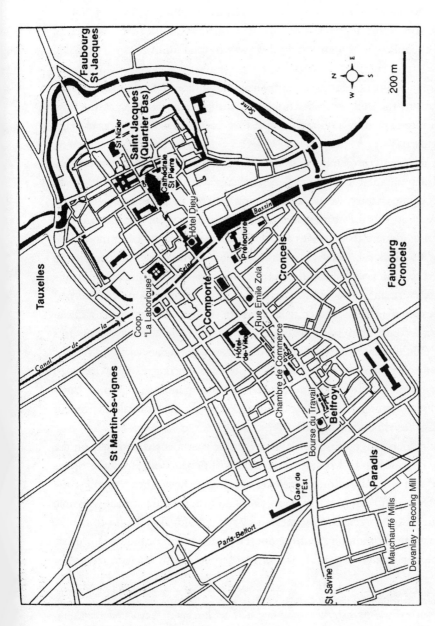

Figure 4   Map of Troyes in 1882, from *Nouveau guide de l'étranger dans Troyes et le département de l'Aube* (1882). Neighborhoods and landmarks within the Bouchon de Champagne (champagne cork) defined by the old town walls, and the suburbs outside it, have been superimposed. Courtesy of Colin Heywood and *Oxford University Press*.

minutes to go." This was the start of the morning, because we didn't do eight hours work at the time. Myself, I worked ten and eleven hours at the mill. So as you walked from home—it was still dark— you heard footsteps, the many footsteps on the cobblestones of people who were wending their way to each mill.[3]

In Suzanne Gallois's mind, the ten-hour working day stretched like a continuous path to the mill, from dawn to dusk without a break. In fact, the long day was interrupted by a noon meal pause of one and a half hours, as in many factory towns.

This new pattern of industrial life amid rapid urbanization reflected substantial demographic growth and social changes in the town population. In the preceding chapter we traced the slow process of transition from rural industry to an urban factory system. Here we will consider the formation of an urban working class in Troyes and the development of the labor movement inspired by Guesdist socialists and revolutionary syndicalism. Other groups also vied for the political loyalties of the working class, such as freethinkers (*libre-penseurs*), anarchists, and radicals. The analysis of working-class formation presented in this chapter will stress the different groups and associations that constituted social networks for workers in Troyes during this period. Could such groups be conceptualized as forming a social "class"? The Guesdist socialists obviously thought so. By introducing textile workers to their brand of Marxist socialism, they sought to organize these workers in a revolutionary struggle against capitalist millowners and to mobilize them for their class-based political agenda.

Within Marxism, notions of class have in the past focused narrowly on the primary relationship of workers to the means of production. Recent critiques by labor and feminist historians have demonstrated the need to reexamine the explanatory usefulness of the category *class*.[4] Not only are there many possible components of worker identity, created by the individual's relation to family, workplace, and community, but the uneven development of industrialization, with the persistence of traditional forms of production so characteristic of

3. Interview with Suzanne Gallois, May 14, 1984.
4. For an overview of the debate on class formation, see Berlanstein 1993, introduction, 1–14; and Katznelson 1986, introduction, 3–41; for criticism from feminist historians, see the essays in Baron 1991; and Frader and Rose 1996, esp. introduction, 1–33. For a recent debate on how to "reshape" the notion of class, see Eley and Nield 2000 and the debate with contributors.

France, make it difficult to contend that economic forces predominated over social and cultural ones in class formation. Our concern here is to explain the historical construction of worker identity in Troyes in the multiple sites of this gendered experience: not only in the workplace, but through gendered occupations, family networks, apprenticeship training, café sociability, and shopping at the consumer cooperative. Commonalities, but also differences, were reflected in experiences of mill-town life. Peasant-knitter families, shaped by the residual textile culture of Champagne, formed the core of Troyes millworkers. But others among the workers were former independent artisans, whose children became second-generation apprentices, while still others were migrants from eastern France and elsewhere in Europe. Within the dominant culture of industrial capitalism, millworkers formed an oppositional culture that emerged to resist factory exploitation. A minority, in fact, seemed predisposed to socialism, for reasons that we will explore in this chapter. To further their objectives, they founded institutions that promoted working-class identity. This identity might have appeared contingent, even fragile, in moments when it was tested by elections or collective action such as the great strike of 1900. Yet worker identity in Troyes was steeped in a culture of resistance that persisted well into the 1930s.

THE FORMATION OF THE WORKING CLASS

As in many areas of France, the forces creating a sense of social cohesion among workers were complex. Inward migration from the surrounding countryside had brought peasant outworkers with rural roots and individualistic attitudes, formed in the family workshop, into the urban mill workshops. The fact that these migrants had a common experience of village life and rural outwork in the Aube over several generations created potential social bonds. By contrast, migrants from Alsace and Lorraine who had sought refuge in Troyes after the Franco-Prussian War of 1870 found themselves socially segregated by several factors. Dialect and employment set them apart in the less-skilled textile jobs in spinning mills and dyeworks. Jobs of this kind were poorly paid, more precarious, and involved working in unhealthy conditions, all of which made these workers difficult to organize or to mobilize for protests. Most of the Alsatians clustered in the *quartier bas* near the église Saint-Nizier, a quarter that came to be known as Little Prussia.

Overall, however, residential patterns in Troyes were probably not as important in creating class consciousness as in other textile cities, such as Lille and Lyon, where rapid industrial growth and urbanization created sharply defined workers' quarters. Census records for Troyes in 1851 show that knitters and manual workers were scattered in various neighborhoods and well integrated into the town. Workers and industrialists, merchants and *rentiers*—all lived in proximity in the old town.[5] While the population of Troyes increased by some 71 percent between 1851 and the turn of the century, residential patterns within the inner town limits changed only slightly, with little evidence of social segregation. However, the marked increase in population created overcrowding and difficult living conditions and pushed a larger proportion of workers out into the surrounding faubourgs. According to one estimate, approximately 95 percent of workers lived *intra muros* in 1851, but only 77 percent did so in 1906.[6] The surrounding faubourgs to the west, such as Sainte-Savine, Saint-Julien-les-Villas, and Saint-André-les Vergers, also increased notably in size, and many artisans and factory workers settled near their workplace in these new transitional spaces. Several of these suburbs had been formally annexed to the town by the end of the century. This was the case of the faubourg Croncels, the faubourg Saint-Jacques, and finally the faubourg Saint-Martin, where workers took over the suburb. The problem of affordable housing was aired before the parliamentary commission of inquiry by Emile Clévy, the representative from the knitters' union who would later become mayor of Troyes. He argued that rents were higher in Troyes than in other textile towns, a fact confirmed by the British Board of Trade inquiry on the cost of living in different French industrial towns at roughly the same period.[7]

Within the old town, many working-class families shared crowded lodgings or lived in small furnished rooms. Just how crowded the housing became

5. See Heywood 1990, 116–17. "The source is a systematic sample of every fifth household in census registers. The eight sections into which Troyes was divided were purely administrative in nature. Figures include male and female heads of household, and in the absence of information on income and wealth, they can give only a broad approximation of social structure. The "upper bourgeoisie" consists mainly of property owners, *rentiers,* merchants, industrialists, and professional men. The "white collar" category is dominated by clerks, commercial representatives, the clergy, and *fonctionnaires*."

6. Calculated from census data provided by Heywood (1998) in table 1, "Residential differentiation in Troyes, 1851 and 1906."

7. AMT 4F 530, p. 363. While the index for the cost of food in Paris was 100, the index for Troyes was 96; and for food and housing combined, the cost in Troyes represented 89, in relation to 100 in Paris.

in the *quartier haut* is illustrated by the residence patterns in one central street, the rue du Geoffroy de Villehardouin, over the period between the 1906 and the 1926 censuses.[8] In 1906 textile workers were present in 33 out of the 111 households on the street (about 30 percent). By 1926 nearly three times as many textile families had filled the same space, creating a densely crowded street: 110 out of 165 households had textile workers (some 67 percent). There were also significant changes in worker household patterns during this period. The presence of more women workers living on this street during the second period paralleled their growing numbers in the labor force. While in 1906, most households were nuclear families with very few if any children, by 1926 one-third of textile workers on the street were single, and a significant number were single parents or from stem or sibling households, with an average of one child per family. More important, in 1926 more than one family member worked in the knitted goods industry in nearly half the textile households on the street.

Thus, while the concentration of workers in certain neighborhoods may have increased by the 1920s, overall residence was probably not a determining factor in the development of class consciousness among Troyes workers. More important no doubt was the sense of belonging to a textile trade. While many of the knitters of this generation had once been semi-independent artisans, their children rapidly became millworkers. Once they finished school at age thirteen, they were most likely sent immediately into the mills. In a mono-industrial town like Troyes the labor market made hosiery the *métier obligé*. By the twentieth century there was an almost hereditary practice of work in the hosiery industry, a trend that was particularly evident for women, given the greater demand for women workers in hosiery and garment making. While the 1896 census showed that "male knitters, metalworkers and construction workers who had inherited their trade from their fathers were the exception rather than the rule," by the twentieth century, professional endogamy was certainly the rule.[9] Among the families who lived on the rue du Geoffroy de Villehardouin, only five male or female heads of households in 1906 worked in the same hosiery trade, but in the 1926 sample, thirty-five married couples were both textile workers.[10] Further evidence of professional endogamy comes

8. Based on an analysis of every household on the nominative census list for 1906 and 1926 on the same street. For 1906, n = 276 individuals, including 44 textile workers; for 1926, n = 427 individuals and 186 textile workers (AMT 1F 60, AMT 1F 69).

9. Heywood 1998, 17.

10. AMT 1F 60, AMT 1F 69.

from oral-history interviews. Of the twelve persons interviewed who had worked in the mills during the 1920s and 1930s, eleven had married someone working in hosiery. In five of the families, both parents worked in the knitwear industry; in three, only the mother worked there; and in two, only the father worked in the mills. One of the possible explanations for this pattern of social reproduction among knitters is, of course, the correlation with the low rate of out-migration. The Champenois rarely migrated outside their region during this period. Census date confirms that in 1906, 76 percent of the inhabitants of the Aube were born in the department; in 1931 and 1936, 66 percent of the population represented this pattern.

Class identification with the trade extended outside the workplace and into the community through various mediations. Kin, community, and textile culture provided overlapping social networks, which were all the more evident in the annual celebration of the trade, the Fête de la Bonneterie, held in early September. Long dominated by a masculine craft tradition, the festival was transformed in 1909 by the election of a woman worker as "queen" for the day. From 1909 through 1938, the townspeople of Troyes celebrated their local industry by crowning eight festival queens chosen from among the women workers. At the outset, the festival had celebrated the moral community of work. But over the years it had become a secular expression of community, borrowing from the old craft traditions to reinvent new ones for a modern industrial society. As the town of Troyes became nationally recognized as the knitwear capital of France, millowners sought to publicize their industry in this more commercial way. The festival served to strengthen the industrial community and promote social cohesion in the town, as we shall see in the following chapter. In significant ways, the festival and its queen were instrumental in affirming working-class identity as it evolved over the half century.

As these festivals demonstrated, women workers were an important component of the knitted goods industry. If women's work had been nearly invisible under the putting-out system, because it was organized around a male head of household, by contrast, female workers were patently visible in the urban mill workforce. The growing numbers of women workers employed by the mills maintained a distinct sexual division of labor and it produced a gendered pattern of lifelong employment for women very similar to that of men. This meant that women hosiery workers were also commonly identified with the trade, as *bonnetières,* a term whose usage dates from this period of industrialization. The term *bonnetière* originated as a derivative of the word for the dominant male occupation, *bonnetier,* in a process seen in many French trades. Historical usage of the term suggests that women's gender and class identification with the trade was as significant as men's.[11]

Religion was another factor that could potentially divide or unify the working class. But unlike certain industrial cities in northern and western France, such as Lille and Roubaix in the Nord and Cholet in the Vendée region, Catholicism was rarely a factor in worker self-identity in the Aube. The department was recognized as one of the most de-Christianized areas in France, with one of the lowest practices of Easter duties in the country: 13.8 percent for the Aube as a whole in the period 1875 to 1898, and 9.5 percent for the town of Troyes. These figures further declined in the period between 1907 and 1927, after the separation of church and state: 7.3 percent in the Aube, 7.9 percent in Troyes.[12] For the years 1929 to 1932, more than 40 percent of children in Troyes did not do catechism.[13] In fact, Fernand Boulard described the department as "un pays de mission." In Troyes, workers were often not only passive in religious practices, but also openly aggressive and hostile toward the clergy. Anticlericalism ran high in Troyes among various social groups, such as the Association pour la propagation de la Libre-Pensée (Freethinkers), founded in 1881. Together with the Freemasons, anarchists, and political groups linked to Radicalism, these groups formed the main oppositional force to Catholicism. In significant ways, such groups laid the groundwork for socialism. In their propaganda, socialists openly associated anticlericalism with anticapitalism, specifically targeting bourgeois millowners whose egalitarian aspirations often contradicted their practice of defending the existing moral and religious order. For the Guesdists, religion would disappear when the exploitation of the ruling capitalist class disappeared. To demonstrate their vision of a countersociety, towns with elected socialist mayors instigated anticlerical practices, among them civil burials and the banning of religious processions in the street. Local meetings of the Parti ouvrier français (POF) would often close with cries of "Vive la République! Vive la Sociale! A bas la calotte!"[14]

Other social factors associated with anticlericalism helped to raise the receptivity to socialism in the Aube. Adult literacy had always been high in

11. See Chapter 4.
12. Boulard et al. 1987, 480–83.
13. Ibid., 636.
14. See Cholvy and Hilaire 1986, 25–28; and the speeches of the socialist mayor of Romilly at civil burials in 1889 quoted in Baroin 1970, 71–72. "la calotte" referred to the clergy.

the department, and by the turn of the century it was close to 95 percent.[15] Several associations in Troyes, including the Freethinkers and the embryonic knitters' union, the Chambre syndicale des bonnetiers, were formed around the defense of republican secular schooling. Several were instrumental in founding the Bibliothèque démocratique et populaire de Troyes, in 1879. In this milieu educated and politically conscious workers turned toward social-ism, both as an extension of their existing practices and because of the appeal of new ideas. They would later find in the POF program confirmation of their orientation. A "Comité de vigilance" emerged in 1887, composed of socialists, Freethinkers, Radicals, and anarchists, prepared to offer their support to Jules Guesde. As some of these workers turned to electoral politics, they disrupted the Center-Left dominance in the Aube. The Radical Party was strongly implanted in the upper and petty bourgeois electorate, but also among those millowners, industrialists, and journalists connected with the leading daily newspaper, *Le Petit Troyen*. The Radical constituency, caught between its own egalitarian aspirations and republican principles on the one hand, and its fear of popular opposition on the other, frequently resorted to defending the established order. In the meantime, the growing class polarization in Troyes created conditions for the politicization of the working class and for a class-based socialist movement that established institutions of solidarity in the town. Labor unions and workers' consumer cooperatives became two pillars of the socialist movement in the Aube.

THE POLITICIZATION OF THE WORKING CLASS

The followers of Jules Guesde and Paul Lafargue, known as Guesdist social-ists, first introduced revolutionary Marxism in France and founded the POF in 1882. For their competitors on the left, Guesdists were perceived as doctrinaire and rigidly attached to formulaic principles such as class struggle and collec-tivism. In fact, Guesdists seized on the notions of class conflict and struggle as the basis of their action, and they integrated egalitarian elements of the French revolutionary tradition, notably as adopted from Gracchus Babeuf. The POF advocated the collectivization of the means of production to ensure the just distribution of the fruits of labor and elaborated a political program

15. *Statistiques du recensement générale de la population,* 1906 census.

that targeted bourgeois capitalist property. For this principle alone, Guesdists became known as "collectivists" and were the object of bourgeois hostility. For many Guesdists, class interest alone would lead workers—both men and women—to class consciousness and into revolt and eventually revolution. Firm in this belief, Guesde preached a simplified version of revolutionary Marxism that included a commitment to gender equality, in theory if not in practice. What mattered was creating a structured socialist party (the first of its kind in France) with trained militants, party discipline, and the subordination of organizations such as unions and cooperatives to party political ends. Party militants were firm believers in the value of popular education and propaganda. For this reason they worked tirelessly to popularize and disseminate Marxist socialism, through newspapers, public meetings, and ritual celebrations such as May Day. The aim of their electoral program was for them to win political power at the local level and then gradually take over at the national one. At the outset, Guesdists were opposed to any reformist tactics, such as class collaboration in a bourgeois government, hence their hostility to independent socialist Alexander Millerand's participation in the Radical government of Waldeck-Rousseau in 1899. In fact, POF leaders during this early period directed their polemical attacks at other political groups on the left—Radical republicans, anarchists, and independent socialists—whom they considered serious rivals for workers' political allegiance.[16]

The POF was implanted in several old industrial areas, most notably in the major northern textile cities of Lille, Roubaix, and Tourcoing, but also in central France, in the region of Bordeaux, and along the Mediterranean coast. In the municipal elections of 1892, the party captured control of the industrial cities of Roubaix and Montluçon and obtained representation in many other municipalities, often on the grounds of their social welfare programs.[17]

Guesdists in the Aube adopted many of these national political strategies. They recruited their members from among the many manual workers in the department—small peasant landholders in the Barrois to the south of Troyes, winegrowers in Les Riceys, waged employees of the railroad—but their main constituency was drawn from the knitters and metalworkers of the mills in Troyes and Romilly. It was those former independent artisan knitters who undeniably favored collectivist ideas, as the following article in 1901 in the

16. Stuart 1992, chap. 2.
17. Ibid. See also Willard 1965.

Reveil des Travailleurs reveals: "The small artisans who thirty years ago had to abandon their tools—their individual property that provided a living—forced out by capitalist competition, these artisans know that the development of mechanization has been one of the causes of their loss of freedom and property in their labor."[18] For many former rural artisans in the Aube, this explanation of their new situation must have rung true. Party militants assumed responsibilities in the unions and consumer cooperatives, their political activities extending into the practical organization of class-based collective action. Numbers of them were tireless propagandists, through the written and the spoken word, contributing to socialist newspapers or carrying their message to political meetings. All these means of political organizing would serve to mobilize the working class of Troyes and the Aube.

The Origins of Socialism in the Aube

The roots of socialism in the Aube date from the late 1870s and the existence of embryonic workers associations, called *chambres syndicales,* that were clearly attempting to work within the confines of the 1864 law on associations.[19] The Third Republic had been slow, in fact, to liberalize the right of association and to draft legislation that, while allowing workers to organize, would establish a fine line between professional and political activities. The law of 1884 legalizing unions attempted to accomplish just those very distinctions.[20] In Troyes a Chambre syndicale de la métallurgie was founded in 1876, and an umbrella-type union for the knitted goods industry, called the Association syndicale des ouvriers de toutes les industries se rattachant à la bonneterie, followed a year later. The mayor of Troyes had been opposed to these early forms of unions, fearing that, while the small number of metalworkers could not create a "revolution in town," the considerably larger numbers of knitters certainly could, if they were well organized and a conflict over wages

18. *Le Reveil des Travailleurs de l'Aube,* March 1–8, 1901. The article attacks one of the leading millowners, who boasted that progress in mechanization benefited not only millowners but workers as well. See Chapter 1, p. 55.

19. In 1864, Napoleon III repealed the law outlawing coalitions that had been in place since 1791, but he left strict limits on the size of meetings and type of action that could be undertaken. For contemporary administrators, the law's repeal created some ambiguity about what types of action should be sanctioned. M. Perrot (1974) demonstrates that the law's repeal led to a wave of strike activity (1:74–80). Reddy (1984) argues that historians understand the law to have legalized strikes, but not unions (246).

20. For the parliamentary debate leading to the law of 1884, see Barbet 1991, 5–30.

emerged.[21] In their statutes the founders announced broad general goals, ranging from the defense of their members and the organization of the annual corporative work festival, the Fête de la Bonneterie, to more practical corporative concerns, such as the apprenticeship of workers' children, the placement of unemployed members, and the election of members to the trade courts, les Conseils des prud'hommes. The association also proposed the creation of institutions for social promotion such as a library, training courses, and a craft museum, insofar as resources allowed.[22]

The association took a significant political step. It decided to send a report to the workers' congress to be held in Marseilles in October 1879. Union leaders thus acknowledged their support for the "new ideas" to be introduced at the congress and announced their intention to initiate members to such ideas. The report ended with a paraphrase of Abbé Sièyes's revolutionary pamphlet about useful labor as the basis of citizenship: "The future belongs to all and not to a few. What is the worker at this moment? An instrument. What must he be? Everything, motor and promoter, since he is producer and consumer."[23] While no delegates from Troyes ultimately attended the Marseilles congress, the report sent by the knitters' union demonstrated that its professional action could become a political project. The workers' congress in Marseilles was open to all groups, and at this stage no political party claimed to represent the working class. The congress represented a historic moment for French socialism for two reasons: first, it provided the opportunity for Jules Guesde to launch the POF and Marxist socialism in France; second, for a brief moment in history, feminism and socialism connected, when suffragist Hubertine Auclert found sufficient support to introduce "the woman question" into the socialist political agenda.[24] A resolution by the congress supported equal rights for women within the workers' movement.

By the time of the Marseilles congress, Guesde had already made two trips to Troyes, in August and October 1879, at the invitation of the Comité de vigilance, to obtain support for his party's program, the Programme et adresse du socialisme révolutionnaire français, which had been published in April

21. Letter from the mayor of Troyes to the prefect, 1876, cited by Baroin (1970, 83–84).
22. Statutes of the Association syndicale des ouvriers de toutes les industries se rattachant à la bonneterie, ADA M 791.
23. Didier Berneau, "La naissance du mouvement ouvrier," La Dépêche de l'Aube, October 16, 1984; and Bedin 1977.
24. For feminist readings of this historic congress, see Klejman and Rochefort 1989, 61; Hilden 1987, 288–89; and Sowerwine 1982, 24–25.

that same year in the party newspaper, *L'Egalité*. More than five hundred signatures had been gathered in support of Guesde's program throughout France, including those of sixteen workers from Troyes.[25] However, these early years of Guesdism in the Aube reflected the struggles between various socialist groups within France as a whole. Inevitably, political factionalism within socialism itself made organizing difficult, as evidenced by the number of short-lived newspapers directed at a working-class constituency in Troyes. In 1881, the anarchists split off from the socialists to found a group called les Nivelleurs troyens. In that same year, Jules Guesde returned to Troyes, accompanied by the Paris Commune's well-known leader, Louise Michel, to present his party's electoral program.

The growing appeal of socialism in the Aube corresponded with the historic moment of union legalization. By 1886, knitters in Troyes had founded a new union called the Association syndicale des ouvriers et ouvrières de toutes les professions se rattachant à la bonneterie, headed by Julien Grée, a knitter and member of the Comité de vigilance. Intended to be inclusive at the outset, this new union sought to integrate workers who were seriously divided along craft lines. Women were actively welcomed, according to the statutes.[26] Two workers' consumer cooperatives were also created in 1886: the Sociale, founded by the Guesdists, and the Laborieuse, a more successful venture founded by metalworkers and knitters of socialist inspiration that began with a promising membership of some five hundred workers. Several of these class-based organizations were structured by local Guesdist militants as a means of strengthening working-class solidarity. Their obvious success as class organizations (to be treated in the following section) gave the socialists a solid grassroots base.

In 1888, the POF leadership called upon local socialist militants from the knitters' union and the Comité de vigilance to organize the party congress in Troyes. Breaking with party leaders, the organizers appealed to socialist groups and unions outside the POF all over France to attend. By all reports the workers' congress that convened in Troyes in late December 1888 rallied such a wide diversity of groups from worker federations, craft unions, and socialist

---

25. These included six knitters, three *employés de bonneterie,* three metalworkers, a textile finisher, and a smith (*forgeron*), among others. For the early years of the POF, see Willard 1965; and his biography of Guesde (Willard 1991). See also Compère-Morel 1913, 126–42; and the excellent in-depth study of the Guesdists in Stuart 1992.

26. ADA SC 1288.

factions that for eight days speeches and debate were extremely heated. The presence of some three hundred women confirmed the POF's efforts to put the woman question on the congress agenda, now framed as "women's situation under capitalism." Despite the efforts of POF co-founder Paul Lafargue and other leaders present to overcome sectarian divisions, the congress failed to advance the Guesdists' minority position among the participants. However, the congress did recruit local members among workers in Troyes and succeeded in founding the Fédération socialiste de l'Aube.[27]

Just as competition between socialist factions continued to plague the party at the national level during the 1880s, the newly formed workers' organizations in the Aube remained fragile, divisive, and financially shaky. Guesdism had roots, but needed an eloquent and charismatic leader in order to draw a larger constituency. At this moment local militants called upon Etienne Pédron to join their political campaign. Pédron, a skilled watchmaker who had been organizing for the POF in Reims, arrived in Troyes in December 1889. Over the following seven years, his leadership would create the structures needed to overcome competition from other socialist groups, to shift some workers' allegiance from the Radicals to the POF and to train new militants within the Aube.

Popularizing Marxism

Etienne Pédron (1849–1931) was a gifted political organizer, a committed socialist, and a creative propagandist. All these talents helped to transform the local socialist party structures in Troyes and in the Aube and to create working-class support for the POF electoral program. For the Troyes workers, he was "the wandering Jew of socialism"; for the police who tracked his movements, he was "a ferocious revolutionary."[28] As an orator and propagandist, he possessed a special charisma: one account of the workers' congress in Troyes in 1888 described him as "tall, emaciated, with the head of a prophet and the gestures of a preacher."[29] Militants of this stature could exert a powerful influence, and Pédron was no exception. He left his mark on the labor movement through his reorganization of socialist groups in Troyes, through his tireless

27. See Bedin 1977, 65–67; Willard 1991, chap. 4; Stuart 1992, 39–42.
28. Report of the commissaire spécial of the police des chemins de fer in Troyes, July 3, 1895, ADA SC 340.
29. Quoted from *L'Aube,* January 1–2, 1889, in Bedin 1977, 67.

political meetings in towns and villages, and through the education and training of local militants. Above all, his activity as a propagandist and polemicist
served the POF in its popularization of Marxist socialism.

When Pédron arrived in Troyes in 1889, the Comité de vigilance had already
come under police suspicion. His first action was to subdivide the group
into four neighborhood sections, to create a wider geographical base within
the town: the Travailleurs troyens were to recruit their members in the center
of town, the Reveil social was attributed the left bank and the faubourg
Croncels, the Droit social was implanted in the *quartier bas* on the right bank,
and finally the Groupe socialiste de Sainte-Savine was to organize among
the millworkers of this faubourg. Their objective was to confound the police
and, more important, to create wider networks for political support, relying
on militants who lived in these neighborhoods. But, in fact, the police raided
Pédron's lodgings on April 24, 1890, and found a list of POF members, along
with their strategy for neighborhood networking.[30] The police raid probably
anticipated his involvement in the celebration of the first socialist May Day
in France.

The first May Day celebrations in 1890 were part of an international offensive for hours reform, promoted by the Second Socialist International a movement that had broad support among labor leaders. Guesde and the POF were
instrumental in launching this celebration nationally.[31] Jules Guesde claimed
that shorter hours would put an end to overproduction and to periodic or
seasonal unemployment, the source of a common complaint among jobless
and irregular textile workers during the 1880s.[32] Pédron intended to mobilize
Troyes workers around this symbol of international solidarity and national
worker unity. A tract issued by the knitters' and metalworkers' unions, together
with the Groupes ouvriers socialistes, called on both men and women workers to demonstrate in support of workers' interests and to strike on May Day
if they could afford to do so. The demand for the eight-hour day was the
focus of the protest, to which Guesdist militants in Troyes added the demand
for a minimum wage. This was the logic of their argument: "The eight-hour
workday would benefit the working class because it would put an end to

---

30. Letter from the commissaire central to the prefect, dated September 27, 1890, ADA
SC 340.
31. See the account quoted from *Le Combat* of May 2, 1890, in Rossel 1977, 111–14; see also
Rodriguez 1990.
32. Guesde 1894. See also Lafargue 1883, chap. 2; and the analysis in Cross 1989 (59–64).

fratricidal competition for jobs among hungry workers, thereby obliging manufacturers to employ the unemployed, and thus, by the simple logic of supply
and demand, the decline in the numbers of idled workers would inevitably
lead to higher wages." The eight-hour day, they argued, would also allow time
for leisure, family, education, and hygiene for all those workers whose " labor
produces social wealth . . . for the needs of all society." The demand for a
minimum wage called attention to the special exploitation of women and
children, who were consistently paid lower wages for their work. While the
argument for reform was clearly stated, the peaceful intention of the demonstration was even more explicit. The organizers cautioned workers that the
state would not hesitate to employ the use of force and intervene. From the
outset, the demonstration was intended to be a peaceful show of strength,
characterized as both a protest and a celebration.[33]

The meeting was called for eight o'clock that evening in the hall of the
Saint-Nizier market on the right bank; official authorization from the prefect
and the mayor had been requested. At the very last moment, the prefect
banned the meeting and ordered the hall occupied by the light infantry.[34]
As the crowd gathered, workers arrived in groups organized by workshop
and filled the marketplace. Finally, a dense crowd spontaneously broke out in
song: "C'est huit heures, huit heures, huit heures, c'est huit heures qu'il nous
faut, Oh! Oh! Oh! Oh!" This was Etienne Pédron's song in support of the
eight-hour day, and it galvanized the crowd of supporters.[35] The song had
by then become a lightning rod for mobilization, a declaration of workers'
rights. Then, some four thousand workers, carrying red flags, set out to march
across the town to the faubourg Sainte-Savine, in search of a meeting hall.
What began as a peaceful, festive demonstration unfortunately turned into a
pitched battle, as the infantry followed them across the town and intervened

33. Tract "Manifestation internationale du 1er Mai," Archives Musée de la bonneterie.

34. For the prefect's version of events, see his letter to the minister of the interior, dated May
2, 1890, ADA M 1273. The prefect maintained that there had not been the least sign of trouble
until the evening, when demonstrators contravened his ban on the meeting in place Saint-Nizier
and marched across town carrying "revolutionary emblems and flags." The gendarmerie had to
open fire in self-defense, he maintained, when they became the target of stones and bricks.

35. Pédron's *Chansons socialistes* was published in Lille by the POF in 1906. Writing under the
pseudonym Germinal, the editor argued that this song had played a historic role in preventing
any violence from breaking out during that first May Day celebration in Troyes: "More than one
song would be worth its page in history; without this little refrain, 'C'est huit heures . . . ,' we
would have already had on the first celebration of May Day on the place St.-Nizier in Troyes,
violence like that which occurred at Fourmies [the following year]. It can't be said that songs
have no impact" (Pédron 1906, 7).

in Sainte-Savine. The prefect's reports now qualified Pédron as "a violent and dangerous revolutionary" and accused Guesdist militants of fomenting disorder. Nineteen arrests were made, including those of ten textile workers, on the grounds of their "rebellion and participation in an armed gathering."[36]

In October that same year, Pédron followed up this action with a more typical POF political meeting, featuring Guesde himself as a speaker. The propaganda for the meeting appealed to men and women workers, socialists of all tendencies, union leaders, and anarchists to lay aside sectarian quarrels and unite behind the POF and its electoral program. This appeal was couched in terms of class conflict and stressed that a united bourgeoisie was only too happy to see a divided working class. While organized meetings of this type did not draw the same crowd as demonstrations, they did provide the opportunity for dissident socialist and anarchist groups to contradict the speaker, air their views, and generally create trouble. Leftist political culture made wide use of this "conférénce contradictoire" to train militants in public-debating techniques, common to both the face-to-face verbal battles of working-class self-defense and the sometimes harsh exchanges of parliamentary debate. To be sure, speakers came prepared to face hecklers and detractors. The more heated and animated the meeting, the more lively the political debate and exchange proved to be.

Political meetings, organized under such circumstances, served one of the essential purposes of Guesdist propaganda techniques, the education of the working class. Through their newspapers, reading rooms, public lectures, theater, and songs, Guesdists in Troyes attempted to popularize the principles of Marxist socialism. In 1892, Pédron founded *Le Socialiste Troyen,* which published theoretical articles by Guesde, Lafargue, and other POF leaders, as well as chronicles of party activities and life in the mills around France. Local militant Hébert Corgeron replaced Pédron as editor in 1896, changing the paper's name to *Le Reveil des Travailleurs de l'Aube.*[37] Socialist publications were sold hand to hand, but they were also available on newsstands and in a special library and reading room at the Maison du Peuple in the center of town.

Pédron knew how to reach workers through songs and short theater sketches, many of which he wrote himself. Several of his revolutionary songs were composed in Troyes and evoked mill life in stark, human terms; among

36. Police report, May 2, 1890, ADA M 1273.
37. The *Reveil des Travailleurs de l'Aube* was actually printed at the POF press in Lille.

these were "Huit heures" and "Le Caffard" (1890), but also "Le chômage" (1898), "La Troyenne" and "La Romillonne" (1895). Drawing on the world the workers knew, Pédron contrasted the poverty and humiliation under capitalism with promises of a better world under socialism. Some songs, such as "La Troyenne," represented a call to arms against bourgeois exploitation in the strident terms of class war, while others, for example, the 1895 "La Romillonne," celebrated socialist victories at the polls.

> N'insultez pas la canaille qui passe,
> Bourgeois, il faut même au nom de vos lois,
> Vous incliner: notre parti de classe,
> A Romilly, vous vaincra chaque fois.
> Car son drapeau, qui flotte magnifique,
> Porte ces mots: plus d'exploitation,
> Egalité, Liberté, République,
> Enfin, celui de la Révolution.

Refrain

> Au chant de notre Romillonne,
> Il faudra bien que l'on nous donne
> Nos droits, car désormais personne
> N'arrêtera nos bataillons.
> Au nom de la classe ouvrière
> Contre le crime de la guerre
> Et le fléau de la misère
> Debout! debout! les Romillons.[38]

Here, Pédron called on the ruling bourgeois class to respect the rules of democratic order and accept that a legitimate working-class party could govern locally with an agenda of social justice, as in Romilly in 1895. This march served at the same time to galvanize support among workers for the POF's notion of a social revolution, based on unitary class interests, envisaged within the social Republic they sought to create.[39]

38. From "La Romillonne" (Pédron 1906, 32).
39. See Stuart 1992, chaps. 7 and 8.

In an age when work songs strengthened a culture of community, Pédron's work was significant and enduring in creating a sense of political identity.[40] His song in favor of the eight-hour day depicted a system of low-wage slavery that drove mothers to work twelve hours in the mills and allowed millowners to use repression to reduce wages even further:

"La faim force nos compagnes
A laisser seul nos marmots . . .
Pour aller douze heures en bagne
Enrichir les aristos."

C'est huit heures, huit heures,
C'est huit heures qu'il nous faut!
Oh! Oh! Oh! Oh!

"Pour baisser notre salaire
On nous montre des flingots . . .
Pour réfréner la misère
Malgré gendarmes et sergots . . ."

C'est huit heures, huit heures, [etc.].

"Assez vivre en bêt' de somme
Trop longtemps courber le dos
Huit heures de travail pour l'homme
De loisir et de repos"

C'est huit heures, huit heures, [etc.].

There is little connection in this song between working hours and real wages. Pédron's argument was presented in moral terms rather than economic ones. The power of his song lay in its claim for a universal worker's right to eight equal hours of work, leisure, and rest.

Pédron's theater, however, was clearly more ephemeral. Only police records survive to recount the political sketches that he performed with a small troupe, often in private cafés or backrooms to escape censure. One such piece, called *Le combat social,* dramatized millowners' actions in Troyes, contrasting them to

40. For the role of songs in the textile working-class culture of the Nord, see Marty 1982, 197–206; and Reddy 1984, chap. 9.

what would exist in millwork under socialism, and ended with the historical and political significance of May Day for worker solidarity. The police commissioner covering the performance in the line of duty found the pointed caricature of the millowners distasteful, because Pédron had singled out the best known among them, scarcely hiding their names: Auguste Mortier became "Mortout," the polemical Léon Poron became "Potpointu" (newspaper cartoons of bourgeois millowners unfailingly showed them as fat bellied), and Maurice Mauchauffée was "Maufroité" (a pun implying both unsavory company and someone not to get entangled with).[41] Theater of this kind was intended to educate while entertaining and was a form of propaganda more likely to reach a wider audience than those of strictly political meetings. Such performances often closed with the audience joining in song. Henri Millet, socialist mayor of Romilly, praised Pédron's performances as artful propaganda: "[His plays] are undertaking the dramatization of 'La sociale,' which depicts so completely the drama of this fin de siècle, . . . bringing to life, before the assembled workers, these hideous types of insatiable bourgeois and renegade workers that playwrights of every period have always carefully dissimulated. To make art an element of struggle, a revolutionary force, to oppose old melodramas, where Providence and God play the principal roles, with this new artistic conception that consists of representing human life in its daily manifestations, this is an enterprise worthy of a party that expects to triumph on the sole basis of revealing truth."[42] As Millet observed, theater in the service of socialist politics empowered workers by committing them to collective struggles. But Etienne Pédron's plays also combined a special blend of caricature of the bourgeoisie and the dramatization of the experience of labor that fueled individual aspirations and formed a culture of resistance.

All the male leaders of the POF were public figures, well documented by the police. A number of them had been early socialist activists and members of the Comité de vigilance.[43] Julien Grée was a knitter who joined the POF and the knitters' union in 1886. As a recruiter for the party, he organized public

41. Letter from the commissaire spécial to the prefect, July 3, 1895, ADA SC 340. Other theater pieces performed by Pedron include *Le naufrage de la bêtise humaine,* a satire on republican notables; *La fête d'Eloi,* another satire on republican lawmakers; and an anticlerical play called *Le Jesuite et le Libre-Penseur.*

42. Report of the commissaire spécial to the prefect, July 5, 1895. The police quoted an article by Millet in a socialist newspaper (ADA SC 340).

43. Biographical data on each of them can be found in Compère-Morel 1913, 126–42; Maitron 1976; Willard 1965, 602–51; also ADA SC 340, 365.

meetings and socialist congresses within the department, working from the Maison du Peuple, which he also helped run. Another knitter and POF militant, Ernest Lozach, developed his talents as an orator and propagandist within the Aube. He became a committed union leader, frequently presiding over strike meetings. Lozach later served as assistant to the mayor of Sainte-Savine and municipal counselor. Hébert Corgeron (1859–1930) was a more important figure in the local POF. The son of a knitter in Estissac (Aube), he became a coiffeur, an occupation that secured a precarious livelihood but allowed him time for politics. He was one of the founders of the Maison du Peuple and the POF in Troyes, along with Etienne Pédron. In 1896 he replaced Pédron as editor of the POF weekly, *Le Reveil des Travailleurs de l'Aube*. In this role he was indicted for inciting soldiers not to fire on workers and was tried before the Cours d'Assises in 1906 but finally acquitted. He was also a POF candidate for municipal elections in May 1900. Poverty and persecution finally forced him to move to Paris in 1908.

Two other POF militants experienced better fortune with electoral socialism and managed to win national or municipal office. Emile Clévy was the leader of the knitters' union, delegate to the annual congress of the Fédération nationale du textile, and active at the Maison du Peuple. His strong support of the SFIO finally won him election as mayor of Troyes in 1919. The following year, he would serve as a delegate to the historic Congress of Tours. Finally, Céléstin Philbois, another knitter by trade, was trained by Pédron as a propagandist, orator, and organizer for the POF. He presided over the daily strike meetings in 1900, urging workers to hold out for a unified settlement in solidarity. Philbois joined the SFIO in 1905, running as the socialist candidate in several local elections before finally being elected deputy from Troyes in June 1914. All these committed militants, who had been trained by Pédron, had political careers as socialists lasting through World War I and beyond. Their first-generation militancy carried through to the formation of a second generation, whose leadership would subsequently be tested by the socialist party split in 1920.

In December 1893, the POF established its headquarters at the Maison du Peuple in the center of town, at the place de l'Hôtel de Ville. Access to the building was through a narrow passage that lead to a courtyard, around which were offices and meeting rooms used for a variety of political activities. The Maison du Peuple housed the offices of the unions and the POF weekly paper, *Le Reveil des Travailleurs de l'Aube,* a printing press; a library; and an adjoining reading room. Since the party served a working-class constituency, there were also offices for job placement and counseling for the trade courts (Conseils des prud'hommes). The POF had founded two organs to promote and finance party activities, but both encountered difficulties. *Le Reveil des Travailleurs de l'Aube* came under attack for expressing political positions considered seditious. When the editor, Corgeron, was taken to court and subsequently fined, the party complained bitterly that the government's censorship was an attempt to silence them. The POF, in fact, relied on the good offices of the local daily Radical newspaper, *Le Petit Troyen,* to communicate notification of party meetings, urgent announcements, and direct appeals to members. The workers' consumer cooperative, the Sociale, founded by Pédron and Corgeron in 1886, operated on the ground floor of the Maison du Peuple. While a portion of its profits were returned to members, most of the earnings served to finance party activities and the rent of the building. But mismanagement of cooperative funds and its inability to compete with its main socialist rival, the Laborieuse, forced the Sociale to close in 1901.[44] After 1906, the Maison du Peuple declined in importance as a Guesdist stronghold. By then the town council had voted to turn the old merchants hall, the Halle de la Bonneterie, into the Bourse du Travail, which became a rival center for labor union activity and job recruitment under the influence of revolutionary syndicalists.

Guesdism and Gender Equality

In their meetings and propaganda, the POF also addressed working women as a special constituency. From the outset Guesdist leaders strongly affirmed equality between the sexes in their theoretical statements in order to distinguish themselves from those currents of the labor movement that were influenced by Joseph Proudhon, which contested women's right to work outside the hearth and home. The fact of Guesdism's implantation in two major textile regions, the Nord and the Aube, speaks to the strength of this egalitarian appeal to women textile workers. Yet in both regions Guesdist political leaders failed to put their theory sufficiently into practice. This was particularly true in those unions, discussed in a following section, that were dominated by the notoriously paternalistic leader Victor Renard. At best, Guesdist rhetoric on the "woman question" was confusing, but most often it was contradictory.

44. Report of the commissaire spécial, February 24,1896, ADA SC 340. See also Bedin 1977, chap. 3. The growth and development of the Laborieuse is discussed in Chapters 5 and 7.

Patricia Hilden notes that "Guesdist propaganda reflected [male] negative attitudes along with more positive ones. As a result what working women heard from the party was a confusingly mixed message."[45] By the turn of the century, POF leaders found themselves contested on one side by a growing feminist movement for women's rights and suffrage and, on the other, by revolutionary women from the Commune generation, who found POF positions on social reform not revolutionary enough.[46] In this context, the POF's overt commitment to gender equality declined after 1900, when issues of socialist unification and electoral politics became its major concerns.

In all fairness, both Jules Guesde and Paul Lafargue were early supporters of women's rights, as was manifest in their political statements from the party's inception in 1882. However, by the time of the POF's merger into the SFIO in 1905, the two leaders' positions on "the woman question" had evolved in different directions. Guesde had embraced gender equality and women's right to work as early as 1878 in *L'Egalité*, in which he argued that women's work was a necessary means of their economic independence and that, for women, as for men, work would become a means of liberation as society was transformed under socialism.[47] In this same article, Guesde disavowed Proudhon's characterization of a woman as a "housewife or harlot," on the grounds that this view was "contrary to socialism." Women's place was not confined to the home, he contended, but alongside men within the socialist movement. Many of these ideas found their place in the POF program of 1882, which included a firm commitment to equality between the sexes.

Guesde further elaborated his position on this question in a long article devoted to the question of women's work, reprinted in *Le Reveil des Travailleurs de l'Aube* in October 1898. In this article he attacked those who thought that "women's real place was in the home," and he underscored their double exploitation: "More than anyone, workers, whose civil and political emancipation should allow them to measure the deceptiveness of any freedom that is not based on economics, should be unwilling to prolong the economic subordination of one sex by another. This would render woman the proletarian

---

45. Hilden 1987, 286. Robert Stuart contests Hilden's analysis of Guesdist policy toward women workers. See Stuart 1996, 57–82; and 1997a, 107–29.

46. For the struggles between socialism and feminism during this crucial period, see Sowerwine 1982, esp. 54–66; and Zylberberg-Hocquard 1978. For a further discussion of the Guesdists' discourse on women, see Stuart 1996, 57–82; and 1997a, 107–29.

47. Jules Guesde, "Le travail des femmes" *L'Egalité*, January 27, 1878. See the discussion on Guesde's positions on women in Hilden 1986, chap. 5, esp. 176–80.

of man, while removing all dignity from sexual relations entered into without freedom." Guesde then defended women's right to work, as he had done in the past, although couching his defense in less explicit terms than before: "No, the place of woman is no more in the household than elsewhere. Her place, like that of men, is everywhere, where her energy can and wants to be employed. . . . Why, on what grounds, wife and mother if we so wish—while not denying those who are neither one nor the other—could a woman not determine herself socially in the context she so desires?"[48] It is obvious that the question of women's equality had pursued Guesde from his earlier public statements in favor of women's political and social rights, but by century's end he found it difficult to integrate his concern into an electoral program. Workingwomen were left to define their own position within the party and to defend their right to work. Like many of Guesde's articles, this one had probably appeared in a revised form several years earlier in the socialist press and was being recycled for workers in Troyes at an opportune moment. Local militants might have reprinted it in order to sustain Guesdist appeals to women textile workers. In all his statements, Guesde, like other socialist theoreticians, reiterated the message that women's emancipation from various forms of inequality would only be accomplished through a socialist revolution.

POF co-founder Paul Lafargue (1842–1911) wrote more amply on the woman question, borrowing heavily from earlier socialist works by August Bebel and Friedrich Engels.[49] In his early work he defended women's right to work as the basis for a future communist society in which women would no longer be economically dependent on men. But by 1904, he had turned to exalting motherhood and traditional women's roles in the spirit of Proudhon. In a pamphlet devoted to women's rights, titled *La question de la femme* and published that year, Lafargue claimed that the socialist revolution would liberate women to fulfill their natural inclinations as mothers and housewives.

Party leaders and workers' associations maintained close political contacts between the two textile regions. Both Guesde and Lafargue were elected deputies from the Nord, and Guesdist policies toward women workers in this region followed a pattern somewhat similar to those in the Aube. However, the working class was distinctly different in the Nord, and so were several Guesdist practices. The three large textile towns of Lille, Roubaix, and

48. *Le Reveil des Travailleurs de l'Aube,* September 24–October 23, 1898.
49. August Bebel, *Woman and Socialism* (1879); Friedrich Engels, *The Origin of the Family, Private Property, and the State* (1884).

Tourcoing contained a diverse working-class population of French and Belgian immigrant workers, primarily practicing Catholics. Rapid industrialization and urbanization had created overcrowding. Textile millowners exercised specific paternalist policies, often religious and charitable in nature, to control their labor force. Patricia Hilden argues that Guesdist policies toward women workers shifted from an initial commitment to gender equality and women's right to work to subsequent party practices that effectively marginalized women workers.[50] The shift came in the 1890s as the POF focused on an electoralist strategy containing an implicit recognition that women workers could not vote. Party leaders' theoretical and political statements concerning questions of gender equality and women's right to work became more ambiguous, even contradictory. At issue were working women's special status as "double proletarians," at home and in the workplace, and their class identity as workers.[51] Marxists insisted on the primacy of class over gender interests, so that any autonomous action by women could be interpreted as divisive to class struggle. In Lille-Roubaix-Tourcoing a conflict emerged on which principle to adopt with regard to integrating women into party activities. Autonomous women's groups within the party had emerged in the 1890s to campaign for free school meals and to discuss women's issues. But by this time, Guesdist leaders were no longer responding to working women's expectations and were mobilizing all their efforts to win electoral campaigns in which disenfranchised women carried no weight. Hilden concludes that Guesdist leaders attempted to organize women according to two separate principles that she contends conflicted in theory and practice: women were more frequently treated as wives and mothers, rather than as waged workers, when in fact they were both.[52]

The Troyes working class experienced industrial capitalism differently from workers in the Nord. As we have seen, common roots in rural industry created a potential for class consciousness, but divisive elements persisted, especially among semi-independent artisan outworkers. The greatest challenge for POF

50. Hilden 1986.
51. Ibid., chaps. 4–5, esp. 200–223. Hilden contrasts Guesde's theoretical commitment and concern with women's equality with Lafargue's peculiar vision of how capitalism had destroyed the working-class family. But she underscores that women militants such as Aline Valette and Paule Minck were no less successful in defining a coherent policy on women's emancipation within the class struggle. Minck at least attempted to put into practice some of the POF party decisions in favor of women's political equality by agreeing to stand for election in 1892 as a candidate for both the POF and a socialist feminist group, la Solidarité des femmes.
52. Ibid., 200–223.

militants was to build solidarity between millworkers and industrial home-workers, and across craft lines. For this purpose, in the 1890s Guesdist strategies to promote an inclusive class-based program were consistently directed at both men and women workers. Party propaganda addressed female workers as having the same class interests as male workers, and the approach seemed somewhat successful. During the great strike of 1900, women millworkers organized according to occupation or craft, as male workers did, and joined massively in the strike action. Their solidarity was never really seriously questioned. Tensions in gender relations most commonly arose over wages in those women's occupations that were among the lowest paid. Guesdist slogans of "equal pay for equal work" helped to encourage working-class unity. Given the sexual division of labor in the trade, women's specialized tasks never raised the issue of women's competing for equal wages with men. The issue for all was a living wage.

There is no trace of autonomous women's groups within the Guesdist movement in Troyes, similar to those that existed in Lille and Roubaix.[53] Women workers were active in POF meetings, where the police always signaled their presence. During the great strike of 1900, there were at least four women on the strike committee, and many more were designated by their mill workshops as delegates to present grievances to public officials.[54] For the most part, women workers during these years remained part of the faceless crowd, those who have left no historical record. However, two women militants can be identified for their political support for the Guesdists around 1900. The first was Lecolle Carabin, a seamer in the Raguet mills, whose militancy led her to sign the strike declaration as delegate from her workshop and to represent the general strike committee at the meeting with Premier Waldeck-Rousseau in Paris. Carabin was born in Nancy to humble parents whose social origins indicate a precarious existence. In 1896 Lecolle had married Auguste Carabin, a shoemaker, and legitimized their son. Probably shortly thereafter, the family of three moved to the *quartier bas* in Troyes, where they appear in the 1906 census. Other than her active militancy during the strike, her presence was noted at a May Day public meeting in 1900, where she acted as a POF official.[55]

53. Ibid., 200–208.
54. See the list of delegates drawn up by the Juge de la Paix during an attempt at arbitration in AMT 2J 47.
55. See Chapter 1. Lecolle Carabin was born Marie Eugénie Cognevaut in Nancy to a proletarian family (her mother was an *enfant trouvé* [foundling], her father a day laborer). At some

These fragments of her story suggest a persistent struggle for a better life for herself and her family. The second woman militant, Louise Lamblin, appeared as an orator at a 1899 POF meeting, where she was introduced as "Marianne," and as working at the *Reveil des Travailleurs de l'Aube*. She spoke on the subject of religion, treating it in the manner of many anticlericalists and freethinkers, decrying it for its role in spreading submission and ignorance among the working class.[56] The fact that Lamblin spoke in a public meeting as a young woman of twenty-two suggests that she was among the more educated women party militants. Yet her social origins locate her with the textile workers of the *quartier bas*: her father was a bleacher, her mother a cloth finisher, both living in the rue des Bas Trevois in 1906.[57] Louise Lamblin later married into the family of an artisan hosiery manufacturer in Normandy.

At no point did these local women militants exercise leadership. In fact, the term *auxiliaries* best characterizes the role of women in the POF, since there were very few women in national leadership positions.[58] Several women militants from the generation of the Commune came to Troyes for public lectures and meetings or wrote articles, reprinted in the local press, that reached women textile workers. Paule Minck, a longtime political activist committed to the struggle for women's equality, came to speak in August 1897 to an audience of some four hundred workers, a third of whom were women and children. Her message on religion and its relation to the capitalist oppression of workers singled out the religious practices that were imposed on women millworkers in certain factories in the Nord and promoted by a Catholic association called Notre Dame de l'usine.[59] Minck urged women workers to

---

point, perhaps after the strike, the Carabin family moved to a socialist suburb of Paris, Ivry-sur-Seine, where Lecolle died in 1952. Etienne Pédron worked as secretary at the mairie d'Ivry from 1896. When the Carabin family moved, and whether she continued her militancy for the POF in Ivry, are open to speculation.

56. ADA SC 340.

57. Louise Lamblin was born in Troyes in 1878 to Alexis Eugène Lamblin, *blanchisseur* from Palisy (Aube), and Augustine Giey, *apprêteuse*. She married Aimé Claude Victor Baloud, a hosiery manufacturer in Falaise, Normandy, who died in 1906. In 1907, she remarried; her second husband was her brother-in-law, Paul Victor Alexandre Eugène Baloud, also a hosiery manufacturer.

58. Charles Sowerwine (1982) argues that in these early years of socialism before unification there were very few women of "leadership calibre in the POF. . . . Revolutionary women like Minck preferred to concern themselves with revolution, like men; women who were workers . . . could scarcely take part in serious political work. Even if they did not have, as most of them did, the double burden of factory and housework, the political concerns which enabled some working-class men to become active in the parties were not part of their roles" (66).

59. See Hilden 1986, 114–16.

turn toward the freethinkers and the socialists for their moral and material emancipation.[60]

Aline Valette, another militant who was popular with women workers, was the only woman to serve on the POF national council. From 1895, she wrote as a journalist in the Guesdist press, and her articles were often reprinted in the *Le Socialiste Troyen*. As a former labor inspector, she wrote frequently about issues of women's work and protective legislation. In one article titled "Ce qui vaut une loi," she emphasized the ways in which millowners were circumventing and flouting the law of 1892 that shortened women's working hours to ten a day and banned them from night work. She noted that a recent governmental decree allowing garment industries to employ women up to eleven o'clock at night during rush periods, practically nullified the law. Denouncing the ways the government catered to capitalist interests, Valette urged workers to unite against such practices. While Valette was a staunch defender of women workers' interests, she was not in the long run effective in recruiting women for the party. At the party congress in Romilly in 1895, Valette issued a call to revive the working-class family, weakened by industrial capitalism, which had "dragged women into the waged labor force . . . far from their children, far from their kitchens, far from their households."[61] She urged *all* members of the POF, not just women, to make an effort to unionize women workers. To be sure, hers was a lone female voice on this subject, her words directed at a predominately male audience, but ironically her message sounded remarkably similar to that of other Guesdist militants who wanted to return working women to their homes.

It is interesting to note how socialist ideas on women were recycled and reworked, and even incorporated within the revolutionary republican tradition. For example, Etienne Pédron's son, Paul, reported in *Le Socialiste Troyen* on a special meeting for women held by Paul Lafargue at the end of the POF congress in Roubaix in 1893. Addressing a hall packed with women workers from the local mills, Lafargue spoke on the topic "Woman and Socialism." Paul Pédron noted that the action of POF women in Lille, Roubaix, and Paris was exemplary of political struggle at the municipal level, even implying that

60. Report by the commissaire spécial to the prefect, August 16, 1897, ADA SC 340.

61. Cited in Hilden 1987 (298). Valette wrote regularly for *Le Socialiste,* but her bourgeois origins no doubt made it difficult for her to relate to working-class women. For a critical treatment of Aline Valette's contribution to socialism and feminism, see Sowerwine 1982, 59–66; and Hilden 1986, 197–99.

the party might support women candidates for the municipal elections in the capital. The main obstacles to women's emancipation, Paul Pédron argued, had been their lack of education and the fact that men had continued to consider women as inferior. Young working-class women's education had been especially neglected, since working mothers often left their daughters home to sew, mend, and knit instead of sending them to school. But women were breaking these chains with the help of the POF and organizing to defend their interests within the class struggle. "No doubt our women of today, like their ancestors in 1789, will be powerful auxiliaries of tomorrow's Revolution and will one day march on all the Versailles of this world to overthrow all the kings and tyrants."[62] By invoking the women's march on Versailles in October 1789, Paul Pédron reclaimed working women's historic role as auxiliaries of the revolution.

In Troyes, as in the Nord, Guesdist rhetoric and the practice of gender equality were often opportunistic in the attempt to mobilize women workers to their cause. At party congresses, men greatly outnumbered women as delegates so that even women of stature from Troyes, including Etienne Pédron's wife, Lucie, seemed not to have had a voice. The language of both politics and work was decidedly masculine. When Guesdists were interested in swelling their numbers at meetings and in recruiting union members, they made direct appeals to women. But large numbers of unpoliticized women textile workers were unreceptive to Guesdist Marxist formulas except during strikes and moments of significant collective action. And in such cases, since the Guesdist rhetoric of formal equality was not sustained by any concrete measures in favor of women's political rights, women workers as disenfranchised citizens remained outside electoral politics.[63]

Electoral Socialism

What political success did Guesdists have in the Aube? Problems arise when considering how politics actually worked at this time. The analysis of the electoral situation is rendered difficult by the political volatility of the workers.

62. Paul Pédron, "Le mouvement féminin," *Le Socialiste Troyen*, March 18–25, 1893.
63. Stuart (1996) contends that "the POF believed that women exercise a decisive influence in electoral conflicts upon 'their loved ones, fathers, husbands and brothers'" and that the "electoral fever of the 1890s actually encouraged a Marxist interest in the female non-electorate" (61 n. 12). I have found no evidence of women's participation in electoral politics in Troyes for this period.

Electoral outcomes masked a whole range of political behavior, from a core of dedicated militants to a substantial number of casual adherents. Moreover, given the factionalism within French socialism during these years, electoral lists in Troyes carried confusing party labels to distinguish dissident groups from former allies. As the *Reveil des Travailleurs de l'Aube* warned its readers in May 1896, candidates often claimed to be something they were not: "yesterday's reactionaries declaring themselves republicans."[64] But by any measure, Guesdist electoral success in the Aube was limited during this early period, until the party joined the independent socialists in the SFIO in 1905.

The POF project was to gain control over certain industrial towns, and from these local bases build national support. Between 1890 and 1893, party militants in the Aube attempted to build such electoral bases. Although their candidates received only 5.7 percent of the vote in the 1893 legislative elections in Troyes, they won control in municipal elections in Romilly in January 1895 and in Les Riceys and Sainte-Savine in 1896. Romilly and Sainte-Savine would remain socialist strongholds throughout this early period. In the legislative elections of 1898, the POF received between 11 and 16 percent of the vote (from among registered voters) in the three electoral cantons of Troyes and 16 percent in the town itself. While this relative electoral success did not lead to mayoral victory in Troyes in either May 1896 or May 1900, several municipal counselors were elected on the POF list. The elections of 1900 marked the peak of Guesdist success in the Aube, notably in towns with a worker constituency, among them Romilly, Troyes, and nearby Aix-en-Othe.[65]

As its rationale for gaining power at the local level, the POF program for municipal government claimed to express the interests of the proletarian class. In the Troyes municipal elections of May 1896, the POF sought to distinguish itself from its political rivals on the left, including the Radical incumbent mayor, Louis Mony, by denouncing them as Opportunists in disguise who did not act in the workers' true interests. The POF advanced two major arguments to win voter support: first, its winning power locally would serve to defend and protect industrial workers from the abuses of capitalism; and second, the election of worker candidates to local office would prove the capacity of the working class to govern, as it had already done so successfully in Montluçon, Lille, and Romilly. The latter argument was an attempt to counter attacks from the Right and to demonstrate that an electoral mandate was not

64. *Le Reveil des Travailleurs de l'Aube*, May 1–8, 1896. See also Chapter 1.
65. Willard 1965, 243–49 and 495–98. See also Baroin 1970, 264–71.

a monopoly of the bourgeoisie.[66] Among the candidates presented by the POF for these local elections were many skilled manual workers, but also several *employés* (white-collar workers), small shopkeepers and businessmen, and eight knitters from the union. The POF electoral program, largely drawn from the party's experiences in Lille and Montluçon, proposed a long list of social welfare and reform measures that would improve working-class life. At the top of the list was a program to provide school lunches, and the distribution of shoes and clothing to poor families, followed by measures to ensure that landlords would repair and rehabilitate insalubrious housing. Such measures were part of an overall program designed for greater social justice in everyday life.

Why did many workers in the Aube, and especially in Troyes and Romilly, embrace Guesdist socialism? Several historians have attempted to answer this question by emphasizing that Guesdism was primarily a provincial movement and that its principal stronghold was among the textile workers of the large industrial cities of the Nord. Strong support existed among textile workers, then, strengthened by the industrial textile workers' union, the Fédération nationale du textile, based in Roubaix and headed by a loyal Guesdist, Victor Renard. But while textile workers might appear to have predominated in the Guesdist constituency, its base was, in fact, much more diverse. According to Robert Stuart, the POF embraced "a startlingly diverse array of supporters and militants, mobilising highly paid metallurgists from the engineering works of Montluçon and impoverished textile workers from the mills of Roubaix, laborers from large-scale industrial plants and tradesmen from tiny workshops, artisans from the traditional trades in the great commercial cities and raw recruits from the 'green-field' site of the second industrial revolution, 'white-collar' employees from counting houses and 'blue-collar' laborers from construction sites."[67] The apparent openness of its appeal, its dogged attempts to diffuse and popularize Marxist principles, and the strength of its local organizing certainly contributed to the party's success during this period of economic recession and sectarian competition between the parties on the left.

Historian Claude Willard has attributed the Guesdists' strength in the Aube to two primary factors: their strong ties to the labor movement, and the role and commitment of militants such as Etienne Pédron and Henri Millet, the latter a young knitter converted to socialism by Pédron who became mayor of Romilly. Millet was, in fact, an exemplary case. He lost his job as a knitter

66. *Le Reveil des Travailleurs de l'Aube,* May 1–8, 1896. See also Chapter 1.
67. Stuart 1992, 45.

because of his socialist activism when he was municipal counselor. As a journalist, orator, and campaigner, Millet was an intelligent and dynamic spokesperson for the POF, until his early death while he was a candidate in the midst of a campaign in 1902. For Willard, such militants gained support for the party by their "constant concern for theoretical principles and doctrine, by their uncompromising defense of workers' interests."[68] However, Willard's arguments accord too much weight to a labor movement that was in fact weak in numbers and obviously still divided by craft, as we shall see below. In the case of the knitters, the union ultimately split after the failure of the great strike in 1900, and many members turned to direct action and revolutionary syndicalism. Moreover, Willard underestimates the strength of other political forces in Troyes, notably the local revolutionary syndicalists among the young rebrousseurs who sparked the strike in 1900. Their union had invited two anarchist leaders, Fernand Pelloutier and Paul Tortelier, to hold a meeting in Troyes in October 1896, a gathering that drew some three hundred people. Both speakers attacked electoral socialism for its claims to reform workers' lives. Both argued that the general strike was the only effective weapon against capitalism.[69] A public meeting the following year drew a crowd of some fifteen hundred people to hear Sebastien Faure, founder of the anarchist newspaper *Le Libertaire*. Beyond the anarchists, there were larger numbers of influential Radicals to contend with, and some workers did in fact vote for Radical candidates.

The Guesdists recruited support primarily through collective action and campaigns for local election. Mass demonstrations, such as those that took place on May Day, 1890, and during the great strike of 1900, were in most cases more effective mobilizing tactics than were political campaign meetings and elections. Guesdists sought to create a socialist counterculture in opposition to the bourgeois republican one. The predisposition for such a counterculture already existed among freethinkers, anarchists, and anticlericals of other persuasions who laid the grounds for socialism. Guesdist militants shaped this counterculture into disciplined organizations subservient to their party. Colin Heywood has argued for the significance of oral propaganda in mobilizing workers in Troyes, although ultimately, he concludes, the Guesdists failed overall to win their loyalty. Certainly he is right to underscore the importance

68. Willard 1965, 249.
69. Report by the commissaire général de police to the prefect, October 12, 1896, ADA SC 365.

of the spoken rather than the written word in appealing to workers.[70] Militants trained in the rhetoric of class conflict had to make their voices heard in the rough-and-tumble political meetings and demonstrations of the period. This required the considerable rhetorical talents of such speakers as Pédron and Millet. While "class war" became an obvious political slogan of the communists in later years, Guesdist militants also used it effectively to channel confrontation from the social to the political arena. Whether or not the revolutionary rhetoric of class war convinced workers in the long run, it did serve to distinguish the POF agenda from that of its opponents. In the polemical politics of the moment, most militants were probably prepared to use body language, that is, their physical presence in protests, to channel the latent violence of class conflict in Troyes that often broke out in the workplace. In many cases, male textile workers preferred the physical face-to-face defense of their rights in the street to lengthy political meetings, as the many demonstrations during the 1900 strike suggest. Suzanne Gallois, CGTU militant in the 1920s and 1930s, emphasized that she could always mobilize workers to attend a union meeting if she promised to organize a street demonstration to follow.[71]

In the complex interaction between strike movements and political mobilization for elections, the simplified Marxism, party discipline, and electoral socialism advocated by the Guesdists did not succeed in winning textile workers' lasting political allegiance at the ballot box. Revolutionary syndicalism would have a far wider appeal, with its empowering message of direct action to create greater worker autonomy on the ground.

Revolutionary Syndicalism

The great strike of 1900 had failed to organize textile workers in Troyes into a disciplined Guesdist-inspired union. Subsequently, many workers turned toward direct action in an effort to create the type of autonomous institutions that would provide the solidarity and material well-being they wanted within the dominant capitalist society. For revolutionary, or direct-action, syndicalists, as they were also known, class solidarity was far more important than organization. They emphasized working-class culture and the "importance of

---

70. Heywood 1998, 20–31.
71. Suzanne Gallois, interview, May 14, 1984. She argued that Troyes was an open town, that felons had been permitted to settle there, and that the workers liked "la bagarre," making them difficult to discipline and organize for political work.

involving workers across craft and industry lines, and without regard to skill, gender or national origin."[72] For this reason, strikes were instrumental in winning increasing numbers of workers to their side. According to CGT leader Victor Griffuelhes, strikes were regenerative acts of revolutionary practice, and because they functioned within the unions they were a better educational tool than libraries: "[A strike] educates, it trains for battle, it mobilizes and it creates."[73] When Griffuelhes became leader of the CGT in 1902, unions were vying with political parties for workers' allegiance; unions represented an alternative strategy of empowerment. Moreover, government officials now intervened in strikes; they subsidized the creation of the Bourses du Travail, a movement led by anarchist Fernand Pelloutier, and they promoted unions and collective bargaining as means of integrating workers into the social order and of curbing labor radicalism. This situation changed in 1906 when Radical prime minister Georges Clemenceau led the repression against labor. Government use of troops against strikers only made the revolutionary syndicalists more hostile to parliamentary government and to electoral politics run by "politicards," as Emile Pouget called them.[74]

Pouget's weekly Parisian newspaper, *Le Père Peinard,* had a local correspondent in Troyes who reported news of work conflicts in the knitting mills of Troyes, notably during the great strike of 1900. The author accused the visiting socialists of being "endormeurs" for urging strikers to remain calm and not to react to millowners' provocations. Preaching passive resistance at this time, the writer argued, was an attack on worker dignity and only served to weaken workers' resolve in the increasingly humiliating confrontation caused by the millowners' lockout. Such advice, he suggested, could only have served socialist interests in the electoral campaign for control of the Troyes town hall.[75] In fact, revolutionary syndicalists advocated abstention in the upcoming elections. A "Groupe abstentionniste" had been organized in the *quartier bas* to create propaganda for the electoral campaign period. Its success can be measured by the fact that more than 20 percent of registered voters, evenly distributed in all neighborhoods of the town, abstained in the municipal

72. Friedman 1997, 160.
73. *L'Action Directe,* April 15, 1908, as quoted in Julliard 1988, 49.
74. Friedman 1997, 155–81. See Julliard 1988, 32–40; *Le Père Peinard,* September 4–11, 1892, and especially April 15–21, 1900. Pouget invented epithets to characterize the parliament: the National Assembly was the "aquarium," deputies were styled as "dépotés" to emphasize the nature of the office as a club, and socialists were called "bouffe-galettes socialards."
75. *Le Père Peinard,* March 11–18 and April 1–7, 1900.

elections of May 1900.[76] Those workers who abstained now believed in direct action for achieving their goals of greater autonomy and a counterculture of resistance that would sustain working-class values.

Revolutionary syndicalists also addressed women, claiming that female workers would participate in professional unions in a future society on equal footing with men. In Pouget and Emile Pataud's postrevolutionary utopian society, "woman was no longer obliged to be 'housewife or harlot,' to use Proudhon's brutal terms," nor would she need to seek the vote as did her bourgeois sisters, the suffragists, in order to affirm her equality with men. True to socialist promises, woman would be liberated under the new organization of society to be free individuals: "woman could remain a woman—in the most feminine and human sense of the word—without aping men."[77] Moreover, by defeating capitalism, the new socialist society would abolish one of capitalism's worst abuses, the sexual exploitation of women workers. Reports from the Troyes mills in *Le Père Peinard* were filled with stories of foremen and managers taking sexual advantage of young women workers.[78] In many respects, then, revolutionary syndicalism as practiced during these early years of the CGT reached out to women in more concrete ways than did the vague theoretical principles of Guesdism.

SOCIALIST UNIONS AND WOMEN WORKERS

Only a small fraction of the French working class belonged to unions. Moreover, labor organizations in France were generally weak, factional, and subject to conflicting political pressures. Labor historians have offered various explanations for this numerical weakness of unions. Some insist on the distinctive path of French industrialization, its slow pace, and the resilience of small-scale artisans and dispersed units of production.[79] Others focus on the diversity of trades, the coexistence of skilled and unskilled, rural and urban, factory workers and homeworkers, men and women, in the labor force.[80] Still others

76. ADA M 132. See Chapter 1.
77. Pouget and Pataud 1995, 173–74.
78. *Le Père Peinard*, nos. 220 and 223 (June 1893).
79. See Lenard Berlanstein's (1992) excellent overview of French labor movements (660–85).
80. This is the basic position of Gerard Noiriel (1986). He emphasizes the constant renewal of the labor force through the peasantry, the absence of uprooting and proletarianization until the second industrial revolution at the end of the nineteenth century.

argue that union membership is not an index of worker combativity and that French workers based their collective action on class solidarity against hostile employers, rather than on revolutionary principles, divorced from the workplace and therefore ineffective.[81] Among feminist historians, there has been a strong interest in looking at the gender dimension of this problem, notably the relative neglect by the labor movement of women's potential membership. Women's consequent reluctance to join unions, complicated by the fact of their lack of suffrage until much later in the twentieth century, raises the important question of when their right to work was legally recognized by the unions themselves.[82] These early decades of union organizing, then, present special historiographical challenges.

For most of the fledgling unions at this time, self-definition was complicated by relations with socialist parties. The 1890s represented a period of intense political factionalism and competition between socialist sects that had repercussions in the labor movement. The POF ostensibly encouraged and supported formal unions as a necessary means of organizing workers' defense. Further, it advocated unions' political neutrality, at least in theory. In practice, however, the party openly tried to politicize unions, to win them to their goals and subordinate them to party action. The contradictory nature of these partisan practices fueled tensions with other groups, among them the revolutionary syndicalists, that were intent on preventing Guesdist hegemony. But the POF's strength in textile centers made it a powerful ally of the Fédération nationale du textile, with its headquarters in Lille, headed by Victor Renard.[83] In Troyes, Guesdist militants maintained their dominant position as union leaders and supporters of the POF program until the failure of the great strike of 1900. They had initially strengthened union membership after a six-week strike at the Mauchauffée mill in September 1888, when workers had called upon union leaders to negotiate a settlement. When the millowner had refused to negotiate with the union and had prepared a lockout, the prefect had interceded, while townspeople firmly took the side of the strikers.[84] Mauchauffée was obliged under public pressure to concede the workers' major demands. The success of this strike had been clear, as a vast movement of local

81. Cottereau 1986, 111–54.
82. The basic work of reference is Guilbert 1966a. Since this pioneer work, see Zylberberg-Hocquard 1978; Downs 1995; Frader 1998 ; Rogerat 1995, 165–82; Chenut 1998, 35–51.
83. See Stuart 1992, chap. 6.
84. Even the municipal council had been supportive; it had voted a subsidy of five hundred francs to textile workers forced into idleness as a result of the strike (ADA M 1273).

solidarity gave the workers the support they needed and the union gained new members.

However, in 1894 the Guesdists attempted a new strategy to recruit members, one that required splitting the Syndicat des bonnetiers de Troyes into three separate "sections" according to trade occupation. They were then federated within an umbrella-type union, the Association syndicale des ouvriers et ouvrières de toutes les professions se rattachant à la bonneterie.[85] Membership remained low in this mixed-sex union, which effectively grouped all occupations within the trade, except the spinners and dyers. Statistics for 1895 showed some 1,100 union members in the Aube, but only 250 in Troyes.[86] However, union membership figures for these years should be treated as only approximate. In assessing the numerical importance of women in these unions, it is essential to recall the low rate of unionization even in 1900 in France nationwide (2.9 percent), and in the Aube (1.06 percent). Madeleine Guilbert's pioneering study on this prewar period provides the basic data for the department as a whole: in 1900 women represented 13 percent of industrial union members in the Aube, but they constituted 32.8 percent of the working population. By 1911, women's union membership had declined to 6.8 percent, despite the overall increase, to 38.5 percent, in the number of women in the working population. Guilbert concluded that "there is a constant and considerable discrepancy between the percentage of women in the workforce and the percentage of women in unions."[87]

Another set of figures suggests the evolution of female membership in the mixed-sex knitters' union in relation to the total membership for the period 1894 to 1909.[88] Although the accuracy of these data are somewhat uncertain, they convey the apparent volatility of women's commitment. On the whole,

85. The statutes of 1894 refer to a corporation that was divided into four sections, each composed of members in the same occupation (*métier*), with headquarters at the Maison du Peuple. See ADA SC 1288.

86. ADA M 2352. In 1895, the prefect complained of the difficulties of verifying any information on union membership. Given the police surveillance of socialist meetings and militants, union leaders' reluctance to allow further control of membership seems understandable. On the legalization of labor unions and an analysis of legislators' intentions on the law of 1884, see Barbet 1991, 5–30.

87. Guilbert 1966, 28.

88. The source for these figures is the annual self-declaration by the unions to the mayor of Troyes, based on a questionnaire distributed by the Ministry of Commerce and Industry via the mayor. The prefect expressed his extreme reservations on the accuracy of these figures as he transmitted them. Data is provided for the Association syndicale des ouvriers et ouvrières de toutes les professions se rattachant à la bonneterie (AMT 7F 32–42).

women textile workers seem to have entered the union somewhat later than men, with particularly large numbers joining in 1898. By 1900 female workers constituted nearly half the total membership (almost four hundred of eight hundred members), confirming the fact that they joined the union massively during the great strike. Overall, their participation remained stabile under the domination of the revolutionary syndicalists until 1905, when it fell dramatically, most likely in reaction to socialist unification in the SFIO at the national level. Membership rebounded somewhat at the time of the CGT congress in Amiens in October 1906, but then dropped again when National Textile Federation leader Victor Renard's proposal to work closely with the SFIO was defeated. The Congress of Amiens voted overwhelmingly for union independence from political parties at this time, a vote that constituted a historic defeat for Guesdist-dominated organizations such as the Troyes textile union.

A Problematic Relationship

The dependence of Troyes manufacturers on women's labor made the question of government regulation of working conditions and wages a contentious issue. By the turn of the century, gender-specific protective legislation had passed in the Chamber under pressure from social Catholics, socialists, and other reform-minded groups in favor of state intervention. Legislation in 1892 and 1900 had shortened women's working hours in factories and regulated night-work, without stipulating a minimum wage. In 1900 a woman's wage was slightly more than half a man's in the Troyes mills.[89] If we consider that women formed an absolute majority in the labor force in the Troyes knitted goods industry at this time, their low rate of union participation raises a number of basic questions about the appeal to women of Guesdist union leaders. What efforts were made to recruit women union members? How were women's issues addressed? What tensions arose between gender and class interests? Unfortunately, sources addressing these questions are only fragmentary.

A union tract addressed specifically to women workers in Troyes, and calling upon them to join the Association syndicale de la Bonneterie, provides some sense of Guesdist recruitment strategies. The tract probably dates from sometime after the POF national congress in Romilly in September 1895, at which Aline Valette made a special plea to delegates to unionize women. The

89. Calculated from the average wages provided by millowners in the parliamentary commission of inquiry in 1904.

tract's appeal was formulated precisely to attract women workers as mothers to join the union: "Comrades, think what could happen if you wait until you are in complete poverty, your children could hold you responsible for this situation that prejudices their future, for it will be your fault and it will be too late to remedy it." Thus, joining the union would protect both the family's interest and that of women, as workers. The tract then pointed to the latest strike victory that had been won "especially thanks to the energy of women workers and their timely solidarity." The appeal reached out to include women in terms that identified them as both women and workers, enumerating one by one the female occupations in the knitwear trade: "Mothers, wives, and young women, show a good example to your husbands, to your brothers, so that our union will be the largest in the region."[90] Finally, the text announced that women workers would be invited to a special union meeting for the purpose of creating a women's section within the union. Union leaders evidently intended to include women as a special constituency, within the existing union structure and subordinate to it. The granting of separate and subordinate status within the socialist union was part of a strategy that attempted to channel women's action in terms of class solidarity. Such a strategy would become standard practice later in the twentieth century.[91]

Articles in the POF press also provide insights into party leaders' attitudes toward women workers. Between 1898 and 1900, *Le Reveil des Travailleurs* published regular columns on union activities directed at female textile workers, together with more serious theoretical pieces on "women's emancipation," written by national Guesdist leaders and local POF militants. Guesde's followers in Troyes showed some theoretical concern for the question of women's wages and the right to work. But in most cases, militants seemed to make unsophisticated pronouncements of principles that had little practical relation to the situation in Troyes. For example, Hébert Corgeron, editor of *Le Reveil des Travailleurs,* raised the equal wage issue in the paper in April 1898, as part of a discussion of the POF national program that incorporated this demand. He observed:

> Following the principle that women's needs are the same as men's, and accepting that the effort expended for the work is the same, we

90. ADA M 2292.
91. See Frader 1996b.

consider that a minimum wage should be established for women workers, the same as for men.

If we examine the work in the knitting industry in our town, we wonder in all sincerity if the work of women seamers, winders, etc. is not as painful as that executed by male knitters? And that often the work accomplished by women could not as well be done by men? That is why we state, equal pay for equal work [*à travail égal, salaire égal*]. In this manner the worker would never fear competition from his mate.[92]

Corgeron's conclusion only confounded the wage issue. He clearly read wage inequality as competition between the sexes. Given the marked gender division of labor within the trade, it was highly unlikely that men would accept doing women's work as he intimated they would. The proposition alone would have provoked a revolution. By alleging competition from women workers, he confused the position of local Guesdist militants, who were struggling against the disparity in piece rates between the various mills. Women's work in this trade posed no economic threat to men. It was in fact the greater discrepancy in wages between factory workers and homeworkers during this period that ultimately drove wages down. Consequently, in the 1900 strike Guesdists struggled against this divisive system and sought to mobilize textile workers around the issue of uniform piece rates. Guesde's followers, while affirming their agreement with the principle of equal pay for equal work, retrenched behind a defensive stance on workers' wages without distinction of sex. The union never publicly condemned the fact that a woman's wage was slightly more than half a man's in the Troyes mills.

By separating out women's roles in this way, Guesdist militants could more easily marginalize them and respond to some male workers' hostility toward women working outside the home. The National Textile Federation issued contradictory statements on women's right to work and to strike outside the union. Indeed, Victor Renard's personal attitude toward women in the textile union betrayed a shift in Guesdist efforts, from encouraging the recruitment of women to supporting protective legislation that would restrict women's and children's labor.[93] The political reasons behind this stance will be analyzed

92. *Le Reveil des Travailleurs de l'Aube,* April 16–23, 1898.
93. For an analysis of this shift as it concerns women textile workers in the Nord department, see Hilden 1986, chap. 4.

in the following section, against the background of competing union strategies. But in Renard's case, it is fair to say that he often considered women workers' protest behavior as divisive.

Overall, the socialist unions' problematic relationship with women workers during these early years revealed the weakness both of syndicalism itself and of women's identity as industrial workers in relation to men. Syndicalism needed a reliable political ally to obtain legitimate recognition from employers and the state, and women were still disenfranchised citizens. Many women workers in France attempted to unionize separately from men during this period, with the support of Catholic employers or bourgeois feminists such as Marguerite Durand. This was not the case in Troyes, where women textile workers never attempted to create separate single-sex unions. In the long run, small, relatively weak French labor unions established a historical pattern of marginalizing women within a predominately male organization, and Guesdist-dominated unions in Troyes followed this pattern. Issues such as how to recruit women members, how to integrate them within existing structures, and the special nature of many women workers' demands would resurface in labor struggles after 1920. In Troyes the public presence of women textile workers alongside that of men clearly demonstrated that class issues predominated over gender ones before World War I. However, tensions would emerge over gender differences as the process of the feminization of the labor force became irreversible after the war. Socialist parties and labor unions would then have to compete with other groups for working women's allegiance.

Limited Suffrage for Working Women

Nevertheless, working women's rights made important formal gains during this prewar period, thanks to a number of legislative reforms voted in their favor. It is true that most of these reforms were inspired by a protectionist logic, as seen in the law of 1907 granting married working women free disposition of their earnings, and in the law of 1909 instituting an eight weeks' maternity leave without pay.[94] However, during this period of increased militantism in

94. On the ambiguities of the law of 1907 as a way of correcting the Napoleonic Civil Code's enshrinement of the husband's authority, see the analysis by Florence Rochefort (1998). The law concerned 95 percent of couples who were married under the "régime de la communauté des biens," under which the husband had control over his wife's property, including wages, unless a contract stipulated otherwise. Rochefort argues that the law had limited application, because the husband could still make claims given the fact that the 1907 law did not abolish "la puissance

favor of women's suffrage, both in France and in neighboring countries, the fact that French working women were granted limited suffrage in elections to the local trade boards (law of March 27, 1907), and became eligible for election to these boards a year later (law of November 15, 1908), did not go unnoticed. These trade boards, known as the Conseils des prud'hommes, had been established in 1808 in order to hear, arbitrate, and conciliate workplace disputes. By that time, the Revolution had abolished the guild system, and the *prud'hommes* councils were instituted to bring together elected representatives, from merchants and manufacturers on the one hand, and labor on the other. Historically both men and women had brought cases before the courts for arbitration and settlement.[95] The new measures of 1907–8 that allowed working women equal voting rights with men in the *prud'hommes* elections were undoubtedly linked to the notable increase of women in the French labor force. According to the 1906 census, women represented 37 percent of the total working population in France, and some 52 percent in the Aube. It is paradoxical that women working in industry and the trades were the *only* women who could legally exercise the right to vote on equal terms with men at this time. But did they actually do so?

Voting requirements for the *prud'hommes* elections were the following: holding French citizenship, registering to vote, being at least twenty-five years old, and having exercised an occupation in the same trade for at least three years. Records for these prewar elections in Troyes show that initially only a few isolated individual women even registered to vote, and that participation by male workers was not particularly high either. In 1910, out of twenty-eight hundred men registered, fewer than five hundred actually voted.[96] The weakness of the unions at this time, and their outright ambivalence toward recruiting women

---

maritale" (the husband's ultimate authority). The reform to the Civil Code that removed this power, a cause advanced by radical feminists, was not instituted until 1938.

95. On the unique structure of these French arbitration courts, or "local trade councils," see Felkin 1867, 480–81. See also Cottereau 1986.

96. AMT 1K 311. Records for the *prud'hommes* elections for 1913 in Troyes, for example, show 2,828 men registered to vote in the first category (industrial worker, textile trades), of whom 412 voted. The fact that no women were registered for this election is hardly significant, since only three *bonnetières* had done so in 1910 for the very first time. By 1929, 25 women were registered in industry and commerce, and 15 voted; and in 1935 there were 122 women registered in the same trades out of a list of 4,396 registered voters. Such voting figures for women workers seem insignificant and should be seen in relation to their low membership in the textile union. But these same figures do highlight the effort by the local suffrage society to bring women workers out to exercise their vote in 1914.

workers, probably account for women's lack of interest in these local trade board elections. It was only in 1929 that there was a significant increase in the numbers of women workers registered to vote for the *prud'hommes,* a trend that continued into the 1930s. By this time, unions were especially interested in increasing their numbers and were actively recruiting women workers. As we shall see in a later chapter, there was a clear commitment in the CGTU propaganda to educating women for political responsibility.

The demand for suffrage was most closely identified with a number of feminist or women's rights organizations of various political tendencies founded at the end of the nineteenth century.[97] But Marxist socialists, and working-class organizations in general, routinely characterized feminism, and suffrage within feminism, as middle class or "bourgeois." In Troyes, a small local chapter of the Union française pour le suffrage des femmes (UFSF) was founded in 1913.[98] The national UFSF organization, much like the moderate British suffrage organizations, had consistently supported a gradualist strategy on woman suffrage. The local UFSF group in Troyes, led by the woman director of the *école normale* and several primary school teachers, clearly had a reformist, republican, and moderate agenda. But the group's leaders recognized the need to cross class lines by reaching out to local women textile workers through UFSF propaganda. There are several examples of such outreach action. Through the local press the leaders publicized draft legislation under discussion in the National Assembly concerning working women, such as a minimum wage for women homeworkers. More important, because the UFSF leaders were so keenly aware that working women formed a major audience in their town, they wanted women workers to exercise even their limited right to vote. In January 1914, with the support of the Syndicat du textile, they distributed leaflets at factory gates to women textile workers, urging them to vote in the upcoming local elections to the *prud'hommes.* This specific initiative, as we have seen, had little effect. Further actions were undermined by the

97. Two excellent studies of the feminist movements for the period exist: Klejman and Rochefort 1989, and Bard 1995.

98. Private archives were recently found for the Groupe de l'Aube de l'Union française pour le suffrage des femmes. These records consist of a manuscript notebook in which the secretary of the local Aube chapter of the UFSF consigned the minutes of their meetings for the period running from March 11, 1913, when the group was created, to December 24, 1915, the date of their last meeting, with only three members present. The minutes of the last meeting reveal both a sense of powerlessness to influence events at that time, and the belief, held by many moderate suffragists, that their conduct during the war would plead in favor of their enfranchisement at the war's end.

outbreak of war several months later. The subsequent indifference to the cause of women's suffrage among local electors came as no surprise to UFSF members under the circumstances, since Troyes was on a war footing from August 1914. Unfortunately, there is no record that this local suffrage organization ever regained sufficient momentum after the interruption of the war. Yet some women, among them Marie Bonnevial, a militant syndicalist and socialist who had brought funds to striking workers in Troyes in 1900, remained convinced that women's suffrage was inevitable. "The problem," Bonnevial argued in 1914, "is not knowing if women want to vote, because the reality is that women must vote."[99]

A DIVIDED LABOR MOVEMENT

The period leading up to World War I was one of both heightened labor militancy and government repression in France. While Jean Jaurès eventually managed to unify competing socialist factions within a single political party, he clashed openly with Jules Guesde over important issues involving socialist support for the bourgeois Radical coalition government. The Millerand crisis in 1899 was only the first of many challenges to test Guesdists' loyalties. To be sure, tensions broke out when some socialists voted with the republican government in condoning the use of military troops to break strikes. But socialist struggles at the national level reflected critical differences over political strategy: Guesde maintained that any class collaboration with the bourgeois government was unacceptable, while Jaurès attempted to pressure more-progressive Radical leaders toward social reforms that would benefit the working class. But ultimately, in 1904, Jaurès was forced to abandon his efforts at class collaboration. The following year Guesde agreed to merge his forces with the independent socialists into the SFIO.[100] However, when Radical Georges Clemenceau became premier in 1906, he did not hesitate to use troops against labor unrest. This was the national political context in which Troyes workers struggled to obtain a greater share in the growing prosperity of the Belle Epoque.

99. In response to a press poll of women readers. As quoted in Corradin and Martin, eds. 1999, 151.
100. See the historic debate between Guesde and Jaurès at the Amsterdam socialist congress in 1904, in Goldberg 1962, 326–29.

In Troyes, millworkers had many reasons to protest. A number of their grievances consisted of unresolved issues from the great strike of 1900. At the forefront were the young rebrousseurs who went on strike regularly to demand wage increases. At issue was the mode of payment, contested in the 1900 strike, that made it difficult for them to earn a living as subcontracted pieceworkers. They continued to demand a daily wage. In August 1905, the police reported that rebrousseurs had gone on strike for the same wage increase they had been demanding "each month for the past year." By October 1913, their anger had turned against management. The work stoppage spread from the Mauchauffée mill to other sites in town. When the rebrousseurs finally obtained a small wage increase, they returned to work, only to be faced with threats of sanctions in case of further disorders, and with the firing of nine leaders of their movement. Workers responded to these threats by organizing action against one of the mill managers: more than a thousand workers angrily marched him to his home in town, a practice known as a "conduite de Grenoble." Management retaliated with a three-day lockout that forced more than two thousand workers from their jobs. The Syndicat du textile de Troyes, along with the mayor, intervened to bring union representatives and the managers of Mauchauffée together to resolve the conflict. By accepting a plan to allow union-designated delegates in each workshop to bring grievances forward, management hoped to forestall further action of this kind.[101]

In 1911 protests also broke out in the mills over wages in relation to the sharp increase in the cost of living resulting in conditions known as "la vie chère." Bad weather, low agricultural production, and an outbreak of hoof-and-mouth disease all created scarcity that drove up prices for dairy products. The resulting rise in food costs suddenly changed ordinary workers' perception of how well their nominal wages could provide for their families' needs.[102] While there were no riots or disruptions in the marketplaces by women to secure better prices, as there were in the north and northeast of France, women textile workers in Troyes did demand higher wages to feed their families.[103]

101. See police reports on these strikes in AMT 2J 48, also ADA SC 819, and the account of the October 1913 strike in *L'Ouvrier Textile,* December 1913, which emphasized the role of the textile union in restoring order.

102. For a discussion of the relation between strikes, wages, and the cost of living, see M. Perrot 1974, 1:124–32. Perrot affirms that the subsistence riots of 1911 marked the first time that strikes became a form of protest against the cost of living. See also the discussion in Glickman 1997, chap. 3.

103. For a discussion and analysis of the women's riots in 1911, see Hanson 1988, 463–81.

Most of these strike actions and protests were not instigated by the unions, which remained numerically weak.[104] Rather, they took place spontaneously, in ways that both reflected and confounded union divisions over strategies. The great strike of 1900 had changed the political landscape for the craft unions in Troyes. The main victim of the strike had been the Guesdist-dominated federation of knitters' unions in the Aube, which had split into two factions, the larger one voting to join the CGT. This national confederation was dominated by union leaders who asserted their independence from socialist parties and politics. As revolutionary syndicalists, they distinguished themselves through a set of beliefs that appealed to many of the young workers and knitters in Troyes. Their pro-strike strategy was relatively effective until 1907, when previous government support abruptly turned to repression under Clemenceau. The rise in prominence of the new Bourse du Travail in Troyes, inaugurated in 1906 by Jean Jaurès, symbolically confirmed the loss of POF influence over the unions.

In fact, a struggle ensued between two competing notions of syndicalism that played itself out both in Troyes and within the Fédération nationale du textile, the national textile union, founded in 1902 through the fusion of an existing national organization and the strongly Guesdist textile union of the Nord. Victor Renard, head of the new national textile union and a Guesdist militant, took a firm position against spontaneous unplanned strikes that, he argued, hampered union organizing and the achievement of material gains. Renard's strategy, typical of mutual aid societies in the past, was to increase union membership by offering workers strike funds and unemployment benefits. Renard's opponents criticized this strategy as reformist. But the union leader insisted that only a numerically strong union could exert gradual pressure for reforms such as the eight-hour day, protective legislation, and a minimum wage.

However, a competing strategy, supported by a minority of revolutionary syndicalists within the national textile union, called for direct action through strikes, notably a general strike. Emile Pouget, leader of the CGT, clashed openly with Renard, asserting that strikes were spontaneous expressions of worker solidarity and that Renard's reformist and passive programs impeded collective action. Within the Aube knitters' unions, Franco Caiti, from Romilly; Gustave Batisse, from Troyes; and many rebrousseurs all backed a revolutionary syndicalist strategy. Such internal struggles became open debates on certain issues

104. The author of an editorial in *L'Ouvrier Textile* of March 1909 reported that there had been 247 strikes in the textile industry in 1907, producing some 33,348 strikers, of whom 70–80 percent were unorganized or nonunion members.

that challenged Renard's leadership and ultimately affected union membership. When Renard managed to swing the national textile union toward a reformist strategy in 1905, union membership in Troyes dropped notably as we have seen, and only recovered when the national union voted to support the CGT, thus restoring a more pluralistic and inclusive orientation.[105] If we consider just three issues—strike strategy, the eight-hour day, and the minimum wage—we can understand how these divisions over the notion of syndicalism and forms of collective action affected men and women textile workers in Troyes.

One of the most divisive issues concerned whether strikes constituted an effective weapon against capitalist millowners, and the desirability of joining a general strike if called upon in solidarity with the CGT. A debate on this question took place in August 1908 at the national textile union's congress held in Troyes. Victor Renard argued that such action not only would be economically disastrous, given current unemployment in the textile industry, but also would destroy workers' organizations and exhaust their strike funds. Ultimately, he swayed the delegates behind his position in favor of active union recruitment and against "any movement, not only a general strike, but a generalized strike, that would constitute a tactical error . . . and an inconceivable blunder."[106] But while the congress endorsed Renard's position, unorganized textile workers, notably certain groups of women workers who went out on their own, continued to strike.

This was the case of the women textile workers in the Isère, under the leadership of militant Lucie Baud, who had organized a union among the silk weavers of Vizille in 1902 and had led them on strike in 1905. When she complained by letter to Renard that the Fédération nationale du textile had not shown them any solidarity, Renard refused to publish her letter in L'Ouvrier Textile.[107] However, in 1911 an angry exchange took place between Renard and revolutionary syndicalist Emile Pouget of the CGT over women strikers in the jute industry in Dunkerque. Pouget accused Renard of suppressing the strike through his attack on women workers' spontaneous action against employers who had fired union militants who were presenting legitimate grievances.

105. AN F7 13819. See the letter from the prefect to the minister of the interior, August 17, 1905, that characterizes Renard's action as a "coup de théâtre." However, the CGT asserted a nonpolitical stance the following year in its Amiens charter, which was an effort to promote the union's autonomy and pluralism.

106. La Défense des Travailleurs de l'Aube, August 21–28, 1908; L'Ouvrier Textile, September 1, 1908; Letter from the prefect to the Ministry of the Interior, August 20, 1908, AN F7 12767.

107. Baud published her letter and opened a debate in the CGT newspaper, La Voix du Peuple. See M. Perrot 1978b. A short account can be found in Jonas 1994, 137, 162.

The strikers were predominately women, most of whom were nonunionized. Pouget took advantage of the strike's collapse to attack Renard's reformist notion of syndicalism on the grounds that it resulted in guarding strike funds like savings in the bank.[108] The increased incidence of women textile workers' militancy during this period, even if it represented a minority trend among strike movements, is important.

The demand for the eight-hour workday originated in the first May Day celebrations in 1890, and it reappeared for discussion on the agenda of each annual congress of the national textile union. Renard was prepared to work gradually for this reform in concert with other labor unions, even at the European level. Inevitably the eight-hour-day movement encountered strong opposition from employers, but it also engendered a certain ambivalence among workers despite its political appeal. Shorter working hours were more strongly supported by labor activists than by unorganized textile workers, until the reform was tied to a guaranteed minimum wage. Subsequently, the two demands topped the May Day agenda in Troyes. However, few millworkers in Troyes actually answered the union's appeal to stop work on May Day in 1911.[109] By 1912, however, the knitters' union in Troyes was endorsing a new agenda for May Day, calling for a reduction of working hours through the introduction of a shorter workweek, known as "la semaine anglaise," that would give workers Saturday afternoon free. Julien Grée, in the name of the CGT, exhorted workers to celebrate May Day by stopping work and demonstrating in favor of the union's campaign for the shorter workweek. Most of the arguments advanced to promote this reform underscored the advantage to women workers, who could use the Saturday afternoon to do their household chores, leaving Sunday for family leisure and rest. In this respect the union's argument was specifically designed to mobilize women workers to support the new reform.

As for the demand for a minimum wage, the issue was confounded by the diversity of wage scales practiced in the textile industry as a whole, by the strict application of the piecework system in branches such as knitted goods and hosiery, and by the initial demand for a unified wage scale. The complexity of the system was daunting, compounded as it was by gender and social divisions

108. Exchange of letters in *La Guerre Sociale*, February 8, 1911; press cutting found in AN F7 13820.
109. According to police records, only 2,437 workers out of a total hosiery workforce of 8,740 were listed as "inactive" on May 1, 1911, while many of these were employed in three mills that closed for inventory that day (ADA SC 330). See police record of CGT tract signed by Julien Grée, and the list of strikers in the knitting mills compiled by the police in Troyes.

of labor within the textile industry itself and by regional differences that some-times exacerbated competition between workers. This issue was debated at several textile congresses as delegates sought to document their own experi-ences and wrestle with possible solutions. At the Congress of Fourmies in 1912, Franco Caiti, head of the knitters' union in Romilly, called for the suppression of piecework altogether, rather than for a unified wage scale. Such a suppression would put an end, he argued, to the cause of many of the divisions between workers, that is, the rivalry to produce more. Since no con-sensus emerged on this question, a resolution was approved that satisfied everyone without offering a solution. Underlying this debate were two differ-ent notions of syndicalism, a reformist and a revolutionary one. Caiti spoke for the revolutionary minority by insisting that "the union is an organization to combat employers and capitalism, not a mutual aid society. Its goal is to make men conscious, ready to accept any effort and sacrifice."[110]

Several recent French labor historians have attempted to put the distinctive-ness of the French labor movement in historical perspective, looking back to the Revolutions of 1789 and 1848 as providing the framework for a "vision of the future socialist society as a federation of democratic self-governing trades that collectively owned the means of production." This vision of a "republic of labor," they maintained, dominated the French socialist and labor movements until World War I.[111] While Guesdist socialists and revolutionary syndicalists in Troyes might have shared a similar vision of the social republic they wished to create, each advocated different means to achieve this end. Moreover, each had to mobilize and discipline a diverse, often rebellious working class to work toward their goals. A majority of Troyes textile workers, with roots in rural community and family workshops, were predisposed to resistance to urban factory exploitation. But only a minority seemed to embrace Marxian socialism, which defined such resistance in terms of class struggle. From their perspective, Guesdist militants had hoped to convince male workers that they could create a cooperative socialist society through the parliamentary sys-tem. To realize these aims, Guesdists helped forge an emergent class identity

110. *La Bataille Syndicaliste,* August 18, 1912. See also his article in the same CGT paper on July 17, 1914, calling for support for the revolutionary syndicalists' position within the Fédéra-tion du textile at its next congress in Caudry.
111. Sewell 1980, 275–76. Sewell cites Bernard Moss and his own agreement with him in this respect; see Moss 1976.

through political propaganda that prioritized and dramatized grievances of working-class life. Gender solidarity formed one component of this strategy, although women workers were increasingly marginalized from political action. In the end, Guesdists failed in their efforts to create a disciplined political party and a worker constituency that could ensure electoral victory over the established forces of the moderate Left in the Aube. As their political project lost favor, their followers failed to dominate the knitters' union and to manage successfully the workers' consumer cooperative the Sociale, which was to have helped sustain party activities.

The subsequent shift of Troyes knitters toward revolutionary syndicalism revealed their desire to rebuild class solidarity through direct action in the mills and in the workers' community. While the revolutionary fervor of the general strike declined, strike action did not. Those young workers who had no faith in political parties or in a bourgeois-dominated republican state continued to strike. Other workers invested their energies in labor unions and in the consumer cooperative the Laborieuse that would become one of the instruments of socialist transformation. In opposition to the growing government repression of strikes and to bourgeois commercial capitalism, workers would create local cooperative associations for collective action based on their egalitarian desires. This utopian political vision would help satisfy workers' need for greater workplace autonomy and control over their lives.

To be sure, at the century's end industrial and commercial capitalism continued to dominate in Troyes, as it did in the rest of France. As the bourgeois republican government attempted to integrate workers into the political system, revolutionary syndicalists rejected these efforts. Textile workers in Troyes based their resistance on a counterculture that affirmed working-class values and cooperative socialism. The real diversity of workers' interests—between homeworkers and factory workers, artisan outworkers and young apprentices, skilled and unskilled, men and women—made organizing political solidarity difficult. Social transformations of this kind, as Jacques Julliard has noted, closely linked workers' culture and political autonomy: "The aspiration for political autonomy, the vision of an alternative society, emerges from a lived experience, the experience of exclusion, which is transformed into a claim for a new identity."[112] This complex process of an emergent working-class culture was integral to the experience of class.

112. Julliard 1988, 32.

4

A CULTURE OF TEXTILE PRODUCTION

When knitter Emile Caillot celebrated the virtues of a small knitting machine (*tricoteuse*) that he had seen on display at the Paris World's Fair of 1900, he imagined all the ways that it could be developed in the mills of Troyes and employed at home. Addressing millowners, he predicted that

> the *tricoteuse* would be the queen of the hosiery industry and would be used all over France. The superiority of the *tricoteuse* over our large knitting machines is striking. One worker can operate ten such *tricoteuses,* since they stop automatically. But its main advantage is that it has a domestic use and can be employed in many households. And little training is necessary to operate it for either producing knitted goods for the home or for sale. In ten years all families could own one, like they own a sewing machine today. Well, gentlemen, buy this machine, have it examined by your best workers, don't hesitate about spending a few thousand francs, you will see your efforts crowned by success. Your skilled workers will make you a marvelous one. You will see that this new knitter can be operated easily. . . . It's as light as a sewing machine so that a woman could operate it without tiring.[1]

1. Report by Emile Caillot, knitter, delegate to the Paris World's Fair of 1900, AMT 2F 47.

The unique machine that Caillot described conformed to his idealized vision of the artisan's life. This little machine would revive and perpetuate the tradition of industrial homework, embedded in the large-scale manufacturing system in Troyes. Indeed, for Caillot the immediate advantage of such a machine would be to maintain his family's working together at home.

The purpose of this chapter is to consider the ways in which the specific culture of textile production in Troyes was shaped by gender, class, family, and community.[2] The aim here is not to suggest that the mode of textile production itself specified a particular cultural order. If we consider culture to be a system of shared beliefs, symbols, and values that order one's experience, then productive work, as anthropologists have shown, clearly plays a recognized part in the formation of culture.[3] Long-term patterns and conventions governing the social and sexual division of labor form part of the dynamic process by which culture is transmitted from one generation to another. The persistence of industrial homework played an important part in the production process in Troyes, and it also had a formative impact on workers of both sexes. Assigned tasks, shared *savoir-faire,* recognized skills, a common language of textile techniques of production—all contributed to perpetuating a work culture and establishing worker identity with the trade. Much of textile work was linked to social practice and the production of material goods, but it was also inscribed in the symbols and representations of a shared community in the town. An analysis of some of these cultural constructs and symbols that mediated the knitters' trade forms an important part of this chapter.

While the technical knowledge of the trade created significant social bonds, it also established differences between workers. Craft and community in Troyes created an implicit system of internal ranking in the mills in terms of occupation and skill. This hierarchy shaped a gendered work identity for men and women, valorized by class and community in the town. As one French ethnologist has observed, "[W]hen a town is the site of industrial production in which *savoir-faire* govern the social position within production, that same social position is transposed to urban status; in the same social class, groups

2. Leora Auslander (1993) has characterized what she calls "the culture of production" among furniture makers as a site for craft knowledge, transmission of skill, and aesthetic concerns of the trade. Her very sensitive reading of artisan voices historicizes technical craft culture and poses the problem of workers' multiple identities, their diversity and change over time.

3. From the enormous literature on this subject, see Godelier 1980; Geertz 1973; Hunt 1989; Bonnell and Hunt 1999; Sewell 1999, 35–61; Williams 1977, esp. 7 and 8; Tabet 1979.

become ranked in relation to each other."[4] Given the growing feminization of the labor force by 1900 and the strict sexual division of labor, one of the questions that will be examined in this chapter is how notions of gender inflected worker identity. If skilled work was gendered masculine in the mills, how did women workers' skills become defined and valorized? What role did technological innovation play in transforming traditional gender patterns of work? Gender segregation within the workplace raises further questions of social and cultural representations of men's and women's work and how these are produced. An analysis of both men's and women's occupations in the knitted goods industry from a gender perspective follows in this chapter.

Any analysis of manual work must necessarily include reference to the body, to the gendered body, and to the physical gestures of work. This is indeed the case here. We will look at the ways in which men's and women's work was circumscribed in separate spaces and subjected to sex-specific observations concerning the physical effects of industrial work. In many cases, women's bodies were subjected to special scrutiny on the assumption that it was "unnatural" for women to work in factories.[5]

Finally, in Troyes the revived craft festival, the Fête de la Bonneterie, constituted a unique ritual that celebrated the trade from 1909 through 1938. Examining the festival allows us to consider how new cultural meanings were transmitted to the event. We will follow the different versions of this craft festival, beginning in this chapter with the festival of 1909, which inaugurated the election of a woman worker as "queen" for a day. In subsequent chapters I will show how the festival was transformed in different political contexts, as it incorporated new cultural elements with the old. This craft festival stands as a privileged moment for exploring the manner in which the experience of work and gender were continually reinterpreted and reconstructed.

GENDERED WORK

Chapter 2 described the world of factory work in 1900 and traced the increasingly complex process by which knitted goods were produced. Not just knitted fabric, but also socks, stockings, underwear, and garments of cotton, silk, and wool, were produced by specialized machines and skilled labor. One

4. Vallerant 1982, 226.
5. Scott 1988, "'L'Ouvrière!'" 139–63.

way to visualize this process, and the hierarchy of *métiers* (occupations) in-volved, is to analyze the representation of the trade on a commemorative post-card of the 1909 festival parade (Fig. 5). Mounted on a float were the various skilled *métiers* of the trade. The *bonnetier* (knitter) is shown at the top, work-ing on a hand-knitting frame similar to the one invented in Britain by William Lee in 1589; just below, a second knitter operates a circular knitting frame that was invented and perfected by Jean-Auguste Delarothière, an artisan mechanic from Troyes. These two male figures are surrounded by women employed in female occupations—spinners, winders, hand seamers, and menders—who are depicted with such various symbols of the trade as *bonnets* and stockings. In the lower right corner sits the young *rebrousseur* (male apprentice), whose task it was to transfer stockings from one frame to another on the knitting machine. The process of production formally depicted here is domestic man-ufacture, represented as a pyramid of gendered occupations, with the skilled male knitters at the top and center, surrounded by women auxiliaries finishing the knitted goods. Overall, the float depicts the trade as a visual unity.

A similar hierarchical representation of the trade is encoded in the names of the various *métiers*. Their nomenclature also reveals the gendered nature of textile work, since the French terms are either masculine or feminine. Tracing the history of such terms provides a sense of their social evolution over time. For example, the masculine term *bonnetier,* designating a knitter working on a mechanical frame, originated in the seventeenth century.[6] These framework knitters must be distinguished from the *bonnetiers au tricot à l'aiguille* (hand knitters), whose corporation existed before the invention of the knitting frame in 1589. Thus from the moment of its invention, the knitting frame was con-ceived as a gendered tool, reserved exclusively for men. Skill, in fact, was his-torically significant as a marker of both gender and work identity. Women, in contrast to men, were ostensibly excluded from the techniques and *savoir-faire* of the most important tool of the trade, a tool that Diderot appraised in the eighteenth century as "one of the most complicated and the most important that we possess." In fact, he devoted many pages to describing the complexities of the knitting frame in the *Encyclopédie*.[7] While women were not historically associated with the knitting frame, the masculine term *bonnetier* in French did

6. The authoritative source is Franklin 1906, 69–70.

7. Denis Diderot and d'Alambert, *L'encyclopédie, ou Dictionnaire raisonné des sciences, des arts et des métiers,* 17 vols. (Paris, 1751–72). We also owe to Diderot the traditional image of the sex-ual division of labor under the ancien régime: the man seated at the knitting frame, his wife working on the spinning wheel, representing a self-sufficient household. See Chapter 2.

Figure 5   Commemorative postcard from the first Fête de la Bonneterie in 1909 that depicts a float from the festival parade, representing the different occupations in the trade. Author's personal collection.

have a feminine counterpart, *bonnetière,* recognized by the Troyes industrial community. Its usage dated from the factory period of industrialization and conveyed the notion of a female independent wage earner in the Troyes mills. It connoted complementarity in the gender division of labor, similar to that employed in many French trades. One can find many examples on the *livret ouvrier* (work passports) and even in the nominative lists of the nineteenth-century census.

However, in the historical process of engendering skill, this construction of difference gradually stigmatized women hosiery workers. By 1939, social connotations of these terms had changed: *bonnetier* still referred to a skilled male knitter, but *bonnetière* had become an increasingly disparaging term for the local factory girl, tarnished by vulgarity and by her association with men in the workplace.[8] According to a recent linguistic study of the vocabulary used

8. The term *bonnetière* was also narrowly used to designate women workers who operated a small circular knitting frame, a practice not widespread in the Troyes mills.

in the knitted goods industry, the term was "little used, [was] often confusing and is only understood in reference to the masculine term '*bonnetier*,' more evocative and prestigious." Remarked an official involved in the local professional training center: "In the street, *bonnetière* is considered pejorative."[9] Several of the retired women millworkers I interviewed who had been operatives during the 1920s and 1930s were conscious of this devalorized image of their occupations over time. Yet they maintained a stubborn pride in their *métier,* an attitude that contradicted their humble station in the mill and the de facto devalorization of their tasks.[10] This insistence on a positive identity with the trade reveals the problem of defining women's skills in relation to a normative male model and highlights the fact that once an occupation was feminized, it took on the subordinate status of the women who practice it.[11] The changing representation of the bonnetière from the turn of the century on was just one way in which the townspeople of Troyes constructed the social image of the local mill girl. In fact, not one, but several, models of the mill girl circulated in the community.

Gender Segregation in the Workplace

Clearly, then, men's work and women's work in the hosiery industry were constructed very differently both socially and technically. Ultimately, such gender distinctions would act to circumscribe women's work and establish boundaries. The principal and most obvious way in which boundaries were marked was through the spatial segregation of women and men within the mills.

The knitting-machine workshop represented a world of men: knitters, rebrousseurs, *commis-bonnetiers,* and mechanics worked together on the machines in an atmosphere of noise, grease, and dirt. Jacques Valdour, a social reformer and medical doctor, left an account of mill life in Troyes in the late 1920s

9. Perdriset 1980, 74. This same connotation was reiterated in a local journal: "The bonnetier was a highly skilled worker, proud of his work and well paid. Women were, at best, knitters. To say, 'she's a bonnetière' took on a derogatory meaning for a long time in that it relegated the woman to the level of women of doubtful company" (*Folklore de Champagne,* no. 92 [April 1985]: 15).

10. One retired bobbin winder responded to my question about the pejorative sense of the term *bonnetière* with these words: "No, at the time I worked, well, I was a bonnetière, men were bonnetiers and the women were bonnetières . . . no, seamers, menders, we were all considered bonnetières. Even when I was married, it was marked, 'occupation: bonnetière'" (testimony of Mme Fournet, interview, 1986).

11. See Phillips and Taylor 1980; Chenut 1996b.

based on participant observations.[12] Unlike the social investigators of the nineteenth century, Valdour became a silent observer of working-class life by hiring on as an ordinary laborer in factories. He openly acknowledged that his own subjectivity constituted part of his critical observations. Writing during a period of deep ideological division, he made no attempt to hide his conservative Catholic beliefs and anticommunist political agenda. Valdour was hired in August 1930 as a laborer in a Troyes hosiery mill that employed some three hundred men and women workers. He left the following description of the male world of the knitting workshop:

> My job is to clean one of the workshops with another day laborer, a sixty-year-old former knitter who has been forced to leave his machine due to a work accident. Two big contiguous workshops, well lighted, maintained at a high temperature and humidity necessary for the yarn to remain flexible. Two long rows of knitting machines fill the two rooms. A knitter, assisted by a rebrousseur, an adolescent or young man, operates the machine, an extremely complex one, six or seven meters long, that costs up to one hundred thousand francs and knits a dozen stockings at a time.[13]

The strict sexual segregation that we find depicted in period photographs is here confirmed. Valdour also insisted on the particular sociability of the male workshop, based largely on the complicity of "vulgar" language and the ample use of profanity.

Women workers were carefully segregated in large, open-space workshops, in a separate world supervised by *contremaîtresses* (forewomen). Grouped according to their place in the work process, women operated different types of sewing machines for finishing cut-and-sew garments. Few photographs of such women's workshops for this period seem to have survived. But oral testimony from women operatives active in the 1920s stressed the importance for them of a particular form of sociability. Management in several mills tolerated their right to sing as they worked, recognizing the positive effect such

12. Jacques Valdour (1934) was the pseudonym of Dr. Louis Martin (1872–1938). He wrote a series of some sixteen works, mostly accounts of his factory observations, but also an explanation of his method (Valdour 1924). I am grateful to Georges Ribeill for bringing Valdour and his text to my attention.
13. Valdour 1934, 171–72.

collective habits could have on their productivity. However, such tolerance was not practiced in all the mills. Suzanne Gallois recounted that when she was newly hired in a small mill workshop, her co-workers recognized her and greeted her by singing the "Internationale," but the occurrence of such political songs was most certainly a rare event.[14]

This form of sociability practiced in women's workspaces escaped the attention of Jacques Valdour. His appreciations of women workers' behavior were focused on their interactions with men. According to Valdour, the fact that women bonnetières were accustomed to mixing with men made them very flirtatious in their gestures, gaze and words of address. In his opinion, the factory was a place of corruption for women, and only a very few could remain "honest." Nevertheless, his observations on the ways in which women workers occupied their work space remain insightful:

> Many women have a little mirror near them into which they glance from time to time, examining their teeth, their eyes, their waved hair, their complexion. These glances to check their appearance are repeated a quarter of an hour later. Sometimes, one of them has brought in a few flowers and placed them in a glass filled with water. In the afternoon, they snack on bread and chocolate, or fruit, without stopping their work. . . . With their heads bent over their work, they still have an eye on every corner of the workshop, on their co-workers, on the comings and goings of service personnel, on the two male laborers assigned to their workshop, on the flowers or candy belonging to other women workers, the clothing of a fellow worker. Nothing escapes their gaze.[15]

Valdour's presentation of women workers as self-conscious, even narcissistic, in front of their mirrors contrasts sharply with the image of sociability so dominant in women worker's oral testimony of their mill experience.

14. See testimony from Mme Aubron, interview, 1982, and Suzanne Gallois's testimony. In mill workshops that I visited in 1996, young women seamers were seated in single rows so that they could not communicate with their neighbor in front of them. Many wore headsets and were listening to tapes.

15. Valdour 1934, 186.

Gender and Skill

Historically, skill (*métier*) was an important component of worker identity, and it was recognized almost exclusively as a male attribute or "property."[16] Labor historians still debate the degree to which skilled workers in France became "proletarianized" during the second half of the nineteenth century and, in the process of becoming wage earners, lost control over their craft status and skills. In the search for explanations of when and how deskilling happened, the general assumption has been that skill is gendered male or, at best, is gender neutral.[17]

Feminist historians have used a different approach by seeking to explain the sexual segregation of women's work and its consequences (including unskilled labeling, low wages, lack of mobility, and devaluations) in other than purely economic terms. They have attempted to demonstrate that Marxist categories of economic analysis have been, as Heidi Hartmann has stressed, gender blind.[18] In seeking to explain the nonobjective and noneconomic nature of such workplace discrimination, Anne Phillips and Barbara Taylor argue that the construction of skill is a key category in the meaning of work: "Skill definitions are saturated with sexual bias. The work of women is often deemed inferior simply because it is women who do it. Women workers carry into the workplace their status as subordinate individuals, and their status comes to define the value of the work they do. Far from being an objective economic fact, skill is often an ideological category imposed on certain types of work by virtue of the sex and power of the workers who perform it." These authors point to the arbitrary way that women's subordinate position in society has been used to explain women's unskilled label and low wages.[19] Several

16. See Rule 1987. Rule is attentive to the exclusion of women from the category of skilled labor.

17. There is an enormous literature on this subject. Yves Lequin (1992) argues that workers' concern for the dilution and loss of their skills appeared with the first signs of Taylorism, which he dates from the 1880s. Studies of skilled artisans stress the relation between the increased division of labor, changing working conditions, and the growth of class consciousness. Two different positions are represented by Johnson (1979) and Cottereau (1980). Some historians have examined the patterns of resistance to industrial capitalism in various industries; see M. Perrot 1974 and Scott 1974. Still others assume worker resistance to industrial discipline to be the norm and seek to understand the meanings of a whole range of grievances and conflicts, from informal to the more formal collective action of strikes. This is particularly the approach of Cottereau (see Cottereau 1986).

18. Hartmann 1976.

19. Phillips and Taylor 1980, 79–88.

historians develop this analysis further by demonstrating how gender distinctions were constitutive of job composition and workplace organization. For Sonya Rose, for example, such distinctions created antagonism within the working class and operated as a capitalist strategy to divide and control workers' loyalties.[20] Joy Parr, in her comparative study of the knitting industry in Canada and England, examines the gender construction of skill in relation to many variables. She notes that the sex labeling of specific tasks is contingent, and she points to knitting as a prime example of contested gender terrain: "In the midlands and in Ontario, knitting was made men's or women's work through a complex interaction which combined tradition from the workshop and the early factory with social prescription about who was entitled to work for wages at all and characteristics of the local labor market and labor organization and of both the product market and the prevailing technology."[21]

In the French hosiery industry, the male model of *métier* predominated as a definition of technical aptitude, mastery, and craft.[22] The meanings attributed to the term were shaped by changing historical conditions in the trade, so that the introduction of new technology gave employers an opportunity to erode the craft knowledge and ability that workers had struggled to maintain in their jobs, the same skills that union leaders defended as training and experience. Wage demands, in fact, often masked contested meanings of skill.

Women's skills in the Troyes mills became redefined in a specific industrial and historical context: after 1900, knitting frames operated by men and geared to mass production created more task-specific jobs for women, as they became loopers, seamers, quality-control workers, and finishers. Certain female occupations became categorized according to machine-specific skills, as we shall see. The fact of operating a specialized machine did not necessarily confer a skill label, but mechanization of special female tasks did allow women to master new skills and to perform as machine operatives just as men did. In this sense, jobs that were identified with operating a machine conferred status. Between 1880 and 1914, in the early phase of mechanization, women's occupations were named according to their place in the production process and to technical evolution in the industry. The feminization of the workforce in

20. Rose 1992, esp. introduction and chap. 2; 1987. Rose uses the English hosiery industry to demonstrate how men and women often competed for jobs.

21. Parr 1990, 60; 1988.

22. For a longer development of this issue, see Chenut 1996b.

Troyes was linked to the increased specialization and professionalization of women hosiery workers. They were no longer auxiliaries or contingent workers. Their skills in this sense were in demand, needed to execute the increasingly fragmented tasks of sewing and finishing knitted clothing.

But the technical mastery of a machine was not the only measure of skill. Women workers were also recognized as having different skills from those of men. This gender difference was sometimes valorized as "natural feminine aptitudes" or was sometimes diluted to a mere symbolic distinction, but it was always perceived as constituting a different but complementary work identity for women.[23] At one end of the social scale were semiskilled, physically demanding jobs, in which women were in close proximity to men. At the other end was the only women's occupation requiring hand skills and artistry, the mender, closely identified with a feminine ideal and highly prized by mill-owners as the most skilled of women's hosiery jobs.

The Work Process: From Bobbin Winding to Machine Knitting

In order to explore workers' lives in Troyes, it is important to follow the different stages of textile production, making use where possible of the testimony of men and women workers themselves. The first step in the work process was the preparation of the yarn. The bobbin winder (*bobineuse*), who was always a woman, worked in tandem with the knitter and provided him with the raw material—the spun yarn—for his machine. She worked on a *bobinoir* to rewind yarn from the spinning mill. The regularity of the knitting process depended on the quality of the yarn on the bobbins. However, the job was badly paid, being almost exclusively calculated on the weight of the bobbins wound. One of the difficulties bobbin winders faced was dealing with certain raw materials that were fragile or became entangled once they had been dyed and that required special preparation by hand before being wound. Such time-consuming work was often not taken into account in the pay the women received. The job also required controlling the way the bobbins were wound and intervening to tie broken threads, using the weaver's knot, a special operation that required dexterity and coordination if it were to be executed rapidly.

Much of the oral testimony about this job stressed its hard physical labor: the bobineuse worked in a standing position, her arms and legs in constant

23. Scott 1988, "Work Identities," 107.

motion. The technology, as it evolved, created even more problems by imposing a faster work pace. One bobineuse remarked that the only technical innovation that marked her working life was the introduction of the "American
winder" at the end of the 1930s. It was such a high-performance winder that
it produced in one day what used to take one week to turn out. But in human
terms, the new winder forced her to move much further at an accelerated pace:

> To keep up with the machine we walked more than twenty-five kilo-
> meters in a day. . . . The work wasn't more difficult, but it was ex-
> hausting because the more we did, the more spindles they gave us to
> do, the more work there was to be done. . . . We began with fifteen
> spindles, afterward they gave us twenty, then twenty-five, etc. Well,
> there comes a moment when—you know a woman is not a machine—
> you can't follow. I stopped working when bobbin winding started to
> decline, and I was working on a winder with thirty spindles.[24]

This image of a "woman-machine" recurred in the scientific management
studies carried out at the end of the 1930s concerning job composition for
bobbin winding. Time and motion study experts were interested in analyzing
the different movements required by this job, just as mill management envisaged establishing production norms.[25]

The testimony also often stresses the striking discrepancy between the
bobbin winders' own conception of their *métier,* and the devalorized social
image of the job. One bobineuse explained the situation in these terms:

> When people talk about a bobineuse, they talk about a worthless
> woman, on a level with a prostitute, because, you see . . . the work
> was extremely hard. Then you had to work in the mill at temperatures
> of thirty and thirty-five degrees [Celsius], so that most of the time a
> woman worker would wear just a little blouse over her underwear,
> something that at that time was considered immodest. . . . So when

---

24. Testimony from Mme Chailloux, interview, 1983.
25. The first attempts at rationalizing bobbin winding in the Troyes mills date from the
late 1930s. An apprenticeship manual for the textile industry published in 1945 included a professional time and motion study sheet/checklist, detailing the operative's requisite physical,
intellectual, and moral qualities, as well as a deconstruction of the movements to be timed by
stopwatch (Labriffe 1945).

you were called a "bobineuse," you were being described as a woman worker of the lowest category in the knitted goods industry.[26]

Indeed, historically, any female job in a mill involving contact with men connoted promiscuity and moral weakness on the part of the woman worker. For nineteenth-century male social reformers, the exposed female body provoked reactions of immodesty that shocked their bourgeois sensibilities and made such exposure socially unacceptable. Clearly, such attitudes persisted into the twentieth century.

The *salle de bobinage* was separate from the male knitters' workshop and, rather like the female arena of the public street market, was considered a space reserved for women. A foreman described the room in these terms: "[I]t was a bit as if you were in the marketplace, listening to vulgar remarks and all that loose language."[27] Jacques Valdour's observations give a similar impression. This denigration of the bobineuse as "vulgar" might be explained in part by bobbin winders' status as the lowest-paid women workers in the industry. But the fact that these same women frequently displayed very combative behavior in collective action suggests another explanation for the devalorization of their occupation. Bobineuses often went out on strike in conjunction with the knitters, whose work was linked to theirs in the production process. They were also more often unionized than menders, for example. It could be argued that moral suspicion and charges of vulgarity were more likely to be directed at such women as bobbin winders, who voiced work demands and protested in the street.[28]

Unlike bobbin winding, the operation of the knitting machines themselves had long been a masculine preserve. The technical skills most prized for their prestige and productivity were those that had developed out of the craft tradition. The Cotton patent knitter or (bonnetier Cotton) operated a machine, described as a technical marvel, that revolutionized knitted goods production over a period of sixty years.[29] The originality of this flatbed machine consisted in a series of multiple heads that could knit several fully fashioned articles simultaneously, resulting in the increased production of quality goods.

26. Testimony from Mme Laborie, interview, 1987.
27. Testimony from M. Desvignes, interview, 1985.
28. Improved technology at the spinning mill has since made this women's occupation redundant. Finely spun bobbins are now delivered ready for knitting.
29. Poisat 1982b, 111. Building on the work of French sociologist Michel Freyssenet, Poisat analyzed the process of skilling and deskilling in the industry since World War II.

Subsequent improvements to the Cotton patent knitting machine diversified production. As the technology evolved, the worker had to specialize in the operation of one type of machine. When the Cotton knitter was first introduced, the work required some physical strength in order to engage the gears of the machine between operations. These operations were rapidly automated, and the operation of the machine then became principally a job of overseeing, making adjustments, fixing breakdowns, and most commonly, replacing broken needles. The worker could sit down on the job while waiting for the machine to stop automatically between operations. "We usually watched the machine operate by itself," explained a former machine operator.[30] The pace of the knitter's job increased notably when management made knitters responsible for overseeing two machines, and then introduced a much longer flatbed knitter with twenty-four heads. Nevertheless, the knitter had the possibility of intervening in the knitting process, and he maintained his technical know-how. A mill foreman explained the meaning of the knitter's continued autonomy, stressing the worker's ability to adjust the machine: "He could fix small breakdowns, changing a broken needle, for example. This ability to intervene meant that he loved his work. When there is no longer any possibility for intervening in the work process, there is no reason to love one's work."[31] The knitter's job required a long period of training, involving an institutional apprenticeship with its rites of passage up the occupational ladder. All these elements strengthened the Cotton patent knitter's status within the mill workshop. It was an occupation that evolved, that became reskilled over a period of some sixty years, and that remained identified with the modern hosiery mill and mass-production technology.[32]

From the beginnings of the factory system, the young male rebrousseur was an essential link in the knitting process. Fully fashioned stockings were knit on the Cotton patent knitter in two stages, requiring the transfer of the article from one machine to another, to turn the heel, for example. This was the job of the rebrousseur, whose work was subcontracted by the bonnetier, with whom he worked in tandem. It was considered a training position for adolescents, and as such was poorly paid piecework. It took many years before technological advances made this occupation redundant, when finally a knitting

30. Testimony from M. Laborie, interview, 1987.
31. Testimony from M. Desvignes, interview, 1985.
32. Today's new machinery now has a digital operating system that has all but eliminated the need for human intervention. For the effects of this new development, see Poisat 1982b, 448 ff.

machine could produce the entire fully fashioned stocking on a single machine. In the Troyes textile culture of production, the rebrousseur was nicknamed *le caffard* (cockroach), because the work sometimes involved crawling underneath the machines. Rebrousseurs were also represented in the local culture as young rebels and protesters—it was their initial walkout that sparked the great strike of 1900. In fact, the emblematic figure of the "caffard" was to Troyes what the young revolutionary "Gavroche" was to Paris, that is, a symbol of rebellion. Etienne Pédron composed a song in honor of these apprentices, celebrating their carrying the red flag in the first May Day celebration of 1890. The song depicted in local workshop slang their cocky, rebellious, ebullient behavior; rough and ready, they were ripe for battles in the street. It also celebrated their revolutionary spirit by touching on a number of socialist themes, among these proletarian unity and the end of wage slavery.[33]

Men also oversaw small circular knitters of different gauges and diameters that were reputedly simpler to operate. These machines produced knitted fabric or ordinary tube socks and stockings. In other countries, the job was, in fact, a mixed-gender occupation. But in the Troyes mills, the initial experience of using women to operate the machines—during World War I—was not conclusive.[34] Few women workers in the Troyes mills seemed attracted to this occupation, possibly because they could not emulate male knitters, who were allowed to fix and adjust their machines. Such tasks were reserved for workshop foremen or mechanics, since women were assumed to have neither the tools nor the training to make even simple repairs.[35]

The Finishing Process

The finishing process in the knitting industry—seaming, looping, mending, and quality control, all labor-intensive subdivided tasks—were overwhelmingly the province of women. The skills required were good eyesight, good taste, the dexterity needed to work with the elasticity of knitted fabric, and knowledge of the knitting process. As we shall see, millowners prized one group of female workers above all others: skilled menders (*raccoutreuses*), trained in the

33. See Pédron 1906, 45–47; Reddy 1986, 364–94. Reddy argues that workers suffering during the early period of industrialization used songs laced with farce and irony to transcend the poverty and moral suffering that was their lot. See also Marty 1982.
34. For a comparative perspective based on the Canadian hosiery industry, see Parr 1990.
35. Testimony of M. Desvignes, interview, 1985.

fine needlework skills of repairing flawed or damaged goods. When one considers that such goods included the expensive luxury silk stockings of the Belle Epoque, it is easy to understand how manufacturers ranked this work as highly profitable. The final operations, from matching pairs to packaging, were also mainly executed by women.

The fact that seaming and garment making were only partially mechanized led to the creation of many specialized tasks. Sewing was, in fact, rationalized into piecework in the mid-nineteenth century, before becoming mechanized.[36] Each technical innovation in the finishing process created a new division of labor. Knitted garments were put together along an assembly line made up of women operating machines that were specialized in one operation, such as hemming or button sewing. Manual tasks were assigned to women who became known as "petites mains." It could be argued that because of the very abundance of women workers trained for this type of garment work, mill-owners were never sufficiently encouraged to search for technical solutions that would have mechanized such manual tasks. Much of the garment industry today relies on hand, as well as machine, sewing skills, carried out by women workers.

Le remmaillage (looping) was akin to seaming on a sewing machine, and for that reason it was assigned to women at the outset. The work done by a *remmailleuse* (looper) consisted of joining two edges, stitch by stitch, onto *poinçons* (hooks) and sewing them together. In the nineteenth century this work was done by hand with a crochet hook. It became mechanized around 1880, when the sewing machine was adapted to the seaming of knitted goods. The introduction of a specialized machine allowed women to master new technical skills. Apprenticeship on this specialized machine took place in the factory, but a significant number of women loopers were trained in the family workshop or by their mothers at home. One obvious advantage of this small seamer was its compact size and shape, allowing it to fit easily into a domestic environment. As we have seen, many loopers were outworkers, combining child care with industrial work. Millowners organized the delivery of dozens of socks and stockings, to be sewn to outworkers in town in exchange for finished work. Mme Fournet, whose sister trained her as a looper on the family workshop machine, began her professional life as a looper in her father's workshop. In 1923, she entered the mill to do the same sort of work and

36. For the history of sewing and women's work in the garment industry, see Coffin 1996b, Green 1997.

remained until the birth of her first child. Subsequently, she worked at home, combining paid work and child care for her four children. Finally, in 1945, she returned to the mill. Work patterns of this kind were typical for many women workers in Troyes.[37]

While the looper's machine-operative skills were recognized, there were hidden difficulties to the job that were less obvious. The manual dexterity and good eyesight needed to produce a flat, invisible stocking seam that could stretch around the heel, for example, made the looper's job a delicate one. The looper worked with her eyes riveted on the tiny metal *poinçons,* which reflected the light; working with black thread on fine knitted goods diminished her productivity; and problems with the tension of her precision machine could prevent her from making her quota for the day. In principle, loopers were not supposed to adjust their own machines, since management considered the seamer a high-precision machine. Loopers were paid by the piece, and they had to pace themselves to make a living. By the 1930s, millowners gradually forced the pace; and after 1945, a looper's productivity was controlled by a stopwatch. She had no career ladder to climb, no technical improvements to master, only an accelerating productivity norm to meet.

Raccoutrage (mending) is a technique specific to the knitted goods industry. It involved fine, delicate work, consisting of repairing the slightest defect in stockings or knitted fabric. Such quality-control work required good eyesight, dexterity, good taste, and extreme patience, for the slightest flaw spread to the entire fabric. Each slipped stitch had to be reworked by hand. One of the millowners described the skills he thought the job entailed: "[W]ork executed by hand by trained specialists. Delicate work, since the defects when repaired should appear invisible. The women menders use only the very simplest of tools—needles and bodkins. In order to succeed, you need consummate skill."[38] Mending was highly prized by hosiery manufacturers because it allowed them to preserve a quality product, particularly if this product was knit in an expensive fiber such as silk. According to a former mender, women workers in this *métier* were considered "show-offs," doubtless because they were at the top of the women's occupational skill ladder.

Consequently, menders commanded good wages. A former mender remembered having brought home 320 francs for a two-week period in 1925, high

37. Testimony from Mme Fournet, interview, 1986.
38. M. Hamant, "Les diverses opérations de fabrication et le matériel de finissage et d'apprêt," Conférence faite à la Chambre de commerce de Troyes, April 10, 1944, p. 16.

wages at the time—and an amount that aroused her mother's suspicion that she was cheating on the job.[39] Jacques Valdour noted their earnings at twenty-five francs a day, or three hundred francs for two weeks, in 1930, calculated on a base salary and a productivity bonus. However, the aptitudes prized in this work—perfectionism and the ability to bring out the finished quality of the article—tended to militate against production norms. To take into account the difficulty of their work, they were often paid by the hour, rather than by the piece.

Menders definitely had a sense of their *métier* and possessed recognizable skills, technical mastery, the ethic of turning out finely finished work, and the capacity to intervene in a positive way to make a quality product. The utility of the menders' work was combined with the pleasure of taste and fashion: "[W]e had the impression of saving the article we were working on," related one woman mender from the 1930s.[40] In the past she had worked on silk stockings, quality raw material that was fine and supple to the touch. Her work followed fashion changes: she made *grisottes,* embroidered patterns running up the ankle of silk stockings in the 1920s. The introduction of synthetic fibers such as nylon, used in tights, broke with this tradition of quality production.

No doubt mending was also prized because it entailed a relatively long on-the-job apprenticeship and required practical experience with knitted fabric, which during the interwar period could take sixteen to eighteen months in the mill workshop. Apprentices had to learn to identify flaws in the finished knitted product, then reconstruct the stitches in such as way as to render the repair invisible. Rozsika Parker has remarked that "the art of embroidery has been the means of educating women into the feminine ideal, and of proving that they have attained it."[41] The skilled menders in the Troyes mills certainly embodied such a feminine ideal.

Troyes millowners held this *métier* in such great esteem that they organized a skill competition in 1930 to reward their best women menders. It was an exceptional event, organized at the initiative of the local deputy and millowner Léon Boisseau. The competition was designed to test technical, manual, and artistic skills in both male and female occupations: for men, the test combined pattern making, laymaking, and cutting garment pieces from knitted fabric; for women, mending with consummate taste specific flaws in the pattern of

39. Testimony from Mme Aubron, interview, 1982.
40. Testimony from Mme Binet, interview, 1983.
41. Parker 1984, 1.

finely knit silk fabric and creating an openwork design. Both tests were to be executed in the best time. The all-male jury consisted of millowners, overseers, and workers. The women laureates received prizes of fifteen hundred francs (a sum representing five times their biweekly pay at that time), and the remaining women competitors were each awarded a pair of silk stockings. Newspaper accounts centered almost exclusively on the extraordinary artistry of the menders, whose openwork designs were comparable to those of the best lace makers.[42] The commentary tells us more about gender distinctions than about the women who performed the work: "Our women workers are really little fairies . . . daughters of Penelope with prodigiously nimble fingers," the local newspaper boasted.[43] When the vocabulary of skill is applied to women's work, it evokes mythical images of patience, perseverance, and silent craft. After millowners lavished praise and recognition on the two prizewinners, both women returned to the mill, requested promotion, and were refused.[44]

Technical progress in the knitted goods industry after 1945 considerably changed the status of menders in the mills. The invention of a new tool to pick up slipped stitches partially mechanized the repair process. And finally, the introduction of cheap, resistant synthetic fibers in the production of stockings made mending less important. Nylon stockings with snags or defects were discarded, not repaired. Thus the decline in the production of luxury goods, changing fashions, the introduction of modern synthetic fibers, and new norms of productivity all led to the progressive compression of work in this very skilled women's occupation.

APPRENTICESHIP IN THE TRADE

The transmission of a textile culture of production from one generation to the next provided an important element of social cohesion in Troyes. In fact, both

42. The comparison was drawn by the commentator in the *Tribune de l'Aube,* which co-sponsored the competition. See *L'annuaire de la Tribune de l'Aube* for details of the competition; see also Chenut 1996b.

43. *Tribune de l'Aube,* June 28, 1930.

44. In oral-history interviews with both women, I learned how difficult it was to obtain promotions in this highly skilled profession. After many years of waiting, one mender was finally moved to a training position in 1947 where she was to instruct apprentices in her trade (testimony from Mme Aubron, interview, 1982, and Mme Binet, interview, 1983).

millowners and millworkers had a great deal at stake in terms of family fortunes and work identity in the legacy of the knitted goods industry. In this section we will look more closely at the technical training and apprenticeship in the trade that was inherited from the artisan workshop and family networks.

Beginning in the 1880s training in the hosiery industry followed two separate channels. Formal training of foremen and technicians in the industry took place for the most part at a professional school founded by the millowners in 1888, the Ecole Française de Bonneterie. Informal training in the trade was provided by emulation and example from family members, or on the job with experienced workers in the mills. Obviously the second route, informal and family apprenticeship, has left little written record for historians to evaluate. We have only the experienced hand, or what one French worker called *la mémoire de la main*.[45] From a gender perspective, women's technical knowledge and skills were often transmitted in this way. Consequently women workers suffered from lack of recognition of their skills, often because what was prized was the product of institutionalized knowledge, and only men benefited from institutionalized apprenticeship and training.

Institutionalized Training: The Ecole Française de Bonneterie

Troyes entrepreneurs combined foresight and personal interest in establishing the Ecole française de bonneterie in 1888. Many of them had attended engineering schools or the regional *école des arts et métiers,* and this experience led them to seek state and municipal aid for their project. Emmanuel Buxtorf, a mechanical engineer and inventor of several auxiliary machines in the industry, became the school's first director. The purpose was to train young men to become captains of their industry, with a training modeled in part on that of the army.[46] Millowners were committed to a two-to-three-year general and technical education program to train a small male elite for their immediate needs in the mills. Two-thirds of the some twelve students enrolled each year had scholarships, but the millowners maintained absolute control over admissions. Most important, selective training of this type also allowed employers greater control over recruitment in the mills.

45. This phrase comes from a watchmaker and was quoted by François Caron during a French thesis defense in June 1986.

46. Emmanuel Buxtorf as director expressed their aim in these terms: "[F]oremen are to industry as noncommissioned officers are to the army" (AMT 1R 257).

When the school's directors requested an annual subsidy from the municipal council in 1892 to ensure scholarships, the debate revealed the professional stakes for the working class. M. Douine, the director of a large spinning mill and an elected municipal counselor, contended that the school would render a service to the working class and fulfill a need:

> [it would provide] methodical and systematic training of production workers or foremen, for imagine how this training now takes place. Most of the young people now leave primary school and enter the mills directly, learning the trade by themselves or with the help of willing fellow workers; they begin at the lowest jobs, slowly and painfully attaining the better-paid positions, more through their intelligence, their conduct, and their morality than by way of their technical knowledge. They do not posses the bases of real industrial knowledge about the workings of machine parts, the cause and consequence of certain operations, knowledge that allows a worker to acquire personal competence, proper skills, to operate to his advantage the machine assigned to him in the best conditions for production.[47]

The industrial norms promoted by M. Douine concerned only a small male elite that was to be trained for the explicit needs of the local knitted goods industry. These norms of technical knowledge were to be sanctioned by a diploma.

What was at stake was the kind of professional *savoir-faire* and autonomy that artisan knitters had sought to protect against the inroads of industrial capitalism. Millowners passed over in silence the technical aptitude and competence required by textile operatives that was in the family workshop. For their part, workers perceived the school as an attempt by manufacturers to train their own sons in the specialized and technical knowledge of the trade, thereby dividing the workforce even further into supervisors, technicians, and manual operatives. One worker from Troyes who was a delegate to the Paris World's Fair of 1889 had argued in favor of training that would transmit an integral vision of the trade, together with a general education, free and guaranteed by the state.[48]

47. Excerpt from the register of deliberations of the Troyes Municipal Council, September 24, 1892, AMT 1R 257.
48. Report by Louis Foin, AMT 2F 46/B.

The norms established by millowners for the administration of their private professional school in Troyes were contested by the socialist municipal counselors in 1895, but the town's subsidy was never seriously called into question. Rather, local elected officials sought to strengthen the technical education programs of the public schools, offered in the *lycées techniques d'état,* and called upon individual public-spirited entrepreneurs to make inspection missions and recommendations. The Ecole française de bonneterie maintained its autonomy as an industrial training institution, gradually evolving to meet the research and development interests of the industry after World War II. Thus employers' monopoly over high-level technical training also represented a particular form of paternalism, devoted to the promotion of technical knowledge that kept the local industry alive and committed to technological progress.[49]

Informal Apprenticeship

Informal and family apprenticeship provided most production workers entry into the mills. Like many nineteenth-century trades, the Troyes knitting industry was grounded in endogamous intermarriage, which ensured the continuity of work skills and *savoir-faire* from one generation to the next. Children were initiated into the proper skills and work processes of the trade in the family workshop. As head of household, the father trained the members of his own family. But some mothers who worked as outworkers, seaming socks and stockings at home, also trained their children to help finish certain manual tasks. Once young workers entered the mills, most were further trained on the job to acquire the factory experience that qualified workers of both sexes in the eyes of the foreman. Family networks served to facilitate access to this type of employment as early as age thirteen (the legal school-leaving age).

In this two-stage learning process, the family workshop experience played a primal role for many young workers in Troyes. This world of the family workshop has been documented and preserved thanks to a rich series of turn-of-the-century photo postcards presenting interior scenes of families at work. In Figure 6, family members are shown standing next to their machines. At a glance we can inventory the machines and the work process. The workshop is clean and orderly, the tools are laid out on display, the family dressed up

49. See AMT 1R 257 and Bernard Savoie, "L'Ecole française de bonneterie" in *Centenaire de l'Enseignement Technique,* Histoire et actualité dans le Département de l'Aube 1745–1988 (Troyes: Centre Départemental de Documentation Pédagogique, 1988).

in Sunday clothes for the benefit of the photographer. This is no sweatshop, rather an orderly and respectable world of productive work. Other photographs of family workshops confirm the separation of male and female occupations, represented by segregated work spaces and gender-specific machines. Women workers who relied primarily on this type of informal family training, combined with short on-the-job factory experience, suffered most from the lack of recognized apprenticeship.

A shortage of skilled labor in the knitted goods industry after World War I urgently raised the question of professional training for millworkers. Up until then, few measures had been taken to promote apprenticeship outside the mills. To be sure, several initiatives to promote general technical training were established between 1913 and 1922, including the opening of a commercial and industrial section in the principal lycée of Troyes and the creation by the town of a Chambre des métiers that offered professional training courses. A private Catholic school, l'Ecole St.-Joseph, opened a general technical apprenticeship center in 1921 for the sons of workers and employees, but enrollment remained relatively low in comparison with what was needed in the industry.[50]

While the informal outwork sector continued to thrive into the interwar period, apprenticeship for male occupations increasingly took place in the mills. In fact, technical progress gradually imposed this logic of mass production. Ultimately, the state stepped in to establish the norms that would give legal status to apprenticeship. The state school system was to coordinate the various forms of professional training and would administer examinations. These directives were embodied in the law of 1928 on apprenticeship. There was a price to pay, of course; testimony from workers confirmed that their families had to advance young people money for their apprenticeship, especially since no wages were earned during the training period.

The law of 1928 afforded some recognition of family apprenticeships, notably in cases in which children were employed in the family workshop. However, as apprenticeship now had both a legal and an institutional status, the family workshop could be considered inferior training by comparison with professional courses then offered. From the employers' viewpoint, the debate on this question was inconclusive, if we are to judge from an article that appeared in the leading trade journal, *La Maille Moderne,* in 1928. The author

50. François Velut, "De l'école d'apprentissage au LPETP Saint-Joseph de Troyes," in *Centenaire de l'enseignement technique,* Histoire et actualité dans le Département de l'Aube (Troyes: Centre Départemental de Documentation Pédagogique, 1988), 63–74.

recognized that technical schools tended to train foremen and managers, while production workers were what the industry really needed. If it were admitted that the two forms of instruction were complementary, a solution might be found by establishing "centers for family training that would have no pretension of being professional schools." The critical shortage of young production workers concerned the "natural" skills that one generation possessed and transmitted to the next: "the assimilation of a *métier,* the knowledge of raw materials, instilled into a child in a natural and progressive manner by the father represents a factor of economic wealth in our industry," the author argued.[51] Such recognition and praise for the role of the traditional artisan family, in relation to training and the diffusion of technical knowledge, appeared to address this crucial issue too late to prevent an exodus of young workers into the Parisian labor market.

No reference was made to training women workers in this debate. Women's occupations did not benefit from either institutional training or long apprenticeship in the mills. When women's work was first mechanized, on-the-job training directed by an experienced worker or forewoman provided the only formal training outside the family workshop. By the 1920s, women workers spent three to six months acquiring the skills and speed necessary to earn their living at piecework. This relatively short training period implied lower skill content and contrasted noticeably with the longer training required for men's work. The increasing subdivision of women's work into fragmented tasks diminished their opportunity to learn and improve their skills. The total absence of formal institutional training for the women's occupations in the hosiery industry disadvantaged women in relation to men. Formal training for young women was introduced only in 1937, when the lycée technique d'Etat founded a section of *ateliers-écoles* (workshops) for women in domestic science and infant care, together with introductory courses on knitting machines (*couseuses, remmailleuses*), raccoutrage, and sewing. After World War II, a formal professional training center for women was established and backed by the state. In this postwar period of economic reconstruction, the need for formal institutionalized training for a whole new generation of women workers in hosiery was finally recognized.

Interviews with men and women workers who had done their apprenticeship during the interwar period reveal striking differences in the skill ladder

51. *La Maille Moderne,* March 1928, 195.

and career patterns of this generation. The only common denominator in most of these personal accounts was the acknowledgment that the local industry provided *le métier obligé*, or practically the only professional trade in town.

Le Métier Obligé: Entering the Trade

Most parents who worked in the mills wanted to ensure their children a job by the time they reached the school-leaving age of thirteen. The choice of occupation was generally left to the young worker's own personal inclination. A former bobbin winder explained her choice in the following terms: "My father didn't want me to be a bobbin winder. He wanted me to be a raccoutreuse, and I just couldn't sit still at that age. I was a real live wire, so I managed to get the job I wanted, to become a bobbin winder."[52] She had a short apprenticeship on the job with three other apprentices, overseeing a bobinoir with some twenty spindles. Similar testimony came from Mme Laborie, a former bobbin winder who insisted on the fact that her apprenticeship had been both rapid and insignificant. Her sister, a bobbin winder then working at the Mauchauffée mill, both recruited and trained her, showing her what she needed to do as she worked alongside her. She learned everything she knew through working on the job. The rare firsthand accounts of apprenticeship by women textile workers all confirm this short period of on-the-job training under the guidance of more experienced women.[53]

But other women workers explained that their occupational choice came from emulation within their families. Mme Aubron, a raccoutreuse, wanted to follow her aunt's example: "I admired the work she did, and I told her that I would like to learn to be a raccoutreuse, so I spent the afternoons at her house and she showed me how. When I entered the Mauchauffée mill for my first job, I already knew how to retrieve slipped stitches. There I perfected this technique, and learned how to attach stitches, to do it right . . . ; then I learned how to make *grisottes* and other decorative designs. In fact, I had five days of apprenticeship in all."[54] This short apprenticeship was, in fact, exceptional. For this occupation the usual training period in the mill was

52. Testimony from Mme Fournet, interview, 1986.
53. Jeanne Bouvier's autobiography is one of the rare published nineteenth-century narratives. She started work at age eleven in a silk manufactory, learning from another woman worker how to unwind and rewind skeins of silk. For thirteen hours in the mill, she was paid fifty centimes a day in 1876 (Bouvier 1983, 56–57).
54. Mme Aubron, interview, 1982.

much longer, and the job required considerable practice with manipulating knitted fabric, with ripping out and reconstructing stitches. At the outset, Mme Aubron's capacities were recognized, and she was immediately hired as an apprentice raccoutreuse. In her case she had, in fact, considerable skill and talent, which she proved in 1930 by winning a skill competition in her occupation. But she had also apprenticed in her father's family workshop, working alongside five other children.

The needlework skills required for this occupation could also be learned through traditional apprenticeship to a seamstress. This was the path chosen by another mender, who also won an award in the skill competition of 1930. Mme Binet's mother placed her in an eighteen-month apprenticeship with a seamstress so that she would know how to "work with a needle." Then the daughter entered the Gillier mill, where she learned from an experienced woman mender for some sixteen months. During her apprenticeship she was paid by the hour, until she could work fast enough to earn piecework rates. Mme Binet chose her occupation based on her own taste for manual work. Working on a seamer as her mother had done never appealed to her at all.

The increased specialization of women's occupations and the progressive rationalization of tasks as they became mechanized favored an accelerated on-the-job apprenticeship. Women operatives learned directly on the machine under the guidance of an experienced worker or forewoman. In the case of garment making, women operatives assembled knitted fabric to stitch on sewing machines, which were similar to the ones used by their mothers at home. It could be argued that there was a transfer of skills, from operating the generic Singer sewing machine to working on the more specialized machines for stitching more supple knitted fabric. But Suzanne Gallois's experience as a *piqueuse* underscored the necessity of undertaking a rather long, specific apprenticeship, at her own expense, and continuing in it until she could meet production norms.[55] Judith Coffin cites Jeanne Bouvier's long struggle to acquire sewing skills that, she maintains, were not commonly learned at home.

55. Suzanne Gallois had been hired by the Singer sewing machine company in Troyes to do a training program designed to demonstrate its machine in a local salesroom. When this office closed, her mother, who worked as a *piqueuse* (seamer), obtained a mill apprenticeship for her daughter during which Suzanne had to pay to learn the necessary skills. Finally, one of the directors offered her a second apprenticeship as an "ourleuse" (involving more delicate work hemming knitted fabric), paid by the hour, until she could meet production norms. But her experience with Singer had taught her to adjust her machine, a skill that opened up the possibility for her to direct the work of other young women operatives. Testimony from Suzanne Gallois, interview, May 14, 1984.

Coffin argues that historians have wrongly sited the origins of such skills in the household, when in fact most women may have been trained in industrial waged-work settings.[56] The issue cannot be satisfactorily resolved, because most women's apprenticeship in sewing and needlework trades took place on the job, in workshops situated at the blurred boundaries of industrial home-work. The real issue is that such women's skills were undervalued.

Despite the diversity of personal itineraries in these apprenticeship narra-tives, all do have several themes in common: the preference for traditional women's work, the transmission of technical knowledge from one generation of women to the next during a relatively short on-the-job training period (from one to sixteen months), and the assumption by management that such brief training was sufficient. It was only with the introduction of Taylorization in the knitted goods industry at the end of World War II that professional apprenticeship training for women operatives was recognized as both desir-able and necessary.

By contrast with women's apprenticeships, those of male knitters and mechanics entailed much longer training periods. Before he could operate a knitting machine, a young man had to climb a prescribed skill ladder. He usually began as a rebrousseur, around the age of thirteen, a stage during which he learned how machines operated and how knitted fabric was made. When he was eighteen or twenty, the young man left the mill to fulfill his military service, another masculine rite of passage. Upon his return, he was given a knitting machine to operate as a "commis" (apprentice knitter). His apprenticeship lasted some three to six months, depending on the complexity and the gauge of the machine and his own aptitude for this type of work. He had to learn to adjust the machine, locate possible points of breakdown, and repair bent needles. It was a learning process by stages, spread out over a period of six years and geared to specialization on one type of machine.

Becoming a mechanic necessitated an even longer apprenticeship for acqui-sition of the requisite technical knowledge. M. Desvignes began at age eleven as an apprentice in a small firm in Troyes.[57] He remembered this first work experience with pleasure because, with a three-year contract, he had the luck of working with a mentor who offered him a substantial technical initiation into the world of machines with access to the mentor's personal library, and

56. Coffin 1996b, 138–39.
57. Testimony from M. Desvignes, interview, 1985.

who even enrolled him in evening courses in industrial drawing. At the end of his contract, his employer found him a job with the Lebocey knitting-machine-construction company, one of the leading manufacturers in Troyes. His job entailed a second apprenticeship with a skilled worker who taught him how to assemble machines. Little by little he climbed the skill ladder, and by the age of eighteen, he was repairing and adjusting machines in the region around Troyes. After seven years of technical training, he could consider himself skilled, even if his training had not been sanctioned by a diploma from the Ecole française de bonneterie.

This example is far from unusual. Many of the foremen and mechanics of this generation were trained in the technical culture of knitting machines in a similar way. Long-term intensive training of this kind, spent in the acquisition of technical knowledge from oral and written sources, provided such men with both professional and social recognition of their *métier*. When we examine the modes of transmission of this dominant male textile culture and compare them to the incomplete, discontinuous, and often unrecognized training for women operatives, it becomes clear how the historical process of conferring skills operated to valorize male knowledge and professions in the trade. It also helps to explain women's subordinate positions in production and the undervalorization of their work.

Gendered Technology

Historians have focused more often on the general social effects of technology than on its gender implications. Yet mechanization and technological innovation have constantly transformed traditional patterns of gender relations and created new divisions of labor. By the mid-nineteenth century, the introduction of machines to replace human strength in the early textile mills had raised the possibility of employing men, women, and children interchangeably. Machines were understood to simplify work, so that even unskilled labor could be rapidly trained for certain tasks.[58] But artisanal forms of work far outnumbered factory jobs in France even at the beginning of the Third Republic. Under these conditions the male model of the skilled worker persisted long after the actual erosion of working conditions and the dilution of skills. By

58. Scott 1988, 148–52. For another approach based on the gendering of textile tools and machines, see Freifeld 1986, 319–43; Robert 1980; Rose 1992, 24–30.

the turn of the century, French unions in many trades clearly articulated the notion of a skilled male worker whose identity was increasingly threatened by technological advances and by women's employment.[59]

During the long process of mechanization in the knitted goods industry, new machines were introduced according to a certain technical, but also social, logic that would govern their use. At the same time, meaning was assigned to these machines in gendered terms. Two periods concern us here. The first, from 1890 to 1914, was one during which mass-production technology was introduced and perfected as a legacy of the nineteenth century, and millowners increasingly specialized in luxury goods. During these years, mechanization affected both men's and women's work by increasing specialization. Fewer men were needed to tend the mass-production Cotton frame knitters imported from England. Moreover, the unevenness of technical change and fickleness in the demands of fashion resulted in slowdowns in production and layoffs. The second period, from 1914 to 1945, was characterized by the introduction of new textile fibers, but also fewer mechanical innovations and a more diversified production. During this latter period the knitted goods industry became even more dependent on its female workforce. The number of specialized tasks in garment making, tasks that remained semi- or nonmechanized, increased as women's finishing work was subdivided into gender-specific jobs. During these interwar years, employers were bridging technological gaps in the production process with semiskilled women's jobs. Production shifted from hosiery to a greater diversity of fashion clothing made from cut-up knitted fabric sewn together along an assembly line.

Anthropologists have taught us to question the meaning of certain cultural exclusions and to reflect on the implicit rules that govern the sexual division of labor in society.[60] An Italian anthropologist, Paola Tabet, has posited that male domination over women has been constituted and maintained by the prescriptive use of tools and techniques for the production of goods, leading to the exclusion of women from use of the most productive and perfected

59. For textile workers' views, see the reply of the Fédération nationale ouvrière de l'industrie textile de France to the parliamentary inquiry of 1902,: "Workers' technical mastery in the textile industry is today eliminated by the progressive substitution of automatic machines . . . for hand labor and dexterity, in sum, for everything that constitutes men's technical mastery, which has been displaced by the employment of women and children" (AN C 7321)

60. Tabet 1979, 5–61. Feminists working in disciplines other than history have borrowed insights and notions from anthropology to look at technological change and women's work. See Cockburn 1983.

tools in society. Tabet contends that this long-standing "technological gap" has allowed men a monopoly of advanced technical knowledge and has constituted one of the bases of male power. She contests "the natural character, the notion of complementarity and reciprocity in the division of labor." When women had access to the appropriate tools for their tasks, she argues, they were often badly equipped in relation to men, employing more rudimentary tools. In fact, women possessed the tools that men attributed to them as a consequence of men's having designed and manufactured them. This gap—between the more complex and productive tools controlled by men, and the more rudimentary hand tools attributed to women—broadened during the industrial age.[61]

Tabet's argument sheds new light on our analysis of gendered knitting technology. We can understand the exclusion of women from the knitting frame in the eighteenth century and appreciate the economic power that men subsequently held. But her argument also helps to explain how men preserved the technical knowledge and skills in the trade that allowed them to reskill as improvements were made to their machines. The techniques employed by women in production, taking place outside the knitting process, hardly benefited from technological innovation. When asked about the strict gender boundaries between men's and women's work, most workers interviewed acknowledged that such was the "custom" in the trade. The weight of custom, however, does not sufficiently explain the male monopoly of the knitting frame. Its attribution to men had been supported at the turn of the century by the need for physical strength (standing position, distance covered to oversee long flatbed knitters, strength required to change gears), and by the risks for women of catching their skirts in the driving belts of flatbed knitters.[62] But these machines were rapidly fitted with automatic functions, eliminating the need for strength. Why, then, did women not operate knitting machines?

In Troyes the gendering of technology strengthened the traditional sexual division of labor, thus preserving occupational segregation and the skilled status of male knitters on the Cotton frame. Mill management offered only one job that was designated as mixed gender, or "swing," that is, for either men or women knitters. The job consisted of tending small circular knitters that were purported to be simpler to operate and less tiring to oversee. However, women textile workers in Troyes were not attracted to operating knitting

61. Tabet 1979.
62. Arguments advanced by Ricommard (1934).

machines of any size. Rather, they used the domestic tradition to emphasize their feminine skills, and they sought to improve their technical knowledge in their own occupations. Many women who had worked in the 1920s expressed the desire to have benefited from retraining and reskilling.[63] Instead, employers restricted women to increasingly semiskilled finishing tasks. Moreover, the attitude of the male-dominated textile unions was to try to eliminate economic competition between men and women workers by demanding higher wages for women while preserving existing male prerogatives. In the long run, the existing gender division of labor and technology was codified in the collective bargaining agreement of 1936. At that time, male union leaders negotiated an agreement that favored protecting men's jobs.

If we consider this same issue comparatively, the gendered construction of skill becomes more obvious. The resistance among male knitters to women operating the knitting machines was much more explicit in England than in France. Women in Leicester were, in fact, employed on the same circular knitting frames as men, but they were paid less. Disputing the issue, leaders of the Leicestershire Amalgamated Hosiery Union proposed in 1888 that the smaller, six-headed knitters be designated "women's machines," and the more productive, eight-headed ones be reserved for men. Furthermore, the same union barred women from operating the Cotton patent knitter, threatening them with expulsion from the mixed-gender union if they did so. As Sonya Rose demonstrates, this artificial distinction was made to maintain male jobs when a wage dispute forced male knitters into competition with female ones.[64] James Holmes, secretary of the union, implicitly acknowledged to a parliamentary commission that the distinction between men's and women's machines was artificial: "[I]t is so convenient for men to believe that women cannot do certain things until they do it and then they find that the impossible is done."[65] Once the machines were effectively gendered, male knitters also acquired the task of supervising female knitters' work.

As machines became gendered in the hosiery industry in Troyes, those assigned to women had certain recognizable characteristics: they were small in size, were easy to handle, required a short apprenticeship, and could often be used in the home. The boundaries between factory work and industrial homework remained blurred. Troyes millowners relied heavily on the outwork system

63. Testimony in particular from Mme Aubron, interview, 1982.
64. Rose 1997, 1992. For the Canadian case, see Parr 1988, 511–33; 1990, chap. 3.
65. The quotation is from 1906 Earnings and Hours Inquiry, as cited by Rose (1987, 173).

and working-class women's need to continue to work while raising children. Male knitters also saw the advantages of such small domestic machines, which allowed women to work at home, as Emile Caillot so eloquently stated in 1900.

Such arguments on the virtues for women of industrial homework, embedded in the family workshop, represents one important tradition in Troyes that needs to be examined more closely. It would be easy to dismiss family workshops as a sentimentalized ideological construction, but they formed a fundamental practice of the trade. Yet knitting-machine manufacturers targeted working-class families, and especially women homeworkers, just as sewing machine makers sought to create a female mass market for their product.[66] The advertisement for *la tricoteuse,* manufactured by J.-D. Clad in Mulhouse in the 1920s provides a clear case in point. A woman homeworker, dressed patriotically in Alsacian costume, is seen busily knitting on a small machine, all the while nursing her baby and minding her older child. The manufacturer proudly claimed that this was "how to raise one's children, supervise housework, and earn a living."[67] All these domestic chores were presented as compatible with femininity, productive work, and family life. There could be no clearer representation of working women's two attributes in French society—motherhood and home work—than those superimposed in this image.

INDUSTRIAL HOMEWORK

Work and family were indissociable in the households of Troyes textile workers. The parameters of the two worlds were rarely strictly defined, since family members worked together and often in the same mills. The household constituted the basic economic unit and was structured by many individual variables, as the census data revealed. No one family structure predominated, although survival was certainly easier inside than outside. In general, the family constituted a network of support within the larger urban community, and in times of conflict, it became a site of resistance to industrial capitalism. The profiles of many different types of families emerged from oral testimony, from archival sources such as inventories after death, and from census household data.

66. For the sewing machine as a gendered consumer product, see Coffin 1996a.
67. Instructional brochure, undated, and bearing the inscription "independence and prosperity through homework." Both the distinctive Alsacian costume and the decorative layout suggest the 1920s. Kindly lent by M. Becker in Troyes.

Throughout this period, most married women worked either in the family workshop or in the mill. No marriage bar existed, as it did in certain English hosiery towns, and women's status as workers was never really challenged.[68] On the one hand, male workers recognized that two wage earners were needed to ensure a family livelihood, and, on the other hand, millowners acknowledged that women's productive work was vital to the commercial success of the local industry. Despite the fact that women workers moved back and forth between mill workshops and home, it was their family role that ultimately determined their primary status in French society. As wives and mothers, women workers were the object of specific paternalist measures, based on prescriptive gender norms. But male workers also had to demonstrate their compliance with a masculine code as breadwinners and heads of household.

Laid out in the following sections are two idealized representations of the working-class family, the first constructed from the male, the second from the female, viewpoint. In each case, the ideal represented will be confronted with the multiple realities of working-class families' lives and these families' strategies for maintaining a livelihood.

The Male Artisan Ideal

In Troyes the family artisan workshop (*atelier de façonnier*) represented a symbolic site of resistance to industrial capitalism. As Emile Caillot himself observed, a family's living and working together as a self-sustaining unit was projected as the preferred form of family life. Underlying this ideal was a problematic fantasy of autonomy and semi-independence in a world predating the factory system.[69] Caillot's vision of the artisan workshop was predicated on the knitter's regaining control of his knitting frame, since mechanization on a large scale had robbed him of his independence, an experience that was tantamount to a loss of masculinity. One may question how many male textile workers harbored this artisan's dream, but such imagined alternatives lived on

68. For the marriage bar in England, see Rose 1992, 45–47.
69. "Imagine," Caillot said, "this old city of Troyes rejuvenated by forty years, to the period when men and women worked at home, their children raised under their own eyes. There would be no debauchery, no more contagious diseases like tuberculosis, no more injustice in the workshop, no more strikes, because workers who work at home with their families are opposed to strikes [*anti-gréviste*]" (AMT 2F 47). For an analysis of the role of the World's Fairs and the problem of worker consciousness in the decline of the culture of production, see Auslander 1993.

Figure 6   A family workshop in the village of Estissac, southwest of Troyes, c. 1910. On the left, the Paget knitting frame, and on the right, the Cotton patent knitter. Archives départementales de l'Aube.

well into the 1930s. There is little evidence, however, that women workers ever explicitly shared this idealized vision.

Many social reformers of the late nineteenth century painted a similar, if somewhat modified, ideal, which was related to bourgeois notions of moral improvement. The father should assume responsibility for the household both as paterfamilias and as independent artisan or foreman. His wife was to assist him in production and assume domestic and child-care tasks as her primary attribution. The children would work alongside their parents, until such time as they decided to found their own *foyer*. It was just such an artisan family portrait that E. Jamerey presented in his monograph on Mazières-la-Grande Paroisse, a village where he worked as a primary school teacher in 1900. The family was composed of the father, aged forty-seven; the mother, aged forty-three; and their two children, twenty and eighteen years old, respectively. The daughter worked as a seamstress, while the three other family members worked together in the family workshop, producing hosiery for the Doré-Doré company in nearby Fontaine-les-Grès. According to Jamerey, the parents had worked in the same trade since their childhood: "The head of the family, who had ten brothers and sisters, began hosiery work at age eleven under his father's guidance, and has continued ever since. At age twenty he paid his debt to his country, did six months of military service, then at age twenty-six . . . married a young woman of twenty-two, a knitter [*ouvrière en bonneterie*] like himself, founded a family of whom he can be proud, because this family lives in harmony and peace, finding happiness in their work." The author of this flattering family portrait considered the father an exemplary head of household, since the latter had worked and saved enough to buy both a knitting frame and a sewing machine on credit. As a provident father, he had subscribed to the mutual aid society to provide for his family's future. The family itself was self-sufficient thanks to the work of its four members, and Jamerey's description of the work distribution actually accounts for the wife's contribution in monetary terms. However, he depicted her actual productive work as secondary to her housework: "The mother does not work exclusively as a bonnetière in the sense that she cooks and does housework (the two children are sufficiently grown now so that these chores are much lighter). When the housework is done, she rewinds bobbins and *rebrousse,* and is thus occupied all day long like the men are." We can recognize in this family portrait the attention given to household chores and note the emphasis on social harmony through work, so familiar in the monographs of the Le Play school.[70]

The Feminine Ideal of Domesticity

Paternalism spawned complementary ideals of domesticity for women workers. As we have seen earlier, Léon Vitoux expressed special concern for his women millworkers in his address to the parliamentary commission of inquiry in 1904. His proposals to accommodate his women workers' double day and to provide a crèche for child care revealed a self-styled philanthropist and a "modern" boss. For Vitoux, the factory system had altered the domestic environment by separating home and work. As a result, life was more difficult for his workers than it used to be: "Everything has changed today, since all work is done in the factory, so what has happened? Husband, children, interior, all this is sacrificed for work." The solution he proposed, a shorter working day

70. See also the description of an artisan family workshop producing *passementerie* in Saint-Etienne by Mathilde Dubesset and Michelle Zancarini-Fournel (1988). They note that the mother appears in a service role like a "poor slave" or a "precious auxiliary" from the moment she does not operate a loom.

for women, would protect them and preserve their families, by allowing them to be "good wives, good mothers, and good homemakers while working in the mill." In his view these two roles for women were compatible: marriage and motherhood were no obstacles to mill employment. They were also in the interests of the hosiery industry.

In his role as a modern mill manager, Vitoux presented a hyperrealist vision of women workers' exhausting daily routine:

> To arrive at the mill when it opens, generally around 6:30 A.M. (sometimes even earlier), they have to get up at 5 A.M., wash up a bit, wake the children, take them to the care provider or the crèche, or prepare them for school, then arrive on time at the mill if they want to avoid a fine; they are forced to leave the beds, the housework in disorder for lack of time. Once inside the mill, work begins, they need to eat something because there was no time to do so before leaving home. At noon, they run to make lunch (nothing has naturally been prepared in advance), stopping at the butcher, the baker, the grocer, where they are obliged to pay more. Around 12:30 they sit down to eat, as best they can, then at one o'clock the children return to school, and the parents to the mill until closing at 7 P.M.; at a quarter past seven, everyone has returned home, and the mother has already worked fourteen hours; her work continues as she prepares dinner, makes the beds, tidies up the rooms, repairs clothing, sometimes prepares food for the next day, etc. She is busy therefore until 10 P.M., so that between millwork and housework she spends some sixteen to seventeen hours every day, doing the same humdrum routine.[71]

In fact, Vitoux's description of the bonnetière's double day paints a picture of an elastic work time that never ends, all in the service of the family. The moralizing observations on her leaving her home in disorder and buying ready-made food from the grocer, implying that she is spending more money than she should and not saving, reveal the bourgeois norms against which this hypothetical woman worker was being judged. He proposed that by looking after their homes, women workers would encourage men to abandon

71. AN C 7318.

the café-bars in town, noting that "the most welcoming sign for a man return-ing from work is to find the table set, his home cared for by his loving wife." The social construction of motherhood and domesticity Vitoux projected for his women workers did not correspond to their lives of struggle. To be sure, some women workers must have dreamed of spending more time at home, living a more comfortable home life.[72]

In reality, how did women workers organize their family lives while work-ing? Testimony from women operatives in the 1920s and 1930s revealed the importance of neighborhood networks of class solidarity and the critical sup-port of family, which helped in the organization of services and subsistence. Suzanne Gallois described the daily routine of a bonnetière in very different terms from those of Vitoux:

> Every morning early you saw a mother on a bicycle, with her child all wrapped up, his sleepy eyes showing above his scarf; she was taking him either to his grandmother's or to a neighbor's house in the next street—there were no crèches, there were no nursery schools. So mothers who needed to work had to leave their children somewhere. Once the children were left off, mothers returned to fetch them at around noon; the husband did the food shopping on the way home, because they did not necessarily work in the same mill, so he had to buy the bread. . . . Everyone ate lunch rapidly, the wife made the meal, often standing up to eat, because the child had to be taken back [to the caregiver] before returning to work.[73]

During this period there were, indeed, very few crèches in Troyes to provide child care for the many married women textile workers. Before 1945, only three crèches existed in town, two in the center and one in a quarter near the mills. The first was founded in 1876 at the initiative of Catholic nuns in a convent in the rue Louis Ulbach; the two others, operated by the munici-pality, were founded in the 1920s. The total capacity for all three was listed as 115 children in 1946.[74]

---

72. See Cottereau 1980, 32–40, 80–87. Cottereau decodes the household patterns of Parisian artisan workers' wives from employer Denis Poulot's descriptions and groups them in an inter-esting typology of workers' families.

73. Testimony from Suzanne Gallois, interview, May 24, 1984.

74. The three crèches—Rue Ulbach, Les Mitaniers and Les Trevois—could never have met

Given the absence of child-care facilities, women workers had to rely on their families or stop working while raising their children. Statistics for the Aube region, indicating the percentage of women active in the labor force in relation to the number of women of working age, demonstrate an exceptional continuity in the female work pattern for the period 1921 to 1936. Women in the Aube worked throughout their lives, and most notably during the years of child raising, a work pattern strikingly identical to that of men.[75]

Among the women workers I interviewed, most relied heavily on their families for child care in order to continue working. Mme Chailloux, who, as a bobbin winder, did shift work, took her son to stay with her mother in the nearby suburb of Saint-André during the week, returning to fetch him on Friday evenings. When her son was ill, she stopped working, even though her husband's wages were not sufficient to support the family. Mme Laborie, also a bobbin winder and the mother of three children, preferred to be employed in small workshops in her neighborhood that offered greater flexibility of hiring and hours than did the bigger mills. Working near her home allowed her to prepare the noon meal for her children. However, Mme Binet's mother, widowed young, worked at home as a seamer in order to raise her daughter. Then, when Mme Binet married and went to work in the mills, she was able to continue working as a mender thanks to her mother, who looked after her two children. But family strategies also included providing income for one's aging parents. Mlle Henon, a single woman and white-collar worker in the Valton mill, had to work beyond the age of retirement to provide for her mother.

The solution most often adopted by women textile workers in Troyes involved a combination of millwork, interspersed with one of the many forms of industrial homework. Mme Aubron left a job as a skilled mender in one of the mills to raise her three children, but divorce quickly forced her back to work, this time in her family's workshop in the neighborhood. For eighteen years she worked with her brothers and sisters in three shifts, or *les trois huits* as they are called in French. "We began work at five in the morning, five [A.M.] to one [P.M.], one to nine, and then nine [P.M.] to five A.M. Well, often my children were asleep when I went off to work at five in the morning,

---

the needs of the large working population. It was only in the 1960s that the town increased the number of crèches, which it did fourfold. See Imbert and Combes 1978.

75. Based on statistics from INSEE, *L'annuaire statistique régional,* Direction générale de Reims, 1957, 138–39.

but then at eight I came home to get them up and give them breakfast." This type of schedule organized around the family provided flexibility to meet the children's needs, but it also made for long hours. After World War II the family workshop declined, and Mme Aubron returned to work day shifts in the mill, but she soon found the schedule incompatible with her responsibilities as a divorced mother. She was forced to quit after nine months: "I earned a good living, and I left because of the children." When she was able to return to the mills, the choice was a positive one, since she had experienced working in the family workshop as a "dead end." Working outside the mills left little possibility to learn new skills or to experience technological advances. Moreover, she missed the sociability of a women's mill workshop. Many women textile workers in Troyes expressed a preference for working in the mills, rather than at home, the latter an experience they had chosen at one time or another in their lives.

Industrial homework (*travail à domicile*) was ubiquitous in Troyes, particularly among seamers and menders. Delivery and collection of manual finishing work was regularly organized by the mills. Homework of this type provided at most a means of subsistence, or a *salaire d'appoint* (extra income). Mme Chailloux combined shift work in the mills with homework to pay her son's medical bills: "When I went back to work in the mill, I worked the early shift, then picked up extra work to do at home in the afternoon; I worked from, say, two in the afternoon until eight at night cutting up lace or sewing on buttons."[76] Many women textile workers remember as children helping their parents finish or deliver work. During their childhood there were no clear boundaries between homework and millwork.

While millowners tended to present homework as an "ideal solution" for combining work and family, women textile workers lived the contradictions that were inherent in the system. The case of Mme Binet's mother, a young widow who worked as a seamer at home, reveals how this system affected homeworkers. Mme Binet remembered that her mother had worked against her watch, pushing herself to seam a dozen stockings in ten minutes, as if she had been working in the mill. In order to earn a livelihood, she had interiorized the production norms of the piecework system that were applied in the mill. Other homeworkers reported that they, too, had to produce the same quantity at home as in the mill. Under such conditions, these women

76. Testimony of Mme Chailloux, interview, 1983.

homeworkers lived factory constraints within the space and time of their own homes. Moreover, at this time, homeworkers had a relatively marginal social status, which was exacerbated when millowners distributed homework during work conflicts, using women homeworkers as scabs.

WORK AND COMMUNITY: LA FÊTE DE LA BONNETERIE

Despite these different and divisive forms of production, many of the cultural practices in Troyes contributed to a broader sense of community. One of the most important of these was this textile town's annual craft or corporative festival, the Fête de la Bonneterie. Long dominated by a masculine artisan tradition, the work festival was transformed in 1909 by the election of a woman worker as queen for the day. From 1909 to 1938, the townspeople of Troyes celebrated their renowned knitting industry by the crowning of eight festival queens. The Fête de la Bonneterie apparently originated with the founding in 1505 of the hand knitters' guild, the Confrérie et corporation des bonnetiers de Troyes, whose members fixed the date of their patronal festival on September 8, the date of the Virgin's birth.[77] The traditional celebration of the patron saint's festival day included all members of the trade at all levels—apprentices, journeymen, and masters together. The religious nature of the festival required that all work be stopped and that all join in the celebration of Mass to renew the oath of solidarity. There were processions to and from the church, followed by a ritual sharing of food.[78] In the 1870s, the festival organized by the local Confrérie des bonnetiers in Troyes included a mass at the cathedral, a banquet, and a ball for its members. In this way members of the trade perpetuated the ritual of what they identified as a moral community of skilled workers. It should be noted that historically this festival tradition was overwhelmingly masculine. As best as we can tell, women were excluded from these rituals.

The new version of the festival, initiated in 1909, differed in two significant ways from the earlier tradition. First, it was organized by the millowners rather than the workers; and second, it gave a central, symbolic role to women workers. It was launched at a time when Troyes millowners were attempting

77. BMT, QI, fol. 280–83, "Statuts de la Confrérie des bonnetiers de Troyes." See also Ricommard 1934.

78. Ricommard 1934, 34–35. See also Bibolet 1997, 67–68.

to consolidate their gains, heal social strife, and develop commercial support for their industry. And what better way to do this than to transform the local work festival into a unifying, even leveling force in Troyes, symbolized by the election and crowning of a woman worker as queen for a day?

Queen for a Day

Rural French society had practiced the ritual of electing temporary queens from among the young unmarried women of the village at special ceremonies, held most commonly in May.[79] However, from its origins as a work festival, the Fête de la Bonneterie belonged more to the tradition of urban industrial France than to the rural religious festivals of prerevolutionary society.[80] In 1909, millowners stated that their purpose in renewing the festival was to endow the local industry with a "Muse," a nineteenth-century allegorical figure invoked as inspiration for any enterprise in poetry or the liberal arts.[81] The festival of 1909 associated art nouveau symbols of decorative and organic femininity, "la femme-nature," with the historic pageantry of sixteenth-century royal France. Representations of the festival, then, projected both backward and forward in time. The festival program evoked the gracious festival queen looking down over the historic center of Troyes (Fig. 7).[82]

Yet the millowners certainly had other intentions in their promotion of the festival and its queen. Their speeches during the festivities stressed the paternalist values of class collaboration in the interests of prosperity and emphasized the development of local commerce and industry. It was also hoped, they stated, that the festival would provide popular entertainment, keeping workers in town during the three-day holiday and discouraging an exodus to the countryside for a prolonged weekend.[83] Two local working-class charities in

79. These women were called "rose queens" or "May queens" and were associated with both virginity and virtue. See Maza 1989; Segalen 1982.

80. See especially Alain Faure's (1978) study of Carnaval in nineteenth-century Paris. Faure traces the evolution of Carnaval in Paris from a gargantuan feast of popular consumption taking place outside the gates of Paris before Haussmannization in the 1840s, to the largely commercial and spectator festival. He reported the crowning of queens by the Parisian washerwomen.

81. *La Tribune de l'Aube,* September 13, 1909.

82. AMT 1J 154.

83. *Le Petit Troyen* on September 13, 1936, gives this account in a short history of the festival. But this interpretation is also suggested in *Le Petit Troyen* on September 12, 1910. There were some thirty thousand visitors reported at the festival in 1909, according to E. P. Verville (1909).

Figure 7 Poster from the first Fête de la Bonneterie in 1909. At the top left, a representation of Henry IV's entry into Troyes in 1595, and at the bottom left, the festival parade of 1909. The colors of the French republican flag float behind the festival queen. Archives départementales de l'Aube.

aid of children, la Goutte de lait and l'Allaitement maternel, were also to benefit from the profits of the festival. Public statements by millowners and local notables repeated as a constant refrain: "What is good for the working class is good for the knitting industry."[84] While their critics on the left attacked the festival as a diversion from social reality,[85] the organizers praised it as an expression of the benefits of industry for the whole of society: "Festivals like today's are not improvised to mask decadence or poverty. On the contrary, they mark the excellence of our production, so well-adapted to the necessities of modern life."[86] In this sense we could interpret millowners' desire to bring together different social groups and to promote social peace through the crowning of a working-class queen.

On another level, the organizers of the festival of 1909 were eager to establish Troyes's reputation as the capital of the knitted goods industry. In sum, they wanted to establish an identifiable industrial trademark for their town. The local Radical paper, Le Petit Troyen, boasted, "Troyes is to the knitted goods industry as Lyon is to the silk industry." To this end, the festival organizers created a woman worker as queen for the day. They dressed her in a royal white satin gown with a long court train, covered by a red velvet mantle that was lined with white satin and decorated with hermine. This royal regalia was displayed beforehand in the shopwindows of the Magasins Réunis, the largest department store in town. The visual effect masked the queen's working-class origins and imparted an illusion of social equality, so redolent of the whole festival enterprise. Yet the message mediated by the queen's regalia was also one of material comfort and prosperity through the local industry. Over the following decades, the worker-queen would indeed become a marketing symbol for a host of services and commodities, all related to an increasingly commercialized festival.

The election of the first festival queen constituted an event in and of itself. Millowners established the simple criteria that the queen was to be elected by her co-workers and that she must be "a minimum of eighteen years old and entirely worthy of the honor to be bestowed upon her."[87] In sum, their criteria were virtue and virginity. Women operatives were to designate two

84. Verville 1909.
85. See the socialist weekly newspaper La Défense des Travailleurs de l'Aube, August 21–28, 1909.
86. Le Petit Troyen, September 12, 1909.
87. AMT 1J 154.

delegates from each workshop, and these women would then select the queen from among themselves in a second or third round of voting. The fact that the vote was decidedly theirs is attested by ballots distributed in the workshops.[88] Women homeworkers even wrote to the organizers of the festival, expressing their desire to participate in the queen's election and citing the fact that they were retained at home by their double day. The importance of this first election lies in the fact that through their ballots, women workers defined the criteria of what the queen was to represent. These criteria were embodied in the first queen.

The records of the first Fête de la Bonneterie identify the inaugural queen as Renée Kuntz, who worked as a skilled mender (*raccoutreuse*) in the mills.[89] In the hierarchy of women's occupations, as we have seen, the mender was highly ranked in terms of skill, social esteem, and the wages she earned. Newspaper reports confirm that she was "young and beautiful." The journalist who came to interview her in the mill after her election in August 1909 left the following portrait: "The festival queen is happy, but she keeps her happiness to herself; her intense joy is interiorized. Infinitely modest, Miss Kuntz refuses to believe that she is pretty and her reserved manner of speaking lets us know the gratitude she feels toward her co-workers."[90] Visibly moved and "intimidated," to use the journalist's own words, she could only smile and refused to speak. It is easy to imagine the emotion of this young woman worker who found herself suddenly carried before the public eye and who throughout the ceremonies, according to all reports, did not utter a word beyond simple expressions of gratitude.

Miss Kuntz's co-workers in the mill, however, invested a great deal of themselves in her symbolic triumph. For many of them, the positive image of a working-class queen conveyed the message that women's industrial work was acceptable, even honorable. It strengthened their conviction that a woman could be virtuous and still work in the mills. The day after the election, her co-workers organized a ceremony in the mill yard, forming an honor guard to acclaim her as she left work, presenting her with a basket of flowers and accompanying her in a procession along the streets to her home in the center of town. In this way, other women operatives shared in her joy and marked the event with a sign of social and gender solidarity. From a historical

88. Ibid.
89. *Le Petit Troyen*, August 4, 1909.
90. Ibid.

perspective, this popular tradition of an honor guard and procession had been handed down from the Mardi Gras celebration. But the honor guard (*conduite*) also had its roots in the tradition of the *compagnonnages*. Skilled workers of the Tour de France were thus escorted upon leaving a town for their next destination.[91] The festival clearly drew on many traditions to recast women workers in the values of modern industrial society.

The citizens of Troyes demonstrated their enthusiasm for the queen during the three-day festival in September 1909. She was paraded along the streets of Troyes on a float and crowned by the town's mayor at a special ceremony. While all the magical symbols of power were present—scepter and diadem, royal red cloak—the speeches echoed the incongruity of royalty being associated with work, and the ephemeral quality of both power and beauty. Addressing the queen as "Sa majesté du travail," the mayor of Troyes continued to mix his metaphors: "Even if you lose your fairylike royalty, attached to your regalia and crown, you will maintain another, one that comes from your colleagues' esteem in a vote whose meaning is not ephemeral; they have consecrated your grace, together with your merit and virtue."[92] For the millowners, the queen represented a gendered symbol of working-class dignity, rising above political divisions and class struggle. M. Doué, president of the organizing committee and a prominent merchant manufacturer, voiced his perspective at the crowning ceremony: "We have the conviction that in collaborating with working-class charities, we will reach our second goal, that is, to highlight and acknowledge the importance of the major industry of Troyes and its products, since what is good for the worker becomes good for the knitting industry."[93] The political purpose of this speech, with its call for working-class collaboration, escaped no one at the time, least of all the Guesdist socialists, who treated the festival with undisguised irony.

The socialists, in fact, seized upon another image of the queen. She was represented in the socialist newspaper, *La Défense des Travailleurs de l'Aube*, as "l'élue du peuple," a real working-class Cinderella forced to return to the factory the next day. They quite naturally stressed her identity as a worker in the class struggle, noting, "[W]e are the slaves and you are one of us." But the socialists were particularly attentive to the way the festival organizers had co-opted one of their own revolutionary symbols, Etienne Pédron's famous song

91. Barret and Gurgand 1980, 456.
92. *Le Petit Troyen*, September 13, 1909.
93. Ibid.

"La Troyenne"; they had replaced Pédron's words with others in praise of the two local products for which Troyes was reputed—the knitting industry and the *andouillette* sausage! *La Défense des Travailleurs* subsequently published the original version of "La Troyenne," a masculine combat song written in 1890, at a time of great socialist fervor in the town.[94] In general, the socialists targeted the festival's contradictions; it was a luxurious moment of feast and celebration in the midst of unemployment and hunger. Yet, in the transgressive spirit associated with Mardi Gras, they also represented the festival as a means for the working class to escape their condition for three days of rejoicing. They even ironized that the festival provided an opportunity for the worker-queen to exercise symbolic power in Troyes, a town that the socialists had lost in the municipal elections of 1900.

The Corporative Tradition

If the novelty of the 1909 festival and its break with the past was everywhere apparent, evident also was the continuity with the historic corporative tradition. The festival opened with the pageantry of a torchlit procession through the old town, led by a costumed Henry IV on horseback followed by his men-at-arms. The reference here was to the good king Henry IV who had granted craft statutes to the merchant knitters, but also to the same king's historic visit to Troyes on June 1, 1595. The festival parade the following day was a re-creation of Henry's sumptuous and triumphant entry, together with floats that evoked the illustrious counts of Champagne and artisan inventors of knitting machines from Troyes. Trade and commerce dominated the parade. The most popular float represented an elaborate historical depiction of the skilled occupations in the hosiery industry, a float analyzed earlier in this chapter. Still another float featured the queen and her *demoiselles d'honneur* (the runners-up in the election) on a royal dais decorated with the shields of the town of Troyes and its major industry. While the old trade corporation, la Confrérie des bonnetiers, participated in the renewal of the festival, it maintained a separate ritual: the traditional mass in the cathedral, followed by a concert and ball in the evening for its members. This skilled craft tradition, which the *confrérie* tried to preserve through such practices, became increasingly marginalized by commercial interests as the festival evolved over the following decades.

94. *La Défense des Travailleurs de l'Aube,* August 21–28, 1909.

The festival of 1909 was an overwhelming popular success, bringing together different communities in Troyes and attracting visitors from nearby villages and towns. By 1900, rural workers had swollen the ranks of the urban workforce and overflowed into the new industrial suburbs. The 1909 festival took place within the historic urban center, the Bouchon de Champagne. From within this recognized social space, celebrations spread to several quarters of the town, with public balls, parades, and fireworks. As the festival was transformed over the following two decades, it spilled over into the suburbs as well. Festivities in local neighborhoods took on greater significance, and townspeople multiplied the number of young women designated to represent them, electing queens, mascots, and "queen bees" to reign over the celebrations. This inflation of feminine symbols in the popularization of the festival was only one indication of how the Fête de la Bonneterie was to evolve until the demise of the Popular Front in the late 1930s.

As we have seen, the crowning of the first queen represented a confusion of attributes and contradictory values. Originally elected in 1909 by her female co-workers as the queen of working-class values, she would become, by the 1930s, a beauty queen chosen by an all-male jury, as we shall see in subsequent chapters. In the process, popular participation would be channeled toward leisure and commerce as the festival was recast to promote the values of a modern consumer society.

In this chapter I have relied heavily on evidence of the experience of men and women knitters, to describe and analyze the multilayered culture of textile production in Troyes. Their written and oral testimony helps to underscore a technical culture that represented cultural capital for millowners and mill-workers alike. Embedded in this system were the *savoir-faire*, skills, and values that workers had appropriated and transformed for themselves. However, gender distinctions in the construction of skills devalued women's work, making their skills contingent on their power and status in society. Yet women's work was vital to working-class communities as women filled their various roles: as millworkers alongside their husbands and children; as skilled seamers, menders, and finishers of luxury garments; and more publicly, as festival queens who helped market the goods they produced. "Made in Troyes" became a quality label for knitted goods because of the town's skilled workers who made them. Workers' identification with the trade extended beyond the factory gate to the knitted goods and the commercial market that distributed them.

Worker delegates who went from Troyes to the Paris World's Fair of 1900 took pride in the quality goods they produced, compared to those manufactured by hosiery mills in France and in other parts of the industrial world. Many affirmed their satisfaction that their town's production was far superior to their competitors' on display at the fair. Emile Caillot was one such spokesman for the culture of production in Troyes. Relying on his discerning eye and skilled hand to judge quality, he asserted: "[A]ll these knitted fabrics were enclosed in display cases, and it was therefore impossible to touch them, and in the hosiery industry, the feel of the fabric ["le toucher"] is essential to knowing if it possesses all the qualities that the eye beholds."[95] While there could be no better advocate of the skilled knitter in his trade, Caillot focused his observations on the better-quality goods that reflected the narrowness of commercial vision still predominant among textile manufacturers in Troyes.

Technological advances in Troyes had been adapted to a specialization in the production of quality luxury goods—silk and cotton stockings embellished with embroidery and openwork, for example—for a protected domestic and colonial market. Even Auguste Mortier admitted, in discussions at the Chambre de commerce de Troyes in 1903, that the local industry should compete for foreign markets and revise their preferences for luxury goods: "Sheltered by high tariffs, which some would say are too high, we have been able to work for eight to ten years in the quietude of protectionism; we have crammed and saturated the national market, forgetting perhaps that external markets are a condition of life for us."[96] Troyes millowners were slow in shifting their production toward a two-tiered market, one that catered not only to the bourgeois tastes of the Belle Epoque, but also, more important, to a second domestic market of more standardized goods for the modest consumer, goods that even the millowners' own workers could afford.

95. Report by Emile Caillot, ouvrier bonnetier, AMT 2F 47.
96. Auguste Mortier, Chambre de commerce de Troyes, *Compte rendu,* 1903, p. 183, as quoted in Heywood 1994, 180.

5

WORKERS AS CONSUMERS

Louis Foin, a knitter in the mills of Troyes and an administrator of the workers' consumer cooperative the Laborieuse, was sent as a delegate to the Paris World's Fair of 1889. In his report to the municipal council, which financed his trip, Foin made the connection between the increased productivity of the new knitting machines displayed at the fair and the decline in worker wages and purchasing power. He noted that "there is overproduction and workers who are underemployed cannot even consume the goods they need, and those who have no work at all are at the mercy of public charity, and there is talk of reducing wages in order to increase sales." Foin argued for the subordination of production to social needs, identified with those of citizen consumers like himself: "It is workers who are the most serious consumers because their consumption is not motivated by luxury and whim, but by necessity. . . . The more wages are lowered, the more workers as natural consumers will be unable to consume, and consequently there will be less demand and need for production."[1] Foin's argument pairs the notions of production and consumption, linking technical progress to the growth in productivity that in his opinion threatened to reduce wages and create unemployment. He urged millowners in Troyes not to target the luxury market at the expense of the "natural consumer," that is, workers like himself. From what he had learned

---

1. AMT 2F 46. Louis Foin had several overlapping roles: he worked as a knitter in the mills; he was one of the worker delegates to sign the petition (with Pédron) to meet with the prefect on the first May Day celebration in Troyes; and he was an administrator of the Laborieuse.

as both a producer and a consumer cooperator, Foin recognized that mill-owners in Troyes practiced a form of industrial and commercial capitalism that maintained control over the distribution and marketing of essentially luxury goods. Foin reasoned that better wages would enable workers to satisfy their needs and would in turn spur industrial production.

From the late medieval sumptuary laws concerning the distribution of lux-ury goods and the preservation of social distinctions, to the Revolution's pre-scriptions on dress, each century has addressed the ethics of consumption in its own historical terms.[2] Over the course of the nineteenth century, patterns of consumption had become liberated from the constraints of religious moral-ity and political authority, and bourgeois values prevailed to a large extent. The expansion of industrial and commercial capitalism further changed the terms of the debate over what to produce, what to consume, and who could consume what. Many forces were active in producing and marketing a greater variety of goods. During this same period, debate turned to the nature of needs and the role of fashion in stimulating consumer demand for certain lux-ury goods—objects desired more as status symbols than for their usefulness— and the possibilities of their diffusion among working-class consumers.[3] By the late nineteenth century, the emerging debate on "social needs" helped to maintain a narrow domestic market and a marginal place for workers within it. This debate, involving moralists, economists, and intellectual elites, informed much of the thinking about French cultural traditions, and even penetrated manufacturers' assumptions about which commercial markets to pursue.[4] It

2. See Braudel 1981; Schama 1988; Rosalind Williams 1982; Roche 1994.

3. Recent historians of consumption have focused more on the Paris market and have centered research on the aristocratic or the bourgeois consumer. See D. Roche 1994; Auslander 1996b; Lipovetsky 1994; Rosalind Williams 1982. See also Fairchilds 1993, 228–48. Fairchilds argues that by the mid-eighteenth century, Parisian workers had the possibility of buying cheap copies of aristocratic luxury items, goods that she termed "populuxe." Fairchilds included stock-ings among the goods that had become cheap, as a result of consumer demand and a parallel marketing system outside the guilds.

4. Several thinkers can be cited in this turn-of-the-century debate: Georges d'Avenel, an aristocrat and historian of private life, who wrote essays in *La Revue des Deux Mondes,* notably a series called "Le mécanisme de la vie moderne," published between 1894 and 1905, that chroni-cled changes in material culture and consumption during the Belle Epoque, and a book titled *Le nivellement des jouissances* (Flammarion, 1913); Veblen (1994); and Charles Gide, economist and principle theorist of one strand of the cooperative movement, who elaborated a notion of solidarity inspired by science and religion. See his *La coopération: Conférences de propagande* (Paris, 1900); and *Principes d'économie politique* (Paris, 1905). For more recent accounts of this debate, see Rosalind Williams 1982; Beale 1999; Tiersten 2001. For a critical assessment of French businessmen's cultural attitudes and resistance toward modern marketing strategies and consumer markets, see Landes 1951.

was not only a cultural critique of the marketplace; it was equally an economic one. In the case of Troyes, the mills had produced in the 1870s essentially basic, utilitarian goods—underwear, socks, and stockings in cotton or wool— but by 1890, production had turned toward more diversified luxury articles in the form of fine silk lingerie and stockings, and knitwear emblematic of the Belle Epoque. Many of these goods were designed for the export market. Mill-owners' unwillingness to cultivate the popular domestic market demonstrated their resistance to the social and cultural leveling of goods. They staked their reputation, as well as their profits, on quality luxury products.

The social meaning of clothing, and its distinctive status as an object of consumption, raises a number of fundamental questions concerning consumer behavior in relation to class and gender, questions that form one of the sub-texts of this chapter. Over the centuries, clothing has served a dual function: both to protect and to adorn the body. The tension between these two func-tions, as Daniel Roche has noted, is embodied in the human condition, and has been expressed through individual adherence to dress codes. Controversies over appearances have traditionally involved the interplay between conformity to social rank and nonconformity or individual desire.[5] Obvious questions of economic constraints, of poverty and necessity, have further complicated dress choices within the moral economy of working-class culture. In the late nine-teenth century, worker clothing was a marker of both social class and economic inequality. Workers wore the uniform of their trade, and they were easily identifiable in the street going to and from work, especially in the provinces. There was little visible blurring of social distinctions. Their clothing revealed their status as workers within a bourgeois-dominated society and formed still another cultural manifestation of class consciousness. Yet a tension persisted: that between dressing according to one's rank and the desire for more egali-tarian self-expression.

The purpose of this chapter is to explore workers' demands for leisure and the right to consume during the period 1880 to 1914. As we saw in Chapter 3, there are a variety of indicators, including the resurgence of labor unrest and rising expectations of greater equality, that suggest the growth of class con-sciousness among workers during these years. The precariousness of employ-ment and the prevailing low wages, described by Louis Foin in his report on the Paris World's Fair of 1889, help to explain why workers felt excluded from

5. D. Roche 1994, chap. 1.

the bourgeois market economy. French industrialization had progressed rapidly thanks to new sources of energy and the introduction of mass-production technology, which increased productivity. By the century's end, the availability of more standardized goods, especially ready-made clothing, and the development of credit systems strengthened both commercial capitalism and consumer demand. With the French economy showing such vigor, workers mobilized through collective action to claim a greater share in the increased prosperity, demanding shorter hours and higher wages. Several strands of the labor movement organized consumer cooperatives to defend workers' right to consume, forming a subculture with a separate set of consumer practices. Cooperatives provided a "community of consumption," a community that clearly adopted spending practices and sought objects for common use, which set them apart from other groups in society.[6]

The focus of this chapter is the material culture of working-class life. Using a variety of sources, it will examine particular patterns of clothing consumption and suggest social practices that were dictated by needs and economic constraints, but also motivated by individual desires and collective action. Desires are never simply needs, and as workers like Louis Foin observed the urban world around them, their gaze consumed the new commodity culture.[7] If there was to be a democratization of demand, it had to be matched by a democratization of supply. As Nancy Green has shown, the rise of standardization and sizing in the production of men's clothing from the mid-nineteenth century had stimulated popular demand for ready-mades.[8] But, in fact, demand preceded the industry's capacity to supply. Technically, garments had to be produced in series to ensure affordable prices and a democratization of supply. Then, there was the question of distribution. The workers' consumer cooperative movement that emerged in the 1880s was conceived as just such a collective means to ensure a more equitable distribution of goods than that available

6. De Grazia 1989, 225. De Grazia cites, in fact, Daniel Boorstin, who refers to the transformation of communities in America that were "created and preserved by how and what men consumed." See Boorstin 1974, 89–164. Boorstin observes that there were many overlapping communities of consumers in late nineteenth-century America that became more homogenized by the common use of standardized goods.

7. I owe these insights to discussions with Judy Coffin and Vanessa Schwartz.

8. Green 1997, 77–86. Green shows how the production of military uniforms contributed to the standardization of sizing and ultimately the simplification of production of men's wear from the mid-nineteenth century, while women's wear was less standardizable. She dates the "take-off" of women's ready-to-wear to the 1880s and 1890s in France, when the department stores helped to spread clothing patterns and styles.

through the capitalist marketplace. Yet to meet their consumption needs, workers' families in Troyes still relied partly on their own resources and labor, for women workers still produced some food and clothing for the household. Other class networks and institutions, ranging from neighborhood shops to consumer cooperatives, constituted a fabric of urban relationships that set workers apart from other townspeople. How did textile workers in Troyes perceive production changes in the mills, and how did they react to the emerging market culture of luxury goods? What clothing did they actually own during this period? What forms of consumption were available to them? How did they define their own needs and desires in terms of clothing? Answers to these questions will help us to determine the extent to which Troyes textile workers may have become consumers of the goods they were producing by the interwar period.

THE RIGHT TO CONSUME

Recent historians have studied consumption from many different angles. My preference here is for the approach taken by Giovanni Levi, whose micro-historical analysis provides a way of examining and analyzing incremental socioeconomic change and individual strategies.[9] Levi contends that consumer behavior is a more complex social phenomenon than can be accounted for by any one model, and that overall there is no entirely satisfactory economic logic to consumption. Social strategies that attribute meanings to goods have been far more common than economic ones in determining consumer spending.

9. Levi (1996) gives a critical overview of recent studies on consumption, showing the weakness of interpretative models. He identifies three ways in which historians, in their search for analytic frameworks, have tended to reduce consumer agency to fit a preconceived model. First, they have focused on production at the expense of consumption, approaching consumers as mere economic and political agents of production (Braudel 1981). This model is predicated on the assumption that economic growth and technological progress tend to determine income distribution and consumer behavior. Levi questions whether there could have been no mass consumption before the industrial revolution.

Second, historians have centered on the critical moment when a putative consumer revolution created the condition for a mass market of goods and a commodity culture (Brewer, McKendrick, and Plumb 1982). Studies based on this approach, according to Levi, neglect the variety of cultural practices that prepared the way for such a revolution. More important, such historians implicitly accept an integrated society, with more uniform consumer practices resulting from this process. And finally, a third approach has sought to emphasize consumer behavior as a process of social emulation that trickled down from the elite to the masses, an approach that reduces individual agency (D. Roche 1994).

Levi's preferred sources are inventories after death, wills, and family account books, documents that reveal family, even individual, strategies, many of which rely on informal systems of credit and exchange. An important starting point for measuring any step-changes in socioeconomic inequality is to determine the level of material goods and subsistence: what workers actually owned. The next step is to discover how they spent their wages and establish the meanings they attached to specific goods. Yesterday's luxuries could become today's needs. Moreover, as Levi convincingly claims, there has never been a model of consumption common to both the elites and the masses. Why would workers want to emulate the bourgeoisie, even if they had the means to do so? Levi reminds us that goods are invested with different valences by different social groups. His approach reaffirms consumer agency. Historians, therefore, need to observe a plurality of social practices within given groups in order to understand consumer strategies and the extent to which they were motivated by solidarity, desire, conflicts, and even survival. Similarly, to understand how consumer practices function in relation to social mobility, historians must examine the interrelation between available forms of consumption, social class networks, and the social meanings of goods.[10] By examining the range of consumer practices within the working-class community, we can learn, as Levi suggests, how individual workers met their social needs.

Leisure and Consumption

If workers such as Louis Foin felt the need to defend their right to consume, it was also because they had little leisure or disposable income that would have allowed them to exercise it. Socialist thinkers had long argued against the brutal factory regime, which imposed either long hours under extenuating work conditions or periods of layoffs and underemployment that kept workers' wages low and living precarious. Guesdist leader Paul Lafargue popularized the notion of leisure as a remedy for industrial crises of overproduction and unemployment, by casting it in the appealing terms of "the right to be lazy." His pamphlet of that title, written in 1883, was one of the most widely

10. Levi is interested in the diversity of social practices of consumption within culturally homogeneous social groups. This leads him to redefine the questions and to ask how consumer expenses vary in function of income within such groups. His examples are drawn from a study of family budgets in seventeenth-century Venice, in which he emphasizes the subjective choices of goods in relation to what he sees as a patrimonial strategy in terms of family survival or prestige (Levi 1996).

published and read of Guesdist works. It was certainly to be found in the reading room at the Maison du Peuple in Troyes, and it was regularly advertised
in *Le Reveil des Travailleurs de l'Aube*. Lafargue's pamphlet criticized the working class for believing in a "dogma of work," in sum, for their acceptance of
the capitalist work ethic, which only confounded the crises of overwork and
overproduction.[11] In arguing in favor of leisure for workers, or as he phrased
it, freedom from the discipline of work, Lafargue also gave economic legitimacy to workers' right to consume. In his eloquent justification for women
textile workers as potential customers for the very textile manufacturers for
whom they worked, he wrote: "Monsieur Bonnet, here are your workingwomen, silk workers, spinners, weavers; they are shivering pitifully under their
patched cotton dresses, yet it is they who have spun and woven the silk robes
of the fashionable women of all Christendom. The poor creatures, working
thirteen hours a day, had no time to think of their toilette." He then exhorted
the leading textile manufacturers to clothe their workers, citing each one by
name and identifying their known specialty fabric: "Put at the disposal of your
working girls the fortune they have built for you out of their flesh; you want
to help business, get your goods into circulation—here are consumers ready at
hand. Give them unlimited credit."[12] However sardonic Lafargue's formulation of the right to consume might appear, his assertion that workers were natural consumers, because of their needs for the basic necessities, had received
little recognition up until then. By 1900, production in Troyes was almost
entirely geared to bourgeois luxury consumption. Workers' needs, Lafargue
asserted, were social needs that should determine what was produced. Workers' right to leisure and a living wage would allow them to consume.

As we have seen, militant socialists linked their demand for the eight-hour
day to the notion of leisure, as a time to rest from long working hours. Simultaneously, various Catholic and social-reform groups were also exerting pressure to liberate Sunday as a day of rest from industrial waged work. Arguably,
one of the principal objectives of the secularized version of leisure was to facilitate the possibilities of consumption. Thorsten Veblen has shown that by the
late nineteenth century, the concept of leisure itself took on greater economic
importance as commercial capitalism came to dominate industrial production

11. For a discussion of the ambiguities within Marxist ideology on the notion of liberation
through work, highlighted by Lafargue's pamphlet, see Stuart 1992, 65–67; for similar ambiguities raised by workers, see Rancière 1986.
12. Lafargue 1883. The quotes are from the English edition 1907 (25).

and control the marketing of goods.[13] While the leisure classes were visible consumers during the Belle Epoque, workers' use of the limited time spent moving between work and home remains somewhat elusive. What conceptions of leisure did workers have? How did consumption fit into individual free time? In fact, the use to be made of shorter working hours and subsequent leisure was the subject of much contemporary debate.[14] There were a number of spokespeople within the unions and the workers' consumer cooperative movement in Troyes who articulated the link between leisure and consumption in significant ways. Many of them, including Louis Foin, were socialist cooperators who had undoubtedly been influenced by Guesdist leader Paul Lafargue's arguments. Nevertheless, our evidence for the prewar period suggests that only a minority of textile workers actually thought about nonwork in consumerist terms.

The battle over shorter hours and the debate on the uses of leisure took several forms. As noted in Chapter 3, the political appeal of the eight-hour-day movement of the 1890s did not prevent its being met with strong opposition from employers and a certain ambivalence among workers. Ordinary workers more easily understood the link between wages and the cost of living than they did the relation between shorter working hours, increased productivity, and thus higher wages. Those pushing for another reform proposal, in favor of the *semaine anglaise* (Saturday half-day holiday), successfully proposed social time for family needs that even conservative employers might support. Consumerist goals were indeed embedded in this notion of free time. In 1913, the CGT textile union in Troyes distributed a May Day tract that stressed in gendered terms the advantages to women of liberating the Saturday afternoon for household chores and provisioning.[15] The union clearly saw the *semaine anglaise* as a way of recruiting women and moralizing men. Posters and propaganda circulated by the CGT in favor of shorter hours and the *semaine anglaise*

13. Veblen was somewhat of a prophet in this respect, arguing that commercial capitalism drove consumer demand, and especially the "conspicuous" consumption of the privileged classes. His major work, *The Theory of the Leisure Class,* was not translated into French and published until 1970. See Aron 1970.

14. Gary Cross (1989) maintains that "the historical relationship between leisure and consumerism is more tenuous than labor historians have claimed" (12–14). Cross examines the theory of the "modernization of labor," which posits that workers relinquished control over the labor process for access to greater leisure, increased income, and a higher standard of living. He argues that there is little historical evidence for this "trade-off" before 1945. Short-hours movements preceded mass consumption, and "neither employers nor workers thought predominantly in terms of consumption when the eight-hour day was won in 1919" (14).

15. Tract on the *semaine anglaise* signed by Julian Grée, ADA SC 330. See Chapter 3.

conveyed a specific family ideology: if given more free time, fathers would renounce the café-bar for happiness in the family home. The posters portrayed two distinct working-class households, one in which alcoholism, poverty, and tuberculosis lurked, the other in which family life prospered in an ordered domestic environment.[16] But in that same year, 1913, millowners in Troyes expressed their opposition to a Saturday half-day holiday, reasoning that this reform proposal had come either too late or too soon. In a conjuncture of heightened competition from foreign manufacturers, Troyes millowners considered shorter-hours proposals to be unrealistic without an international agreement.[17] The Saturday half-day holiday was finally instituted in 1917 after an intense campaign endorsed by the Fédération de l'habillement (Federation of Clothing Workers), many of whose members were seamstresses, whose strike in Paris had forced the union to take up the issue. At the outset, however, it was to have limited application.[18]

The question of free time was primarily an economic issue, but it also raised social and cultural factors that fueled debate over consumption. Workers clearly voiced the demand for social time, for mixing in the street in clothes that did not segregate them as workers. The bourgeois habit of Sunday promenades in parks and boulevards required an appropriate change of clothes. As early as 1873, the Chamber of Commerce in Troyes had noted that knitters maintained their practice of the Saint Monday (taking the day off from work) because "they lacked clean or appropriate clothes to wear on Sunday in the midst of a population *en toilette*."[19] Similar sentiments were echoed by the socialist newspaper in Troyes, *Le Reveil des Travailleurs*. The paper published the following commentary in 1897 on the lack of worker attendance at evening popular education lectures: "Why don't workers attend? . . . Because those who work have dignity, and he who creates riches through his labor is often himself more than modestly dressed and feels sovereignly uncomfortable to mix in a milieu where aggressive elegance is the rule, beginning with the professors giving the talks. . . . Because *le peuple* [who] leave work at eight in

16. See "Réduisons les heures de travail," CGT (1978), no. 63.

17. Chambre de commerce de Troyes, "Sur l'opportunité de l'adoption de la semaine anglaise dans l'industrie de la bonneterie," April 4, 1913, Archives du Musée de la bonneterie. Millowners did agree that Saturday free time would have been a preferable reform to the shorter daily hours legislated in 1900. By 1913 competition from foreign textile manufacturers made any shorter-hours proposal much more problematic.

18. Coffin 1996b, 194–95.

19. AN C 3018, Aube, report dated October 16, 1873, "Enquête sur la situation des classes ouvrières 1872–1875," as quoted in M. Perrot 1974, 1:226.

the evening, tired from labor, want physical sustenance before the intellectual nourishment that they reserve for Sundays."[20]

But for working people, the transition between labor and leisure not only depended on having disposable income with which to afford a decent change of clothes; it also required a locker (*vestiaire*) to facilitate a change of clothes before leaving work. Workers no longer wanted to be identified as workers upon leaving the job. The notion of dignity, even respectability, depended on the possibility of changing one's identity and melting into the crowd. By the turn of the century, workers' strike grievances included just such a demand for lockers, and in 1908 a public-administration regulation provided for the compulsory installation of lockers in certain factories.[21] Indeed, by 1913, the Troyes Chamber of Commerce noted that workers frequently used work time to change their clothes on arriving and leaving the mills.[22] In many respects, the very possibility of changing out of one's work clothes represented a new and measurable transformation in working-class culture.

Spending Patterns

The right to consume, then, raised issues that emerged from the workplace and spilled out into the social spaces of urban life. Shorter hours, leisure time, higher wages, and disposable income were all interconnected, placing material constraints on consumption that were played out in the family budget. Recent studies of working-class family budgets for this period reveal a fairly complete picture of how some workers spent their wages, and the share allocated in their incomes to food and clothing. Michelle Perrot used data from fifteen family monographs by the disciples of Catholic reformer Frédéric Le Play, published in the series *Les ouvriers des deux mondes,* to calculate the following average expenses allocated by working-class families for the 1890s: 62.8 percent for food, 16.5 percent for clothing, 12.3 percent for housing, and 8.3 percent for miscellaneous expenses.[23] These figures confirm the fact that food constraints

20. Quoted in Morlot 1986, 364.
21. M. Perrot 1974, 1:227.
22. Chambre de commerce de Troyes, "Sur l'opportunité de l'adoption de la semaine anglaise dans l'industrie de la bonneterie," April 4, 1913, Archives du Musée de la bonneterie.
23. The average for clothing was based on a low of 8.5 percent and a high of 30.8 percent. See M. Perrot 1974, 1:215. Maurice Lévy-Leboyer, working from a variety of nineteenth- and twentieth-century sources, calculated budget allocations for food and clothing among workers as follows: 62.8 percent on food and 16.5 percent on clothing in 1880 for France as a whole, and

continued to dominate workers' budgets during this period. The sudden rise in the cost of living in 1911, a period known to contemporaries as "la vie chère," changed ordinary workers' perception of how well their nominal wages could provide for their families' needs.[24] But it did not significantly change their priorities. Without an increase in income or a decline in food prices, there could be little change in the allocation for clothing. Spending on both food and clothing remained imperative if workers were to maintain their collective life both inside and outside the home. During this historical moment of transition in consumer patterns, worker clothing in Troyes was clearly a visible sign of class and a marker of the relative measure of social change.

The sociologist Maurice Halbwachs, in *La classe ouvrière et les niveaux de vie,* published in 1913, confirms these spending patterns in important respects. Halbwachs's primary focus, however, was not the family, but social class. He demonstrated that social classes were differentiated not only by income, but also by material needs, and that these needs were socially and culturally determined.[25] In his view, social needs were largely defined by contact between social classes, in a process of interaction that took place not in the workplace, but in the street and in society at large. Since it was society that attributed meaning to goods, consumer spending was also determined by a sociopsychological rationale. For Halbwachs, workers lived on the periphery of French society, both alienated by the nature of their factory work and marginal to modern life. Consumption represented a primary mode for their integration into society through the system of exchange of goods and values. Therefore, the key to understanding workers' relation to contemporary social codes was to examine their behavior as consumers, their needs, and what he called their "level of living."

For Halbwachs, the locus of consumption was the family. Like Le Play, but free of the latter's conservative ideological assumptions, he examined family

---

64 percent on food and 14 percent on clothing in 1907 for major cities. He argued that reductions in food expenditure allowed workers to buy available ready-to-wear clothing in the 1880s and 1890s, replacing their habit of trading in used clothing. See Lévy-Leboyer and Bourguignon 1990, 41–44.

24. The rise in prices in 1911 was caused by an outbreak of hoof-and-mouth disease that affected meat and milk and dairy products. For a discussion of the relation between strikes, wages, and the cost of living, see Perrot 1974, 1:124–32. Perrot affirms that the subsistence riots of 1911 marked the first time that strikes became a form of protest against the cost of living. See also Glickman 1997.

25. Halbwachs 1913, 118–27. For recent assessments of Halbwachs's work, see Baudelot and Establet 1994; and Coffin 1999.

budgets, wages, and spending. In his 1913 study, Halbwachs showed that no matter what their income, manual workers tended to spend more money on food than did, for example, *employés* (white-collar workers) with the same income. During this period the largest expense in workers' budgets was for food (more than 50 percent), a long-standing priority in working-class life. Food represented not only a physical necessity, but also an important means of family sociability, for example, around the evening meal after work.[26] Clothing represented the second item in the family budget, absorbing between 11 percent and 13 percent, followed by housing and related expenses. Halbwachs inferred from these choices that workers would sacrifice on housing comfort to buy clothing, an expression of their strong desire to mingle in the streets, cafés, and other sites of social integration. Their clothing needs were increasingly changing, he argued, in relation to their social life, their income, and their desire to mix. In the transitional space between home and work, those who could afford to do so frequently wore an intermediary costume in the street, reserving a significant change of clothing for Sundays or holidays. Yet he recognized that their dress would rarely be so "radical that workers in the street could not be distinguished from nonworkers."[27]

In this initial study, Halbwachs viewed French workers as relatively isolated and self-contained, with class-specific needs. From this perspective, their integration was important to social cohesion. Because Halbwachs did not venture to observe workers in factories, as later generations of French sociologists would do, his rather mechanistic account of industrial labor ultimately shaped his definition of worker identity. His personal vision of a fixed cultural identity, and ultimately a homogeneous working class, seems overdetermined by the nature of industrial labor. By the 1930s, however, his vision would significantly change, as we shall see in a later chapter.[28] Halbwachs's significant analysis of working-class consumption drew several important insights from his contemporary Thorsten Veblen. Both men understood needs as socially defined. However, Veblen more clearly theorized the way women functioned as conspicuous consumers of clothing in a commodity culture. By contrast, Halbwachs scarcely gave a role to women. More serious criticism can be

---

26. Halbwachs 1913, 420–22. The evening meal also strengthened patriarchal authority, Halbwachs argued, as if there was only a male breadwinner. As Judith Coffin (1999) so rightly observes, notions of gender are absent from Halbwachs's work.

27. Halbwachs 1913, 425, 432–39.

28. Ibid. See Chapter 8.

leveled at the way in which Halbwachs's emphasis on material constraints, low wages, and class consciousness in workers' lives left little scope for collective action. In fact, as we shall see, many workers' motivations to consume stemmed from egalitarian desires and collective action. The growing workers' consumer cooperative movement provided an alternative, albeit minority, vision, dominated at the outset by socialists concerned with a more just distribution of goods and necessities in French society. Halbwachs's insights into the importance of clothing for working-class sociability will, however, inform to some extent my analysis of workers' wardrobes.

WORKERS' CLOTHING

Direct knowledge of the household economy of ordinary textile workers in Troyes, male or female, at the end of the nineteenth century remains scarce, since many died young or appeared to have little disposable income for more than a basic wardrobe. Inequality in terms of basic material needs and life expectancy had manifestly already set them apart as a distinctive social class. Moreover, direct access to workers' social practice of dressing is difficult given the fact that clothing remained a fragile acquisition somewhere between necessity and desire. Our sources for this section provide two rather different perspectives on working-class life. The first, derived primarily from inventories after death and observations by contemporary social reformers, emphasizes individualized consumption within the couple or the family unit. The second, based on period photographs, offers a normative vision that contextualizes the individual within a social setting at a particular moment in time. Both approaches can be construed as obtrusive ways of looking into workers' wardrobes and closets. But the lens of the public notary is not the same as the lens of the street photographer.

Looking into Workers' Wardrobes

For contemporary social scientists and reformers of various political persuasions, questions of class and consumption converged on the working-class family. Two family monographs by disciples of Catholic reformer Frédéric Le Play concern the Champagne region: the first, a study of a skilled spinner and his family at the rural factory of Val-des-Bois near Reims, was published in the series Les ouvriers des deux mondes in 1896; and the second, a study of a family of rural knitters in Maizières-la-Grande Paroisse by the village schoolteacher, was prepared for the Paris World's Fair of 1900.[29] Both these studies furnish inventories of everyday objects, together with family budgets detailing expenses. For this reason they provide some measure of material change in workers' lives, when compared to our sample of inventories after death for the 1880s.[30] Both these monographs reflect social scientists' interest in the interconnections of wages, expenses, household unwaged labor, and the purchasing power of the working-class family. The focus of both researchers remained the family, still envisioned as the basic economic unit of French society. However, each author consciously addressed the contemporary debate on women's work and protective labor legislation.

Because of their nature and function in French society, inventories after death pose several problems as sources on working-class material culture. Above all, the inventory served to protect the rights of heirs and creditors and to provide an evaluation of possessions for estate tax purposes. As such, it can provide only partial evidence of a person's fortunes at a moment in time. During the nineteenth century, declarations by household, under the marriage regime of the *communauté des biens,* suggest a systematic underestimation of items such as clothing, which was considered of lesser material interest than furnishings or land by both the notaries and the *commisseurs priseurs* drawing up the inventories. But by far the greatest problem concerning workers is the absence of property of any significant kind to declare—how can one constitute a representative sample when most workers were too poor to own property?[31] Few had possessions of any value, and these inventories reveal a bleaker picture

29. The first study is Guérin 1896; the second, Jamerey 1900. See also Jamerey's discussion of the family workshop in Chapter 4. For an analysis of Le Play's position in French sociology, see Coffin 1996b, chap. 7; 1999.

30. An earlier monograph on a rural agricultural laborer in the Champagne region, dating from 1856, paints a stark picture of poverty. Clothing represented 46 percent of the value of the family's total effects, a considerable portion of the budget for a family of four. Most of this wardrobe can be attributed to the wife, who worked as a seamstress, hired for the day or for piecework. She sewed, repaired, and laundered all the family clothes. Among the husband's possessions were a heavy worsted jacket, a new blue smock, a woolen vest, and six pairs of woolen socks; his wife owned a dress and two skirts in wool, a corset, two printed calico scarves, and four pairs of wool stockings. The author of this study noted that the clothing "was chosen exclusively in terms of utility; no special style, almost all of them made of cotton, patched until totally worn." More significant, none of the clothing bore any "affinity with bourgeois dress" (Delbet 1983, 51–52).

31. For a discussion of the problems posed by inventories after death, but also their richness as a source, see D. Roche 1994, 17–18, 70–75.

of provincial working-class life than do our other sources, the family monographs and period photographs for the region. My sample privileges a small minority of artisan knitters and those who had sufficient property for the state to evaluate.[32] Notarial records, gleaned from the Table des successions après décès for the periods 1878–80 and 1896–99, showed that in virtually every case for both periods the property in question was of minimal value.

My sample of detailed inventories is based on twenty-eight individual cases, eleven for the earlier period, seventeen for the later. While the overall sample is relatively small, the data brings vividly to life some aspects of what would otherwise remain a disappearing and silent world. In many ways, the inventories of goods evoke an intimacy and feeling for individual behavior that other sources cannot reveal. For both periods, roughly four out of five workers had such meager possessions that they were designated in the register as having a "certificat d'indigence."[33] Understanding this poverty is made easier when we correlate the estate data with the age at death. According to hospital records, the major cause of death among textile workers was tuberculosis.[34] There was a huge discrepancy in life expectancy for textile workers, notably among women, by comparison with the general population of the town. For the period 1878–80, women textile workers died an average of twelve years earlier than the women in the general town population. Indeed, a third of women textile workers died before the age of thirty. A similar pattern holds true for the later period (1896–99) and continues into the 1920s.

Given the short life expectancy among textile workers, it is not surprising that few had accumulated possessions of any value. Among the urban artisans, several owned knitting machines, while their wives had sewing machines or winders (*bobinoirs*) at home. Only a very few owned land or the house in which they lived; even fewer possessed any savings. For both the 1880s and

32. ADA 3Q, Table des successions and Table des mutations après décès. I took a systematic sample of textile workers with names beginning with *B, C, L,* and *M* for the periods 1878–80 and 1896–99, looking for age at death, marital status, sex, occupation, and whether or not there was an estate. Unfortunately, for the postwar period I was only able to consult the general tables that list the overall value of an estate for the years 1924–27; more detailed estate records were not yet available, as notaries conserve their records for one hundred years.

33. The registers, or Tables des mutations après décès, for these two periods indicated an overwhelming number of textile workers of both sexes who died without leaving any property of value: 87 percent in 1880 and 89.2 percent in 1899. My sample for 1878–80 was based on 136 workers out of a total adult population of 1,522, and for 1896–99, 158 workers out of 1,297 (ADA 3Q 8218, 3Q 8226).

34. ADA H dépôt 387/1662, H dépôt 387/1664. I looked at all deaths for the years 1902, 1909, 1924, and 1934. See Chapter 3.

the late 1890s, working-class couples in our sample owned clothing averaging about 17 percent of the total value of their personal effects. In the earlier period, basic wardrobe items—shirts, socks, stockings, and *jupons* (petticoats)—were prevalent. But significantly, by the 1890s new items, such as *corsages* and *camisoles* for women and *jacquette fantaisie* for men, were appearing in wardrobes. Very few inventories carried any reference to body linen, which had been such an important sign of cleanliness and luxury in eighteenth-century Paris.[35] Undoubtedly, in late nineteenth-century Troyes, such items were assumed to be without value. Overall, by 1900 there is evidence of a wider range of apparel, even if there is little quantitative increase in the number of clothing items possessed. Therefore, by the late nineteenth century, more material comfort existed among those textile workers who had enough possessions to necessitate a declaration.

All the inventories provide a distinction between everyday work clothes and Sunday or festive attire. During the nineteenth century, it was a sign of bourgeois respectability for men to dress in dark, or black, clothes, a code eventually adopted by all social classes by 1900. Baudelaire gave this dress code a political explanation. He noted mournfully that black frock coats were a visible sign of growing equality.[36] The inventories show that Sunday clothes for men in the 1880s were of predominately dark, mostly black, worsted, a sign that solidity and durability mattered in the choice of fabric. By 1900, the earlier nineteenth-century *habit* and *redingote* had been replaced by a *costume de drap noir* (black suit) and a *pardessus* (overcoat), signaling most likely the standardized ready-to-wear goods now available for all men. But by far the most significant change occurred with regard to work clothes. In the early 1880s, men still wore traditional blue cotton smocks (*blouses bleues*), the distinctive uniform of the working class, but by the late 1890s, new garments, among them loose jackets (*paletots*) and knitted vests (*gilets*), became basic items. By the late nineteenth century, workers' wardrobes included clothing that did not identify their social rank and could be worn in the streets.

35. As a factor in hygiene, cleanliness, and ultimately class distinction, personal linen was an eighteenth-century conquest that, according to Daniel Roche, transformed behavior. Linen was beyond the budget of the laboring classes, in terms of both price and laundering expenses. See D. Roche 1994, chap. 7, esp. 157–63; 1987, chap. 6.

36. In Baudelaire's own words, "a uniform livery of grief is a proof of equality" (cited in Harvey 1995, 26–27). Harvey's study traces the transition to black clothing in the nineteenth century in a fascinating work that combines the meaning of the color and the clothes in European history. He suggests that dark menswear signified work and professional dignity and that bourgeois women, who were excluded from the professions, were color coded in white.

Evidence from one of the family monographs also confirms these changes in male workers' dress. In the wardrobe of the skilled spinner, working at the Manufactory of Val-des-Bois near Reims, "all trace of regional costume has disappeared; the traditional worker's smock is worn only in the workshop, and indeed many have already abandoned it. Not only do these workers wear loosely fitted jackets [*paletots*], but also top hats that seemed to be the prerogative of urban men."[37] This man's family shopped at the local consumer cooperative run by his Catholic employer, Léon Harmel, and he could thus presumably afford ready-made clothes. Not so for the rural knitter's family in Maizières-la-Grande Paroisse, whose basic wardrobe in 1900 was still socially marked. The author observed: "The knitter's clothing is not luxurious, but it is made of a fabric that wears well. On weekdays the father wears a vest with sleeves and a blue cloth apron; on Sundays a worsted jacket; on festival days, four or five times a year, a black *redingote*."[38] Clearly, rural workers had less disposable income, and less access to ready-made. In this family, clothing expenses represented 24 percent of their annual budget.

Women's basic work wardrobe consisted of the *chemise* and the *tablier* (apron), worn over a skirt and one or more petticoats. Women's work clothes had scarcely changed since the early nineteenth century. However, the fabrics were lighter-weight cottons and were more varied in color than men's clothing. In general, women dressed with greater fantasy than men. Gaily colored cottons, known as *indiennes* (calico), provided contrast to more sober everyday clothes, while such items as ribbons, lace, silk scarves, and hats were fashion accessories. The prevalence of cotton clothes over heavier, more solid fabrics, was a consequence of the nineteenth-century textile revolution. As Michelet observed in *Le Peuple* in 1846, cotton had brought a revolution in hygiene to poor households:

> Little remarked on, but important, a revolution in cleanliness, an improvement experienced by poor households; body linen, bed linen, table linen, curtains, were all owned by whole classes for the first time in human history. The great and capital revolution was *l'indienne*. The combined efforts of science and art had been necessary to force a stubborn, unwieldy fabric, cotton, to undergo daily such brilliant

37. Guérin 1896, 96.
38. Jamerey 1900.

transformations, but once they succeeded, it spread everywhere, making it accessible to the poor. Every woman used to wear a blue or
black dress that she kept for ten years without washing it for fear that
it would fall to pieces. Today her husband can cover her in flower-
printed cotton for the price of a day's wages.[39]

The wearing of cotton not only improved bodily hygiene, it also diversified
women's wardrobes, because of its cheapness, versatility, and printed colors.

Among women, the staple item of dress clothing was the black merino
wool dress, found in virtually all female wardrobes from the 1880s to the turn
of the century. We can speculate that the color black for women was a sign of
respectability, but that it was not necessarily dictated by fashion as it was for
men. Working women owned white cotton stockings, rather than the more
expensively dyed black ones, and by 1900 the urban *bottine* (ankle-high boot)
had replaced the rural clog.[40] Similarly, brimmed hats signaled a certain refine-
ment in wardrobes where bonnets and modest scarves (*fichus*) had previously
been workingwomen's lot. Shawls of various materials and colors completed
their dress costume. Both family monographs noted earlier confirm that
mothers and young women were spending more than men in following fashion trends, but also that they were using their garment-making skills to recycle and refashion clothing that had seen earlier use. In the case of the spinner's
family, the wife made a substantial contribution to the family budget through
industrial homework as a knitter. Moreover, this model housewife had pur-
chased her knitting machine at a price well above that which a worker could
ordinarily afford (fifteen hundred francs). Her earnings thus provided the
means for the family to purchase ready-made suits and dress clothes. For the
contemporary observer, fashions made at the mill seemed to drive this family
to spend some 8 percent of their annual budget on clothing. The author reasoned that the mill in Val-des-Bois manufactured "fabrics that [had] become
the passion . . . launched on the [fashion] market by the company itself."[41]
By this time fashion clothing appeared to be within the reach of at least some
working-class women.

39. Michelet 1973, 80–81.
40. Black was more expensive because of the costly dyeing process. By the end of the century new aniline dyes made the process both cheaper and more durable. For an analysis of the
social role and meaning of black in women's nineteenth-century clothing, see Pellegrin 1994.
41. Guérin, 92. The author of this study estimated the family's annual clothing expenses as
three hundred francs. The industrious wife's earnings averaged some five hundred francs a year,
that clearly covered clothing for the family of four.

The inventories after death reveal little about the purchasing strategies of the goods assessed. We are left wondering about what items of dress might have been prized in these humble wardrobes, and speculating on how certain valuables entered the families' possession. For example, the presence in the inventories of watches and jewelry raises perplexing questions. Silver watches were found in one-third of the male textile workers' estates in our sample for the 1870s, and nearly two-thirds by the 1890s; by contrast, very few watches or jewelry were found for women textile workers for either period. What purposes did these objects serve? Their presence in our sources suggests a number of social meanings and possibilities, ranging from their being status symbols to their more likely use as deposits for small loans in the event of declining fortune. As E. P. Thompson observed, "[T]he time-piece was the poor man's bank, an investment of savings: it could in bad times be sold or put in hock."[42] No doubt jewelry served the same purpose for women workers.

Sorties d'Usine

A second representation of working-class life is found in popular postcard photographs for the period 1904 to 1914.[43] These photographs offer a normative vision that contrasts sharply with the image of poverty that is revealed in the inventories. In this popular format, workers figure in street scenes, at times grouped in front of cafés or mingling with shopkeepers, but more commonly in "sorties d'usines," when leaving the mills.[44] Such genre photographs of social groups were produced commercially, in response to popular interest in urban everyday life. As postcards they served to advertise and document the authenticity of their correspondents' lives. The popularity of such images among workers themselves ensured their circulation from the moment of their purchase at the neighborhood shop, to reception by friends and family. One worker in Auxerre wrote to his father on the back of a postcard: "I'm sending a photo of a group of workers in the place where I work. There's my father-in-law who was hired with me as my helper. We're photographed at the return

42. See his now classic essay (1967). This second explanation is also suggested by Giovanni Levi (1996) as a survival strategy (201).
43. For historians' treatment of visual materials, see Perlmutter 1994, 167–81; Samuels 1994, 315–36; for Walter Benjamin's reflections on the the relation between history and images, see Schwartz 2001.
44. See Zeyons 1997 for striking examples of the subjects of these popular images during this period. The first photo postcards appeared in Troyes in 1897.

to work after lunch. Several of us had put on our work clothes."[45] What interests us principally here is the way photographs construct representations of working-class life in particular social sites. For example, the factory gate, as Maurice Halbwachs remarked, appeared to be a greater social barrier than the front door of the home; it marked the separation of workers from social life.[46] A close look reveals that many *sorties d'usine* record workers' sense of release at the gate from the discipline of physical labor. Still others document the sexual segregation imposed by certain Catholic and state employers, whose moral concerns about women workers did not stop at the factory gate.[47] Almost all figures were intentionally posed by the photographer. The ritual posing is most obvious in the case of mill workshops, with their rows of seated and standing workers. But in the more informal settings, photographs of this type emphasize class, occupation, and social space, all frozen at a particular moment in time.

The first image examined here (Fig. 8) depicts a crowd gathered in front of the Café de la Cloche, rue Largentier, in Troyes, showing men and women workers employed at the nearby mill, the Société Générale de Bonneterie, around 1905. Street clothes predominate over work clothes. Even in this mixed crowd, female workers stand out distinctively, with their aprons (*tabliers*), high-collared blouses (*corsages*), and the mere absence of hats—they are "en cheveux"; that is, their long hair loosely crowns their heads. Male workers can be distinguished by their caps (*casquettes*), jackets (*paletots*), and shirts generally without collars and neckties. Despite the café setting as a center of sociability, the photo represents a sober image of workers' lives, expressed through their serious faces and their dark clothes. Two figures emerge from the group that suggest occupational rank; they can be identified as a mill foreman (on the far left) and a forewoman (center) by their more formal clothing and hats. The presence of young children and a worker with his bicycle remind us of family life outside the mill. Bicycles were more common by 1914, but in 1902 their cost varied between two hundred and four hundred francs, an expense that represented well over a month's wages for a knitter.[48]

45. Ibid., 38. For further examples of the genre in Troyes and commentary on the epistolary practices engendered by these photo postcards, see Bérisé 1993, 1999.

46. See Halbwachs 1913, 425.

47. *Mixité* (gender integration) was proscribed in the spinning mills of Val des Bois operated by Léon Harmel, at the Menier chocolate factory in Noisiel, and at most state-run tobacco factories, even as women workers left the mills (Zeyons 1997, 53).

48. Ibid., 30. The price cited is from the 1902 catalog of the Manufacture des Armes et Cyles de Saint-Etienne.

Figure 8 Men and women workers from the Société Générale de Bonneterie mill in front of the Café de la Cloche, rue Largentier in Troyes, c. 1907. Collection Claude Bérisé.

Figure 9 *Sortie d'usine* at the Poron mill, rue des Bas Trévois, c. 1908. Collection Claude Bérisé.

In the transitional space between the mill and the street, workers at the *sortie d'usine* in the second image (Fig. 9) pose informally in front of the Poron mill, rue des Bas Trevois, in 1908. As in the previous photo, this group of workers can be clearly distinguished by their clothing, especially the women by their long skirts, aprons, and uncovered hair. The two young women to the left smile playfully and hold hands. To the right, a group of young male *rebrousseurs* (apprentices) in caps are dressed similarly to the adult male knitters with whom they worked.[49] The man in the bowler hat at the back can be identified as a white-collar worker whose monthly wages afforded him a hat three times the price of a worker's cap. There is a notable mixing of sexes and ages that gives this industrial landscape the flavor of an environment with a sense of community.

If we compare these two photographs with a third one (Fig. 10) of the management at the Valton mill in 1909, social hierarchy and class distinctions become more apparent because of the bourgeois clothing. All but the women have adopted the social prerogative of the suit. Seated solidly in the front row is the director, André Valton, flanked by his white-collar managers. All the men are dressed in black, fitted, three-piece suits; some wear ties; many are making some effort to hide their hands. They give every appearance of self-assurance and being at ease in their tailored clothes. The four women are *contremaîtresses* (forewomen), who oversaw the workshops of women seamers. All wear the air of bourgeois respectability.[50] The contrast is striking between these men in their tailored suits, and the male workers in the previous photographs, whose ready-made street clothes bear little affinity to the bourgeois dress code featured here.

The following photograph (Fig. 11), showing the personnel of the Vitoux-Derrey mill in 1904, provides an alternative view of working life. It seems that here millworkers have been invited to dress as they would like to be seen, in street rather than work clothes. This particular photograph is drawn from an album documenting the Vitoux-Derrey mill in 1904. The date indicates that it was probably commissioned for the visit to Troyes that same year of the Parliamentary Commission of Inquiry on the Textile Industry and that perhaps it

---

49. The young apprentice in the Troyes textile mills, known locally by the epithet "le caffard," was the subject of a song by Etienne Pédron. The published edition of his songs carries an illustration of the apprentice dressed exactly like the young men in this photograph. See Pédron 1906, 45. See also Chapter 3.

50. From Boucraut and Boucraut 1986, 54.

Figure 10   Millowners André and Xavier Valton (front row center) with mill managers and foremen/women in 1909. Boucraut and Boucraut, *Pierre Valton et ses fils* (1986).

was intended as a gift.[51] As we know, Léon Vitoux showcased his mill for the commission's visit. The women are all grouped in front, the men segregated in the rear in a sea of caps and others spilling out from a doorway into the courtyard. Overall, the clothing is more fashionable, less marked in terms of class. Some women workers have opted to wear hats that might have been norms in the street, but were not so in the workshop. There are secondary signs related to fashion, more subtle distinctions of accessories and coiffure, that characterize these women as workers. But overall the greater diversity of dress reveals the individuality of certain figures, in striking contrast to what is seen in the previous photographs.

51. The photograph is part of an album dated 1904, obviously taken by a professional photographer for the purpose of documenting the entire mill, machinery, workshops, and personnel. There is no text to explain the circumstances for this special vision of mill life, except that Léon Vitoux, the millowner, invited the members of the commission in 1904 to visit his mill, at the same time that he gave them a copy of his lecture on women's work in the industry. See Chapter 2.

Figure 11   Personnel of the Vitoux-Derrey mill posing in the courtyard, c. 1904. Archives départementales de l'Aube.

These genre photographs convey a remarkable collective portrait of working-class life for the period after 1900. The mechanical eye of the camera manifests details that are usually invisible, very similar to the inventories after death discussed above. But these photographs, in contrast to the inventories, operate to integrate workers into social space and to identify the very communities of work and leisure in which these workers lived. It is somehow fitting that industrial workers became the subjects of photography at the moment that photography itself entered a new industrial age. Today's use of photographs as a source for social history corresponds to a moment in time when these very communities, faced with significant social change, attempt to reconstruct their roots and identity in the past.[52] For our study, these photographs at the factory gate attribute broader social meaning to the street clothing worn outside the mill. Despite the absence of the distinctive smock, or *blouse bleue,* we can knowingly distinguish them as workers. One question we might ask of these photographs is, Why is the class of these workers so apparent as a subject?[53] To answer this question we need to look for clues in the increasing democratization of demand among class-conscious consumers.

THE CLASS-CONSCIOUS CONSUMER

The multiple social meanings attached to clothing, its role in fashioning individual, class and gender identity, all confirm the importance of dress in social life. How did workers perceive their own needs in terms of clothing? What dictated their choices? Was there some motivation to transcend class identity through dress? The desire for greater social mobility, and, in individual cases, to emulate bourgeois dress or to adopt *la mode,* are complex social factors that explain the transition toward an increasing democratization of demand, which, as I will argue below, took place in the 1920s and 1930s. However, this

52. The photo postcards appearing in this section and in Chapter 7 are drawn from two volumes compiled by Claude Bérisé (1993, 1999) from his personal collection and published as *La mémoire de Troyes.* I wish to acknowledge his very generous help in documenting working-class life in Troyes.

53. John Berger (1980) asked this question of a series of photographs by August Sander in an essay titled "The Suit and the Photograph," an inquiry into class hegemony through clothing, in particular the bourgeois suit of the nineteenth century premised upon a sedentary lifestyle (27–36). Maurice Halbwachs (1913) commented on this question of workers adopting bourgeois dress by insisting that it was nonfunctional (433).

prewar period can be characterized as one of gradual transition during which numerous consumer practices were at work. The existence of such practices suggests, furthermore, that social aspirations promoted greater diversity of dress, even if it was not immediately affordable. The central marketplace in Troyes included a number of commercial shops, privately owned speciality stores that catered to working-class customers through regular advertisements placed in *Le Reveil des Travailleurs de l'Aube*. Some offered discounts to members of certain trades and occupations; among these shops were Aux 100,000 Paletots on the main street, rue Emile Zola, and the Maison des Travailleurs, which sold ready-made work clothes from the well-known Lyonese manufacturer Adolph Lafont.[54] Two department stores, Magasins Réunis and Jorry-Prieur, located in the center of town, displayed a wide variety of more expensive goods in their shopwindows and sidewalk stalls. Such commercial shops offered the pleasures of window shopping and a spectacle of urban modernity even for those who could not afford to buy.

But there existed in Troyes an alternative to commercial capitalism, a worker-owned and -operated cooperative, the Laborieuse, which formed a significant counterculture for class-conscious consumers. Part of the appeal of the workers' cooperative was its self-conscious stance against bourgeois millowners, several of whom were connected to other retail cooperatives in town. Cooperators at the Laborieuse prized working-class solidarity and an alternative vision of consumer society. And for workers in a provincial town such as Troyes, who had little access to the Parisian marketplace, their store offered a class-based incentive to buy the goods they needed and to satisfy their desires for novelty fashions at affordable prices.

The Laborieuse

The notion of workers' cooperatives for the production and consumption of goods had its roots in the utopian socialism of the 1830s. Cooperatives were envisioned as the practice of socialism in everyday life. The first workers to organize consumer cooperatives recognized that exchange relations and the

54. The socialist paper *Le Reveil des Travailleurs de l'Aube* had a list of recommended shops from among their advertisers, but so did other associative papers, among them the *Bulletin de l'Association Amicale des Instituteurs et Institutrices Publics Laiques de l'Aube*. Founded in 1901, the *Bulletin* carried eleven pages of advertisements in its fourth issue, and by 1913 some twenty-four pages of ads. I wish to thank Jean-Louis Humbert for locating this source.

distribution of goods were shaped by political power. The solutions they proposed contained a critique of competitive industrial and commercial capitalism and offered an alternative. In France, consumer cooperation evolved from two strands of thought, resulting in two different types of organization: the socialist strand, created in conjunction with syndicalism, committed to political action against capitalism; and the reformist strand, with its roots in mutualism and based on the ideals of social protection and worker education. After 1885, two organizations embodied these divergent conceptions of consumer cooperation: the Bourse des coopératives socialistes (BCS), and the Union coopérative (UC). These two organizations competed from behind different ideological positions that corresponded to opposing visions of a social Republic. The apostle for the UC was Charles Gide (1847–1932), a Protestant and an economist, whose vision of cooperation was an expression of the doctrine of solidarism that infused much of the social-reform legislation of the early Third Republic. From Gide's perspective, cooperation would transform economic and social life, subordinating production to consumer needs and harmonizing social relations in the process. Cooperative education would instill citizen consumers with a collective social consciousness that would result in the peaceful transition to a Cooperative Republic.[55] In short, Gide's answer to the social question was consumer cooperation based on solidarism. In turn, socialists considered Gide and the UC as reformists who denied the class struggle through their precepts and practices of class conciliation and collaboration. Despite the continued differences and sometimes sharp debate between the two organizations, by 1912 the UC and the BCS fused, forming the Fédération nationale des coopératives de consommation (FNCC). Prior to the merger, agreement was tentatively reached on a stance of political autonomy.[56]

Although mutualism among workers had a long history in Troyes, what interests us here is the socialist strand as practiced among knitters and metalworkers. From the outset, consumer cooperation of a socialist inspiration was conceived as a means of worker liberation. In certain cases a part of the cooperatives' budgets were allocated to supporting strikes and political propaganda, but practices varied widely. Jean Jaurès described political socialism,

55. The phrase is Gide's, outlined in a historic speech at the Paris World's Fair of 1889 before the Congrès international des sociétés coopératives de consommation. See accounts in Rosalind Williams 1982, 267–315, and Furlough 1991, chap. 4.

56. The history of consumer cooperation in France has been the subject of two important studies: that by Ellen Furlough (1991), and an earlier study by Jean Gaumont (1924) who played a role in the FNCC; see also Lavergue 1923.

labor unionism, and cooperation as the "three pillars of socialism," equal and interdependent elements within the labor movement.[57] But not all socialists would have agreed with this broad vision of cooperation's role. Guesdist socialists held a more hierarchical and instrumental view. They conceived of consumer cooperatives as a political tool, subordinate to their party's ends. In fact, they advocated membership in worker consumer cooperatives on the same terms as those that applied to participation in labor unions; that is, membership was a political commitment that would help finance the Parti ouvrier français (POF). However, Guesde himself remained critical of the consumer cooperative movement as a whole on the grounds that it could serve other than socialist ends. He stressed that employers had already used cooperatives in the past to co-opt and win over workers to the employers' own purposes. Guesde expressed his doubts in these terms: "I wonder if this idea of cooperation that has been so diluted in several sauces—conservative, clerical, bourgeois here, socialist and revolutionary there—would not end up by revealing that cooperation in itself is absolutely not a socialist idea. Cooperation or the cooperative becomes socialist when it is made to serve the ideals pursued by socialism."[58] For Guesde, the consumer cooperative, like the union, should be subordinated to the political party. "It is not the party that should aid cooperatives" he contended, "but it is the cooperatives that have the moral obligation to sustain the party with all means possible."[59] Moreover, Guesde rightly reasoned that all cooperatives, by the very fact that they were operating within a competitive capitalist system, would be forced to adopt capitalistic practices; this meant selling to the general public to make a profit.[60] In sum, for Guesde, the cooperative system lacked ideological purity and an effective means of political control.

For most socialist militants, the primary motivations for adopting cooperation as an alternative to commercial capitalism were to defend the right to consume, to broaden access to goods, to educate the citizen consumer, and to strengthen organized labor. The history of the socialist cooperative movement provides several examples of cooperatives founded by Guesde's partisans along these lines, but it also reveals militant practices in different regions that were

57. *La Revue Socialiste,* April 1904, as quoted in Furlough 1991, 139.
58. Jules Guesde, *Questions d'hier et d'aujourd'hui,* quoted in Compère-Morel 1913, 40.
59. Ibid., 45. See also the discussion of Guesdist attitudes to both cooperatives and unions in Stuart 1992, chap. 6, and Furlough 1991, 120–22.
60. Ibid., 42–43.

much more varied in their response to local needs.[61] In fact, several cooperatives were founded in Troyes during this period, including a fairly short-lived
one, the Sociale, which was closely linked to the Guesdist POF and which
floundered in 1902 because of bad management. These attempts notwith-
standing, the dominant workers' consumer cooperative in Troyes remained the
Laborieuse, whose socialist-inspired activity spanned nearly fifty years, from
its founding in 1886 to its transformation into a regional cooperative in 1935.

The Laborieuse was founded by metalworkers, who sought to defend their
economic interests in a context of low wages.[62] Their principal objective was
access to goods at affordable prices. They created the cooperative in 1886 at
the same time that labor unions were legalized, effectively linking their right
to work to the right to consume. According to its statutes, the cooperative's
purpose was "to buy wholesale, explicitly in cash, food and goods of all kinds,
directly from producers or importers when possible, and to distribute them
exclusively among its members in exchange for cash." By buying directly from
worker-controlled producer cooperatives, consumer cooperatives could harmonize production, distribution, and consumption. They could also avoid the
expensive middleman, the wholesaler. The statutes explicitly ruled out "any
discussion or function that was not related to the purposes of the cooperative."[63] This provision was meant to signify the political autonomy of the cooperative in relation to any political party. From the outset, however, the goals
were clearly socialist and broadly defined. The administrators of the Laborieuse
did not confuse worker identity with partisan political action in the POF, and
they purposely sought a much broader political base. In June 1898, when the
Laborieuse was legally constituted as a *société* (company), it included 2,079
members. An analysis of membership at this time reveals significant working-
class homogeneity among the cooperative's customers; more than 40 percent
were workers in the textile and related industries (spinning, dyeing, machine
construction).[64] Many of the cooperative's administrators in these early years

61. Guesdists in the Nord founded several consumer cooperatives: La Paix in Roubaix and
l'Union in Lille. See Furlough 1991, esp. 175–88. But successful socialist cooperatives existed in
Paris, for example, la Bellevilloise, and in other parts of France.

62. La Laborieuse, *Statuts* (Troyes: Imprimerie Martelet, 1890), 1. The metalworkers who
founded the cooperative worked in the construction of knitting machines.

63. Ibid. Article 5, p. 2. See also ADA SC 21102.

64. ADA SC 21102. In June 1898, when the cooperative was legally constituted, the register
of members showed, among other male occupations, masons, carpenters, metalworkers, fitters,
farmers, stonecutters, and primary school teachers. Among the women members the occupations
ranged from domestics, laundresses, glove makers, and housewives, for example, to primary

were machinists or knitters, among them Louis Foin. While the statutes defined membership in inclusive terms, without distinction of sex or occupation,
individual membership for women was typically limited to single or widowed
women, since the statutes stipulated one vote per household, that vote usually
being that of the husband.

A class-conscious consumerist ethic helped build both membership and
services as the Laborieuse expanded its economic activities from the initial sale
of groceries only, to that of fabric, clothing, and shoes and, by 1904, other
staple items such as meat, wine, and bread. The early success of the cooperative was evidenced by the purchase of expanded shop space over a period of
ten years, and by the growing membership. This steady increase in members
should also be read as a measure of labor militancy and class solidarity. For
example, socialist principles clearly inspired members to vote in favor of support for the great strike in the industry in 1900. Cooperators donated 1,000
francs in aid to strikers and some 1,246 francs to cooperative members who
were strikers or simply unemployed because of the millowners' lockout.[65] In
addition, small loans worth more than 10,000 francs were financed by the
Caisse des Prêts during the strike year. The increase in membership represented a proportionally larger number of workers, since most men adhered
as heads of households. Thus the 2,079 members listed individually in 1898
probably represented a total of 7,000–8,000 individuals. Women could become
members, although they could not hold posts of responsibility or vote in
assemblies unless they were heads of households. This was the case of some
90 single and widowed bonnetières who were listed as shareholders in 1898
(out of 843 members working in hosiery).

The Laborieuse operated according to socialist cooperative principles, which
were in opposition to capitalist consumer ideology and commercial practice.
The cooperative sold only to members, not to the public at large. Members
received a yearly bonus return from the cooperative's profits based on a percentage of their annual purchases, a sum that could amount to 10 percent
savings; the remainder of the profits were placed in a common reserve fund

---

school teachers and postmistresses. The administrators of the cooperative were overwhelmingly
metalworkers and knitters at this time.

65. La Laborieuse, Rapport du Conseil d'administration, AG, August 18, 1900, ADA M 2352.
For similar acts of class solidarity during strikes, see Ellen Furlough's (1991) account of aid to
striking textile workers in the Nord in 1901 and 1906 by the workers' consumer cooperative la
Fraternité (191–94).

that served to purchase goods, services, and shop space for the cooperative.[66] Thus members became the collective owners of their cooperative store, delegating management tasks to regularly elected administrators from their own ranks. The statutes explicitly ruled out purchasing on credit, a principle that applied to all cooperatives of socialist inspiration. Credit was considered servitude—like wage slavery, it created dependence. But a small-loan fund and a *caisse de secours* (relief fund) were created in recognition of the uncertainties of working-class life. Cooperation was thus conceived as an ideal economic organization of society that would abolish, through a system of solidarity, such conflictual economic relations as those between capital and labor, creditor and debtor, and merchant and client.[67] This ideal was symbolized in the cooperative-handshake symbol and in the motto "Tous pour chacun, chacun pour tous" (All for one, one for all).

To be sure, such a project contained a great part of utopian faith in the future of socialism, particularly at this historical moment when commercial capitalism was showing its strength in France. Tensions existed between class-conscious consumerism and the growing commercial consumer culture at large. Much as Guesde had foreseen, the Laborieuse had to contend with local cooperatives based on different and competing ideologies and visions.[68] To deal with this competition, cooperators had to rely heavily on one of the touted virtues of cooperation: educating the citizen consumer.

Cooperative Practices

Persuading the consumer to join the cooperative and to adopt new purchasing practices were prime goals of the administrators of the Laborieuse. They began by stressing commercial education in the management and administration of the cooperative, through lectures and special programs in special study groups called Cercle d'études coopératives. These lectures were addressed to

---

66. Members' attaining savings of 10 percent was the case in 1903, as administrators announced a cash bonus of 8.6 percent to be returned to members, and 1.4 percent to be held in individual savings. Not all years showed such prosperity in sales. Rapport du Conseil d'administration, August 14, 1903, ADA M 2352.

67. See "Les douze vertus de la coopération" 1894, 5–28.

68. Two of the Laborieuse's biggest commercial competitors were l'Economat, run by employees of the Compagnie des Chemins de Fer de l'Est, and the Ruche Troyenne, founded by a local manufacturer and selling to the general public. Ultimately, the latter proved a long-standing rival, developing into chain stores called les Etablissements Economiques Troyennes before World War I.

both men and women and stressed the responsibility of individual citizen-cooperators to shop at the cooperative store. Ideological commitment and loyalty to cooperative goals were to ensure its success. Cooperators targeted workingwomen who were viewed as potentially important consumers, but who needed guidance and education. To create trust in this new system, administrators emphasized the immediately tangible benefits that cooperative practices brought to consumers' lives:

> The cooperative is aimed at transforming society and creating a better industrial and commercial system, in which each citizen will play a responsible role. To this end, it is of the utmost importance for cooperators to educate themselves and to understand what the best methods are to achieve their ideal. The advancement of a cooperative system depends on the development of their cooperative education. . . . Such education begins in the store, where the consumer meets different commercial practices: no more dishonest weights, no more fraud, no more lies, no more expensive credit, no bargaining over prices. Cooperators have no reason to cheat themselves.[69]

Cooperatives thus claimed publicly to practice honest, direct dealing; to satisfy needs, not produce profits.

Administrators of the Laborieuse tended to model their commercial strategies on those of other consumer cooperatives in France. Given the long working hours at the mill, store hours had to correspond to factory time. In 1886, when the cooperative started, the store was open only in the evenings. By December that same year, administrators had managed to hire sales employees and keep the store open three or four days a week. However, in 1900, as a result of an assessment of shopping patterns, store hours were rescheduled to coincide with peak hours of demand. Since most customers shopped between noon and one o'clock, and in the evenings after work, new store hours were adjusted to factory closing times at the *sorties d'usine*.[70]

In 1903, the Laborieuse opened a bakery, confident that the cooperative's administrators could organize better and cheaper bread for members on the basis of cooperative practices, that is, grouping their purchases of flour with

---

69. *Bulletin Syndical et Coopératif de l'Aube*, February 1906, ADA M 2352.
70. *Almanach de la coopération française*, 1894, and Rapport du Conseil d'administration présentée à l'Assemblée générale, August 18, 1900, ADA M 2352.

those of other regional cooperatives and producing items for sale themselves. They even offered a home-delivery service and payment by customers at the end of the week. The bakery rapidly turned a profit and rewarded steady consumers with a 7 percent bonus at the end of 1905.[71] In addition to this obvious financial success, the cooperative's initiative carried a highly symbolic weight. Given the importance of bread in workers' diets and the historical pattern of unrest over its provisioning, worker-collective ownership of a bakery constituted a psychological victory.

Still another strategy to attract workers as customers was to open branch stores in several working-class neighborhoods. The first such branch was opened in 1907 in the faubourg Croncels; the second in La Vacherie the same year. By 1911, the Laborieuse had successfully established five such branch stores, the sales from which represented almost 40 percent of the cooperative's total sales for that year.[72] Here the administrators of the Laborieuse were imitating a strategy that had already been launched by commercial capitalism. General grocery stores such as Felix Potin had founded what were known as "sociétés à succursales multiples" (chain stores) that were in direct competition with cooperatives for working-class customers.[73] Chain stores sold a range of goods similar to those at the cooperative and attempted to capture the popular local market. Under commercial pressure from these competitors, in 1907 administrators of the Laborieuse denounced what they termed "all-out warfare among chain stores."[74] But the cooperative also found itself vying for workers' business with small speciality shopkeepers and, to a lesser extent, with department stores.[75]

By far the clearest indication of the cooperative's success was its expansion of products and social services, provisioning workers' lives with bread, coal, wine, and even medical services, all of which required the acquisition of additional building space. The main shop occupied thirty-two hundred square meters between the quai Dampierre and the rue de Preize near the city center. Early photographs reveal a modest building that bears little resemblance to a store (Fig. 12). The interiors were also plain, with little effort to create an ostentatious or exotic environment through the display of goods, in strict

71. Rapport du Conseil d'administration, AG, March 3, 1906, ADA M 2352.
72. Rapport du Conseil d'administration, AG, September 2, 1911, ADA M 2353.
73. Furlough 1991, 69–72; see Chessel 1998, chap. 4.
74. Assemblée générale, February 23, 1907, p. II, ADA M 2352.
75. For caricatures of such competition, see Royer 1978. See also Zola's novel *Au Bonheur des Dames*.

Figure 12   Main store of the workers' consumer cooperative the Laborieuse, quai Dampierre, in 1906. Collection Claude Bérisé.

contrast to the commercial practices of the department stores. In fact, the cooperative purposely avoided any display of luxury, to distinguish socialist values from those of commercial capitalism. Cooperators clung to the popular image that contemporaries held of the cooperatives "as the *grands magasins* of the working-class."[76]

By 1906, the cooperators of the Laborieuse had begun to collaborate with the local unions in the CGT to publish propaganda in the *Bulletin Syndical et Coopératif de l'Aube*. Then in April 1907, the Laborieuse hosted in Troyes the national congress of the Bourse des coopératives socialistes (BCS), a national meeting that grouped 146 consumer and producer co-ops from all over France. The issues concerning pricing policies raised for discussion in Troyes reveal the difficulties of applying theory to practice within the cooperative framework.[77] For example, despite the BCS's efforts to purchase directly from member

76. Furlough 1991, 228.

77. See Gaumont 1923, 389–91; also *Almanach de la coopération socialiste illustré pour 1910*, 26–31; and BCS de France, 6e Congrès national tenu à Troyes, March 31, April 1 and 2, 1907, ADA M 2352.

producer cooperatives, thus maintaining socialist principles and eliminating costly intermediaries, several wine-producer co-ops had infringed the rules against commercial practices. Relations with syndicalism could also be problematic, since syndicalists tended to view consumer cooperatives as reformist institutions, clearly not engaged in the class struggle, while cooperatives charged that syndicalists treated them as a "vache à lait" (milk cow) for political party activity.[78]

Women and the Laborieuse

In the socialist cooperative movement as a whole, special propaganda was directed toward educating women workers to become consumers. Cooperation, like socialism itself, was promoted as a means of liberation for women, just as for men. However, women were the object of somewhat patronizing solicitude from male cooperative leaders, especially those who argued that political goals overrode all others. Women workers' lack of full citizenship rights cast them as subordinate to men, and therefore secondary actors. Moreover, because women lacked such rights, they were viewed as passive and indifferent to social issues. The woman worker, it was argued, had to be won over to shopping at the cooperative, just as she had to be persuaded to join the union.[79] Movement leaders, in both the reformist and the revolutionary strands of cooperation, recognized women as important to cooperative goals. But, as Ellen Furlough has amply demonstrated, the cooperative movement remained male dominated in terms of both organization and leadership.[80] Obviously, nowhere in the French political sphere did women participate fully and equally with men at this time.

While male cooperative leaders continued to address women consumers with special and often patronizing concern, there is little evidence that such rhetoric had any effect on women's behavior. Recent feminist scholarship on gender and consumption has critically examined nineteenth- and twentieth-century representations of women's relations to consumption and commodity culture. At issue in these accounts is the gender identification of men as

78. See, for example, an exchange under the title "Syndiqués et coopérateurs" in *La Bataille Syndicalist*, October 1911, between administrators of the Parisian cooperative la Bellevilloise and its unionized staff. At issue was the cooperators' sentiment that syndicalists considered the cooperative to be "la vache à lait de leur parti."

79. See esp. the brochure, published by the BCS, by Alice Jouenne (1911), who took a particularly condescending attitude.

80. See Furlough 1991, esp. 219–24.

producers and women as consumers that several feminist historians see as operating in the nineteenth century, and extended into the twentieth.[81] Furlough
has argued that the cooperative movement cast working women solely as consumers within the family. Men, by contrast, were seen as both consumers *and*
producers. She states, "The gender identification of femininity solely with
consumption and of masculinity with both production and consumption
undermined the transformative potential of consumer cooperation since it
imagined consumption as a separate women's activity without a link to production."[82] This blanket gender-coding of women solely as consumers might
have operated at the level of male leadership rhetoric and cooperative propaganda circulating nationally in both strands. But it is questionable whether
this language had indeed any effect in local cooperatives. Clearly, among the
members of the Laborieuse, both men and women workers were recognized
equally as producers and consumers. It stands to reason that women textile
workers used the cooperative to benefit their everyday lives, and that some
were even employed as saleswomen and administrators.[83] The status of single
and widowed women as heads of households and nominal shareholders gave
them voting rights within the cooperative. It was married women who were
especially problematic, since they were represented within the family. But I
would argue that women were targeted differently from men in cooperative
propaganda for this very reason. It was the family as a whole that the cooperative movement targeted as the ideal consumer unit. And workingwomen were
acknowledged as controlling the family purse strings. Women militants in the
cooperative movement, such as Alice Jouenne and Marie Bonnevial, regarded
family ideology as the ideal strategy to attract women to cooperation, and
both urged cooperators to draw women and children into the movement
through structured leisure and educative activities.

At the BCS congress in Troyes in 1907, Marie Bonnevial, an active socialist
and feminist propagandist in this field, spoke of the need to bring women into

81. See Auslander 1996b, 1996a. See also the review essay by M. L. Roberts (1998, 817–44);
Tiersten 2001.

82. See the articles in de Grazia with Furlough 1996, especially that by Leora Auslander
(1996a), who argues that "the production/consumption dichotomy is misleading, that the bourgeoisie of both genders were cast as consumers, albeit consuming to different ends" (79).

83. Reports from the administrative council refer to saleswomen working at the cooperative, and lists of elected administrators record that several widowed textile workers served in
this capacity. See the register of members and administrators in 1898, when the Laborieuse was
constituted as a private company, ADA SC 21102.

the cooperative movement through education and specific responsibilities that would integrate them as class-conscious consumers.[84] Social forces, among them religion, education, and laws, had conspired to keep individual women from emancipating themselves. Participation in cooperation's collective goals, she contended, would revalorize women's economic role within the family and become a means of emancipation. Men organized subsistence, she argued, while women controlled the purse strings and sustained family life.[85] Bonnevial characterized the cooperative as "an extended family," constituted by beehives of consuming families. For workingwomen, she urged the creation of special women's workshops within the cooperative, similar to those organized by the Women's Cooperative Guild in England; for children, activities that would socialize them into the community values of the consumer cooperative. The latter proposal prefigured the vacation camps, or "colonies de vacances," that the Laborieuse and other cooperatives would adopt in the 1930s. However, Bonnevial did not address the central contradiction of married women's position within the cooperative, the fact that they had fewer rights than single or widowed women. In her view, the family and the socialist cooperative provided a basis for solidarity that would help emancipate all women.

What little we know about working-class women as consumers has to be gleaned from sources similar to those analyzed earlier in this chapter. Both inventories after death and family monographs demonstrate how basic material needs significantly dominated more social ones and show that women workers still produced much of what the family consumed, particularly in terms of clothing. The uncertainty of women's wages, the importance of food in their budget, and lack of credit, for example, made purchasing new ready-to-wear clothing problematic. As a result, many workingwomen, restrained by deeply ingrained habits of thrift, made do with secondhand clothes or sewed and refashioned their own. Yet educating women consumers to adopt socialist cooperative practices was overall a successful strategy for the administrators of the Laborieuse. It involved convincing individuals to satisfy their desires in ways that transcended material and class constraints. We need now to consider how workers perceived their own needs and desires in terms of clothing.

---

84. "La femme et l'enfant," in Bourse des Coopératives Socialistes de France 1907, 96–97. Marie Bonnevial attended the congress as a delegate from the Maison du Peuple de Petit-Quevilly and as a propagandist for the BCS.

85. Ibid., 96.

Clothing Workers

The clothing for sale at the Laborieuse visibly catered to workers' immediate and basic needs. From its inception, the cooperative store had a clothing and fabric department, with a section for shoes, work clothes, and ready-to-wear items, managed by a commission that reported regularly to members. All clothing sold in the store was bought directly from manufacturers or from special suppliers in an effort to avoid costly intermediaries. In 1903, a garment workshop was created, run by a professional cutter who put out piecework to wives of cooperators in town. The workshop provided made-to-measure shirtwaists and blouses, goods that were popular and easy to sell. Some fashion items specifically for women were also offered. But the clothing department had to deal with the same problems that their competitors faced. The loss of workers' purchasing power during periods of unemployment and "la vie chère" had repercussions for sales in the cooperative, as in the economy in general.[86] Similarly, fashion changes for women were capricious and never seemed to follow any logic that produced a profit, resulting in unsold items accumulating as stock. One such example of women's apparel was cited by the commission—the blouse (*corsage*): "[T]he classic example, a beautiful selection in black synthetic satin; it's really an unproductive item, what remains in stock from one year to the next is no longer saleable."[87] Appeals for solidarity were then made to women consumers to do their duty, and by 1906 there was a permanent section for items on promotional sale.

But sales also depended on successful retailing techniques and more aggressive merchandising efforts than just political appeals. Thus in the winter of 1897, after amassing a deficit of ten thousand francs on its sales, the clothing commission appealed directly to its women clients in these urgent terms: "*Citoyennes,* don't allow yourself to be tempted by the frenetic propaganda of the department stores, for never forget that the future of our cooperative stores is in your hands."[88] Citing competition with the more luxurious department stores in town was, in fact, misleading. Cooperative customers had already complained of the lack of display space highlighting the clothing for sale. Moreover, the Laborieuse placed few advertisements in the local newspapers. No wonder customers did not flock to the store to browse and buy.

86. Compte rendu de l'Assemblée générale, September 2, 1911, ADA M 2352.
87. Compte rendu de l'A.G., March 3, 1906, ADA M 2352.
88. Compte rendu de l'A.G., February 19, 1898, ADA M 2352.

There was little visual encouragement to do so. In 1906, the commission re-quested permission to reduce the clothing in stock by putting on sale all items that were considered out of fashion or difficult to sell. All the items in ques-tion were women's apparel. Several arguments were advanced to explain the decline in sales, including fashion changes, the lack of loyalty among women cooperators, unemployment, and finally the marketing practices of the coop-erative itself. In fact, by 1911, the administrators of the Laborieuse realized that their branch grocery stores in the outlying working-class neighborhoods had kept women from shopping for clothing in the main cooperative store downtown.[89] In the best of times, women cooperators would be characterized as wayward consumers.

The accusations against women as bad cooperative consumers focused pri-marily on their vulnerability to fashion. For this reason, women's relation to consumer cooperation was said to be more tenuous than men's. Many argu-ments were advanced to discipline them to be more responsible class-conscious consumers. Authors of one article in the CGT newspaper, *La Bataille Syndical-iste,* sought to ridicule the fashions of 1916, depicting them as a false identity for working women. The writers argued: "*Citoyennes,* readers, you have often looked down with pity on those professionals of false elegance when they teetered around on their high-heeled boots, their chests open to the wind, a foolish smile on their lips, and a toque, biretta, or ostrich feather stuck on their heads, all of which are totally out of character with the gracious flowering-rose headbands of our old legends. No, you're not one of them, but you should avoid their indifference to consumer cooperatives. Become a co-op member!"[90] The authors appealed to women workers' class consciousness by ridiculing bourgeois fashion and lifestyle. The very fact that women's fashions raised issues of class identity at this time suggests that gender identity might also have been questioned. It is telling that the issue of women's dress had been treated as a feminist issue at the International Congress on Women's Rights in 1900. Radical feminists had even proposed "more rational dress, possibly pants" for women workers at that time.[91] It is easy, then, to read union militants'

89. Compte rendu de l'A.G., March 4, 1911, ADA M 2352.
90. Amédée and Frieda Boutarel, "Femmes et coopération," *La Bataille Syndicaliste,* October 9, 1916.
91. Feminists of several persuasions were experimenting with *jupes-culottes* (Eugénie Potonié-Pierre), pants, and men's suit jackets (Madeleine Pelletier) in ways that troubled the more con-servative elements of French society, who were concerned that any blurring of sexual distinctions was a sign of moral decline. See the debate among feminists in Klejman and Rochefort 1989,

appeals to women workers on fashion questions as an effort to counteract feminist proposals. Workingwomen's clothing appeared a contested terrain of competing meanings. Identity questions aside, CGT militants' advice to shop at the cooperative also carried a far more convincing argument, one that sought to empower women workers as the real economic agents in the family. They hailed working-class women as the financial managers of the family. Such union appeals to influence women workers as consumers, urging them to be discriminating buyers during a wartime period of rising prices, were also calls for class solidarity. But the question remains of how effective this rhetoric was in influencing workingwomen's spending in terms of dress.

Working-class clothing as represented by the apparel shop at the Laborieuse appeared markedly basic, solid, and utilitarian. Standardized and ready-to-wear clothing predominated over customized goods. Generally, the apparel conformed to workers' station in life. Work clothes such as overalls and *cottes* (tunic jackets in blue cloth) for men, and *jupons* and *tabliers* for women, sold especially well. But street clothing for men also made its appearance in the shop: in 1899 the clothing department advertised "a black jacket . . . clean and handsome, that men could slip on after a hard day in the workshop."[92] In this special fashion appeal, the cooperative reached out to its male customers to promote respectable black dress for social mixing after work. Similar fashion statements were addressed to "housewives" to encourage them to buy the shop's fantasy-colored *corsages*. The workshop for made-to-measure shirts, vests, and aprons continued to thrive and produce a profit. As a general rule, luxury goods were eschewed as a sign of the corruption of urban life, but furs were nevertheless offered for sale in small quantities and on consignment. Overall, the clothing sold at the cooperative affirmed workers' class identity and reflected a preoccupation with preserving class distinctions rather than blurring them.

If we observe not the content but the volume of clothing sales at the Laborieuse, the tension between wages and prices provides another perspective on the priorities of workers' spending. The evolution of clothing sales from 1893 to 1911, as reported biannually to cooperators, was remarkably steady, almost static, with no real upward expansion. There was a notable slump in

---

99–100, and esp. 141–42, on the discussion at the Palais du Costume at the International Congress on Women's Rights in 1900.

92. Rapport du Conseil d'administration présenté à l'Assemblée générale, August 19, 1899, ADA M 2352.

1898, and again in 1911 during the period of la vie chère. Except for these two years, the volume of clothing sales ranged between 206,000 francs and 235,000 annually. In fact, annual clothing sales appeared to keep pace with bread sales at the cooperative bakery. If we focus on annual household clothing purchases for selected years, the figures confirm a familiar pattern of restricted spending: 81 francs per household in 1893, a high of 115 francs in 1896, 84 francs in 1907, and a low of 61 francs in 1911.[93] These figures suggest that even with little disposable income, workers supported their store through increased membership and a steady volume of purchases.

It is useful to compare the evolution of clothing sales in the Laborieuse for this period with those of another type of workers' consumer cooperative that developed from a different commercial strategy. The case of the social-democratic Vooruit cooperative in Ghent is significant because it was a commercial success prior to 1914 on the basis of more capitalistic commercial practices, selling both to members and to the general public.[94] The cooperative was founded by supporters of the Belgian Social Democratic Party and inspired by reformist principles for social change. The cooperative prided itself with maintaining low clothing prices through a dual retailing strategy: wholesale buying of ready-to-wear apparel manufactured abroad, and production of its own garments at a putting-out workshop. The resulting wide selection of stylish goods at low prices was not directed solely at working-class customers, since sales were not restricted to members. Vooruit's clothing sales grew steadily from 1889 to 1913, increasing approximately "8.5 percent per year."[95] A significant leap in sales occurred in 1895, when Vooruit opened a splendid new store, with an elaborate facade, in the city center. In fact, their store resembled, in both its architecture and its elaborate commercial displays, commercial department stores such as the Bon Marché in Paris. Clothing sales slackened only slightly with the increase in the price of cloth in 1898, but overall, stylish goods promoted the continued growth of sales until World War I.

When compared to Vooruit's evident commercial success, clothing sales at the Laborieuse obviously stagnated because they restricted sales to workers whose individual purchasing power limited their shopping. However, the

93. These figures are based on annual clothing sales in relation to membership, from data in ADA M 2352. By way of comparison, Halbwachs calculated the annual clothing expenses for Parisian workers' families for 1907 as 183 francs. See Halbwachs 1939, 440.

94. Scholliers 1999.

95. Ibid., 86–87.

steady volume of clothing sales in Troyes can be read as a class-conscious commitment to the cooperative store and its community of consumption. The
politics of distribution so clearly defined by socialist principles of solidarity
would prevail, ensuring the success of the Laborieuse until long after the war.
However, its socialist vision would be tested in the postwar period by competition with capitalist merchandising techniques, practiced by such retailers as
prix uniques and chain stores, which also targeted working-class consumers.
But it would also be contested by local communists who feared that the cooperative would move toward the more reformist practices of the national federation (FNCC). In the process, critics contended, workers would no longer act
like class-conscious consumers. In fact, in the postwar period, the Laborieuse
would have to adopt new commercial strategies, expand its services, and imi-
tate its competitors in order to survive.

In 1893, the Guesdist leader Henri Ghesquière commented in *Le Socialiste
Troyen* on the election to the National Assembly of the Montluçon stonemason Christophe Thivrier, noting with satisfaction that he had worn his
blouse to the opening ceremony.[96] Thivrier's entry was greeted by a general
uproar among the bourgeois leaders in the Assembly in a reaction that in
Ghesquière's view verged on insult. The presence in the Assembly of a worker
"en blouse" appeared, paradoxically, both to reinforce a social-class boundary
and symbolically to break it down. The author was quick to point out that
the "social question" should not be reduced to the metaphor of appearances:
"Oh! To be sure, it is far from our intention to lower the social question to a
petty struggle between the smock [*blouse*] and the jacket [*paletot*]. We are far
too conscious of social problems to ignore that poverty lurks equally under a
black frock coat as it does under a jacket." Commenting with irony on dress
as a political statement, the author claimed: "Nevertheless, we think, unlike
many of the opposite opinion, that a clean blue smock has every right to be
worn in the Assembly, as does a frock, because if clothes do not make the man,
neither does the frock make the legislator. . . . Today, in the name of the Social

96. H. Ghesquière, "Il n'y a pas de sots métiers," *Le Socialiste Troyen,* September 23–30, 1893.
Elections in late August 1893 had sent a handful of workers as deputies to the Assembly, including the stonemason Thivrier (1841–95). His entry in the Chamber *en blouse* was greeted by
an outcry from petit bourgeois deputies. He had promised his electors to take his seat in the
Chamber: "My electors do not want me to disguise myself for the opening session. They gave
me a mandate to go in Sunday clothes, wearing my smock over my jacket as I ordinarily do"
(Declaration to the *Jeune République* cited in Maitron 1976, 15:217–21).

Republic, the smock like the black frock has the right to vote, and claims its seat in public places of power!" Thus, Thivrier's clothing spoke for his class, his occupation, and his constituency.[97] While he did not have to dress like a legislator, his very presence *en blouse* sufficed to test the existence of equalitarian values and practices. The exercise of democratic suffrage under the Third Republic had not reduced visible social distinctions.

From another perspective, this incident signaled the fact that the spread of bourgeois clothing had done little to effect a democratization of the dress code. The bourgeois who cried out against Thivrier's being *en blouse,* as Henri Ghesquière noted, "had an ineffable fear of revenge from the smock and the jacket, from the disinherited and the scorned." Arguably, the question of whether such a bourgeois hegemonic dress code existed, is misleading. Social emulation of bourgeois consumer values and tastes clearly did not conform to working-class reality at this point in time. What some textile workers as consumers wanted in Troyes was to avoid social segregation through dress. As we have seen, cooperators at the Laborieuse prized solidarity, and they had little desire to emulate bourgeois dress. As Victoria de Grazia has argued, spending choices for clothing, when disposable income was available, were still largely determined by social-class factors until after World War I. Working-class consumption remained "separated by castelike differences in tastes and needs" that continued to set workers apart in a world of their own.[98] Moreover, the democratization of supply of affordable goods lagged noticeably behind demand. Throughout this period, Troyes millowners maintained their commercial strategy of manufacturing and marketing essentially luxury goods for domestic consumption and export.

Yet a real transformation did take place among men during this transitional period at the century's end: the progressive abandonment of the *blouse bleue* first by urban, then by younger generations of rural, workers. Then came the collective desire to shed work clothes at the factory gate and adopt street clothes that allowed workers to mix in the social space between work and home. Greater individuation would gradually become the norm. As the demands of public socializing imposed new standards, the color blue continued to identify work clothes (*vêtements de travail*), but it was no longer an

---

97. See the incident involving Feargus O'Connor dressing in a fustian suit as an unmistakable emblem of "class" for a mobilization of Chartists in 1841, described by Paul Pickering (1986, 144–62).

98. De Grazia with Furlough 1996, 152.

attribute of class.[99] By World War I, the *casquette* (cap) had become the emblem of male worker identity in the street. It would remain a political statement of class for men until the end of the Popular Front. Women workers, however, would have to await the simplification of postwar fashions to abandon their apron at the factory gate. The new female silhouette of the 1920s would serve both as a symbol of liberation and as a force for individuation. Whereas femininity in dress had seemed to be the prerogative of the upper and middle classes, the new fashions promised women workers a more glamorous, youthful identity that broke through class and gender boundaries.

The transition toward more unified consumer patterns, as Giovanni Levi argues, was a long process of incremental changes that implied a point in time when the revolutionary elements of the working class no longer sought to impose their own values and tastes.[100] In this transitional prewar period, workers patronized their cooperative out of class loyalty, and in turn, the managers of the Laborieuse continued to shape worker identity through the goods they sold. After the war, cooperative consumers would turn more resolutely instead to demanding the workers' share of the bourgeois market and greater access to affordable goods. In this chapter I have argued that, on the one hand, working-class consumer behavior was dictated by socially determined needs and class identity. But on the other hand, there is evidence of more complex motivations for some workers to break class ranks into a larger consumer market that was increasingly driven by standardization, fashion, and affordability. Local retail merchandising and advertising increasingly targeted the worker as consumer, driving a plurality of social practices for those who could afford to spend. But in 1914, workers were still caught between the constraints and sacrifices imposed by their social condition and the promise of a more democratic society as citizen consumers of the Republic.

99. Michelle Perrot (1974) maintains that after World War I the term *bleu* was less frequently used to identify workers themselves, and that the term came to designate work clothes.
100. Levi 1996.

6

FEMINIZATION AND INDUSTRIAL EXPANSION

The drama of the Great War represents a turning point in many respects for French society as a whole, but it did not touch all parts of French territory and social groups equally. For the department of the Aube, caught in the strategic position of being just behind the front lines, the war was a dramatic upheaval and presence in everyday life. By August 1914, Troyes was already on a war footing, as troops and refugees from the Ardennes poured into the Aube. The north of the department was invaded on September 8 and 9, and cannons could be heard in Troyes during the decisive moments of the Battle of the Marne. Military hospitals were installed in several lycées in town, bringing the presence of wounded soldiers and the hostilities ever nearer. Ordinary life in the town was suspended as all citizens were called upon to serve. Just how disruptive the war effort became for any political action is revealed in the records of Cécile Chaudron, director of the teacher-training college in Sainte-Savine and secretary of the local group of the Union française pour le suffrage des femmes (UFSF). The outbreak of war had suspended their organizing: "After having gained real momentum [in our movement] in the first months of 1914, after the loss of confidence engendered by the indifference shown our cause by candidates, electors, and elected officials, we have to admit that the war front in our department has struck a real blow to our group."[1] It was presumably a

---

1. Cahier du Groupe de l'Aube de l'UFSF.

blow from which this group never recovered, since there is no further trace of their existence.

In the crisis of war, socialists and labor movement leaders all over France found themselves forced to choose between nationalist goals and revolutionary ones. The assassination of Jean Jaurès on July 31, 1914, followed by the outbreak of the war effectively split the socialist movement nationwide. By August 28, 1914, Jules Guesde had agreed to join the government of national defense. In Troyes, production in the mills was halted when a significant portion of the workforce was mobilized for war. Local workers' unions were weakened by the mobilization of their members, but also by the fact that a minority among the nonmobilized did not fully support the war effort in the mills.

If we focus on the unresolved conflicts in the Troyes mills, the period covered by this chapter can be read as one of relative continuity with the prewar years, despite the major disruption of World War I in the region. The war effort, followed by the intense mobilization of textile workers in Troyes, as in most of industrial France, can then be understood as a continuum of struggle in the mills that culminated in the strike of 1921. During this postwar period of economic instability, manufacturers in Troyes would attempt to return to "normalcy." But the postwar world was very different from the lingering nineteenth-century prewar one. Workers' experience of wartime sacrifice, coupled with the revolutionary historical context, empowered them to demand their fair share. The consequences of this major strike—its impact on labor relations—opened a new period of economic recovery and industrial expansion into the 1920s. For workers, the strike's failure further divided and weakened the labor movement. For millowners, the strike strengthened their resolve not to recognize the unions and to decentralize production through an elaborate outwork system in the countryside. As we have seen, textile employers had had recourse to such a strategy in the past in order to safeguard capital and profits. This time, their principle motivation was to circumvent the unions. In this chapter I will argue that the resulting dispersion of production, plus the proliferation of speculative small-scale hosiery manufacturing during this short period of relative prosperity, compromised the solid growth and modernization of industrial infrastructure. I will show how millowners' policies of economic retrenchment with regard to wages also exacerbated labor relations.

The war, and events in the years immediately following, marked the peak of women's economic activity in France. In fact, the war had brought many women into industrial work for the first time and moved them into sectors previously closed to them.[2] Whereas the pattern of women's employment in Troyes followed a similar increase from the 1880s, it continued at a high level well into the interwar period. The resulting feminization of the labor force became irreversible, forcing unions to reconsider the importance of women's recruitment on the same terms as that of men. Nevertheless, proactive union strategies did little to alter gender roles within the organized labor movement. The fact that French women had not yet obtained equal political rights with men complicated their struggle for social and gender equality in the workplace. However, women workers would find allies in the newly founded French Communist Party (PCF), which would support legislation for both women's suffrage and their right to work.

THE IMPACT OF WORLD WAR I

Mobilization of the male population for war deprived the knitted goods industry of a major part of its workforce. Moreover, there were logistical difficulties in receiving supplies of spun wool and cotton from the mills of Lille, Roubaix, and Tourcoing in the north, further disrupting production. Added to these problems was the presence of some twenty thousand refugees from the Ardennes and a great number of soldiers stationed in the department. Public buildings were requisitioned to bivouac troops, a situation confirmed by one soldier who described in an August 23, 1915, postcard home that he was sleeping on straw in the Bourse du Travail.[3] The mayor of Troyes estimated in 1917 that "out of a prewar population of sixty thousand inhabitants, there remained in town some thirteen thousand nonmobilized men between the ages of sixteen and sixty, including refugees, and about one thousand men mobilized or capable of being mobilized, that is, between the ages of eighteen and forty-nine, deferred from service and working in local factories for the national defense."[4] These figures underscore the shortage of manpower in the knitting mills of Troyes at this time.

2. For an analysis of the shifts in women's employment during the interwar years, see Zerner 1987.

3. Bérisé 1999, 90.

4. Letter from the mayor of Troyes, June 13, 1917, cited by M. Roche (1985, 22).

As a result, women were brought into the workforce in greater number than before, and under special conditions. Before the outbreak of war, there were fifty-eight knitting and hosiery mills in Troyes that employed some 9,500 men and women workers. Out of these fifty-eight mills, twenty-three employed from 20 to 500 workers; five, from 500 to 1,000; and one large mill occupying between 1,000 and 2,000 workers.[5] So when work resumed in the mills in mid-April 1915, a small number of male workers, who were considered essential to industrial mobilization, were recalled from the battle front, and large numbers of women were recruited for factory work. Most of the mills worked both for the national defense effort and for commercial purposes. This was the case for knitting-machine manufacturers such as Lebocey, Société Générale de Bonneterie, and Poron, which transformed part of their production into shells. However, these local constructors also profited from orders for knitting machines to replace those formerly imported from their German competitors. The dyeworks made gunpowder, and the other mills produced basic knitted goods for the military as well as for commerce. According to one local historian, the few spinning mills in Troyes worked full time.[6]

There is little evidence from the records that the mills in Troyes operated full time for the war effort. In fact, there remains a certain ambiguity over how much of the production in specific mills was dictated by commercial interests, and this doubt persisted into the postwar period of labor unrest. The question of wartime profiteering was closely guarded from the public. The dissemination of information, as we know, was closely controlled to mold public opinion, and the local situation evolved in the confusion of movements of troop and refugees, under the constant threat of invasion. In February 1917 the minister of the interior reinforced the security surrounding those factories that were working for the national defense effort, and police gathered for the prefect some estimates of the numbers of workers involved.[7] Even if we accept the figure advanced of some 10,100 workers employed in the mills, it is likely that a smaller number of these actually worked on the wartime production of munitions and gunpowder.[8]

5. Ricommard 1934, 94–96.
6. Ibid.
7. ADA SC 408. The commissaire spécial providing these figures explained that, beyond the first list of some twenty-seven hosiery mills and metalworking factories, employing approximately 10,160 workers, information concerning smaller factories was less reliable.
8. Letter from the commissaire spécial to the prefect, February 16, 1917, ADA SC 408.

Women workers everywhere in France replaced men mobilized for the war, and in many cases this massive influx of women into industry required the reorganization of the work process. This was certainly true in the hosiery mills of Troyes, where men had previously operated the knitting machines. Given the shortage of manpower, women were put to work overseeing small circular and flatbed knitting machines. According to Ricommard, this break with traditional women's work required a special effort: "Women were put to work on the knitting machines, but the task was difficult for them. The job required an apprenticeship, on the one hand, and on the other, one had to take into account the strength needed to release the gears on the machine; the longer the knitter, the more strength was needed. So, in order to use women operatives, the flatbed knitters with twelve to eighteen heads were abandoned in favor of the older ones with six to eight heads."[9] Ricommard underscores the problem of physical strength—an argument that had always been advanced to exclude women from certain tasks—but also the question of apprenticeship. To be sure, women lacked the initial technical training to oversee the machines. But the compromise that was adopted, attributing the small, less complex machines to women, did not in fact change the hierarchy in the sexual division of labor. In the end, foremen and male fitters exercised appropriate supervision and carried out machine repairs.

A wartime innovation of this kind had little permanent effect. Mobilizing women to operate the knitting machines in the Troyes mills did not, in fact, institute a new industrial pattern. Once the war ended women returned to their former production tasks. As Françoise Thébaud observed in *La femme au temps de la guerre de 14*, "[W]hen the question was raised at the end of the war about women's professional future, it seemed obvious to everyone that they would not continue to make munitions or military uniforms, and normal that as substitutes, they return their jobs to demobilized soldiers."[10] Women workers in Troyes returned not to household tasks, but to their former occupations in the trade, to the seaming and finishing workshops in the mills. The fact that the women had operated knitting machines in the absence of male knitters in no way brought recognition of new skills or technical aptitudes learned on the job. Their wartime deployment as knitters was nothing but a parenthesis in their lives that ended when they returned to their former jobs.

9. Ricommard 1934, 96–97.
10. Thébaud 1986, 287.

Such exceptional mobilization of women workers on the knitting machines in Troyes was not a unique case by any means. Everywhere in France where the war effort employed women workers to replace men, work organization was modified to reduce the need for labor and increase industrial output. It was in the wartime munitions factories that most of the techniques for rationalization, or "scientific management" as it was known in France, were experimented with. Taylor's ideas on breaking down the work process into unskilled and repetitive tasks to increase productivity were virtually unknown in Troyes. In any case, scientific management techniques were not well suited to the small-scale production that predominated in the Troyes mills. In fact, no systematic attempt to adopt rationalized production methods would be undertaken in Troyes until the end of the 1930s. However, garment making had long been rationalized to some extent before it was mechanized.[11] Given the shortage of labor, the war effort obviously intensified demands for greater productivity. Under wartime circumstances, women revealed the rapidity with which they could work, and this aptitude for *speed* as *skill* was much appreciated by millowners. After the war, the increased demand for women workers led to a more marked feminization of the workforce.

From all reports, working conditions in the mills did not change during the first years of the war. Most workers did a ten-hour day. When a dramatic rise in prices for staple foods occurred in 1916, workers went on strike, demanding an increase in wages in relation to the cost of living. In May 1916, millowners granted an allowance amounting to an additional 10 percent to all workers (*prime de guerre*); six months later, in response to further demands, an *indemnité de vie chère*—a small bonus to compensate for the increased cost of living—was added to the hourly wage. In fact, every six months, successive increases in this bonus were given, to supplement wages lower than eight francs a day.[12] The increase was calculated according to the evolution of the cost of living. The labor unrest during the war in other parts of France put pressure on millowners to institute such changes in wage policy. The soaring cost of living, and a sense of war weariness, touched off a series of successful strikes among women munition workers and seamstresses in Paris.[13]

---

11. See the analysis of the sewing trades in Green 1997 and Coffin 1996b.
12. Letter from the president of the Chambre syndicale des fabricants de bonneterie de l'Aube to the mayor of Troyes, October 19, 1918, AMT 2J 48.
13. Dubesset et al. 1992.

Union militants had felt the erosion of their organization by the war mobilization. A minority of the Troyes labor movement had refused to accept the national consensus (*union sacrée*) that had been constructed to sustain the war effort. Thus, in June 1916, when threatened by violence, the management of the Mauchauffée mill complained to the mayor of Troyes that their foremen and forewomen were being harassed on the way home from work. The management threatened to close the mill for a week, putting some four hundred men, women, and children out of work, if the police did not intervene against those workers whom they described as an "aggressive and turbulent minority . . . [using] revolutionary procedures."[14] But by October 1916, workers in this same mill had organized their own work stoppage to demand another 10 percent increase in wages. While negotiations were pursued with management, some thirteen hundred workers walked off the job; after the lunch break, four hundred returned to work, including a majority of women. Negotiations continued during the day, both with management and the mayor, resulting in a small gain of several centimes on the cost of living bonus for those earning the lowest daily wages. Such conflicts were symptomatic of the relations between millowners and the labor movement during the war, culminating in the strike of 1921, relations that would shape the terms of war reconstruction and economic recovery in Troyes.

By the end of the war, the industry was facing both reconversion to peacetime production and a severe labor shortage. The labor shortage concerned skilled knitters and apprentices, but also low-paying jobs for women such as bobbin winding. Official war losses for the department were 8,397 dead and missing, of whom 29 percent were textile workers and 41 percent peasants. Moreover, the 1921 census noted a decline of 5.5 percent in the population of the Aube between 1911 and 1921.[15]

THE STRIKE OF 1921

Postwar reconstruction programs were debated among those social partners who had contributed to the victory. Very quickly, traditional social forces within industry and commerce turned away from proposals to remodel the

14. Letter from M. Portal, June 31, 1916, AMT 2J 48.
15. See Antoine 1975.

economy under the guise of reconstruction. Instead they favored a return to a prewar status quo, which included a market free of government control, and no renovation of former business practices. For the Confédération général du travail (CGT), which had become a partner with the government during the wartime effort, the postwar moment provided an opportunity to embrace the modernization of the economy and to include labor in the management of this recovery. In 1919, Léon Jouhaux of the CGT affirmed the need to put an end to the "reign of industrial individualism and economic Malthusianism" that had governed before the war.[16] Jouhaux was convinced that workers would accept new standards of productivity in exchange for higher wages and a role in the management of factory production. Such reorganization of industry would lead to economic expansion and the most effective use of human and material resources. Georges Clemenceau soon buried these ideas for reform, while employers returned to business as usual, rejecting any extension of their wartime collaboration with the state.

For the labor movement in Troyes, the nonresolution of demands concerning wages and working conditions before the war had only postponed a clash with millowners. However, tension was reduced by the fact that the state intervened immediately after the end of hostilities to initiate a national negotiated agreement between employers and workers on instituting the eight-hour day in each industry. The new law, voted in on April 23, 1919, raised the delicate problem of wages by stipulating that "the reduction in working hours could not be a determinant reason for lowering wages." It was also obvious to all involved that in addition to the difficulties of maintaining wages and modifying working hours, there was the problem of the increased cost of living, *la vie chère*. This second problem could hardly be characterized as postwar, since inflation and the decline in the value of the franc had begun during the war and only deepened into a crisis in 1920. Economic instability was a profound experience of everyday life for many people.

Moreover, the postwar recovery era had a revolutionary potential, born of the hopes of the Russian Revolution. A major national strike wave broke out in early May 1920. It was launched by the railroad workers in the CGT, who called for a general strike. They were followed by the miners, dockers, and sailors, and finally by a third wave of construction and transport workers,

---

16. *La Bataille Syndicaliste,* March 2, 1919, as cited in Kuisel 1981, 60.

metalworkers, and gas workers in Paris. This attempt at a general strike collapsed, adding to the disillusions of the postwar period. Soon thereafter, the union movement split, in a break that paralleled events at the Congress of Tours in December 1920, when Léon Blum led the socialist minority out of the congress, leaving the majority to form the Parti communiste français (PCF). The procommunist CGTU was formed as a rival to the CGT. Union membership in the CGT declined dramatically, leaving overall a divided and considerably weakened labor movement. Moreover, a new political force emerged in 1919 in the form of the Confédération française des travailleurs chrétiens (CFTC), which also competed for worker loyalties.

It was against this somber but dramatic background that textile workers in Troyes mobilized in 1921. By all accounts the social and political context in favor of mobilization gave it momentum. As a labor-intensive industrial sector, textiles were rife with labor struggles. While Troyes millworkers were voicing their grievances, a general strike broke out in the Nord against the Consortium textile de Roubaix-Tourcoing. It was provoked by a wage cut and by employers' rejection of arbitration and collective bargaining procedures with the unions.[17]

The Origins of the Strike

In Troyes the old Fédération socialiste de l'Aube and the Union des syndicats had been strengthened by a new postwar generation of militants. Reports of the May Day celebration in 1919 suggest the potential strength of the labor movement before the split in summer 1921. A work stoppage by some six thousand striking workers kept the mills from operating, while a more modest crowd of roughly fourteen hundred workers paraded through the town to a political meeting. Among the old guard socialist leaders present, two had been newly elected to public office in Troyes: Emile Clévy as mayor and Célestin Philbois as deputy. Both had formerly worked in the knitting mills. Philbois had been Etienne Pédron's disciple. Two new militants appeared on the scene as speakers at the May Day rally: Henri Jacob, secretary of the local Jeunesse socialiste, and Lagrange, manager of the Laborieuse. All speakers

---

17. See the analysis by Susan Pedersen (1993) of the consortium's refusal to talk to the unions and their policy of tying family allowances to constant presence in the mills, a strikebreaking measure to manipulate wages and allowances against labor (236–61).

addressed the symbolic protest of the workers' holiday with its list of demands for application of the eight-hour day.[18]

Symbolic of the dynamism of the historical moment was the creation of a newspaper, *La Dépêche de l'Aube,* just days before the historic socialist Congress of Tours in December 1920. The newspaper was the work of new militants, who also established a printing house, l'Emancipatrice, to ensure its future.[19] The editor in chief, René Plard, took a strong editorial position to try to prevent division in the socialist federation. "What would Jaurès have done in this situation?" Plard queried, invoking all factors that would consolidate the socialist union, and committing the newspaper to this goal.[20] Plard, a former postal employee who had been dismissed for striking in 1920, was an educated, intelligent man with a personal following among socialist militants in the town. Thanks to his influence, the newspaper opened its columns to militants, encouraging the airing of opinions that created a polemical debate for more than a year. However, the split within the Socialist Party became inevitable as the struggle between proponents of revolutionary and reformist tendencies played itself out at the union level. Most of the actors belonged to both party and union. Two strikes in the Troyes knitting mills—one in February 1921, the second in September that same year—revealed the divisions leading up to the scission. Opposition between the two strands of syndicalism developed during the course of the summer of 1921, culminating in the split by the end of the strike in November.

The political situation in the Aube became more complex as each left-wing party tried to appropriate for itself the Guesdist legacy. "Comrades, don't you believe that we have remained faithful to our Guesdist roots?" questioned Célestin Philbois, who as deputy from Troyes had joined the first communist parliamentary group in the National Assembly.[21] But union militants

18. Report from the commissaire central to the directeur de la Sûreté in Paris, AMT 2J 48.
19. For this section on the working-class press and the complex events surrounding the split in the socialist movement, I have relied on Bedin (1975). The author follows the day-to-day history of the split and provides a detailed analysis of the role of the newspaper in this process, insisting on the workers' attachment to their newspaper from the moment it was created. See esp. chap. 9.
20. *La Dépêche de l'Aube,* January 1, 1921.
21. *La Dépêche de l'Aube,* July 21, 1921. Philbois, a knitter, had been trained by Etienne Pédron to become an effective propagandist. He shifted from the POF to the SFIO in 1905, and was elected deputy from the first *circonscription* (district) in Troyes in 1914. Reelected in November 1919, he was part of the minority within the SFIO that constituted, after the split in December 1920, the first parliamentary group of the French Communist Party. Philbois attended the Congress of Tours, where he brought forty-six mandates for membership in the

belonging to the "revolutionary" strand tended to distance themselves from prewar tradition, and specially from the CGT, by supporting popular mobilization. The new leader of the communist affiliated Syndicat du textile–CGTU, Henri Jacob, was reported to be a man given to violent speeches with whom employers refused discussion.[22] In February 1921, CGTU textile union leaders called upon workers to mobilize, using such revolutionary slogans as "general strike" and "worker control," which evoked the direct action syndicalists of the great strike of 1900. Moreover, both these left-wing unions were in competition for workers' allegiance with the newly founded Syndicat chrétien des ouvriers du textile de Troyes, which drew its members from the mills owned by Catholic employers.

The economic situation was as explosive as the political one. During these first years of postwar recovery, workers' demands were negotiated in a collective bargaining agreement signed on June 5, 1919, between the Chambre syndicale patronale and the workers' unions in a climate of social tension and unemployment. The agreement provided for the application of the eight-hour day, a work schedule ensuring forty-eight hours of production per week (including half day on Saturday, called *la semaine anglaise*), and the possibility of special temporary dispensations for overtime during seasonal rushes. It also granted a 25 percent increase in wages and maintained, but raised, the wartime system of a fixed hourly bonus (*prime horaire fixe de cherté de vie*) to compensate for the increased cost of living.[23] The entire system was cumbersome, complicated, and potentially conflictual. By September strikes had already broken out in two mills, where the workers claimed that their wages were lower than in other mills. Positions hardened on both sides, and when employers threatened a lockout to provoke a return to work, negotiations resumed to modify the collective bargaining agreement. An amendment dated October 14, 1919, established a joint commission, composed of representatives from labor and management, to observe the variations in the cost of living and to put in place

Third International and twenty-two mandates in support of the Longuet motion, from the Fédération socialiste de l'Aube. See Maitron 1976, 4:255–57.

22. Henri Jacob was born in 1896 in Troyes to parents who were weavers. He went to work in the knitting mills at the age of twelve, joined the socialist youth group two years later, then fought in the war, where he was wounded in September 1918. He received a veteran's pension for 65 percent disability. His postwar militancy led him back to the Fédération socialiste de l'Aube, and in May 1920 he became the secretary of the Syndicat du textile de Troyes. His subsequent commitment to the Communist Party and involvement in aid work to Soviet Russia made him a dangerous man in the eyes of millowners. See Maitron 1976, 32:97–99.

23. See *L'Ouvrier Textile* for July 1919, and ADA SC 2332.

a procedure that would measure both an increase and a decrease in the bonus in relation to the cost of living. As amended, the system was even more complicated than the initial one, resulting in abstract calculations of fluctuations in the cost of living that were often applied to wages with some delay. As a result, this system was riddled with misunderstandings, which contributed to a growing distrust among workers.

The postwar period marked a dramatic shift in wage policy through family supplements called *sursalaire familial*. Social welfare schemes that included measures for child support had been debated since the prewar period in response to what was perceived across the political spectrum as a depopulation crisis.[24] Government delegation of authority to employers for war production had continued to structure the private industrial sector after the war, and therefore employers in Troyes proposed a family supplement amounting to fifty centimes per day, and per child. They also created an employer-managed fund for such contributions, which began operating in May 1920. This private initiative represented a modest recognition of the social cost of children, and a contribution on employers' part to family maintenance. Aid was allocated to the family through the employer, not to an individual wage earner. The welfare fund responded to pronatalist concerns as a recognized priority and social entitlement. But millowners were doubtless seeking to serve other interests as well. In this period of labor shortage, employers perceived family allowances as a means of stabilizing the workforce and of encouraging their loyalty.[25]

While many demobilized soldiers had returned to their previous jobs in the Troyes mills, some categories of workers were idled, awaiting economic recovery. Given the underemployment in all the mills, social tensions remained high early in 1921. In the impending conflict, workers initially demanded that employers accept the principle that wages be calculated in relation to the cost of living. Workers' representation of their wages was linked to inflationary pressures, to their buying power as consumers, and to the family budget. Testimony from a knitter in the Troyes mills whose father worked as a "formeur" at this time, is indicative of how workers perceived their wages: "I remember

24. On the population debate, see Offen 1982; M. L. Roberts 1994; Reynolds 1996. For an analysis of the debate and policies adopted, see Pedersen 1993. Pedersen argues that French employers used allowances for children to control labor and restrain wages.

25. A debate in the town council over strike committee requests for food rations for large families in need in October 1919 is significant in this respect. Socialist mayor Emile Clévy issued a guarded warning to millowners that a lockout might provoke a worker exodus from Troyes in search of better wages elsewhere. The debate turned to the family allowance and the proposal to create a collective welfare fund (AMT 2J 48).

when my father brought his pay home in 1913, we could live on it; he had begun to earn five francs a day! In 1913, five francs a day was good pay! . . . then the war came and the currency began to fall dramatically."[26] Fluctuations in the cost of living and in the value of the franc gave the impression of a growing gap between the nominal wage and the real one.[27] Moreover, many politically conscious workers imputed to their employers partial responsibility for the existing economic crisis. In a well-documented article in the *Dépêche,* one militant knitter denounced what he termed scandalous war profiteering among the millowners.[28]

In February 1921 the joint commission noted a slight decline in the cost of living, and the employers' union immediately announced a reduction in the cost-of-living allowance of twenty centimes per hour. The millowners' decision provoked the anger of union leaders, who called upon their mayor, Emile Clévy, former leader of the knitters' union, to intervene. Clévy urged millowners to "rethink their decision that risked profoundly disturbing social relations."[29] He grounded his arguments in the prices of "those items indispensable to life," and in the increase in rents and the crowded housing resulting from the war. The millowners' response underscored their own difficulties with regard to the reconversion of production and economic recovery. But it also revealed a different logic in relation to wages. They contradicted the mayor's reasoning by maintaining that "the joint commission's findings, which would seem the major influence in your arguments, do not constitute the principal factor in the evolution of wages."[30]

The union's position was equally confrontational. Its demands exceeded the limited framework of wages. In addition to the maintenance of existing wage levels, it demanded recognition of the union; strict application of the eight-hour day; and in the long term, some degree of worker control over mill management to prevent this type of wage conflict in the future.[31] All these principles had been proposed by CGT leader Léon Jouhaux in 1919 and

26. M. Laborie, interview, 1987, who was one of two children at the time.

27. See Lhomme 1968.

28. Article by Mahu, Syndicat des bonnetiers de Romilly, *La Dépêche de l'Aube,* January 1, 1921.

29. Letter from the mayor to the presidents of the employers' unions in hosiery and metalworking, February 9, 1921, AMT 2J 49.

30. Letter from the Chambre syndicale patronale to the mayor, February 11, 1921, AMT 2J 49.

31. Bedin 1975, 105. This last demand was developed by Thibault of the CGT textile union in the *Dépêche de l'Aube* on February 16, 1921.

were aimed at making the union a full partner in postwar economic recovery. Needless to say, the union's position that claimed such recognition and partnership was unacceptable to employers. Thus two opposing logics were headed for a clash in the strike in September 1921.

Millowners temporized while confronted with a growing strike movement that had popular support. They agreed to postpone until March 1 a wage reduction scheduled for February 14 and to lower wages in two stages. Work resumed on February 17 in all the mills, while the headlines in the *Dépêche* read, "A Great Victory for Workers." In fact, the confrontation was postponed. Thibault, leader of the CGT-affiliated Union des syndicats, commented that "today's peace can only be a simple truce in the troubled period in which we are living."[32] The agreement concluded on March 2 between the employers' union and the textile unions was to govern relations for the coming six months. It was to regulate the conditions of application of the cost-of-living allowance. Over the following six-month period, this agreement resulted in three successive wage cuts. Considering such conditions highly unfavorable, the Syndicat du textile–CGTU was not inclined to renegotiate the agreement. During the summer of 1921 two important strike movements broke out in other textile regions: in August in the Nord, and in September in the Vosges. Thus when the time came to renew the agreement between the employers and the unions, textile workers mobilized, despite political divisions within their unions and the economic circumstances that made their situation more difficult. The ongoing labor struggles in other textile centers helped rekindle the strike movement of February.

On September 15 an interview took place between the Chambre syndicale patronale and delegations from the workers' unions, with the notable exception of the CGT. Employers announced their willingness to renew the agreement for another six months, but the union delegates expressed their dissatisfaction with the way it was working. In fact, successive reductions in the hourly bonus had resulted in an overall loss of Fr 2.40 per eight-hour day's work.[33] The unions countered with a proposal to consider a new wage scale that would increase wages uniformly by five francs. Although negotiations were at an impasse, talks were to continue. The following meeting, on September 24, still did not yield agreement, but it was decided to proceed with an investigation into wage averages, and to reconvene on September 26.

32. Bedin 1975, 118.
33. Letter from the prefect to the minister of labor, AN F22 181.

Several hours after these failed negotiations, the Syndicat du textile–CGTU voted to strike in two days' time, that is, on Monday, September 26.[34] On Sunday, September 25, the Union des syndicats, affiliated with the socialist CGT, voted to stay out of the strike; and the Catholic union, the Syndicat chrétien, voted against striking. By deciding to strike while negotiations were ongoing, the Syndicat du textile–CGTU made a calculated move to exert pressure at a political moment. René Plard supported the strikers in the columns of the *Dépêche,* portraying their action as "inevitable."[35] Strike mobilization might have been averted or even taken more time if millowners had not decided to replay the card they had used in 1900—a lockout.

The Clash of Ideologies

The millowners' attitude suggests an overreaction to the radical minority within the labor movement and an effort to cut short any further confrontation by isolating the Syndicat du textile–CGTU. Yet their motives were never clear. Even the minutes of the Chambre syndicale patronale contain no reference to the deliberations leading to the lockout decision, as if members had been sworn to a conspirational silence.[36] Four thousand textile workers were reported to have gone to work on Monday, the morning of September 26, out of eight thousand men and women employed in the mills.[37] By some accounts the strike movement did not appear to have had unanimous approval at the outset. But the lockout, initially announced for one week, constituted a retaliation against the Syndicat du textile–CGTU that in fact struck the entire working class. Millowners justified their action by the unilateral break-off of negotiations, voted for by the CGTU, with which employers had refused many times to negotiate one on one. In fact, the employers' union placarded the

34. The textile workers' union in nearby Romilly voted to strike on September 23.

35. *La Dépêche de l'Aube,* September 26, 1921.

36. On the decision as important as the lockout, the decision taken the morning of September 26, 1921, there exists no trace in the official minutes. No record was kept on discussions between September 24 and October 15, 1921 (Chambre syndicale de la bonneterie et des industries s'y rattachant, *Registre de procès-verbaux,* January 7, 1921 to February 5, 1926, Archives de la Chambre de commerce de Troyes.) As Michelle Perrot (1974) noted concerning sources from employers, "Even the records of the administrative board constitute only a bowlderized version, an intentional version of the record" (2:660).

37. Commissaire spécial to the Ministry of Labor on September 26, 1921, AN F22 181. According to the *Dépêche de l'Aube,* the strike was general on the twenty-sixth and so "the employers' decision to close the mills for a week is evidence of the extent of the strike," as quoted in Bedin 1975, 230.

town with posters attributing responsibility for the nonrenewal of the contract to the revolutionary union: "By prematurely going out on strike, the CGTU union has voluntarily burned all bridges. . . . The Chambre syndicale intends to decline all responsibility under these conditions and on the strength of its rights, declares that it will not submit to any means of intimidation or pressure exercised by a small group of agitators."[38] In these terms millowners sought to discredit union militants, presenting the strike "as a movement that was political in origin and in purpose."[39]

As in the previous great strike, millowners used the lockout as a means to reconstitute employer solidarity. Yet even this goal was difficult to achieve and to maintain, since several mills were not hit by the strike. On two separate occasions the Chambre syndicale patronale was forced to decide to reopen the mills. Moreover, on October 5 thirteen small businesses agreed to the wage increases demanded by their workers. On October 25, the leading Catholic millowner, André Valton, requested his colleagues' permission to reopen because his workers had not joined the strike movement and wanted to return to work.[40] It became obvious that the employers' union could not maintain solidarity based solely on economic interests.

Millowners might have had yet another motive in closing their mills; a fear of violence inside the workshops. The prefect had raised similar fears because of the vehement language voiced by strikers during meetings at the Bourse du Travail. He claimed that strikers were "considering the occupation of the mills and the machines." In the same report sent to the Ministry of Labor on September 30, the prefect judged the situation so alarming that he requested the dispatch of reserve gendarmes. To justify this measure, he affirmed that "there was a political movement under way."[41] Other sources downplayed such fears, that early street demonstrations might degenerate into violence. In fact, when the mills reopened on October 3, only some eight hundred militant strikers tried to incite nonstrikers to join them, while the mass of strikers followed calmly. Serious violence only broke out at the end of the strike, as millowners persisted in their lockout.

The arrival in Troyes of regiments of mounted gendarmes inaugurated a phase of repression that was so unpopular that it turned public opinion against

38. Minutes of the meeting September 24, 1921, *Registre de procès-verbaux*.
39. Bedin 1975, 233.
40. Minutes of the meeting November 5, 1921, *Registre de procès-verbaux*.
41. Report from the prefect of the Aube to the Ministry of Labor, September 29, 1921, AN F22 181.

the millowners for their refusal to negotiate. When the Union des syndicats–
CGT joined the strike movement on October 4, its leaders called for collective
action and solidarity. Strikers then succeeded in enlarging the social base of
their movement by an appeal to peasants and shopkeepers for donations.
From October 14, the union operated two soup kitchens in Troyes and organized the departure of 250 children from strikers' families for the countryside. Such actions dramatized union arguments through a recognized ritual of
working-class culture.

By all accounts women workers supported the strike. In police statistics
provided for the first two weeks, female workers accounted for 41 percent of
strikers, male workers 44 percent, and children 15 percent. But beyond these
initial numbers there is little indication that women were on the front line or
that they played any leadership roles, as they did in the great strike of 1900.
The only woman signaled as a member of the strike committee is a Mme
Fontaine, residing in the rue du Geoffroy-Villehardouin, in a quartier known
to be a knitters' stronghold. Suzanne Gallois, who was 23 at the time of the
strike, stressed the ways in which women workers networked support from
neighborhood shopkeepers in order to organize strike relief for workers' families. She herself obtained milk coupons to nourish her young son. Women
workers would seem to have returned to their more traditional protest roles of
organizing subsistence. However, police accounts of women workers' actions
stressed any behavior that troubled public order. Their reports noted the presence of numerous women, picketing factory entrances, whose language was
judged extremely violent, even shocking. But rarely were women portrayed in
official accounts as defending their own interests as workers. Although massively present among the strikers, women workers did not share the same place
in the strike narrative as men. Because this strike was characterized as "political" by many contemporary observers, from the prefect down to the millowners, it was the male union leaders who appeared as the central protagonists. The old Fédération socialiste de l'Aube, like the Syndicat du textile, was
dominated by men, and internal political divisions tended to personalize their
struggles.

By far the most serious incident is hardly mentioned in the archival reports
on the strike, but it remains a strong memory in the minds of workers and
millowners alike. Henri Recoing, the owner of a large mill, was sequestered
by strikers at the Bourse du Travail when he was found walking nearby. The
version related to me stressed the timely intervention of the Syndicat du

Textile–CGTU when an angry crowd wanted to hang him. Suzanne Gallois saved the situation by proposing to humiliate the millowner in a way that appealed to both popular and feminine imagination, that is, to lock the mill-owner up in a storeroom and make him peel potatoes.[42] The strike commit-tee subsequently escorted him to the town hall and turned him over to the mayor. While it is interesting to reflect on the gendered meaning of this act of humiliation—a man doing women's work—the type of violence expressed during this strike was distinctly prewar anarchosyndicalist action. One of the tasks of the Communist Party would be to discipline and control such violence in later years. But this particular incident revealed men and women workers' strong anger at being deprived of work on the very last day of the conflict, November 3, at the end of a six-week strike, when everyone expected to return to work.

The strike did, however, divide the working class, if we can judge by police reports. In September the unpopularity of the lockout may have swung many men and women workers to join the strike movement. Estimates provided by the conservative newspaper *La Tribune de l'Aube* and the police suggest that a very large majority of workers supported the strike at the outset.[43] One month later, on October 24, an attempted referendum launched by the Comité de chômage provided an estimate of the number of nonstrikers. Out of 8,000 workers registered and approximately 3,300 voters, 3,230 workers voted to go back to work. The police claimed that the number of voters represented "exactly the number of workers who had always showed up at the mills to work."[44] These figures, however, do not reflect the multiple pressures that workers must have felt four weeks into the strike. Both the CGT and the CGTU-affiliated textile unions called on their members to abstain from voting, since the referendum in the mills had been initiated by the Comité de chômage, which was closely connected to Catholic employers.

Despite conciliation efforts from several sources, the mayor, the town council, and the government's labor inspector, the strike dragged on. At this

42. Testimony from Suzanne Gallois, interview, 1984. Her comment highlighted the fact that "it was certainly a woman who thought up that idea!"
43. *La Tribune de l'Aube* estimated the number of strikers as 62.7 percent on September 26 and 59.4 percent on October 3 in the twenty-eight principal mills of Troyes. See Bedin 1975, 232. The administration's strike questionnaire gives the following numbers for the first two weeks of the strike: out of fifty-five active mills, twenty-five were hit by the strike; there were 8,045 strikers, including 4,175 men and 3,870 women, out of a total workforce of 10,625 (AN F22 181).
44. AN F22 181.

point the labor unions positioned their demands in such a way as to obtain something tangible, recuperating the hourly cost-of-living allowance without changing the wage scale. When workers offered these concessions, millowners became more intransigent in negotiating the hourly allowance. Finally the prefect proposed to arbitrate and, after interviewing each party in the conflict, drew up an agreement. After the press had published the proposed arbitration, and the working class was expecting an imminent solution to the conflict that would reopen the mills, the Chambre Syndicale Patronale found a mathematical error in the work contract proposed by the prefect. On November 3 men and women workers showed up for work to find themselves still locked out. The millowners' rejection of the contract and their continued lockout unleashed a wave of violence on November 4 against several millowners' homes and their cars. In their outrage the crowd targeted, not the mills, but obvious symbols of material wealth.[45] Workers did not return to the mills until November 7. The strike had lasted six weeks, and workers had obtained an increase of three cents an hour!

Consequences of the Strike

The strike demonstrated two directly opposed logics with regard to wages. For workers, underemployment in 1921 combined with the two subsequent reductions in the cost-of-living allowance, dug deeply into their pockets. The extremely modest gain obtained at the end of a six-weeks' strike left the working class unwilling to renegotiate an agreement. René Plard expressed their mistrust in *La Dépêche*, underscoring that millowners had proposed an "equivocal" contract and, moreover, that they had tried to "manipulate the calculations."[46] Despite the millowners' mistrust of the joint commission's findings, they agreed to continue discussion and evaluation of the cost of living. To this end, union leaders delegated negotiating roles within the joint commission to women militants, whose daily contact with the family budget grounded their experience. It was in this capacity that Suzanne Gallois found herself delegated by the CGTU to the joint commission "sur la vie chère." Her testimony stressed the problem of obtaining millowners' recognition that workers had

45. The state and the town would subsequently be forced to indemnify millowners for the broken windows and smashed gates that resulted from the worker violence that day. The prefect was rapidly and discreetly transferred to another job.

46. *La Dépêche de l'Aube,* November 2, 1921.

the same need to consume quality food products that millowners had: "We discussed potatoes, and they wanted to have us eat old wrinkled potatoes, but I said, 'Those potatoes are used to feed pigs, so let them go to the pigs, but not to workers!'"[47] Women's experience of the everyday market made them tough negotiators, and such confrontational discussions highlighted social inequalities in consumer behavior. Moreover, it was indicative of postwar social tensions that workers in Troyes felt that their efforts during the war had not been rewarded, and from all appearances, millowners had profited. For this reason the privileged targets of violence on November 4 were millowners' personal property and signs of material wealth.

For the millowners, the ultimate goal was to retain control over wages. The employers' union considered that the wage increases granted since 1914 "corresponded overall to the rise in the cost of living."[48] Moreover, they intended to prove it. They proceeded to devise a comparison of wages between those in 1914 and in 1921.[49] As union leaders' opposition to the proposed contact grew, millowners offered further explanations to gain workers' trust. Thus, before the strike broke out, they had posters put up in town, giving their version of how the figures contained in the work contract would be applied. The posters contradicted an article in the *Dépêche* that, from the employers' viewpoint, misrepresented the proposed contract.[50] But when we look at records of private discussions in the Chambre syndicale patronale in January 1921, we find that, independent of any contract negotiations, millowners were convinced that wage cuts were necessary for commercial reasons.[51] Employers refused to reason in terms of the cost of living or by function of any negotiated agreement signed with unions that they refused to recognize.

If we look at the evolution of textile workers' wages from the 1880s to 1922 and compare it to the larger pattern for France as a whole, based on Jean Lhomme's study of French workers' buying power,[52] we might be able to appreciate whether Troyes workers did actually obtain a fair share of the nation's economic growth over this period, and how women's wages compared

47. Testimony from Suzanne Gallois, interview, 1984.
48. Discussion, September 15, 1924, *Registre des procès-verbaux*.
49. A comparison of wages for the periods of June–July in 1914 and 1919 appears in AMT 2J 48.
50. Reply to M. Alfred in *La Dépêche de l'Aube*, September 15, 1921.
51. Discussions, January 28, 1921, *Registre des procès-verbaux*. This same reasoning was evident in their reply to Mayor Emile Clévy on February 11, 1921.
52. Lhomme 1968.

to men's. It is crucial to bear in mind that the evidence for nominal wage rates comes strictly from millowner sources: the figures available were furnished by the Chambre syndicale patronale and only publicly contested by workers during the parliamentary inquiry commission's audition of union leaders in 1904.[53] Moreover, wage rates available for the nineteenth century do not take into account endemic periods of unemployment, a fact that union leaders underscored repeatedly in their testimony. Prices providing evidence of the evolution of the cost of living have been gleaned from various sources, running from those practiced for staple items at the Laborieuse, the workers' consumer cooperative, to those collected and approved by the joint commission in the 1920s. All this being said, nominal wages in Troyes more than kept pace with the cost of living from 1882 to 1900, then both nominal and real wages stagnated, even declined until 1914. Ironically, wages declined after the great strike. For France as a whole, the movement was approximately the same, with the exception of the 1900–1914 period.[54] If we compare the evolution of men's and women's nominal daily wages for this same period, we find that women's wages rose from about one half men's in 1882 to more than three-quarters by 1922. It can be argued that this increase in women's wages in proportion to men's is related to the postwar labor shortage and to the expansion of garment production in the industry during the 1920s.

The strike of 1921 left two important legacies. The first was an evolution of thinking about wages since the strike of 1900. Workers' perception of wages now included the demand for a living wage, one that addressed their families' needs in relation to society as a whole. Workers would no longer accept being marginalized from the growing consumer market. Millowners, by contrast, saw the advantage of family allowances that would simultaneously help stabilize the workforce, respond to national policy pressures for larger families, and offset radical worker demands for uniform wage increases. An employer-controlled family allowance scheme, moreover, allowed them to disaggregate wages, forestalling more costly overall increases.[55] The second legacy was

53. Wages for 1882 from a form sent by the prefect requesting information on women's working conditions from AMT 7F 4; wages for 1890 from Mortier 1891, 83; wages for 1900 from Chambres des Députés, Procès-Verbaux de la Commission . . . Enquête parlementaire, vol. 5, no. 1922, p. 85; wages for 1914 and 1919 from AMT 2J 48; and finally, wages for 1922 from the unpublished Vitoux mill wage register in ADA 90 J 103.

54. See Lhomme 1968, 69.

55. Susan Pedersen makes this point and demonstrates the motivation for different businesses to use family allowance schemes to different ends. See in particular her case study of the Consortium textile de Roubaix-Tourcoing, in Pedersen 1993, 224–61. See also "Remèdes à la

employers' efforts to test the union movement's political strength. Union leaders had held no illusions about millowners' intentions. As early as February
1921, union leaders had warned the working class: "It is our duty to tell the
population of the Aube that for the past six months employers have pursued
one goal: the destruction of workers' unions by all possible means."[56] While
strike mobilization had permitted unions to overcome their own political divisions and regain provisional unity, popularized in the columns of their newspaper, *La Dépêche,* the conflict severely weakened the labor movement. Bitter
political infighting followed the inevitable split between communist- and
socialist-affiliated unions, behavior that only played into employers' hands.

As in the past, millowners emerged in fighting spirit from the strike of 1921.
Their official interpretation of the strike, published on December 1 and titled
"After the Strike," imputed entire responsibility for "such a grave adventure"
to the workers and their unions. They estimated that the work stoppage over
six weeks "cost millworkers about 5 million francs in wages."[57] The most serious consequence, in their opinion, was that the strike diverted orders from
the Troyes mills to their foreign competitors. However, the principal lesson
that millowners drew from the work conflict concerned the way production
was to be organized in the immediate future. The strike had, they claimed,
"opened the way to the decentralization of knitting production, which by
necessity and in the future would emigrate away from the local labor force, to
its great detriment." Whatever the truth of the argument, the warning was
clear and the decision taken. Moreover, there were obvious advantages for millowners in moving production to the countryside, toward cheaper nonunionized rural labor. Decentralization would require, however, a new organization
of production in which women's work would play a major role.

OUTWORK AND FEMINIZATION

By 1921, the knitting industry in Troyes had reached a maximum concentration
in urban mills. While in 1906 there were thirty mills in the Aube employing

---

vie chère," *L'Ouvrière,* March 1, 1924, in which the author argues that family allowances cost
employers less than an overall wage increase.
   56. Poster printed by the unions on February 14, 1921, and posted in town to explain the
origins of the strike, Bedin 1975, 113.
   57. Chambre syndicale patronale, *Après la grève* (1921), Archives du Musée de la bonneterie.

more than one hundred workers, by 1921 there were some forty, six of which employed between five hundred and two thousand workers.[58] Such figures emphasize the level of concentration of both production and the workforce in Troyes. Several mills had reached a scale that became difficult to manage. So the subsequent restructuring of production that took place between 1921 and 1929 benefited from the general economic recovery and prosperity in France as a whole, but more specifically from new business strategies. Industrial homework was not new to the industry, as we have already seen. The rural population surrounding Troyes had always constituted a reserve labor force. However, the business strategies introduced in the 1920s combined several new structures for production, many of which relied on women outworkers. Millowners initially targeted women as a more docile labor force. But the increased feminization of the industry was also a consequence of both technological changes and consumer demand for knitted clothing.

Decentralization

The decentralized outwork system of the 1920s might seem reminiscent of the nineteenth-century putting-out system, but in fact, it demanded greater capital investment and provided greater flexibility in managing labor. A number of millowners with large capital, such as André Gillier, established satellite workshops and warehouses in the Aube. Some branches were located outside the region in an effort to employ cheaper labor. A number of millowners set up knitting frames with artisan façonniers whom they subcontracted to work exclusively in their employ. Many of these artisans had formerly worked in the mills but now, as war veterans, wanted to be "self-employed." Thus the town of Troyes was surrounded by networks of family workshops as in the late nineteenth century. The only significant difference was that these workshops operated with leased machinery and orders exclusively from one millowner. Finally, an industrial homework system proliferated among the townswomen who took in finishing work of all kinds. The Valton mills, for example, distributed work "either within the town limits or in certain parish *ouvroirs* or workshops, or again in convents and small depositories in places like Bar-sur-Aube."[59] In this case, Valton relied almost exclusively on a female labor force.

58. *Statistiques du recensement général de la population,* census for 1921.
59. Boucraut and Boucraut 1986, 53.

The outwork system afforded an employer specific advantages. First of all, "he had no fears of labor conflicts from scattered workers, as he did from a collective workforce," as historian Julien Ricommard observed in 1934.[60] Similarly, Troyes millowners recognized that young rural women were likely to be nonunionized and more passive than their urban counterparts. The decentralization of production took place as the eight-hour-day law was coming into effect. Once again, the absence of unions in rural workshops meant that work inspectors were less likely to exercise control.[61] In 1923 the CGTU denounced in *L'Ouvrière* the specific exploitation of rural women workers in the Aube in violation of the law. "In the village of Les Riceys women working nine hours and producing the same number of stockings as in Troyes, earn only 9 francs a day, that is, a minimum of 11 francs less than their co-workers in town. Similarly, the seamers in the Mauchauffée mill in Bar-sur-Aube receive only 120 francs for two weeks' pay, while women in the same occupation in the Troyes mill earn from 260 to 300 francs for the same period."[62] Examples of this kind demonstrate that women workers in the countryside were working a longer schedule than the one authorized in the Troyes mills, for much lower wages. A similar work pattern certainly prevailed among artisans in isolated family workshops, who were not yet covered by the new law governing the eight-hour day.[63]

Millowners' policy of decentralization also established a new technical division of labor. During the 1920s, the Troyes knitting industry diversified production, manufacturing a greater variety of goods and developing modern marketing techniques that targeted a broader consumer market. The shortage of skilled labor in Troyes diverted the production of more standardized goods to less skilled rural artisan workshops, or to branch mills operating in the southeast region of the Aube, where knitting had not previously been established.[64] Each branch mill, moreover, included a network of women homeworkers.

During this period of relative prosperity from 1922 to 1926, the shortage of skilled labor in the Troyes mills meant that wages, as well as profits, were relatively higher than in the past. Workers remembered this period as one when

60. Ricommard 1934, 141.
61. Work inspectors were solicited with demands for special dispensation from several millowners who wanted to recuperate the time lost over official holidays.
62. *L'Ouvrière*, December 15, 1923.
63. Ricommard 1934, 138.
64. Ibid.

mills were hiring. "It was the golden age of the knitting industry, profits were good, so anyone who had money to invest did so then in the industry by setting up mills and hiring workers."[65] Several men and women I interviewed had begun their working lives as apprentices in mill workshops during this period. These young people entered the trade as their parents had done: "What do you expect? That's the only jobs there were, we had to work for our living and we didn't think about doing anything else. . . . As soon as we left school, hop, the knitting mill."[66] Despite the appearance of continuity, working conditions were decidedly different from those in the prewar period.

Work Norms

Several sources provide a comparative perspective on working conditions before and after the war. As a general rule, workshop regulations were posted in the mills. Such regulations provide the historian with a general framework of norms that were applied for industrial work at this time. But testimony from workers prove a more reliable source for how such norms were actually followed, and the archives from the Conseil des prud'hommes, the local trade arbitration court, provide an overview of how norms were contested. As a typical example, the workshop rules posted in the Regley Mill in 1924 indicated that the mill manager now delegated considerable authority to the factory foreman to impose work discipline. The usual fines for such nonconformist behavior as absence on Mondays were doubled, and they were also applied to the cost-of-living bonus. Work hours were now controlled through punching the time clock. All worker testimony confirmed this new form of control that was exercised over factory hours during the postwar period.

However, some workers also remembered the positive atmosphere of mill life. Testimony from women workers who apprenticed during this period related the fact that singing while working was permitted in the all-female workshops in several mills. In fact, these women were singing popular songs of the period, not the socialist "Internationale," but at most mills not even this practice was allowed. As a woman mender, recalling her apprenticeship, put it, "One had to work; we were supervised. What I really appreciated was that there was no background music like there is today in the mills, so we sang

65. Testimony of M. Labourie, interview, 1987.
66. Testimony of Mme Fournet, interview, 1986.

while we worked. It was permitted, and I assure you that this encouraged us to work. We sang while we were doing our work and I found that beautiful." But the same woman mender stressed that conditions were not the same in every mill: "Conditions were stricter [in another mill] and we didn't even have the right to lift our heads from our work. We had to keep our heads bowed over our work. Actually, I had the right to lift my head up occasionally because I was working on very fine knitted goods, and after a while I could no longer see very well."[67] Work discipline was thus enforced.

Another valuable source for understanding the evolution of the work process is technical trade manuals for apprenticeship that detail the increased specialization of knitting-machine technology during this period. Progress had been made during the 1920s to specialize knitting machines in the manufacturing of specific products. Félix Lamotte, a leading manufacturer in Troyes, explained that this new work process offered the advantages of simplifying product design and improving finishing techniques.[68] In fact, the specialization of knitting machines eliminated downtime lost through resetting the machine for producing another item. Technical innovation had created a more rationalized production process. However, the machine's new specialized capabilities diluted and limited the knitter's skills. Up until then, the knitter had intervened in the operation of his machine, performing tasks that valorized his technical knowledge of the work process. By the 1920s the knitter found himself overseeing more knitting machines, each one with increased productivity. The knitter's skilled status was further threatened by the new authority invested in the foreman, who now imposed production norms. The improved Cotton patent knitting frame needed fewer interventions, and a skilled knitter could now oversee one or even two Cotton frames, with twelve or twenty-four heads.[69] Such new production norms account for some of the numerous conflicts between knitters and foremen that are recorded in the archives of the Conseils des prud'hommes for this period.

The most typical case concerned summary firing, without the customary notice, often in a heated dispute between foreman and knitter that involved verbal or physical violence. The court condemned such behavior, even when

67. Testimony of Mme Aubron, interview, 1982. Suzanne Gallois also remembered the positive spirit created in the women's workshops by this same practice of collective singing while working.
68. Lamotte 1924, 14, a special issue on the department of the Aube. See also Ricommard's (1934) discussion on the advantages of the specialization of knitting machines (105).
69. Ricommard 1934, 123.

women workers were the offenders, as was sometimes the case with bobbin winders. Other disputes involved rupture of the work contract without respect for the usual notice of six working days, called "la huitaine," practiced by both sides in the trade and stipulated in the workshop rules. More frequent were conflicts over arbitrary wage changes by the employer in payment for work that had been agreed upon in advance at a piece rate. Defective work produced by a textile worker, or faulty knitting machines that prevented a worker from meeting production norms, also represented contested terrain.[70] The fact that such norms existed and were strongly enforced as part of the new work discipline increased the likelihood of conflict.

As the economy recovered, millowners introduced shift work to increase productivity and circumvent the limits of the eight-hour law. Knitters working in small and medium-scale factories worked two shifts, in tandem with bobbin winders and rebrousseurs. In 1928 the first recorded time-motion study of bobbin winding took place in one of the large integrated process mills, the Société Générale de Bonneterie. The Syndicat du textile claimed that this mill had been designated to test the application of more Taylorized methods. The union consequently organized a protest strike on the grounds that the increased output demanded of women bobbin winders was accompanied by a cut in the piece rate.

Management's attempts to rationalize the work process ended as the economic situation declined. Perhaps the fact that much of the knitting machinery had not been modernized also played a role. Ricommard suggested that technological advances had been piecemeal and that older forms of production persisted despite modernization efforts made after the war. He specified that there was a great diversity of machinery of all kinds in the Aube, dating from the earliest to the most recent innovations.[71] What is important to note, however, is how little technical progress had been made concerning women's

70. The archives of the Conseil des prud'hommes in Troyes are among the oldest in France and are preserved at the Palais de Justice. I looked systematically at the cases for the interwar years and specifically at the disputes evolving out of the strikes of 1900 and 1921. The employers' union maintained in their testimony before the parliamentary inquiry commission on 1904 that only 10 percent of conflicts settled in the trade courts concerned the knitted goods industry.

71. Ricommard 1934, 117–20. The author discussed a newpaper article published in 1930 that accused Troyes millowners of being reluctant to modernize their machinery, an accusation that Ricommard found "unjust or at least excessive." Whether this criticism was well founded would be difficult to verify, given the lack of access to company records for this period. Ricommard's assessment was based on an inventory of knitting machines identified for tax purposes in 1928.

occupations in the trade. The fact that garment making had only been partially mechanized meant that more women workers were needed to execute special-ized tasks, and that manual jobs such as those performed by "petites mains" for hand finishing still persisted. Incomplete mechanization provides only one of the explanations for the increasing feminization of the labor force.[72]

Feminization of the Labor Force

According to census reports, the numbers of workers employed in the Aube knitted goods industry increased markedly between 1914 and 1930, growing from fourteen thousand to thirty thousand. It is important to stress here the constant increase in the number of women workers employed in industrial trades: women constituted a majority of 51 percent in 1901, and by 1921 they represented 61 percent, an increase identical to that of the national rate (the percentage of women in the working population reached its highest level nationally in 1921). Women remained in the majority throughout the 1920s and 1930s, notably in the category *workers and employées,* where they represented 62 percent of the industrial labor force. In a parallel movement, the number of women "chefs d'établissement" (self-employed) decreased and those listed as "isolated workers" increased to a stable level. This double movement not only demonstrates a substantial feminization of the labor force; more impor-tant, it shows the displacement of women's employment into the category *"worker."* This tendency, already present at the turn of the century, became accentuated during the interwar years.[73]

How can we explain this feminization process? I would argue that the re-course to women's labor was linked, on the one hand, to complex social and technical factors related to the deskilling of millwork in general during this period, and, on the other hand, to labor market strategies adopted by mill-owners. The use of women for specific finishing jobs was dictated partly by technical imperatives in garment manufacturing. Because of the difficulties of mechanizing all stages of making knitted clothing, women were assigned to

72. Martin Vanier (1993) argues that the predominance of cut-and-sewn garments over fully fashioned ones in the manufacture of knitted goods in Troyes after 1918 necessitated "un-skilled handworkers, abundant and cheap female labor" for assembling garments. His technical explanation of the feminization process seems only partially grounded. I offer a more complete explanation in the following section.

73. These figures were culled from *Statistiques du recensement général de la population,* census reports from 1901 through 1936.

the manual tasks for which no accessory machine had been invented: unwinding, preparation for bobbin winding, fine seaming, and embroidery. However, technical evolution cannot alone explain the feminization process. As we have seen, millowners sought to maintain the industrial homework system during the 1920s by preserving forms of work that they considered compatible with child rearing. Thus they aimed at preserving a high rate of women's low-waged employment, even during the years of marriage and child rearing. Such principles had governed labor-management policies since early in the century, and they had come to rely heavily on cheap female labor.

One woman seamer who raised four children worked many years at home on a treadle machine provided by her employer. She explained how she organized her workday: "I had to finish some ten dozen stockings a day. I was given as many to do as if I were working in the mill . . . so I obviously worked later into the evening. Fortunately my mother was there to help me by minding my daughter."[74] What is important to note here is that she was expected by her employer to meet the same production norms as those in the mill, while operating an old-fashioned treadle machine.

The only mill that consistently maintained an outwork system as an integral part of production was the Doré-Doré company in Fontaine-les-Grès, some twenty kilometers west of Troyes. Doré-Doré maintained a network of small family workshops for most of its manufacturing. In 1924 the millowner described the social purpose of this industrial homework system: "Manufacturing quality knitted goods employs a large number of women homeworkers, as seamers, finishers, and embroiderers. These women can thus mind their children, do housework, and occupy their long winter evenings, while doing easy work and contributing to the family budget."[75] Obviously there were not many jobs available in the countryside that allowed women to combine paid work and child care, and such a solution offered women workers flexibility in terms of hours while lowering labor costs for the employer.

Examples of this kind of homework practiced by women workers abound. In knitting manufacturing, as a garment industry, production was organized around the flexibility of women workers as a reliable, gender-specific labor force. The "choice" of working alternatively between home and mill was expressed by many women workers as a family strategy during hard times, but for

74. Testimony of Mme Fournet, interview, 1986.
75. *Illustration économique et financière* (1924), 26.

most of them it was an absolute economic necessity. The feminization of the labor force, attributed by historian Julien Ricommard to "habitual practice" since World War I,[76] was the result of a much more complex phenomenon, based on social, technical and economic factors, as we have seen.

NEW QUEENS FOR A DAY

Following the same logic of this feminization process, women workers increasingly identified with the trade. The revival of the Fêtes de la Bonneterie in 1925 and 1926 provided the occasion for renewed cultural expression of women's role in the industry. This time, the festival was organized by the local tourist Syndicat d'initiative, with the collaboration of millowners and municipal officials. As the economy recovered, commerce and consumption became their more obvious purpose. The crowning ceremony speeches once again set the tone for the festivities. In contrast with the prewar queens, this 1920s version was characterized as "la Reine des Travailleurs," symbol of an almost androgynous worker. The president of the Syndicat d'initiative elaborated on this gender ambiguity further: "[F]or all of us, this festival is not simply a moment of rejoicing, but above all a glorification of work, a tribute to those men and women who, by their professional skill and work ethic have created for our major local industry a universal reputation, and who are the creators of our town's prosperity."[77] Yet this "queen of the workers" did represent a new social reality in the increasing number of women employed in the local industry, who were here identified with the larger mass of women in France's growing industrial workforce.

The queen and her two attendants were once again silent symbols in this festival. Two newsworthy comments from reporters' accounts locate the social and cultural concerns of the 1920s. Although the period was effectively one of relative prosperity in the town, fears of unemployment and economic instability were present. Newspapers reported that the generous queen of 1925 gave the financial rewards of her royalty to local charities. But postwar fashions

---

76. Ricommard (1934) explains the predominance of women over men in the labor force: "During the war, large numbers of women were brought into the industry to compensate for the shortage of men. Once the practice became established, women workers continued to dominate the labor force since this period" (126).

77. *Le Petit Troyen*, September 15, 1925.

involving bobbed hair and shorter skirts provoked more comment and controversy. All newspaper descriptions highlighted the fact that the queen and her court had not succumbed to the dictates of fashion and cut their hair, in what one journalist termed "la barbarie de la tondeuse." By 1926 this was hardly the case, as the commemorative photographs of the queens show. The worker queens of 1926 were dressed by their employers to model fashions perceived as appropriate for a modern fashion industry, in a decided break with the royal past that was invoked in previous festivals. Underlying the postwar fashion for short, bobbed hair was a statement about the "new woman" of modern industrial society, revealing the tensions of gender and political change. The political importance for women of this fashion change in body silhouette and identity has been interpreted in many interesting ways.[78] Women historians have rightly pointed to the self-fashioning by young women who, for feminist or whatever reasons, were challenging the images of femininity traditionally mediated by men. Less well known are the motivations of working-class women to experiment with and adopt such changes. Certainly forming part of the story were the desire to follow fashion and aspirations for social mobility.

Before World War I, most working class-women were identified as being "en cheveu," that is, uncovered in the street. Only if women workers could afford it did they cover their heads with a broad-brimmed hat. By the postwar period some working-class women could follow fashion and cut their hair in a more general movement toward the democratization of la mode.[79] But for the majority, as articles in the CGTU's *L'Ouvrière* stressed in 1926, the constant rise in prices caused by *la vie chère* made new clothing unaffordable for working-class families.[80] Higher hemlines made women's stockings an indispensable item: in 1914 a pair cost Fr 1.50, and in October 1926 they sold for Fr 11.50, an increase of nearly eight times the prewar price.[81] In terms of wages, this pair of stockings represented more than half the daily earnings of a bobbin winder. For many women textile workers of this postwar generation, fashionable items remained unthinkable.[82]

78. Bard 1998; M. L. Roberts 1993, 684.
79. Suzanne Gallois related that she had had her hair cut *à la garçonne* shortly after the end of the war. She proudly announced that she was one of the first women in Troyes to adopt the new style (interview, 1984).
80. F. Meunier, "Pourquoi la vie chère?" *La Dépêche de l'Aube,* February 28, 1924.
81. Index of the cost of living on October 1, 1926, AMT 4F 129.
82. See articles in *L'Ouvrière* on *la vie chère* giving comparative prices for staple items in 1914 and 1926, especially December 11, 1924, February 11, 1926, April 1, 1926, and August 12, 1926. See esp. Marguerite Faussecave, "Les magasins des pauvres," *L'Ouvrière,* February 11, 1926.

ON THE EVE OF THE ECONOMIC CRISIS

In this short period of relative prosperity and industrial expansion, there were signs that economic and social development would slacken. Several were specific to the structures of the local textile industry itself. For example, the lack of renewal in this type of family capitalism, and its confinement within the traditional social and financial milieus of Troyes, hindered restructuring in individual mills, as well as in the local industry as a whole. The generation of entrepreneurs, engineers, and technicians who had previously managed larger mills was dying out, leaving successors who had less training in technical innovation and financial management. The first sign of a break in family tradition was the disinterest for business shown by the third generation in several mill-owning families. At another level, the multiplicity of small knitted goods companies and workshops that had been founded with speculative capital for quick profits in the 1920s proved not to have solid roots. Many of these small firms would fail in the 1930s. Thus, not all the signs of reconstruction-driven industrial growth during the 1920s were solidly based. On the eve of the economic crisis of the 1930s, we need to ask how both management and labor would react to the first signs of problems.

Employer Policies: A Crisis Mentality

Understanding the attitudes and policies of millowners during an economic crisis of the scale they faced in the 1930s is not an easy task. Many of the roots of the crisis were to be found in the economic strategies of the 1920s. For millowners in Troyes, the policy of expansion and diversification of production had seemed highly profitable. Even the principal economic historian of the knitting industry who was writing during this period, Julien Ricommard, insisted on the "normalcy" of crises—they were in many ways characteristic of the industry. According to Ricommard, "[S]ince 1919, except for a few passing crises that recurred periodically, the knitting industry in the Aube had known exceptional prosperity up until 1929." He based his analysis on the classic indicators of growth (high rate of turnover, "high wage policy," and the creation of new factories, among other factors), concluding that the first symptoms of any trouble appeared only at the end of 1929. However, Ricommard was writing in January 1934 in the midst of the crisis, observing the daily decline in industrial activity. Under the circumstances, he privileged an explanation that characterized the crisis in Troyes as a "local manifestation of the [international and national] economic crisis." As a result, his analysis minimizes the causes specific to Troyes, especially the symptoms prior to 1929, the year when the situation suddenly worsened. Moreover, Ricommard adopted the millowners' position on the principal causes of the crisis, that is, the immediate economic context: restriction of the domestic market, the limitation of exports, and foreign competition. He did not look further into the past than 1929 to find the causes.[83]

Many contemporary observers were also convinced that "the international origin of the French crisis emerged from the facts with startling evidence."[84] They affirmed that "the violent drop in prices," which characterized the 1930 crisis, was an international indicator of an approaching crisis. Moreover, they tended to identify the same indicators in countries that had already been hit by the crisis, for example, England and the United States. This interpretation of the French crisis as "derivative, a consequence of a crisis unleashed elsewhere," was semiofficial wisdom of the interwar period.[85] Some reports insisted on the monetary aspects of the crisis, attributing them to "the monetary instability created by the war." Without calling into question this interpretation, it is important to retrace and examine with hindsight certain local phenomena, specific to the textile sector, that anticipated the crisis. Such an approach would consider the year 1929 as a sober marker of economic decline, the signs of which had appeared earlier.

Explaining the crisis in the Troyes knitted goods industry as primarily derivative of larger national and international ones, would seem to mask the weaknesses of millowners' commercial strategies: their preference for cartels to control production, wages and prices; their preference for manufacturing primarily luxury goods; and their dependence since the nineteenth century on an export market, heavily protected by the state. Alfred Sauvy has characterized this entrepreneurial psychology as "economic Malthusianism," and there was a resurgence of such behavior in the 1930s.[86] The economic crisis would thus reveal the fragility of the speculative expansionist policies of the 1920s; and the stagnation of sales could be attributed to the lack of renewal within the industry itself. However, the main problem in interpreting the local crisis

83. Ricommard 1934, 175–76.
84. Letellier et al. 1938–49, 1:24.
85. Ibid., 33.
86. On this question, see Kuisel 1981, 95, 154. See also Sauvy 1965–75, 2:359–78; Boyer 1991, 9.

is the data itself: it is questionable whether Ricommard's sources were at all reliable, as he was writing in 1934 using local sources that are now inaccessible. His account is based almost entirely on mill-production data from 1929 to 1933 that were provided personally and "confidentially" by millowners.[87]

Signs of employment instability and slackening of production that cannot be attributed to the abrupt variations in currency can be found toward the end of 1926. In Troyes, partial unemployment appeared in early 1927 and spread slowly, according to data gathered by the Inspection du travail. The Inspection's reports mentioned the difficulty of obtaining employment information from millowners who were "less and less disposed to provide this information, claiming that the Chambre syndicale patronale was the only authorized source."[88] Nevertheless, the Inspection made its own inquiry and in late March 1927 submitted the following findings to the prefect: out of 17,105 women and men workers employed in the knitting and related industries in the Aube, knitting alone employed 12,237, of whom 3,452 were working less than forty-eight hours a week. Therefore, 28 percent were partially underemployed.[89] According to women worker's testimony, the mills were closed on Mondays and on Saturday afternoons. Thus, unemployment would appear to have been more important than was officially admitted by millowners themselves.

How were these measures to layoff workers in 1927 publicly justified? Only cursory indications were given concerning slackening orders in relation to previous years. Millowners seemed overly preoccupied with the possible consequences of a Franco-German commercial agreement signed in August 1927, which they fought to have revised to prevent the importation of German knitted goods.[90] However, the fact that business recovered in 1928 seemed to confirm that employers had been correct in their policy of diversifying production, that is, manufacturing standard goods as well as luxury ones. The stabilization of the franc by the Poincaré government encouraged a renewed policy of expansion and exportation. In fact, Troyes millowners wanted to guard against foreign competition and any signs of crisis by taking measures that restrained

87. Ricommard 1934; see his notes at 182, 188.

88. Report from the inspecteur du travail to the prefect of the Aube, January 24, 1927, ADA SC 1204.

89. Report from the inspecteur du travail to the prefect, March 26, 1927. This particularly scrupulous inspector had held this post in the Aube since the 1921 strike. He affirmed that his inquiry had focused on "the largest number of mills possible" and for these mills the figures "correspond to two-thirds of the total personnel." ADA SC 1204.

90. Chambre de commerce de Troyes, Rapports sur la situation commerciale et industrielle du département, 1928–1930.

labor and wages. They laid off part of their personnel, put the rest on short time, and cut the hourly bonus. In this way they were able to maintain flexibility in working hours as far as the exemptions to the law of 1919 allowed. Wages appeared to no longer be related to the cost of living, but geared to a collective business strategy. How did workers react to these wage cuts and to short-time working?[91]

The Decline of the Unions

The labor movement had great difficulty in recovering from the strike of 1921. Weakened by the split in both parties and unions, the action of labor organizers was further undermined by personal animosities between union leaders. Moreover, the movement faced the particular difficulties of organizing a more scattered labor force, and a force that involved small-scale family-run workshops. More important, large millowners manifested open hostility toward syndicalism. Estimates of union membership at this time demonstrate the decline. An article published in *Aube Ouvrière,* a weekly newspaper founded by the CGT in August 1928, indicated a dramatic fall in membership in the 1920s: the departmental CGT union had numbered some twenty thousand members in 1919; by January 1929, the total had fallen to forty-five hundred.[92] These figures seem inflated when compared with the estimations calculated from other sources.[93] Whatever the real figures, the marked decline in union membership during these years represented a significant loss for syndicalism. When the labor movement split, the majority shifted their loyalties to the CGTU. Emile Clévy had led the CGT-affiliated unions in Troyes until he was elected to public office in 1919. Subsequently, a figure recognized as far less competent and popular, Louis Thibault, took over the union leadership.

The CGTU was strongly represented among textile workers and metalworkers. Their claim to the more militant tradition was demonstrated by their overlapping membership in both the union and the French Communist Party

91. For a broader national account of slow-time working, gender, and unemployment, see Reynolds 1996, 112–13.

92. *Aube Ouvrière,* January 1, 1929. Union membership was at its lowest point in 1927.

93. Liliane Couvreur (1973) used Antoine Prost's (1964) method for calculating union membership. Using the records of the confederal congresses of the CGT and the CGTU, Couvreur calculated an average number, based on the number of votes attributed to delegates from the Aube, which corresponded to a set number of members. Her results for the CGT Textile were 4,400 members in 1920, 3,500 in 1921, and 175 from 1923 to 1925, followed by a steep drop in membership from 1,325 to 675 in 1929.

(PCF). According to police surveillance records of these years, the PCF in the Aube had some eight hundred contributing members in 1926 and was particularly active in sixty cells organized in the mills.[94] But the CGTU also declined in membership during this period. Its numbers fell dramatically, from 1,725 in 1929 to 750 in 1931.[95] Three important leaders had emerged in Troyes and were active as militants in both the Communist Party and the CGTU. Foremost among them was René Plard, who had been trained as a lawyer by 1923 to defend those militants who were the object of political repression. He also defended individual workers who brought workplace conflicts before the Conseils des prud'hommes.[96] Marcel Cuny headed the metalworkers union, and Lucien Planson, a knitter in the mills, was the leader of the Syndicat unitaire du textile. Suzanne Gallois emerged as the only woman union militant of stature during this period. She had started working in the mills during World War I as a seamer. Under the influence of her father, an early socialist who admired Jean Jaurès, Suzanne militated at an early age, and became responsible for the women's commission of the CGTU textile union in Troyes during the 1930s. In a working-class milieu where there were very few women militants, she played an important role in syndicalism in Troyes. All four militants would play an active part in the Popular Front in Troyes.

Despite the CGTU's concerted action to mobilize textile workers in Troyes, the low turnout at meetings revealed the difficulties of union recruitment at this time. While many of these difficulties were characteristic of the loose organization inherent to syndicalism, political repression also played a major part. As Suzanne Gallois affirmed in her testimony: "Anyone who was suspicious, that is to say, might be unionized, well, you were shown the door without any explanation. 'You have a week's notice, and that's it.' The employer was king; we had a real struggle."[97] Millowners systematically refused to work with labor unions, and union leaders were blacklisted among employers.

94. Note from the commissaire central de police to the prefect, August 17, 1926. ADA SC 4251.

95. Couvreur 1973, 22–23.

96. These cases are documented in the archives of the Troyes Conseil des prud'hommes during the 1920s and early 1930s. For example, in 1934 Plard defended militant Lucien Planson in a case of abusive rupture of his work contract. Planson had tried to bring in the Inspection du Travail as a mediator concerning his employer's posted work rules. The employer accused him of calling union meetings outside the mill and organizing workers inside. Planson lost the case for refusing to leave the mill while attempting to present millworkers' grievances, after the millowner refused to receive the worker delegation.

97. Testimony of Suzanne Gallois, interview, 1984. According to all verbal contracts, workers had to give one week's notice, called a "huitaine."

In these early years, the CGTU addressed specific propaganda to women workers. Its women's weekly, *L'Ouvrière,* founded in 1922, carried regular articles on women's issues and working conditions that aimed at recruitment. Many of these articles were reprinted in *La Dépêche de l'Aube.* The authors of these articles were often newly recruited feminist militants within the PCF such as Marthe Bigot and Lucie Collard, drawn almost exclusively from a milieu of intellectuals and teachers, or radical feminist sympathizers such as Madeleine Pelletier.[98] The principles governing such propaganda for recruitment were class struggle, political education and *mixité* (gender integration). Even the women's commissions (*commissions féminines*) established during the early 1920s were inclusive of party members of both sexes. Nevertheless, there was no general agreement over which arguments might be most effective in recruiting women. In 1924, Henri Jacob from the Troyes textile workers union took part in the women's conference prior to the Lyon party congress and criticized the content of *L'Ouvrière* as propaganda unsuitable for women workers, while representatives of other federations contradicted him.[99] For their part, women militants appealed more directly to women workers' double identity, locating them within both the home and the factory. They contended that political action through union membership concerned women as well as men, in order to defend their interests as workers, mothers, and housewives.[100]

The women's commission presented a list of special demands for women workers to the national congress in January 1925, one that included equal wages for equal work, social and political rights for women on equal terms with men, compulsory and paid maternity leave, the creation of crèches, and abolition of the 1920 law outlawing abortion.[101] The 1920 law had been the subject of several articles by women militants who attempted to counter the propaganda of the "repopulators," by stressing that "today's society punishes but doesn't protect mothers."[102] Typically, articles on women's rights during

98. Marthe Bigot (1878–1962), a primary school teacher in Paris, was a committed feminist before joining the Socialist, then the Communist Party. She attended the Congress in Tour, and in 1921–22 she held a position in the Comité directeur of the PCF with responsibility for propaganda to recruit women. In this context she founded *L'Ouvrière*. Under criticism from the party over her "petit-bourgeois" feminist positions, she resigned or was excluded. See the analysis of these women's roles in the party in Bard 1995, 249–67; also, Corradin and Martin 1999, 147–49.

99. Reported in coverage of the Lyon congress in *L'Ouvrière,* February 2, 1924.

100. "Femmes et politique" *La Dépêche de l'Aube,* January 12, 1924.

101. *L'Ouvrière,* January 15, 1925.

102. See in particular "Une loi sur l'avortement" by Marguerite Faussecave, reprinted in *La Dépêche de l'Aube,* January 12, 1924.

this period emphasized the PCF support for suffrage legislation, claiming that the vote would allow working women to defend their own interests in terms of both class and gender. Invariably these articles contrasted the concrete action of the PCF with that of feminist organizations, represented by the party as "political dilettantes." The vote was presented, not as a panacea, but as part of the class struggle for economic equality that involved both working-class men and women.[103]

The CGT developed a simultaneous campaign to recruit women into the union. Articles in *Aube Ouvrière* in 1928 suggested that women workers' evident disinterest in syndicalism was likely to have a bad effect on the women's suffrage movement (the bill in favor of women's suffrage was before the Senate at that moment). They argued aggressively, "We have reached a stage in the social movement where any neutrality must be considered cowardice or defection. What are you waiting for, comrade women, to come take your rightful place in the proletarian movement?"[104] While women workers were called upon to join the union, men were urged to educate their wives into syndicalism. Thus, at the very moment when syndicalism was at a historic low point, leaders from both unions were proposing their organizations as one of the ways for women to liberate themselves.

While the tradition of struggle was still strong in Troyes, the vast majority of workers remained unorganized. Arguably, syndicalism was not a reliable measure of combativity within the working class, especially during this period when unions were the object of repression. As was their custom, many more workers stated their grievances by work stoppage than by joining unions. A meeting at the Bourse du Travail to celebrate May Day in 1925 attracted seven hundred demonstrators, yet the police reported that 27 percent of millworkers had not shown up for work. The CGTU's strategy was to lead a united-front campaign, together with the other two unions. It was their initiative to form the Comité d'action du textile in February 1927 for a common defense of wages. Already in 1926 the CGTU had taken a public stance on the issue of unemployment; leaders demanded respect of the eight-hour day, the suppression of all special dispensations on working hours, slow-time working rather than layoffs, and measures to protect against wage cuts. In the *Dépêche de l'Aube,*

103. See an article in *L'Ouvrière,* April 15, 1926 that characterized the vote as a "piège féministe."

104. *Aube Ouvrière,* August 1, 1928.

union leaders denounced what they saw as a "campaign to prepare the working class to accept a wage cut" in fear of layoffs.[105]

The twenty-four-hour protest strike called by the Comité d'action du textile for February 4, 1929, provides a more significant measure of grassroot discontent than union membership. The strike represented a change of tactics by the CGTU at a time when political forces seemed unfavorable. The organization of a limited strike to demand a modest wage increase was a response motivated by the expectations of a new generation of young men and women millworkers, who had little significant experience of mill life and labor struggles. In fact, it was young people, among them the lowly paid rebrousseurs and bobbin winders, who formed the majority of strikers that day.[106] The movement touched 30 percent of some 15,300 millworkers, according to police sources, and some 60 percent if we believe the organizers.[107]

However, the twenty-four-hour protest strike revealed deep divisions within the Troyes labor movement. The CGT had refused to participate. It abandoned its role in the Comité d'action du textile, claiming that the CGTU had ordered the strike for the purpose of "political agitation" without consulting workers. By contrast, the Syndicat chrétien supported the movement, which succeeded in obtaining a small increase of fifteen centimes an hour with the prefect's help. However, the CGTU was unable to profit from the strike's success, because the union was deprived of several key militants during that crucial year. Cuny and Planson were arrested and imprisoned for thirteen months as leaders of a pacifist demonstration, and René Plard moved away from the political positions held by national PCF leaders. Plard's political shift had disastrous consequences for the local party organizations until 1934, when the PCF and the CGTU joined other left-wing political forces in an alliance against fascism.

The movement launched by the Comité d'action du textile had been timely and grounded in real worker discontent. Men and women millworkers had accepted the wage cut in 1927, but they expected their situation to improve with signs of economic recovery. Millowners, however, delayed their response to demands for a wage increase, which workers saw as justified by the upswing

105. *La Dépêche de l'Aube,* December 17, 1926.
106. Note from the prefect of the Aube to the Ministry of Labor, February 5, 1929, AN F22 197.
107. Ibid. The police based their figures on those provided by millowners. The Comité d'action du textile announced that "it can be estimated, without exaggeration, that 60 percent of workers, some 8,000 to 10,000, deserted the mills" (*La Champagne Syndicale,* February 1929).

in business and by the rising cost of living. Millowners countered that business had only "momentarily" recovered, and repeated that "wages paid in Troyes were much higher than those paid in other textile centers."[108] The latter argument was the millowners' standard reflex to wage issues.

In an exchange of letters with the employers' union, militants in the Comité d'action du textile affirmed their position in measured terms, claiming that the wages they earned were justified by their skills.[109] "If the wages in Troyes are higher, it is because the knitter in Troyes is more highly skilled and has a right to a higher wage than practiced elsewhere. . . . If you want to keep your skilled workers and maintain the quality of your products, you need to maintain that competitive edge in wages. You have a fine understanding of this issue. The competition from other centers could only harm you if you lost your superiority in manufacturing." Workers' response as wage earners was to suggest that they, too, were trying to anticipate the risks of the economic situation. "If the crisis returns, you will be in a position to deal with it. How about us?" they queried. To counter the crisis, workers appealed to "equity": "Your workers, Messieurs, collaborate fundamentally in the manufacturing of your products. Without them, you cannot produce anything. It is painful to consider your present attitude. You seem preoccupied only with arguing—about reality, probability, and even possibility—about everything except fairness."[110]

These two attitudes toward the postwar instability of economic life and the possibility of a renewed crisis were highly opposed. Millowners had retreated into a postwar policy of economic retrenchment in which wages were hardly negotiable. Moreover, they were reluctant to recognize the social justice of millworkers' demands. They continued to deny that class antagonism existed in Troyes, an argument that socialists in Troyes had developed since the turn of the century. More important, they refused to recognize union leaders or to cede any power to the state or to workers' organizations inside the factory gates. The growing polarization of French labor politics during this period provided renewed grounds for the sharply defined class conflict of the 1930s. In this chapter I have demonstrated that roots for this later confrontation were

108. Letter from the Chambre syndicale patronale to the Comité d'action du textile, December 29, 1928, *La Champagne Syndicale,* February 1929.
109. See Noiriel 1986, 160–63, on the process of deskilling caused by the break in family tradition of handing down trade knowledge within the working class. For a longer development on the process of deskilling, see Chenut 1996b.
110. *La Champagne Syndicale,* February 1929.

obviously present in the 1920s. The political repression of socialists, communists, and organized labor during this decade of instability, recovery, and expansion provided the context in which the textile workers in Troyes would confront the depression of the 1930s.

To some extent the history of interwar France has been largely presented as an ideological confrontation between the Left and the Right, played out in the multitude of social movements of the period, against the background of the economic crisis and the rise of fascism. From this perspective, the historical narrative seems overdetermined by the tragic collapse and defeat of 1940. Political events in Paris overshadow those in the rest of France. In fact, little attention has been given to labor unrest on provincial stages during the interwar years. Gerard Noiriel has contended that there was a decline in the labor movement after World War I, that the strikes of 1921 represented the end of a cycle of combativity, and that the new generation of militants lacked a tradition of struggle.[111] In Troyes, it could be said that little had changed for labor unions since 1904, when Emile Clévy, socialist leader of the knitters' union, claimed before the parliamentary inquiry commission that union leaders were blacklisted and that he himself had been summarily dismissed. Yet by the war's end, Clévy had been elected mayor of Troyes, while Celestine Philbois, another knitter and socialist militant, had been elected deputy. Another generation of socialist militants emerged to take their place on the ground. Noiriel's observation on the decline of militancy in these interwar years does not hold true for textile workers in Troyes. While it is hard not to agree that the socialist/communist split and subsequent dissension caused a dramatic loss in union membership, it can be argued that worker activism continued, taking on new cultural forms that maintained solidarity. What is new in this postwar period is that leisure associations and sports and consumer cooperatives, often in conjunction with political parties, kept working-class culture alive. These less formal political associations helped to sustain worker identity.

In general, militancy continued as the younger generation of union activists met with even greater repression on the public scene in the 1920s and 1930s. Nonrecognition of the unions by employers was fought in the trade courts. Millowners readily infringed on militants individual right to work, and

111. Noiriel 1986, 170. However, private institutions and religious and political associations did to some extent increase the scope of their action in working-class milieu.

the police actively monitored strike pickets and political meetings. Suzanne Gallois's action as a CGTU militant often resulted in her losing her job. In 1935 she went ten months without finding work: "I was really blacklisted, as they say, there was little I could have done. . . . I was laid off everywhere. . . . I was even asking myself if I was really a good worker or not because of this situation! But I was sure of one thing, that I'd never be awarded a work medal!"[112] During these hard times, such harassment accompanied the ebb and flow of union organizing.

Many features of the immediate postwar period were a continuation of struggles for social, economic, and gender equality that had remained unresolved since the late nineteenth century. The postponement of justice for women and workers in terms of rights and recognition, already highly visible in the 1920s, would create a far greater crisis in the following decade. As Marc Bloch observed with hindsight in 1940, "A deep fissure was opening almost before our eyes in the fabric of French social life. The country was splitting into two opposed groups."[113] The depression of the 1930s would test the labor movement's capacity in Troyes to oppose fascism and to elect a Popular Front municipal government in 1936 that might overcome these antagonisms and legitimize their cause.

112. Suzanne Gallois, interview, 1984.
113. Bloch 1968, 165.

7

EXPANDING THE CONSUMER MARKET

World War I had indeed ushered in a new consumer era based on the psychology of marketing and on anticipations of greater material prosperity. The struggle to maintain a living wage and respect of the eight-hour-day law enacted in 1919 were major concerns of the unions in Troyes. Textile workers' demands for higher wages embodied a strong sense of social justice following the wartime effort, a visible dissatisfaction with their share in the subsequent increased prosperity of the mid-1920s. The labor movement became an active advocate of distributionist politics, pressuring the government to intervene in hours and wages disputes, to regulate the economy, and to expand the narrow consumer market. Behind this agenda was workers' belief that they were not benefiting from industrial expansion and increased productivity. Work and wages, time off and consumption, all were the object of negotiation in this interwar period characterized by expansion, then contraction, of the commercial market. Yet in many tangible ways the interwar years provided workers with opportunities for shopping and commercialized leisure that were unthinkable before the war.

This chapter will address one of the central questions of this period: to what extent did workers remain within a relatively closed "community of consumption," represented in Troyes primarily by the Laborieuse, the workers' consumer cooperative, or did they have increasing access, as potential customers, to an expanding consumer market? To be sure, from the workers' viewpoint, the expanding world of French merchandising and consumer goods still appeared socially stratified after the war. In Europe, in contrast to the United States, efforts to maintain well-marked social boundaries through luxury consumption militated against a mass-consumer society, with its stores full of standardized goods. There appears to be little consensus among historians of consumption on this question of how long a two-tiered market persisted in France. Giovanni Levi observed that consumer practices became more socially unified during the twentieth-century interwar period. By that time, he argued, the revolutionary wing of the working class had renounced imposing its own class-conscious consumer behavior and was demanding a larger share in the mass market. This trend is hypothesized as the end of a long process that gradually moved toward more unified consumer patterns.[1] Certainly for such patterns to exist, the distribution and marketing of goods had to match the democratization of demand.[2] Several recent studies by labor historians have centered on understanding the relation between shorter working hours, increased leisure, and consumption.[3] The question then becomes: how and in what ways did mass consumption make inroads into French society? What fundamental decisions did workers make about leisure and consumer choices?[4] At issue is the question of what happened to working-class culture. Were class differences eroded by consumerism, as socialists feared? Was there a loss of community and militancy as workers became integrated into a "mass" consumer society? In fact, when can we speak of a mass, or even a working-class, market?

1. Levi 1996, 194.

2. On this question of democratization of supply and demand in relation to the ready-to-wear garment industry in France compared to the United States, see Green 1997, chap. 1.

3. Cross (1989) and (1993), and his article in *ILWCH* forum (1993b). See also Victoria de Grazia's response in the same issue, 24–30; see also Cohen 1999, 147–69.

4. The debate on these questions has become somewhat polarized. Gary Cross has argued that European workers in the 1920s and 1930s, when faced with the dilemma of choosing between shorter hours or higher wages, opted for more money to spend in the expanded consumer market, much like American workers did during the same period, although for different reasons. In sum, a historic trade-off of time for money. On the other hand, Victoria de Grazia has contended that there were diverse "paths to consumer modernity," much as there were alternative paths to industrialization. She has stressed that the social-democratic path in Europe provided "socialized access to consumption and an austere notion of needs," understood as needs that were strictly related to necessities consonant with class. Efforts by the political left towards "economic redistribution with defense of the subcultural way of life identified with the old craft-industrial working-class" challenged the industrial order, only to be defeated by the wartime totalitarian societies. De Grazia maintains that mass consumerism emerged only in the aftermath of World War II, regulated by state policies of reconstruction, economic planning, and redistribution of income. One of the issues between these two authors is when and in what context did the working-class encounter mass consumer society. See their exchange in *ILWCH* (1993).

To address these questions, this chapter attempts to examine the full range of consumer practices and strategies pursued by textile workers in Troyes during this period. Returning to questions of clothing, we will consider how the fashion changes of the 1920s emerged in working-class culture and what they meant in terms of class identity. Once again, photographs of the period, together with observations by social reformers, document the evolution of dress in relation to class-based consumer spending patterns in the 1920s and 1930s. From this perspective we will follow the evolution of the workers' consumer cooperative the Laborieuse during this difficult economic period in which the cooperative confronted growing competition from commercial capitalism, represented by chain stores and new retailers, called *prix uniques,* that also targeted working-class customers. And finally, we will focus on the multiple actors and commercial strategies in the expanding consumer market during this interwar period. While some millowners slowly adopted new merchandising techniques, including trademarks and advertising, others continued to cling to their traditional bourgeois clientele. For social and cultural reasons peculiar to French society, the marketing of standardized goods lagged behind the demand. Many members of the French cultural elite and those industrialists producing prestigious fashion goods felt threatened by mass democracy and modern consumer culture along the American model. Just in the marketing field alone, Marjorie Beale has shown how early advertisers sought to legitimize their fledgling practice as a science, facing the "problem of communicating in a society as yet only uneasily committed to egalitarian values."[5] Other historians have pointed to the breakdown of traditional cultural values and the growth of a bourgeois consumer marketplace, both of which had, by century's end, fueled the debate over the ethics of consumption and notions of luxury goods.[6]

In this chapter, I raise the question of whether by the end of the 1930s textile workers in Troyes became consumers of the goods they helped to produce. As we have seen in Chapter 5, male workers' demand for street clothes, garments not marked by trade or class, emerged in the late nineteenth century when many could not yet afford them. This demand was largely motivated, I would argue, by egalitarianism. By the 1900s, there is some evidence that

5. Beale 1999, 6, and esp. chap. 1.
6. Rosalind Williams (1982), chap. 6. See also Tiersten (2001), who argues that the late nineteenth-century capitalist marketplace posed problems for the republican political culture peculiar to France, notably by promoting values inimical to civic virtue as defined by the Republic and by eroding French identity as a recognized arbiter of taste.

textile workers in Troyes had access to ready-made clothing, but men more prominently than women. Fashion had compounded the standardization of women's wear, making both style and demand volatile. But after 1918, the concurrent streamlining of women's apparel, the production of a greater variety of knitted goods in Troyes, and the overall expansion of the domestic commercial market all contributed to a democratization of demand during the interwar period, demand that notably reached out into the provinces.

AFFORDING FASHION

The fashion changes of the 1920s signaled a sharp break with the past, a rupture wrought by the war. Just as the war affected men and women differently, so changes in dress reflected a transformation of gender roles. Postwar fashions for women represented a radical difference from the prewar silhouette and embodied new social values that expressed women's growing sense of personal liberation.[7] The simplification of the new line gave way to a different body language that signaled the progressive abandonment of the much disputed corset. Waists disappeared, but so did hips and breasts, within a slim androgynous tunic. Higher hemlines uncovered women's legs, previously hidden, and stockings became visibly important fashion items. Overall, the new fashions allowed for greater freedom of body movement and, arguably, a more active lifestyle. The simplification of styles not only stimulated production in the ready-to-wear industry; it also made dress designs easier to reproduce in the home. The 1920s saw the rise of new marketing strategies, including direct-mail-order-catalog sales of knitting patterns and yarns to working women, wives, and homeworkers. Pattern books and store catalogs diffused the new dress fashions, even to those who could not afford to buy ready-made clothing. And in a sense these pattern books helped to dissolve the boundaries of regional markets and the cultural divide between Paris and the provinces.

New Gender Identities

Feminist doctor Madeleine Pelletier contended in 1924 that female clothing was a form of "social servitude." "Corsets, *cache-corsets,* petticoats, slips, all

7. For a discussion of the relation between fashion and social change, see M. L. Roberts 1994, chap. 3; 1993. See also Bard 1998.

garnished with lace; they all require sewing, washing, ironing, and when one works from morning to night at the mill, the workshop, the office, what time is left for learning?" Her conclusion: "[C]lothing must be simplified."[8] For women readers of *L'Ouvrière,* she recommended wearing less clothing, buying ready-made, and having short hair. Dr. Pelletier's sartorial suggestions were not so much motivated by fashion concerns as offered for reasons of hygiene, practicality, and easy care. Ultimately, simplifying one's dress allowed for spending more time on nonhousehold pursuits such as education and politics, and thus permitted one to share, in her opinion, in the leisure-time goals of the communist Left. But Pelletier also favored what was seen at the time as a masculinization of women's styles. She noted that young men's wear allowed for greater freedom of movement than did clothing for young women, who were often dressed up like frivolous dolls. Postwar fashions were more suited to the active "new woman," more rational for riding bicycles, and more hygienic for factory work.[9] Pelletier herself had already adopted masculine attire to mark her personal challenge to the male world.

The fact that Madeleine Pelletier urged workingwomen to adopt the new forms of clothing suggests that these changes were not immediate and were to some extent class specific. Postwar fashion changes that became emblematic of the new woman were, moreover, controversial short-term phenomena. Critics of these new fashions decried what they viewed as a loss of femininity, seeing them as symptomatic, in fact, of postwar gender trouble.[10] Whereas bourgeois women could more readily afford to adopt clothing that both marked greater freedom of body movement and scandalized at the same time, working-class women's dress choices were more limited by income. Rather than emulate their betters total new look, they were more likely to use their wages to restyle their individual identity through fashion accessories, among these lace collars and cuffs. Articles in the working-class press reveal that the new fashions were adopted slowly and customized according to individual needs and means. The regional cooperative newspaper alternated commentary on Paris fashion novelties with advice on how to restyle older dress

8. Madeleine Pelletier, "Comment s'habiller?" *L'Ouvrière,* March 27, 1924. See also the description of Pelletier in Sowerwine 1982, 110–11.

9. Women's dress had been treated as a feminist issue at the International Congress of Women's Rights in 1900. The congress issued a declaration in favor of workingwomen wearing more "rational clothing, possibly pants" for work, and condemned the corset. See Klejman and Rochefort 1989, 141–42.

10. M. L. Roberts 1994, chap. 3.

Figure 13   Sortie d'usine at the spinning mill la Filature de Schappe, owned by Henri Hoppenot, in 1923. Collection Claude Bérisé.

models.[11] While a mass-market system of fashion for workingwomen did not appear likely in the immediate postwar years, women workers in Troyes did find novelty and advantage in wearing short hair.

Period photographs confirm women workers' changing silhouette, suggesting the appeal of this new feminine identity. The first photograph of a *sortie d'usine* in 1923 at the Filature de Schappe shows that, while many young women spinners had adopted short hair, they had not yet shortened their skirts to follow the postwar fashions (Fig. 13). Their clothing is still primarily made of dark solid fabrics, but there is an absence of aprons, the prewar markers of working-class women. The second photograph in front of the Desnoyers mill, dating probably from 1928, suggests that fashion changes had begun to cross class boundaries by this time (Fig. 14). Here women workers

11. Fashion advice addressed to women in a weekly column, "A travers la mode" in the regional edition of the *Coopérateur de France* from 1929 into the 1930s included information on fashion items and styles, together with advice on ways to appropriate these styles using women's sewing and hand knitting skills. See issues dated August, 10, 1930, and December 5, 1931.

Figure 14   *Sortie d'usine* at the Desnoyers mill, c. 1928. Author's personal collection.

have adopted the fashionable short skirts, cloche hats and short cropped hair *à la garçonne* that easily identify them with their times, but not necessarily with their social class. Stylish shoes have replaced the high boots, or *bottines*, previously worn, and some of these young women workers might even be wearing stockings that had been produced at the mill. In relative terms, they appear to have stepped from the pages of a department store fashion catalog. The presence of several bicycles confirms that women workers had also adopted this individual mode of transport. The large numbers of women in this particular *sortie d'usine* also attests to the growing feminization of the workforce in the 1920s. These women are representative of the larger numbers of female millworkers outside the frame of this particular image.

The transition to interwar fashion was also celebrated at the Fêtes de la Bonneterie in 1925 with its continuing tradition of crowning a queen. The festival queen and her attendants were elegantly dressed in slim silhouette dresses, silk stockings, and diadems, clothing that was an object of class display. Like department store mannequins, they evoked the idealized vision of leisure-class fashion, not of the everyday mill girl.[12] While many such fashionable items were produced in the Troyes mills and featured in the collective imaginary, such goods were inaccessible to ordinary women workers' pocketbooks. By 1926, the festival had become an increasingly commercialized form of leisure that retained little of its prewar industrial character. The queens were actively paraded around town, wearing the luxury silk stockings and jersey dresses that had been produced in the mills; their clothing resembled the stylish goods that were displayed in retail-shop windows.[13]

Yet these same fashions of the 1920s also highlighted the stark contradiction that many women millworkers in Troyes must have felt: their desire for higher wages and better clothing as they worked to produce the luxury dresses worn by their employers' wives. As Suzanne Gallois related, several mills in Troyes specialized in making fashionable dresses of rayon, then known as "artificial silk." One day it was her job to hem one of the first white artificial-silk dresses produced, a model that was to be worn by the millowner's wife, Mme Louis Bonbon, at a trade fair in Lyons. Suzanne Gallois decided impulsively that she, not Mme Bonbon, would wear it first. She disappeared into the restroom and emerged to model the dress for her co-workers. In this case, the luxury dress symbolized both the millowner's personal power and his class privilege, displayed with the same public visibility as the automobiles and homes so violently targeted by angry workers during the 1921 strike. But on this occasion Suzanne Gallois did more than mock the class privilege of the boss's wife—she also claimed for herself the right to wear clothing produced in the mill.[14]

By the mid-1930s, many women workers were wearing colorful ready-made cotton dresses. Popular newspaper photographs of their sit-in strike at the Devanlay-Recoing mills in June 1936 depict a sewing workshop filled by a very youthful group of women, none of whom are pictured bent over their machines. Almost all the women are wearing a *blouse-manteau* (a type of housecoat) to protect their street clothes. This style of fitted shirtwaist dress or housecoat with demure necklines combined femininity with practicality in the workplace. The general effect is overwhelmingly feminine.

12. Christine Bard's grandmother in the Nord worked in a hat shop and wanted to follow fashion. While not denying her working-class origins, she styled herself in a homemade elegant dress much like the ones worn by these worker queens. See her photograph (1998, 47).
13. For discussion of the 1925 and 1926 festivals, see Chapter 6.
14. Suzanne Gallois, interview, 1984. Modeling Mme Bonbon's dress, she explained, was "une petite vengeance."

Popular attraction to fashion change in the late 1920s was more wide-spread and more noticeable for women than for men. But male workers were also affected, probably by the desire for respectability and a new identity that afforded them greater social mobility. Consider, for example, the obser-vations of social reformer and critic Jacques Valdour, while he was working in the mills in August 1930. Valdour concluded that workers were spending all their wages on clothes. Almost all male workers wear caps, he commented, even on Sundays. In fact, the *casquette* (cloth cap) had come to be identified with worker masculinity, and to some extent with militancy. More important, Valdour was struck by what he called their "show of elegance": "On workdays knitters are simply but cleanly dressed; a few young men make a show of ele-gance: suits of the latest fashion, almost new, collar and tie, fine shoes. . . . Only an old machinist remains faithful to prewar workers' clothing: corduroy trousers and a jacket with black cotton oversleeves." A skilled worker with more disposable income was "always meticulously dressed to the hilt: an ele-gant suit, well-creased pants, yellow shoes that shine like mirrors; when he undressed in the mechanics' workshop, he appeared in fantasy striped under-shorts that matched his shirt; his 'bleus' [work clothes] were new and fitted at the waist; he always appeared elegant. . . . All his money was spent on clothes."[15] Valdour speculated that these skilled workers most likely spent their wages on fashionable clothes because they were selfish and had no children. During one Sunday afternoon stroll in town he encountered another skilled mechanic from the mill with his wife, both dressed in fine clothes: "he wore a fantasy suit of the latest fashion, a soft-brimmed hat of a reputable brand name; he was accompanied by his wife who wore silk stockings, light-colored high-heeled shoes, a well-cut dress of the latest style, fur piece around her neck, and a delicate lacework hat. They looked like a rich bourgeois couple in slightly ostentatious dress . . . they wear their wages on their backs and do not want to have children."[16] Valdour's commentary here again reflected a deep-seated moral judgment over what he considered to be individualistic, anti-natalist, even unpatriotic behavior. He clearly decried growing signs of emu-lative spending, inferring that workers who dressed like bourgeois were living above their rank. He laced his comments with reflections against the "materi-alist catechism" promoted by the French Communist Party, a message that he

15. Valdour 1934, 177.
16. Ibid., 220.

felt corrupted young workers.[17] An essential part of Valdour's project was to condemn socialism, individualistic behavior, and the democratizing impulses of the 1930s, which conflicted with his own conservative vision of society, one informed by the religious values of the Maurrasian Right.

Ideology aside, Valdour's more general reading of working-class life in Troyes was based on sharing workers' pastimes and discomforts. His observations on women workers' clothing are less critical of their "weakness" for fashion and more charmed by their desire to display their femininity. He noticed with prudish pleasure that hemlines and sleeves were lengthening in 1930. In his role as a participant observer, Valdour shared meals in modest bistros, evenings at the cinema, and Sunday walks in the center of Troyes, in addition to living his workplace experience as a janitor in the mills. His detailed descriptions of miserable and unsanitary furnished lodgings in Troyes confirm Maurice Halbwachs's findings that workers, motivated by social appearances, would rather spend more money on clothing than on proper housing. However, Valdour failed to make the connection between the overcrowding and lack of hygiene in available housing, and the high rate of tuberculosis among textile workers, a rate confirmed by our data for the prewar period. He criticized workers in Troyes for dissipating their wages on food and clothing luxuries, what he called "extravagant spending," and even for refusing to accept a lower "standard of living."[18]

Some workers were in fact spending more on clothing. But overall the great majority of textile workers in Troyes continued to live near the margins. Of all those dying in the period 1924–27, fewer than one in five (18 percent) had sufficient possessions to leave an estate. By comparison, in the town at large, 30 percent of men and women in all professions had an estate of some positive value. Life chances for accumulating wealth continued to be considerably greater for men than for women.[19] Summary estate records for some twenty textile workers with positive estates, drawn from a larger sample for

17. Ibid., 196.
18. Ibid., 196–97.
19. This fact can be partially explained by the continued high mortality among women. Even among those women who survived beyond the age of forty, the likelihood that they could accumulate wealth was substantially less than for men of their age group. Thus 28 percent of men and only 10 percent of women over forty had taxable possessions. Our sample was drawn from letters A, B, C, and M of the Table des successions for 1924 to 1927, ADA 3Q 14378. The total sample of 966 persons included 136 textile workers, among whom 82 percent had negative estates.

the 1920s, reveal a slightly higher standard of living in relation to the prewar period.[20] Young single male and female workers in this sample left small savings indicating a higher level of disposable income than before the war. Similarly, older textile workers' estates revealed a variety of investments through the banks that included state-sponsored bonds and annuities, as well as shares in consumer cooperatives. Several estates showed property and goods that had been insured. Overall, those textile workers with estates appeared to have had more disposable cash on hand, together with nondisposable income, than before the war.

This same finding was underscored by Maurice Halbwachs in his later work on working-class consumption, *L'évolution des besoins dans les classes ouvrières*, published in 1933. According to Halbwachs, workers' economic behavior had changed in the postwar years, and for this reason traditional household budgets were less pertinent for understanding the distribution of per capita income. Even workers put a small part of their earnings aside in the form of savings in banks and *caisses d'épargne*, to form part of what he called the "collective economy." As for household spending, workers had a whole set of needs that were new in relation to the past, and that were generated by the market and by constantly changing prices. Halbwachs identified *lifestyle* (*genre de vie*) as the most useful category of analysis by which to observe these transformative changes in working-class spending for the period that he had observed both in France and the United States. Inside this new category, one had to examine, not the traditional pattern of household expenses, but the social meaning attributed to certain significant consumer items. "What organic need is satisfied," he asked, "by the purchase of an automobile or a pair of silk stockings?" And he urged researchers to carry out careful inventories of clothing and physical objects that represented a social value together with an economic one. "What objects will attract [workers]? . . . Products that satisfy material needs, or those that distinguish them from other men or other families?"[21] Halbwachs's major finding in this second study is the new economy of needs,

20. Our sample of 23 textile workers who died in the period 1922–24 was taken from the Table des mutations après décès, the only documents available for these years. More detailed inventories of estates, including property and goods, have not yet been deposited by notaries who generally keep such records for one hundred years. Here is the breakdown of the sample: 22 persons, 12 men, 10 women, including five young women and one young man twenty years old and single (ADA 3Q 11389, 3Q 11392).

21. Halbwachs 1933, 14.

the fact that workers were attracted to novelty or imitation luxury items that now seemed accessible. For social reasons, they resisted any effort to lower their standard of living. Needs now seemed to be open ended. Halbwachs's observations engaged him in a number of debates with contemporaries, situated both to the left and the right, over whether workers were being bought out by consumer society or seduced by false material needs.[22]

Halbwachs's second study still retained a notion of socially stratified needs. But he noted the expansion of popular consumption, an increase that indicated a transformation of the working class, now pluralized into several groups. Workers were no longer part of the self-contained, homogeneous class he had described in 1913, isolated from the rest of French society. Rather, they were now involved in a host of social activities outside the workplace that identified them as active citizens. Moreover, he maintained, advertising played to their needs as an economic force in consumer society.[23] As regards clothing, he noted greater uniformity of customary dress in Paris and other urban centers. The fact remained that clothing expenses represented an indispensable item in workers' budgets, and ranked high on their list of socially driven needs.

Another study, carried out in Toulouse in the years 1936 to 1938, focused on changes in purchasing power and consumption patterns among workers and white-collar employees.[24] The author, Henry Delpech, confirmed many of Halbwachs's findings concerning clothing in his own sample of forty workers' households. By far the most interesting observations concern how women workers were spending their money on clothing and where they shopped. His study showed that women were spending more on lingerie, stockings, and shoes during this period, but less so when there were two or more children in the family. Moreover, out of thirty-two workers' households, nearly 50 percent of the women dressed exclusively or partially in ready-made clothing, many at the new *prix uniques* stores, while nearly 20 percent produced all their clothing at home.[25] The important point here is that, given the increasing demand for ready-made women's wear, many women workers were shopping at the new retail stores that addressed their more modest needs. But one-fifth of

22. See Coffin 1999.
23. Ibid., 147–51.
24. Delpech 1938.
25. The figures are as follows: eight women wore exclusively ready-made, seven wore partially bought and homemade, and six made all their clothes at home; we can assume that the remainder of the sample was unknown. The author also noted the large numbers of women who darned their own stockings in relation to those who took them to be mended (ibid., 149).

working women, for whatever reason, continued to customize their clothing at home. It is likely that deeply ingrained habits of thrift in these depression years kept these women from shopping outside the home.

Wages and the Cost of Living

The instability of prices and money both during and after World War I created periods of *vie chère* that eroded nominal wages in relation to real wages (what wages could effectively buy). Workers' experience of inflation was especially damaging after the war effort as the franc continued to decline. The very facts of both monetary instability and worker insurgency over wages and purchasing power gave rise to new concerns for establishing some material "standard of living" in postwar France. Yet the very notion of a "standard" was problematic. As Judy Coffin has noted, the concept emerged at a historical moment when consumption was conceived as a problem of economic behavior that required some form of social, even governmental, intervention.[26] At issue were questions of social inequalities, family welfare, and ultimately social peace. Creating the measures for such a standard entailed the gathering of social statistics, collaboration between the public and private spheres, and more open negotiation between capital and labor than had been the case in the past. As we have seen, social tensions over wages in the Troyes mills had erupted in 1921 in a six-week strike that left deep mistrust over millowners' calculations of wages in relation to fluctuations in the cost of living.[27] Textile workers had felt manipulated by millowners during the bitter negotiations that ended the strike. A joint commission of workers and millowners was then instituted to fix a cost-of-living allowance then recognized as a means to alleviate *la vie chère*. Communist militants represented *la vie chère* as the latest expression of the class struggle, and the cost-of-living index as an invention of bourgeois millowners to dupe their workers.[28] Demands for a living wage by rank-and-file textile workers stressed their families' needs in relation to society as a whole.

Negotiations were affected by three phenomena: nominal wages in relation to inflation, rising prices for staple food and goods, and debate over shorter hours and the application of the eight-hour law. All three were objects of

26. Coffin 1999.
27. See Chapter 6.
28. F. Meunier, "Pourquoi la vie chère?" *La Dépêche de l'Aube,* February 28, 1924.

union action documented regularly in the working-class press. After their wartime sacrifices, workers considered that higher wages were their due, particularly as prices spiraled upward and eroded their purchasing power; the monetary instability of the franc deprived them psychologically of any real sense of control. Records of prices for standardized items were regularly submitted to the joint commission on *la vie chère* by the mayor of Troyes, who frequently based them on retail prices practiced by the Laborieuse.[29] In northeast France the cooperative movement had played a significant wartime role in the struggle against *la vie chère,* earning the movement a justifiable reputation for market regulation. The leader of the Fédération nationale des coopératives de consommation (FNCC), Ernest Poisson, quite rightly affirmed that the movement had set "a public standard of prices."[30] The official benchmark for comparing prices was 1914, when the franc started to depreciate. According to one historian, prices multiplied fivefold between 1914 and 1928, the date by which Poincaré officially stabilized the franc.[31] Prices jumped noticeably between 1923 and 1926, provoking comments in *L'Ouvrière* over the gap between wages and the rising cost of living: standard socks that cost Fr .65 a pair in 1914 were selling in 1926 for Fr 6.50, and shirts that were Fr 2.95 to Fr 4, had by then increased to Fr 25 to Fr 47. The author claimed that some stores no longer dared display clothing prices, but nevertheless exhibited an insolent array of luxury dresses. Working-class women, she maintained, had to make do once again with secondhand clothes.[32] Prices for staple foods were also monitored closely in comparison with those in 1914: bread rose from Fr .45 to Fr 2.75, coffee from Fr 4 to Fr 32, and eggs from Fr .75 to Fr 10.20.[33] Despite the price monitoring, the confidence of workers eroded when they were confronted with the daily gap between wages and purchasing power. In this context, wage issues sharpened dramatically. Women's average daily wages in 1922 ranged from Fr 17.10 for a raccoutreuse to Fr 18.40 for a bobineuse,

29. AMT 4F 129. Many cooperatives located near battlelines during and after the war helped to provision devastated areas, prevent food shortages, and organize relief, gaining a reputation for market regulation that helped to stabilize prices.

30. Poisson 1921, 31. Poisson refers to the wartime role of many French cooperatives that aided the national defense effort, thereby gaining the confidence of public opinion in their prices.

31. Lhomme 1968.

32. Marie-Thérèse Gourdeaux, "Campagne contre la vie chère," *L'Ouvrière* November 25, 1926. The author accused manufacturers of speculation on the export market and thus causing the rapid jump in prices.

33. *L'Ouvrière,* August 19, 1926.

and men's from Fr 13.18 for a young male rebrousseur to Fr 23.35 for a knit-ter.[34] To make ends meet, women textile workers fell back on time-tested methods of managing what they had. Sample menus circulated among women readers in the *Dépêche de l'Aube,* and columnists in *L'Ouvrière* offered readers advice on recycling old clothes to meet fashion changes.

Wage levels were related to the debate over shorter hours that followed the passage of the eight-hour-day law in 1919. Negotiations under duress produced a collective bargaining agreement in the knitted goods industry that set a forty-eight-hour workweek. At issue were productivity (given the shorter hours) and flexibility, both requisite demands for a fashion garment industry from the employers' viewpoint. But in fact a government decree had allowed for exemptions for the busy season in the textile and garment trade.[35] Both these issues affected wages. Workers argued that advances in mechanization had increased productivity, making it possible to maintain production and to shorten working hours. They also claimed that wages had not kept pace with the increases in productivity.[36] As a standard response, millowners opposed restrictions on working hours more vigorously than they fought wage demands. So in the end they instituted shift work (two eight-hour shifts) as a way to circumvent the eight-hour law. But workers' grievances over wage levels did not disappear from public debate.

With the advent of the depression, textile workers reacted sharply to wage reductions imposed by millowners in 1931 and again in 1934. The unions coun-tered employers' arguments concerning the nature of the crisis, underscoring that it was not a crisis of overproduction, but one of underconsumption: they claimed that "curbing consumer purchasing power meant accentuating un-employment and perpetuating the economic crisis." The solution proposed by the CGT was to shorten working hours for all workers in order to harmonize production and consumption; higher wages would then help workers to sat-isfy their consumer needs and also stimulate the economy.[37] This argument propelled workers into the forefront as the motors of a consumer revolution that they claimed would resolve what they understood as an imbalance between production and consumption. Echoing the sentiments of knitter Louis Foin, returning from the Paris World's Fair of 1889, workers thought of themselves

34. ADA J90 103, Usine Vitoux.
35. Green 1997, 83–84.
36. Paul Rives, "La réduction de la journée du travail," *Aube Ouvrière,* September 1, 1931.
37. *Aube Ouvrière,* April 1, 1931.

as "natural" consumers, and they demanded their share in an expanding commercial market.

EXPANDING THE MARKET: THE LABORIEUSE

Consumer cooperation in France expanded rapidly in the 1920s. The war effort had established the reputation of many cooperatives for expertise in organizing the distribution of food relief behind the lines and for establishing price controls. In Troyes, membership in the workers' consumer cooperative the Laborieuse had swelled by 1920 to more than forty-one hundred families, and annual sales had attained 6.5 million francs. The cooperative's commercial success might also be measured by its expansion outward from the center of Troyes to include twelve branch stores in the town and the surrounding area, and by the increasing number of services it offered its members. Its politics of merchandising, clearly defined by socialist principles of solidarity, had prevailed during and after the war. By 1926 membership had increased to roughly fifty-five hundred families and annual sales had doubled. But the war effort had imposed a reconfiguration of both cooperative and capitalist commerce. Wartime economic planning, rationalization of production, price controls, and the rationing of goods had all contributed to a movement toward economic rationalization after the war. Under these conditions, as Ellen Furlough has shown, the umbrella FNCC urged its members to regroup regionally and adopt several new commercial principles.[38] A development society, l'Union des coopérateurs de l'Aube, was formed in 1919 in an effort to concentrate resources and limit the number of competing cooperative stores in the department. But the major problem confronting the Laborieuse was competition from capitalist commerce vying for the same working-class consumer market.

Chain stores had spread into rural areas, while other private commercial shops had opened in the town center. In the 1930s, capitalist commerce launched the *prix uniques* retail stores, challenging the cooperatives to modernize their merchandising methods. Advertisements under the heading "recommended shops" published in both the socialist *Aube Ouvrière* and the Communist *La Dépêche de l'Aube,* provide an overview of the variety of stores serving a working-class clientele in the 1920s. All of them were located in

38. Furlough 1991, chap. 8.

downtown busy commercial streets in Troyes and advertised ready-to-wear clothing, regular promotional sales, and reasonable prices. The Maison des Travailleurs in particular was a depository for a well-known Lyon manufacturer of work clothes, Adolph Lafont. It advertised that it sold directly from the producer to consumer without an intermediary, much as the Laborieuse claimed to do. Other shops also targeted the class connection, among them A l'Ouvrière, a lingerie and notions shop for women workers, and Aux Travailleurs Economes, which sold shoes. Still others played on Paris fashion to attract customers, such as A la Ville de Paris and A la Parisienne, both women's apparel stores selling ready-made coats, shirtwaists, gloves, stockings, lingerie, and other items.[39] Such small privately owned shops specializing in staple items of clothing had never included prices in their advertisements before the war, but they increasingly did so after 1920. Two department stores, Jorry Prieur and Magasins Reunis, also continued to flourish at this time.

To match such competition, the Laborieuse had to adopt the more innovative commercial strategies of its competitors. Challenging private commerce in the city center, the administrators of the Laborieuse opened a number of small speciality shops on the main shopping street, rue Emile Zola, in 1928. These included a clothing and fabric shop, a shoe shop, a hardware store, a bakery, and a mutualist pharmacy. These new stores did not duplicate the branch ones scattered in the neighboring suburbs. Rather, they modeled themselves on the privately owned retail boutiques, on the same street, that boasted elegant shopwindows of goods. However, the cooperative's new specialty shops claimed to sell exclusively to members. While cooperative membership remained strong (6,350 families in 1928), commercial ventures such as these new shops obviously depended for survival on members' steadfast allegiance. In the end, the Laborieuse's real strength came from its rural stores, those scattered in suburbs and villages in the department and numbering twenty-six by 1928. By reaching out to rural consumers, the cooperative spread not only within the Aube, but also to the contiguous departments of the Marne and the Côte d'Or. By 1932 it had acquired a significant part of the regional market.

Commercial competition on this regional terrain was keenest from chain stores, among them Les Economiques Troyennes and La Ruche Moderne, distinctly capitalist ventures but modeled to some extent after the cooperative.

39. The store, A la Ville de Paris, retailed knitted goods manufactured by the Mauchauffée mill. See the mill management's credit register in ADA J39 1119.

They also offered working-class customers a range of staple goods, and they too had expanded their distribution into the countryside. To attract customers and establish a loyal network of clients, chain stores used new merchandising techniques borrowed from department stores. They advertised promotional sales and offered bonus gifts with each purchase, methods considered by some to be "la publicité des pauvres."[40] By creating trademarks for their goods, another advertising method invented earlier in the century, chain stores helped identify and distinguish the quality products they sold. These techniques were apparently successful in developing a working-class clientele, since capitalist chain stores represented a larger percentage of the regional economy than did cooperatives in the Aube. FNCC figures from 1928 estimated that 11 percent of the population of the Aube were cooperative members.[41]

The Laborieuse preserved its distinctive working-class character well into the postwar decade. The new speciality shops in downtown Troyes displayed the cooperative's name in large letters, together with the traditional handshake logo and motto, but no new trademark. By contrast, the FNCC and many of its members had adopted the COOP logo on product labels, advertising posters, and in certain cases, cooperative store fronts by 1920. Instead, the Laborieuse proudly displayed its historic name, long identified with working-class culture. However, administrators now made a greater use of advertising in local newspapers and issued catalogs of items for sale. Moreover, new services strengthened the cooperative's class character and social activism, reinforcing members' sense of belonging to a community of leisure and consumption. In October 1924 the main store on the quai Dampierre made room for a lending library and reading room. This was the historic Bibliothèque démocratique et populaire, originally founded in 1878 by Radical deputy and journalist Gaston Arbouin. The library's collection relocated to the Laborieuse headquarters and opened its doors to the general public. In fact, throughout this interwar period, the Laborieuse organized and structured working-class leisure activities.[42] Many

40. Chessel 1998, 121–29.

41. FNCC, *Annuaire de la Coopération,* 1930, 435–36, as cited in Furlough 1991, 262. Capitalist chain stores represented 35 percent of commerce in the Aube in the early 1950s (ibid., 263). It is interesting to compare the Nord department—another region with a historic tradition of consumer cooperation, where 20 percent of the population were cooperative members—with the Aube. Both departments were, of course, Guesdist strongholds and maintained strong working-class communities.

42. Most of these leisure activities were announced in the local press. For the years 1934–36, they were documented in a scrapbook of newspaper clippings (les Coopérateurs de Champagne, Château Thierry).

of these were sponsored for children through the Groupe des amis de l'enfance et des loisirs de la Laborieuse. From 1927 into the 1930s, the cooperative's administrators proudly sponsored vacation camps for members' children. A public parade symbolically marked the importance of such solidarity initiatives: in 1927 the first children to return from vacation camp were marched from the railroad station to the cooperative's headquarters.[43] Started in these early years as a form of socialist activism and organized leisure, the sponsoring of vacation camps for children, and later whole working-class families, became a social policy under the Popular Front government.[44] Adult leisure programs also sponsored by the cooperative included excursions, photography, bicycle tourism, soccer, and a band (La Fraternelle Coopérative).

Ultimately, the Laborieuse found itself at the center of working-class life in Troyes. It had become recognized in the minds of townspeople as a vital institution promoting class identity and solidarity. One reminder of the cooperative's public role was its participation in the Fêtes de la Bonneterie, a high point of popular sociability in Troyes in the interwar years. The cooperative provided several floats for the ritual parade through the town center, floats that symbolically represented such local services as the vacation camps in 1934; a float presented in 1935 featured an allegorical globe encircled by the handshake emblem to suggest the global strength of the cooperative movement. By this point the administrators of the Laborieuse had become more adept at advertising their cause through modern media. Film screenings became opportunities for recruitment and fund-raising, and regular public meetings with national political leaders favorable to the cooperative movement reinforced this public-service image. At one such meeting in February 1935, Ernest Poisson, head of the FNCC, praised cooperative principles of social solidarity for showing the way to resolving difficulties during the economic crisis.[45] But Poisson also loudly proclaimed the cooperative movement's independence from political parties and the necessity for this to be preserved. Cooperative propaganda eschewed politics and increasingly relied on commercial techniques that appealed to targeted groups of consumers.

43. Letter from the director of the Laborieuse to the mayor of Troyes, October 26, 1927, requesting authorization to parade the children in the streets of the town. AMT Q 305.

44. See Downs 2002.

45. "Une belle manifestation de propagande coopérative," *Le Petit Troyen*, February 27, 1935.

Gendered Consumption

Within the consumer cooperative movement itself, advertising had initially been viewed as an attempt to create false needs in the manner of commercial capitalism. By the late 1920s cooperators openly embraced advertising, giving it a more positive spin. It was highly significant that the FNCC redefined advertising's role and integrated its techniques into the movement's mission. Within this framework, advertising would become an integral part of modernization efforts to strengthen consumers' identification with cooperative goals, products, and services.[46] The adoption of the COOP logo in 1929 was just one example; the creation of sales catalogs, trademarked goods, product labels, and display posters was another. Sales catalogs were a form of advertising that cooperatives had borrowed from the department stores. Looking through these catalogs of items offered for sale provides a window into the cooperative store, and a notion of the targeted shopper.

As we saw in an earlier chapter, women were viewed as primary shoppers for the working-class family. Women militants within the cooperative movement had long promoted a recruitment strategy that would effectively channel women workers' family shopping into the co-op store. Sales catalogs available for the interwar period clearly reflect a conventional gendered vision in their commercial strategy, conveying a message of inclusion very similar to that offered by PCF propaganda at the time.[47] Women were shown to advantage as consumers when they were exercising their roles as mothers. A 1935 sales catalog from the Coopérateurs de Champagne, a regional cooperative that would soon take over the Laborieuse, featured on its cover a mother with two children eagerly opening the catalog to make their choices (Fig. 15).[48] The mother is cast in her role as housewife, caregiver, and shopper. There is no reference to her as a worker producing goods for consumption. By extension the cover could be said to invoke the cooperative image itself as that of one big family. The first four pages inside the catalog were devoted to women's wear, starting with stockings and socks. Goods ranged from utilitarian cotton stockings for everyday wear, to more fashionable ones made of finer cotton called "fil," with chevening (embroidery) highlighting the ankles and calves, priced

46. Chessel 1998, 31–34; Furlough 1991, 269–75.
47. For the gendered images of Communist Party propaganda in 1930s Europe, see Weitz 1996, 311–52.
48. Catalogue général, 1935, les Coopérateurs de Champagne, Château Thierry.

Figure 15   Sales catalog from the Coopérateurs de Champagne in 1935. Author's personal collection.

three to four times more a pair. The following page featured ready-made housecoats and aprons that evoked housekeeping. All items displayed a similar style, one that combined practicality with glamour and serviceability with femininity. Dresses in popular cotton fabrics were fitted at the waist and had relatively long skirts. For those women who preferred to customize their clothing at home, the last page of the catalog showed fabrics that could be ordered from samples visible in the store. Men's ready-to-wear work clothes were displayed toward the end of the catalog, no doubt reflecting the fact that men were considered secondary shoppers. Among the more limited choice of clothing available for men were sturdy imitation-leather pants and jackets, stylishly fitted at the waist, as well as more conventional jackets in blue broadcloth. A long protective overcoat for work appeared as a counterpart to the female domestic housecoat. Also featured were the more emblematic workers' caps and cotton percale shirts, both with and without collars. A whole page was devoted to shoes advertised for their "comfort, elegance, and solidity," together with two different models of traditional clogs. For both men and women, the overall look conveyed a slender, elegant silhouette. The catalog also featured a great variety of useful household items, ranging from dishes to rugs, pots and pans, lamps, and even furniture. This emphasis on homemaking and furnishings was typical of the efforts during the interwar years to rationalize the home and household tasks.

If we compare this sales catalog from the Laborieuse/les Coopérateurs de Champagne with one from a Parisian department store catering to workers, such as the Samaritaine, we gain a broader vision of the popular market in ready-made fashion offered for sale by a competitor for the same year.[49] The catalog for the summer sales at the Samaritaine, which featured on its cover two elegantly dressed women in broad-brimmed hats, one standing on either side of a little girl, was clearly addressed to women consumers. The opening pages showed fashionable printed dresses, made in cotton but also in more luxurious fabrics. More utilitarian housecoats, aprons, and dressing gowns appeared in the following pages, together with children's clothes and basic socks, stockings, and intimate apparel. Men's clothing again featured last, but also included work clothes very similar to those in the cooperative's catalog. In some fifty pages, the Samaritaine catalog offered a much wider selection, not

49. La Samaritaine, Catalogue Soldes d'été, June 1935. BHVP, Catalogues commerciaux, collection Actualités.

only in quality but also in quantity, of household items and accessories for the Parisian consumer market.

Two interesting points emerge from this comparison. First, both catalogs present an elegant, slender, modern silhouette as models for their customers. There is no sign from the opening pages that different goods were designed for different classes, nothing that reflected a two-tiered market. In fact, the models for women's clothing are strikingly similar except for the fact that the Samaritaine catalog carried far more luxury fabrics and accessories than did the catalog for the workers' cooperative. Second, the highly stylized aesthetic of the 1930s helps to represent both the clothing and the consumer in each catalog in a more homogeneous, neutral way. Like mannequins in a department store window, the figures appear strongly unified, almost generic. In both catalogs there is no display of class or appeal to opulence in any way, only slender, form-fitting elegance and femininity.

By contrast, male militants adopted another sartorial style. They wore their clothing as an explicit political statement and as a way to distance themselves from dominant bourgeois society. Daniel Guérin, historian and journalist, encountered such men in 1930 at the Bellevilloise, the workers' consumer cooperative in the twentieth arrondissement of Paris. "On days when . . . I would wander in the corridors and at meetings at the Bellevilloise, the workers' cooperative run by communists at that time, I was happy to find myself face to face with real proletarians. They belonged to the most underprivileged group of their class. But their ruffian-style clothing marked their deliberate desire to burn all bridges with bourgeois society. They illustrated perfectly the ultraleftist slogans of the Communist International: class against class."[50] Guérin's observations were tempered by a critical yet sympathetic stance, a recognition that the "ouvriérisme" practiced by the PCF extended to social appearances and an embodied loyalty to the party line. During these early years of gaining political experience, he self-consciously made note and remembered many of the militants and the way they dressed.[51] In Troyes, a number of male workers followed the same logic, adopting a *laisser-aller* that Suzanne Gallois sought to combat.

For co-op members of the Laborieuse, there was still a strong sense of belonging to a community of consumption. In many ways, the commercial

50. Guérin 1997, 23.
51. Ibid., 34–35.

success of the Laborieuse overshadowed differences within the working class. The cooperative appeared to operate on the basis of a social consensus that belied the divisive tensions so inherent in the politics of the 1930s. But in fact these tensions existed, and their origins can be traced back several decades to the merger between the two strands of the cooperative movement in 1912. The subsequent split in the socialist movement in 1920 brought political issues once again to the fore.

"A Workers' Cooperative Can Never Be Neutral . . ."

The division and political infighting within French socialism during these interwar years had a significant impact on the national cooperative movement. To some extent important political differences had already been patched over by the unification of the socialist and reformist strands of the consumer cooperative movement within the FNCC in 1912. In the process, the proponents of political neutrality had predominated, and consequently explicit references to cooperation as a means of class struggle against capitalism had faded from programs and policies. From 1920 the division within socialist parties and unions further weakened the revolutionary dimension of consumer cooperation. Policy shifted away from exclusively class-based membership and reached out to embrace a general public of "customer consumers."[52] Moreover, professional managers replaced some of the democratically elected cooperative administrators. In significant ways, consumer cooperation was reconceived by FNCC leaders such as Albert Thomas and Ernest Poisson who wanted to move their organization toward "a consumer advocacy group rather than a working-class organization."[53] More important, commercial strategies were increasingly modeled on capitalist objectives and practices in order to compete in the postwar market. Cooperative commerce adopted regional merchandising and distribution schemes, targeted advertising, and created trademarks to identify and enhance goods for consumers. Cooperative stores greatly expanded the range of goods offered to their customers in imitation of what chain stores provided. The administrators of the Laborieuse were not prepared at first to take such

52. Lizabeth Cohen (2003) makes the useful distinction between "citizen consumers" involved in ethical consumption and "customer consumers" who shopped to maximize their personal interests.

53. Furlough 1991, 241. Albert Thomas synthesized this revisioning of consumer cooperation in similar terms.

steps toward capitalism, steps that would compromise their socialist principles and independence.

Finally, in the late 1920s, antagonism between socialists and communists in Troyes affected the policies of the Laborieuse. While administrators were careful to conserve the working-class identity of their cooperative, several new commercial techniques they adopted did imply a shift in politics and policies. Articles in the Communist *Dépêche de l'Aube* in the 1920s warned against what their authors termed a reformist takeover of the whole cooperative movement. But communists firmly supported the Laborieuse as long as it maintained its working-class character and membership. Indeed, they frequently urged workers not to abandon cooperation as a means of collective struggle.[54] Ostensibly their position contained more revolutionary rhetoric than action. Another group identifying itself in the local press as "independent" attacked the cooperative's practices in 1934 as politically motivated, accusing administrators of bending to the PCF and Deputy René Plard.[55] However, by July 1935 communist cooperators openly challenged the management for attempting to marginalize them because of their criticism, and they publicly confronted administrators with rumors of financial difficulties. Communists contested what they felt were undemocratic maneuvers to cover up losses, for example, incurred by the management's expansion of outlying branches and downtown speciality shops. They even charged leaders in the administrative council with evicting communist members, laying off employees, and overriding the wishes of member shareholders.[56] But their main criticism centered on an old ideological issue: they restated their position that "a workers' cooperative can never be neutral or independent of the labor movement, . . . nor can it remain neutral with regard to commercial capitalism."[57] This reemergence of revolutionary

54. A group identified as le Cercle des coopérateurs de la Laborieuse signed two articles calling for a public meeting ("Pour la coopération ouvrière," *La Dépêche de l'Aube*, March 9 and 12, 1928).

55. "Coopération et politique" *Tribune de l'Aube*, February 14, 1934, signed by "a group of truly independent cooperators."

56. The communist press intimated that the director, Marcel Floiras, took over absolute leadership of the cooperative by forcing through a proxy voting procedure that discouraged members from attending the more democratic general assembly and asserting their collective power. See *La Dépêche de l'Aube*, August 31, 1935. In fact, two factors also strengthened Floiras's authority: his father, Alexandre Floiras, had been a founding member and respected administrator of the Laborieuse, and the revised FNCC program had openly encouraged the professionalization of cooperative management.

57. "La coopérative la Laborieuse a-t-elle changé de mains?" *La Dépêche de l'Aube*, July 27, 1935.

principles in the old struggle between a socialist-inspired cooperative movement and a reformist one was primarily inspired by a concern to reclaim cooperative politics for the Left. Given the political context of 1935, the communists
were preoccupied with mobilizing workers in support of the Popular Front
movement, and sought to bring pressure on all institutions that could help
their cause. But one week later, the same newspaper reported that the administrators of the Laborieuse had lead the cooperative into bankruptcy and
were selling out to the regional cooperative, les Coopérateurs de Champagne,
without consulting member shareholders about their actions.[58] The future of
the Laborieuse remained unresolved in press accounts and provoked speculation and anger over the lack of democratic consultation. Administrators tried
to restore trust amid accusations of bad management and falsified accounts.
Finally, a general assembly of members was called for November 3, 1935, to
approve a draft plan for merger with les Coopérateurs de Champagne.

The administrators of the Laborieuse had not publicized their financial
difficulties, despite criticism in the local press over their management.[59] At the
shareholders' meeting at which the fusion was voted on, chief administrator
Marcel Floiras advanced several overt reasons for supporting the projected
plan.[60] He indicated that the cooperative had insufficient capital to continue
on its own and that the FNCC had actively encouraged regional concentration
to strengthen the cooperative movement. Several factors had, in fact, complicated the cooperative's economic difficulties as revealed at the meeting. On
April 23, 1934, the Banque des coopératives de France, an institution that
helped finance FNCC member cooperatives, went into temporary bankruptcy in
disreputable circumstances. News of the bank's difficulties had created a panic
among depositors and had undermined confidence.[61] In the context of the
worsening economic crisis, following upon the political events of February

58. *La Dépêche de l'Aube,* August 3, 1935.

59. The story can be reconstructed to some extent through a scrapbook of clippings from
the local press covering all the cooperative's activities from January 1934 through September
1935 (les Coopérateurs de Champagne, Chateau Thierry). An interview with Marcel Floiras,
chief administrator of the Laborieuse, in *Le Coopérateur de France* in March 1934 gave no sign of
the cooperative's financial troubles.

60. The notarial records of the November 3, 1935, general assembly do not provide dissent-
ing views on the merger plan. The vote showed that 5,561 members out of the 6,212 present
approved the merger (the overall membership was 11,834). The Coopérateurs de Champagne
had five times as many members (Projet de fusion entre la Laborieuse et les Coopérateurs de
Champagne, Maître Henri Menager, notaire à Château Thierry, ADA 1033 W 63).

61. See Poisson 1934, 8–10.

and the general crisis of confidence in the government, the FNCC finally took measures to restore its members' trust. In Troyes, the bank's failure provoked a number of members to withdraw their savings from the Laborieuse. To be sure, unemployment and short-time work had already drastically reduced worker income and thus purchasing power since 1931. But the cooperative's administrators were also at fault for overextending the Laborieuse through their expansionist policies. In particular, the rapid growth of branch stores within the department had proved ambitious even before hard times hit in the late 1920s. Then their extension into the neighboring department of the Côte d'Or in 1932 disastrously stretched their limits, as the region proved difficult to supply from their warehouse in Troyes.

In the fusion with the Coopérateurs de Champagne, the Laborieuse was swallowed up by a much larger and more diverse organization of nearly 55,000 members that operated under more capitalistic principles and practices. In the process the Laborieuse lost its historic name, its socialist identity, and its independence. Preparations had been under way to celebrate its fiftieth anniversary in 1936. At the time the cooperative had some 15,200 members and ninety stores, including forty-five in Troyes and seventeen in the Aube. There is little evidence in the press of further public debate or dissent over the merger immediately after the final vote. Further news of the cooperative appeared in the communist press only on February 29, 1936, when the *Dépêche de l'Aube* finally urged readers to support the new cooperative: "[Y]our duty is to place your confidence in the cooperative movement." Local communist militants tried to explain why, after initially opposing the merger, they had reversed their position. They admitted to having been "caught off guard" by the precipitous revelation of the cooperative's shaky financial position, and even finding themselves "at a loss" to act. But in the end, rather than see the Laborieuse handed over to capitalist creditors, they had voted for the merger in the interest of creating a stronger regional cooperative. They stressed the multiple social and economic benefits to families of belonging to the cooperative. In their words, "[C]ooperation made solidarity a living reality."[62]

When Jean Gaumont, the official historian of the French cooperative movement, reflected back on the demise of the Laborieuse as an independent entity, he considered it to have been inevitable. Sooner or later the necessity to concentrate the movement's strength into larger regional units would have

62. "Tribune coopérative" and "Qu'est-ce que le mouvement coopératif?" *La Dépêche de l'Aube*, February 29, 1936.

brought about the same result. In the end, he argued, the founders' ideals had triumphed in the cooperative's ambition to become more inclusive.[63] It is easy to treat the cooperative's demise on the eve of the Popular Front with irony, as a foreshadowing of the coalition government's inability to ensure a lasting solution to existing economic inequalities. It is perhaps more useful to speculate over the fate of consumerism during a period of capitalist instability and crisis, and to view this transformation of the workers' consumer cooperative as yet one more site of contradictions in class relations. In terms of working-class culture and identity, the Laborieuse lived on in local memory, retreating into the past much like the fading wall advertisement that is still legible on one of its old warehouses in Troyes today. Still another former warehouse has now become a complex of outlet stores for fashion clothing known nationally as Marques Avenue, a pun on *Park Avenue,* one that reveals France's continuing fascination with American marketing techniques.[64]

MARKETING FASHION AND MODERNITY

Raymond Williams dates the rise of modern advertising from the end of the nineteenth century, when industrial capitalism was restructured into larger units of collective ownership and sought "to organize and, where possible, control" the marketing of goods. He identifies it with monopoly capitalism and the attendant manufacture of a growing range of goods. The experience of World War I, Williams argues, introduced new elements of psychological persuasion into merchandising.[65] Just how much and what kinds of psychology were used in France have been the subject of recent studies on the beginnings of the advertising profession in France. Marjorie Beale has pointed out the difficulties for French advertisers to legitimize their trade in a society not yet fully committed to democratic cultural values. Rejecting American-style advertising, they sought to invent a French tradition based on scientific

63. Jean Gaumont, "Il y a 75 ans naissait La Laborieuse à Troyes," *Le Coopérateur de France,* December 30, 1961.

64. *Marque,* the French word for *brand name,* plays on the rhyme with *Park Avenue* to suggest that luxury goods are available at affordable prices in these outlet stores. See the article "Magasins d'usine: Le boom de Troyes," *Le Point,* April 16, 1994, 78–82.

65. See Raymond Williams 1980, esp. 177–89. Williams relates the development of new advertising techniques to the economic transformations of capitalism during this period, and to the new kinds of psychological persuasion that emerged during and after World War I.

models of perception and a contemporary aesthetic, proposed by such French thinkers and artists as Henri Bergson and Le Corbusier. Early French commercial advertising did not attempt to persuade or convince the consumer of a product's utility, as American advertising sought to do. Rather, it aimed to catch the consumer's attention, notably through unusual, striking images.[66] As another historian has noted, the French advertising poster of the 1920s focused on the object, rather than on the consumer.[67] French critics of advertising in the interwar years, among them the writer Georges Duhamel, singled out its power to manipulate the consumer. Many intellectuals, such as Duhamel, identified it with what they regarded as some of the worst attributes and values of American consumer society.

Between the wars, advertising became a significant means of asserting market control, while creating trademark labels or brand names for goods became another. How were the goods made in Troyes represented in the marketplace? For our own purposes a sampling of retail sales catalogs, trade journals, period photographs, and films provide some sense of both the diversity of goods then available on the market for workers in Troyes, and the ways in which such goods were appropriated in terms of class and gender. In other words, we need to understand not only how clothing was marketed, but how it was used.

Made in Troyes

Troyes millowners traditionally sold their products through a network of commission houses and traveling sales representatives, such as the one featured in the photo postcard that served as a visiting card (Fig. 16). These representatives visited shop owners for the purpose of establishing a relationship with their client, collecting credit references and reporting back to commercial services in Troyes and Paris.[68] With the advent of the Paris world's fairs, most of the large mills had moved their commercial services to the capital where a

66. Beale 1999, introduction and chap. 1. Beale situates her discussion of advertising within the broader context of the modernization of French society from 1900, and the ways in which French elites attempted to confront the problems posed by mass democracy, exemplified in large part by American society. See also Chessel 1998, 30–37.

67. De Grazia 1989, 246. De Grazia emphasizes the aestheticizing tradition of European advertising as a whole and cites one French advertiser as claiming that the object sold itself: "No need to construct a scenario: the object, the object alone, the object-king, just solicit it, it will tell its own story" (R. L. Dupuy, "Panorama de la publicité française," *Vendre,* March 1930, 194, cited in de Grazia 1989, 249).

68. Ricommard 1934, 154–56.

Figure 16   Visiting card of a hosiery sales representative. Collection Claude Bérisé.

large market for luxury hosiery and knitted goods was already flourishing. One of the biggest mills, Mauchauffée, sold to fancy-goods shops and notions and knitted goods shops in most of the large and medium-size towns in France, but like many Troyes mills that specialized in luxury goods, it relied heavily on the foreign and colonial export market. George Mauchauffée's colonial sales network extended from Indochina to Madagascar and the West African coast.[69] But in general Algeria absorbed two-thirds of the cotton knit-ted goods exported to the colonies.[70] Industry-sponsored trade fairs within France, such as the one attended by Louis Bonbon and his wife, were impor-tant commercial events for diffusing cultural models of fashion and confirming Troyes millowners' reputation for elegant, quality knitted goods. But despite this significant domestic commercial network, millowners targeted primarily a luxury export market. Only when the worldwide decline in prices in the 1930s called this export strategy into question did millowners shift more serious attention to the provincial domestic market.

Moreover, the domestic market for many items was both socially strati-fied and geographically segmented. The predominance of rural society before World War I—56 percent of the French population lived in the countryside in 1911—militated against a national market. Many peasants lived off their own production, resisted credit purchases, and had little disposable income. As we have seen, low wages kept urban workers from becoming significant con-sumers of ready-made goods. Urbanization during the interwar years and the increase in the numbers of wage earners brought about significant changes in consumer behavior, including a greater social demand for goods. But the structure of the domestic market remained stubbornly regional. The fact that neither a national nor a mass market as yet existed in France, in contrast to the United States, has been explained primarily by the lower income levels and social inequalities that persisted in Europe after World War I.[71] Marie-Emmanuelle Chessell has argued that regional differences in culture and taste, especially for food, helped to maintain compartmentalized regional markets for goods. Regional rural society still produced distinctive food products that

69. Among the Mauchauffée mill archives saved from Dumpster destruction when the mill closed in 1978, there is an early register of clients with careful notes on their credit rating (ADA J39 1119). The register includes the export market organized through agents in European capi-tals such as Brussels, London, Zurich, Bucarest, Athens, and Amsterdam as well as more distant places such as Capetown, Cairo, Buenos Aires, and Saigon. See also Bergeron 1978, 93–94.
70. Hauser and Hitier 1917, 296–97.
71. De Grazia 1993, 26–28; Chessel 1998, chap. 3.

catered to local tastes. Regarding the marketing of ready-made clothing, Nancy Green has observed that the French ready-to-wear industry developed at a slow pace because of both the economic impact of two world wars and a relative degree of cultural resistance from high-fashion designers. Artistic protection of couture design preserved a two-tiered garment market until style copying and pirating made such laws inapplicable in the 1930s.[72] Advertising campaigns were adapted and structured regionally for a host of products. Under these conditions, advertising during the interwar years appeared to have had low visibility in a limited commercial space, with the notable exception of the large Paris market.

How did such market structures affect clothing consumption in Troyes? The simpler fashions of the early 1920s were clearly produced as luxury items in the Troyes mills. Advertisements for silk stockings and fancy socks produced by such reputable Troyes manufacturers as Vitoux, Desgrez, and Savouré conveyed a message of class distinction. Obviously the luxury artificial-silk dress modeled surreptitiously by Suzanne Gallois also targeted a select consumer market. However, by the late 1920s, most mills manufactured a line of leisure sportswear and sweaters that were both more class neutral and affordable. The trade journal *La Maille Moderne* identified sweaters as clothing that clearly corresponded with postwar modern lifestyles, which reflected "the desire to be always comfortably dressed, and except for certain special events in one's life, to choose the most fitting and hygienic clothing. This explains the growing vogue of knitted apparel and underwear, especially the pullover sweater."[73] Manufacturers touted knitwear as the most comfortable clothing for active modern leisure. These new cultural models were mediated through retail-store and mail-order catalogs, but also through the cinema, which represented a growing form of leisure for working men and women. Fashion- and beauty-advice columns appeared regularly in the illustrated leftist weekly *Regards*. As we have seen, ready-made clothes were retailed in Troyes in privately owned shops, department stores, and the shops of the Laborieuse. But wage insecurity during the 1930s made working-class customers poor consumers.

Two key manufacturers in Troyes, Valton and Doré-Doré, sought to capture a more popular consumer market. By adopting new merchandising strategies, creating trademarks for their goods, and diversifying their production,

72. Green 1997, 118–21.
73. "La bonneterie et la mode: Ce qu'on porte," *La Maille Moderne,* July 1928, 611–13.

they were successful in reaching a wider market and promoting a modern image of their products. There were few references to class. It is no accident that the goods they produced were humble socks and underwear, rather than fashionable clothing. The first manufacturer in Troyes to use advertising with a broader marketing appeal was Doré-Doré, a firm specializing in socks and stockings. To show the diversity of its products, it placed an advertisement for socks for bikers in the popular Parisian weekly *L'Illustration* in 1907. Since bicycles were one of the first sports items to be mass produced in the 1880s, Doré-Doré's attempt to identify its product with a popular leisure sport opened up a potential market. By the 1920s the firm was marketing ankle socks for tennis and everyday wear that had earned a reputation for solid dura- bility. More important, in 1926 they created the brand name DD for all their hosiery products. In the interwar years, the brand became associated with clas- sic quality children's clothes, engendering an image promoted by the labeling and packaging of their goods. Advertising first centered on retail outlets, pro- viding systematic promotional displays at counters, and offering bonus gifts or toys carrying the DD label for distribution to parents and children in shops. But in 1933, wall posters advertising DD hosiery were posted all over the French countryside. These graphically striking and visually appealing adver- tisements (Fig. 18) carried a product message together with the manufacturer's trademark.[74] What could convey a more patriotic appeal to "Frenchness" than two little sailor-suited boys in red pompom hats and white socks? Simultane- ously, the ads clearly communicated a universal language of childhood linked closely to the trademark.

Another manufacturer in Troyes adopted similar commercial techniques. One of its first trademarked goods was children's cotton underpants, marketed under the brand name Petit Bateau and manufactured by the Etienne Valton mills. Created in 1913 and officially patented in 1920, the brand name desig- nated a streamlined, comfortable, and hygienic model of children's under- wear. At the same time, Valton launched an advertising campaign targeting mothers, highlighting a distinctive logo that pictured the toy boats seen float- ing in ponds in children's parks (Fig. 17). In fact, the brand name evoked a popular nursery song for very young children. Effective advertising depicted happy, roly-poly children in images that once again appealed to childhood. The brand was an immediate success in the postwar period; sales peaked in

74. Musée de la publicité 1988; Bibliothèque Forney 1999, 164–65.

Figure 17   Advertisement by Béatrice Mallet for underwear manufactured by the Valton mills under the trademark Petit Bateau in the 1920s. Collection Claude Bérisé and comtes of Petit Bateau, Troyes.

1930, just as the depression hit. In 1933, Valton launched a second quality, cheaper version of the same product, distinguishing it under the name Petit-Loup. While it might appear easy to sell underwear even in a depression, Valton advertised his product with easily identifiable images that evoked happy, healthy childhood. Once again, by appealing beyond class to what we would now call family values, the advertising campaign invested standardized underwear with broader social meaning. A concern for bodily hygiene and leisure sports during this period also made these advertisements effective. The Valton mills continue today to manufacture quality cotton children's wear under the Petit Bateau label, which appears to defy time and fashion.[75]

Advertisements for both these products made by leading manufacturers in Troyes attempted to establish connections between their goods and a broad-based consumer market. In this case, by addressing the children's market with standardized goods, they carried a message that was less class specific. There is

75. Boucraut and Boucraut 1986, 67–69, 115–18. See also Bibliothèque Forney 1992, 130, and Cauzard, Perret, and Ronin 1989, 212–13.

Figure 18 Advertisement for socks and kneesocks manufactured by Doré-Doré under the trademark DD in the 1930s. Courtesy of Doré-Doré Fontaine-les-grès.

little text and no reference to fashion. In fact, images of this kind performed like trademarks for the goods they advertised. Both manufacturers relied on well-known advertising artists to create their commercial image. No matter how innovative these advertising campaigns appear in the French context, both firms were concerned to conserve their traditional urban markets, while attempting to reach the mass consumer. Experimental attempts to capture a wider domestic market were indeed risky during the depression decade. As Victoria de Grazia has observed, in the wake of the depression, "advertisers could no longer rely on conventional notions of class and taste to intuit what customers wanted. They needed to find a new language to communicate with mass publics."[76] Compared with more traditional manufacturers in Troyes such as Desgrez and Lebocey, Valton and Doré-Doré were developing just such a new language with their trademarks and product merchandising.

Working-Class Consumer Patterns

Loss of disposable income and wage insecurity during the depression decade forced some textile workers in Troyes to return to second hand clothing or other traditional solutions to meet their needs. The fact that some workers' families suffered during the depression from lack of income for even basic items like warm clothes and socks for their children is confirmed by a primary school teacher who taught in the predominately working-class *quartier bas* of Troyes. In 1930, as unemployment broke out in the mills, the school organized a collection of hand-me-down clothes for children facing the winter cold. Shoes and warm wool socks were the items that were the most worn or lacking, judging by the medical inspector's report.[77] During these difficult years, many women textile workers must also have turned to using their professional skills to sew and knit at home. The simplification of postwar fashion styles had helped to launch a number of women's fashion magazines that were devoted to the latest styles and also included patterns and instructions. Pattern books were distributed in cheap formats, often as supplements to sales catalogs. For example, a cooperative called Les Economats Français, with chain stores throughout France, published in 1929 a sales catalog called *L'Echo des Eco* that displayed basic lingerie, stockings, and housecoats for housewives for

76. De Grazia 1989, 251.
77. Testimony by a primary school teacher, born in Romilly, who taught a class of sixty-nine children aged seven to nine years old (Lacoste 1998).

sale, and included cheap format pattern books as a bonus to customers.[78] Certainly these new pattern books presented an economical way to produce at home what one could not afford to purchase in the stores.

Targeting just such domestic practices, however, required considerable market research and experimentation. One textile manufacturer competing in the north of France launched a novel merchandising strategy of direct sale of knitting yarn by classified ads. Started in 1922 by the Filatures de la Redoute in Roubaix as a way of disposing of stocks of wool yarn, the scheme expanded in April 1925 to include a monthly publication called *Pénélope* that featured knitting patterns and product designs.[79] Within a year, the magazine had brought in 350,000 customers. More than a mail-order catalog, *Pénélope* offered knitting lessons and detailed patterns, fashion news, home decoration advice, and bonus gifts to customers that included free magazine subscriptions. In the space of several years it became a true women's magazine with an educative mission inspired by domestic science, offering advice to women on how to be efficient wives and mothers. Behind the domestic ideology that it conveyed was a clever merchandising scheme. In 1926 the Filatures de La Redoute opened a knitted goods workshop in its spinning mill. The magazine then served as a way to evaluate the impact of new knitted goods and patterns for subsequent catalog distribution. In January 1926, *Pénélope* offered its readers wool stockings and socks at wholesale prices, together with additional yarn to darn and repair them. In 1928, when la Redoute created its first general mail-order catalog, *Pénélope* continued on a separate track as a women's magazine. Then in 1935, la Redoute expanded its catalog services to include a larger range of clothing, knitted goods, layettes, and household goods, in a format very similar to that of today's mass-consumer catalog in France.

The importance of such a mail-order service for women textile workers in Troyes can only be suggested. No comparable merchandising scheme for lowering inventory existed within the Troyes mills, even during periods when sales slumped. To be sure, experimentation with direct sale of this kind depended on the development of a national and a mass market, and both were slow to materialize in France at this conjuncture. It was only in 1951 that a

78. I was able to consult a number of these ephemerals in the private collection of M. Daniel Poulet, collector in Troyes. I gratefully acknowledge his generous help.

79. For the history of the wool manufacturing and mail-order-catalog business of la Redoute, see Petit et al. 1985. La Redoute also published a number of special albums for teaching knitting in domestic-science classes at school.

prototype of factory-outlet stores was founded in Troyes for mail order and direct sale of nylon stockings and other knitted goods produced by small man- ufacturers.[80] Today, however, the town of Troyes is the center of a flourishing group of outlet stores for mill goods and brand-name products from all over France.

For many working-class customers, price inflation, wage insecurity, and loss of income from wage cuts during the depression years restricted their right to consume. Many women continued to make their clothes at home or to refashion and recycle secondhand ones. There was no simple progression of their purchasing power in the interwar years, and thus no lasting changes in consumer patterns. Yet an argument can be made that the fashion changes of this period were adopted by working-class women in ways that rearticulated class identity, and that in the process they employed their domestic skills to sew and knit what they could not afford to buy.[81] Since a truly mass market for women's fashion did not yet exist, workingwomen appropriated the new styles by customizing the patterns to fit their tastes and budget constraints. Viewed from this perspective, women's fashion in particular was a "site of conflicting meanings"[82] within a consumer society still dominated by issues of taste and class-specific values. At the same time, women were experimenting with their visual identity and questioning gender codes of femininity, totally implicated as women in the collective experience of how clothing could express social change. For women workers in Troyes, my evidence suggests that they practiced just such a selective appropriation of style in an expanding market that only partially addressed them.

80. André Massey, a small producer, founded this mail-order service called Bas Nylon Français, then Direct Usine, at a time when he and other façonniers were suffering from lack of business and a shortage of raw materials. The new service rapidly reached sixty thousand cus- tomers through its sales catalog, until growing prosperity and mass distribution finally forced it out of business in 1968. See *Libération Champagne*, 1997.

81. Angela Partington has questioned the commonly held notion that fashion goods "trickle down" from middle-class to lower-status social groups, gradually eroding class differences in a process of social emulation. The upper-status groups then attempt to distinguish themselves by re-creating distinctions, thus provoking a fashion cycle. Explanations of fashion change of this kind are drawn from George Simmel and Thorsten Veblen, both of whom wrote during the early twentieth-century debate on luxury goods. Partington argues that the mass-market system actually provided the conditions for a rearticulation of class differences as working-class women customized the "New Look" of post–World War II fashion in Britain, creating a more complex language of clothing according to their own tastes and preferences (Partington 1993, 145–61). For the 1930s, see Weitz 1996. Weitz stresses how in Communist Party propaganda, fashion was viewed as a "site of class struggle."

82. Partington 1993, 147.

The Worker as Film Hero

During its brief years in power, the Popular Front government inaugurated a richly visual pageant involving ritual mass demonstrations, theater, cinema, and the building of the world's fair of 1937. Pageantry of this kind produced a legacy of powerful photographic images. For the first time workers became inscribed in the collective imaginary of French political life through photojournalism and the cinema. Most photographic images of the Popular Front demonstrations record the sea of *casquettes* (caps) in the dense crowd. Emblematic of male worker identity from the late nineteenth century through the interwar period, the worker in his cap dominated Popular Front iconography as a symbol of mass male militancy. The power of such collective images is strikingly shown on the cover of the left-wing weekly *Regards* for May 24, 1936, an issue that celebrated the popular march to the Mur des Fédérés in commemoration of the Paris Commune of 1871. Against the background of an immense crowd, the cover montage singles out a worker in his cap who is carrying his daughter on his shoulders, her fist raised in a gesture of solidarity with the marchers. In a sense, the new visual medium of the cinema probably had greater popular impact than the photopress, simply because the former reached a potentially wider public. Among those commercial films that portrayed workers' lives, most proposed some degree of documentary detail that conveyed both class identity and difference. For our purposes, we need to examine the ways in which these gendered images of workers functioned and, in particular, how clothing featured in these films to convey more egalitarian dress patterns. But also, what signs of class differences remain?

Clothing figured predominately in *La Belle Equipe* (1936), the story of five unemployed workers who live in relative poverty in furnished rooms, in a *hôtel meublé* run by a stingy landlord who cuts the electricity at night, leaving his tenants *sans confort*. The five men wear work clothes in the street, the only clothes they now own, and the ubiquitous cap as a sign of their estate. But their sudden change in fortune when they win the national lottery unleashes two immediate desires: first, some bottles of cheap imitation champagne (*mousseux*) for a celebration with friends and the residents of the hotel; and second, the purchase of a complete set of new clothes, from head to toe. In fact, their first individual purchases have a transformative effect, clothing them in a new identity that conveys respectability and the possibility of social promotion. Dressed in suits and ties and broad-brimmed hats, they could pass for middle-class businessmen. By contrast, most of the workingwomen represented in these Popular Front films tend to dress and act in seductive ways, using their sex appeal as a means of social promotion. Fine lingerie, stockings, and makeup make frequent appearances in romantic settings, noticeably in *La Belle Equipe*. We are left wondering what social meaning women workers might have attached to these clothes. Overall, working-class women feature less prominently in these films than do men, and almost never as factory workers. In the end, the attention to the material culture and to the struggles of working-class life make these few films iconic, conveying a lasting imprint of 1930s France.

Despite the transformation of the Laborieuse in the midst of the depression, working-class culture in Troyes continued to constitute a strong community of consumption and a political subculture. During the depression decade, textile workers in Troyes maintained their consumer habits, patterned on thrift and the ethics of consumption. However, many aspired to breaking class ranks, as our evidence has shown. The democratic premise of the time, embodied in Popular Front demands for a redistribution of income, inspired new shopping practices. When workers had money in their pockets, they tended to spend more of it on clothes. The observations of Jacques Valdour in 1930 and the evidence from the films cited for the period portray men and women workers' desire for clothing that would allow for greater social mobility. But because prolonged unemployment and social class cleavages so dominated the 1930s, whatever expansion of the market took place during this period only briefly affected their consumer practices. In fact, necessity and thrift continued to regulate their consumer behavior, and many goods remained beyond their reach. To a large extent, working-class culture remained an oppositional culture, structured around institutions of solidarity such as the Laborieuse.

In this context, the social meaning of certain goods acquired status as markers of identity. This defensive posture was also an aggressive one, evidenced in the militancy of the period that sustained the Popular Front movement. At the forefront of the movement's demonstrations were male workers in their caps, their fists clenched in defiance. Popular Front iconography strengthened class difference as a political statement, caught up in the political polemics of the times. And equally important is the fact that nearly all these images were gendered. Militancy was envisioned as overwhelmingly masculine, with few exceptions. Women textile workers were rarely represented as skilled producers, and when they appeared as strikers, the images emphasized their femininity rather than their labor power.[83] Indeed, the photographs of sit-in strikers occupying the women's workshop in the Devanlay mills in June 1936 seemed to suggest that fashion could also be a site of struggle. In reality, women textile workers made a selective appropriation of fashion clothing, customizing their apparel through their own domestic skills and individual tastes, in relation to what they could afford. Yet they, too, seemed eager to adopt new identities, based on the more feminine fashions of the 1930s that shaped and revealed the body.

Workers' access to mass-produced standardized goods was also slowed by a culture of quality and luxury goods, a characteristic Frenchness that had traditionally defined taste and prestige in many parts of the world. Troyes manufacturers followed these principles even into the 1930s, with the notable exception of two firms, which attempted to expand their merchandising to the popular domestic market. Both launched advertising campaigns that emphasized family values and maternalism, social values that were actively cultivated during the period. Overall, the fashions of the 1930s appeared less socially stratified than earlier in the century, a step toward the democratization of supply that was made possible by mass-production technology and standardization. While such modern methods of production existed, manufacturers in Troyes would only fully adopt them in the mills after World War II. By that time millowners were sufficiently challenged by foreign competitors to modernize their production methods, revise their tastes, and envision their own workers as consumers of the goods they produced.

The history of the Laborieuse over the fifty years of its existence as a separate socialist-inspired institution is instructive in this regard. We have followed its evolution as it successfully provided goods and services to the working-class community. As it progressively expanded its network of shops and leisure activities, it never ultimately lost sight of its working-class constituency. But commercial capitalism proved to be a stronger system, even at the height of the depression, and the cooperative foundered. This is not to say that this socialist, and ultimately utopian, experiment in working-class consumer culture was doomed to fail. But it is true that the consumer cooperative movement as a whole struggled to retain its commercial identity at the expense of its politics. Some socialist arguments against consumer cooperatives were

83. See the analysis of Eric Weitz (1996, esp. 328–36).

based on the assumption that consumption was a passive act, a buyout that would integrate workers into bourgeois society, with its more individualistic goals. Yet members of the Laborieuse saw themselves as active and committed class-conscious consumers. In fact, they reacted as producers, gendered individuals, mothers and fathers, and citizen consumers of the Third Republic. In the interwar years, workers found a new positive identity, fostered by the Popular Front movement. It was expressed in fashion, film, and new forms of leisure that accompanied the transition to what would become a modern mass-consumer society in the postwar era.

8

THE DEPRESSION DECADE AND
THE POPULAR FRONT

In the political and cultural imagination of the French working class, the Popular Front emerges as something of a utopian moment, if only for the fact that for a brief period, through the workings of the democratic process, the balance of power shifted in their favor. Looking back almost fifty years later, CGTU leader Suzanne Gallois remembered the social explosion of the strike movement and the spontaneous occupations of the mills as expressions of revenge against a class of millowners whose ultimate weapon over the years of struggle had been the lockout. But she also recalled her hopes, soon cruelly disappointed, that out of this movement the workers' world might be genuinely transformed. There is little doubt that the dominant historical narratives of this particular period, written primarily by left-wing historians and participants, have reinforced a somewhat mythic characterization of the Popular Front.[1] In addition, period photojournalism and film have helped to shape and sustain popular historical memory of these events. In his recent study, historian Julian Jackson underscores the very considerable collective faith and political will that the Popular Front movement had to draw on in order to pursue its mass mobilization against fascism at a critical moment in French history.[2] However, as Jackson notes, the Popular Front had also to confront the immense task of overcoming divisions within the working class,

1. Lefranc 1974, 1966; Guérin 1997.
2. Jackson 1988, xii.

the left-wing parties, and the unions—a task that, as we shall see, would be particularly difficult in Troyes. The very fact that these groups succeeded, however briefly, in creating a Popular Front movement gave the experience a "souffle épique," or epic thrust, that marked twentieth-century French history.[3]

But the era in which the Popular Front movement struggled to assert itself was also a time of economic crisis and depression; this crisis would have a heavy impact on the working classes of Troyes and France in general and would be intimately connected to the emergence of the Popular Front. As many observers have commented, France was less severely hit by unemployment than were many other countries, yet the depression also lasted comparatively longer than it did, for example, in the United States.[4] Recent historians have argued that the French economy made considerable gains in productivity from 1900 to 1930, gains that culminated in what could be described as a second industrial revolution; these same studies also acknowledge that certain traditional sectors, among them textiles, stagnated.[5] The period of the 1920s and 1930s is thus portrayed as a troubled one of transition to modernity, posing particular problems for the working class. Structural changes within production nationwide, whether linked to scientific management methods or not, forced workers to adapt to new norms of productivity. To some extent, and in significant ways, the collective memory of the Popular Front victory overshadowed the recollection of the depression.[6] Yet for Troyes textile workers, the overwhelming reality of those years was unemployment, short-time work, and wage cuts. A great many laboring people, especially women, lost their jobs. Still more—some 75 percent by 1934—soldiered on, trying to get by as best they could on greatly reduced work hours.

The object of this chapter will be to show the strong connections between the legacy of the social antagonisms and stalemate of the 1920s, the experience of the depression, and the conflicts leading to the mobilization of the Popular Front. Workers' testimony strengthens the memory of depression hardship, and underscores the local victories under Deputy Mayor René Plard. The very

3. Wolnikow 1996, 18. Wolnikow underscores the Popular Front experience as a landmark reference for the Left's subsequent outbreak of protest for reform in May 1968, less as a model than as a significant attempt to transform social relations and to influence political change. This latter experience was continued by the efforts to draft a common program of government in 1972, leading later to unity under a government dominated by the Socialist Party.

4. The major texts on this period are Letellier et. al. 1938–49; Jackson 1985; Berstein 1988, chap. 2; Sauvy 1965; Boyer 1991.

5. Noiriel 1986, 121–33. For the debate on these issues, see Boyer 1991.

6. For further examples of this "underremembering" of the depression, see Reynolds 1996.

nature of the crises would raise questions of family survival strategies. Who worked, and how was unemployment experienced by workers of both sexes? And what was the ultimate effect of the Popular Front on the world of work? In particular, since women workers now outnumbered men in the workforce, what was their role in the strike movement, and how were their interests defined in the collective bargaining agreements that figured so prominently in the strike settlements of 1936?

DEPRESSION DECADE

The preceding chapter drew on contemporary interpretations of the causes of the economic crisis in France. To understand the social impact of the crisis in Troyes, it is important to establish a chronology of the decline in industrial production and the rise in unemployment. But the latter phenomenon presents several difficulties for analysis of our sources. First, the organization of unemployment relief depended on several different definitions of *unemployed worker*. Julian Jackson maintains that "the only precise statistics for the total number of unemployed are those of the censuses of March 1931 and March 1936," while the actual numbers of unemployed receiving relief were considerably lower.[7] Several sets of different figures were produced in an attempt to measure aspects of a multifaceted and constantly evolving social phenomenon. Government measures were piecemeal in dealing with unemployment, often improvised as problems arose. Therefore it seems likely that official figures underestimated both the work time lost and the human suffering that resulted. A second set of difficulties concerns the categories used to estimate the extent of unemployment and to determine the eligibility for aid. In his study *L'invention du chômage*, Robert Salais explains the historical problem of the construction of formal categories that, he argues, need to be historicized and relocated in the social logic they were invented to describe and understand.[8] Thus for the French term *chômage* (unemployment), Salais notes a shift in meaning at the end of the nineteenth century when socialism and syndicalism forced the

7. Jackson 1985, 29. The total number of unemployed in March 1931 was 452,800, and 820,800 for March 1936. The corresponding figures for unemployed on relief were 50,800 in 1931 and 465,100 in 1936; the increase in 1936 can be attributed to the fact that more local unemployment funds had been created to deal with the problem.
8. Salais et al. 1986, 20–25. His study is concerned with the history and transformation of this category.

development of a more scientific analysis of work. Syndicalism's defense of workers' right to work influenced the notion of unemployment by imputing responsibility to employers and to capitalism in general. By the 1930s, new ideas of scientific management and the creation of unemployment offices had revised and shaped the concept of "waged worker" and "unemployed worker." The experience of large-scale industry formed the primary basis for observation. Thus, the small-scale mills in Troyes, virtually untouched by scientific-management methods, did not necessarily fit the categories officially devised by the state.

These same categories of the 1930s also present a particular problem for understanding the situation of women workers. The social construction of the category *unemployed worker* conformed to a male model devised by statisticians with reference to the breadwinner, or "head of household," inscribed in the Civil Code. As a result, most existing statistical data considerably underestimated the phenomenon of women's unemployment for reasons that are specific both to the types of jobs women performed and to their civil status. While neither the statistician nor the social worker accurately described the reality of women's unemployment in the 1930s, one contemporary study emerged that was an attempt to give a fuller picture using gendered categories. Gabrielle Letellier, a woman work inspector, collaborated with two male colleagues to produce a three-volume study of unemployment during the crisis. Based in part on an analysis of data from municipal unemployment funds in Paris, Lyon, and Mulhouse concerning a representative sample of 34,174 unemployed workers of both sexes benefiting from relief in 1935–36, their local studies noted the exceptional constancy of women's unemployment in relation to men's: the number of unemployed women in the industrial workforce hovered slightly over 25 percent.[9]

Finally, there is often a difficulty with the types of data collected. It was only in February 1931 that the Ministère du Travail et de la Prévoyance sociale gave specific instructions on how data concerning the labor market and changes in working hours was to be formalized. The monthly record of employment

9. Letellier et al. 1938–49, 2:15. In this study, women represented 22.9 percent of their sample. The authors confirmed what five-year occupational census reports had shown, that from 1896 to 1931 the position of women's unemployment in relation to men's scarcely changed, with the exception of the post–World War I period, when many more women were temporarily unemployed. The census reports gave the following figures for overall women's unemployment: 28.9 percent in 1896, 27.7 percent in 1901, 27.6 percent in 1906, 39.6 percent in 1921, 30.6 percent in 1926, and 31.9 percent in 1931.

undertaken by the departmental Inspection du travail, which provides the most reliable figures, only examined mills with more than one hundred workers and never noted gender variations in the workforce. The fact that the state sought to collect statistics on these larger mills doubtless reflected a concern to understand the bigger picture, but in Troyes only 43 mills fit the one-hundred-worker minimum, according to the 1931 census. The census further noted some 365 workshops that had no paid employees (family workshops fit this description), and 1,050 firms that employed fewer than one hundred workers.[10] But even if some statistics are fairly reliable and accurate, any attempt to reconstruct the total evolution of unemployment in the industry on the basis of data from heterogeneous sources, using gender-neutral categories and variable methods, can only be approximate.

The Evolution of the Crisis and Unemployment

While France as a whole seemed insulated from the impact of the world economic crisis at the outset, such was not the case in Troyes, as we saw in the previous chapter. Already in 1927 there were concrete signs of an economic slowdown, to which millowners had reacted by putting workers on short time and lowering wages. This policy of economic retrenchment conformed to their strategy of limiting production, keeping high profit margins, and sharing markets through cartels. Millowners in Troyes had every reason to limit production for luxury and colonial markets from 1927, since the exports of knitted goods dropped dramatically, some 90 percent, between 1926 and 1932.[11] During the period 1929 to 1931, manufacturers in Troyes cut back basic production of socks and stockings some 60 percent, relying now almost entirely on consumers in the domestic market.[12] By comparison, textile production for France as a whole declined by 25 percent from 1929 to 1932.[13]

10. The expansion of knitted goods production in the 1920s had "tripled the number of industrialists since the war," according to Ricommard (1934), some of whom were "the first victims of the economic crisis" (189).

11. The following figures are given by the president of the French Federation of Knitted Goods Industries in an interview on the economic crisis (*Le Petit Troyen*, January 15, 1936): in 1926, exports of knitted goods totaled 1,200 million articles; by 1932, exports had fallen to 112 million; and by 1935, to 70 million.

12. Ricommard 1934, 181.

13. Berstein 1988, 29. Berstein details particularly the crisis in the Nord and in Normandy, regions hard hit by World War I and slow to recover, and the silk industry that met serious competition from the new rayon fiber. Cotton hosiery production had profited from a large colonial market but it collapsed with the drop in world prices as the economic crisis spread.

The prefect of the Aube confirmed the particular difficulties of the local industry in a report to the Ministre du Travail at the end of 1931: "For reasons that are specific to the local industry, economic problems affected the department very early, and future perspectives are far from encouraging. . . . The industrial crisis is visibly deepening; it has provoked worker layoffs in almost all the mills, a general shortening of work hours, wage cuts, and finally the closing of small workshops notably in the production of silk jersey and elastic fabric."[14] The employment situation was evidently a real concern, but not all branches of production were hit at the same time. The industrial crisis had a selective impact. Production fluctuated in those local industries directly serving the knitting mills (machine construction, spinning, and dyeing), but also in the mills that manufactured different types of knitted products (socks and stockings, underwear, and so on).[15] The spinning mills and dyeworks appeared to have been the hardest hit during this first phase of the crisis. Employment in spinning with a largely female workforce dropped by nearly one-third between 1931 and the end of 1932; jobs in the dyeworks fell some 18 percent, rebounding only slightly in 1933.[16] Moreover, within the forty-three mills employing over one hundred workers in the local textile industry, 20 percent of the workforce had been laid off by September 1932 at the bottom of the first phase of the depression.

In fact, the economic crisis in the Aube can be more easily read by distinguishing two phases: a first phase that extended from 1930 to 1933, and a second one that ran from 1934 to 1938. While the first phase developed progressively, it soon became severe, as reflected in the figures for rising unemployment and short-time work. In September 1930 the Chambre syndicale patronale decided to halt production in the mills one and a half days a week. Progressive layoffs followed in 1931, spread out over several months. Moreover, millowners imposed two successive wage cuts, one in April and another in December 1931, cuts that decreased wages overall by 15 percent. Unemployment increased into the second semester of 1932, followed by a very slight recovery, then stagnation. The larger millowners closed all branches located outside the department, and five branches within the Aube, while many of the

14. Prefect to the Ministry of Labor, December 19, 1931, AN F22 668.
15. Ricommard 1934, 178–79. Ricommard tried to represent the impact of the crisis on employment in the three branches of the local industry from 1931 to the beginning of 1934, when his study went to press.
16. Ibid., 179–80.

rural artisan workshops manufacturing rayon garments for Troyes millowners also collapsed.[17] These closings signaled the end of the decentralization strategy inaugurated after the 1921 strike.

The second phase of the crisis was characterized by a brutal increase in unemployment in the Aube (as in France as a whole) starting in 1934. The decline in industrial production became highly visible as a result of the dramatic increase in short-time work: by December 1934, 76 percent of textile workers in the Aube were employed on short time, compared with 70 percent for France as a whole.[18] Millowners imposed a further wage cut of 10 percent in August 1934, which resulted in an official wage decline of at least 25 percent since 1930. Thereafter unemployment remained stable until late in 1936, when there was a slight improvement, which can perhaps be attributed to Popular Front government reform measures. However, unemployment increased again in 1938, returning to the level of 1935.

Faced with the high visibility of unemployment during this second phase, the Radical government in Paris was forced to renew relief measures. In Troyes, the municipal and departmental unemployment funds that had opened during the first phase, and then closed in 1933, were reopened in September 1934. By then union leaders had constituted a Comité des chômeurs for the purpose of presenting their demands to the prefect. The official institutionalization of the category *unemployed worker* (*chômeur*) and a designated relief fund marked this second phase of the crisis.

Definitions of *Unemployed Worker*

Troyes textile workers no longer lived unemployment as a fatality. Yet not every jobless individual considered him- or herself unemployed and eligible for relief, even if public institutions were now constituted to offer it. In the past, chronic job instability in the trade had forced men and women textile workers to seek better wages through turnover. Changing jobs had long been a means of dealing with unsatisfactory working conditions, including temporary unemployment. Such practices complicate the notion of *chômeur*, both for those trying to define it and those seeking relief. In this section I will examine the official definitions of *unemployed workers*, that is, the essential

17. Ibid., 182.
18. For the national figures, see Letellier et al. 1938–49, 1:100; and for the Aube, see l'Inspection du travail, ADA SC 2312.

characteristics of the category as defined by those institutions responsible for work inspection and relief distribution.

The first task of the Inspection du travail and social workers was to distinguish between *chômeurs complets* (unemployed) and *chômeurs partiels* (short-time workers). Only the former had the right to receive assistance according to the rules governing public relief funds, the guidelines for which had been established by the state. The great majority of workers had to live on vastly reduced wages, resulting from the reduction of work time and the two wage cuts in 1931 and 1934. The category *chômeur* included persons who were eligible for relief: "those who are involuntarily unemployed through lack of work, having been laid off, that is, who have been released from any obligation to their last employer, and are able to accept a future job." This definition clearly excluded "any accessory occupation for the purpose of obtaining supplementary income [*un salaire d'appoint*]."[19] It is clear that the exclusion applied to women homeworkers who were not considered formal wage earners, unless they could prove a recent waged relationship with an employer.

The criterion of "involuntary" unemployment that fixed admission onto the relief rolls called into question certain worker practices, such as changing jobs for better pay. The first police reports concerning unemployment at the outset of the depression indicated that some workers had "left their job voluntarily due to lack of work." In August 1930, Jacques Valdour was struck by the "instability of the personnel": "Thus, on Monday morning, two days after the biweekly payday, I saw three knitters in the same workshop notify their foreman of their departure. They gave no motive for leaving. A laborer told me, "They are all like that. They come, they go, we never know why.'"[20] Whatever their motives, the workers' practice of giving eight days' notice (donner sa huitaine) was their means of regulating the labor market. However, such voluntary fluctuations in jobs without layoffs are difficult to evaluate during a period of depression.

Thus, to benefit from the status of "unemployed worker on relief," one needed to prove an "involuntary" break in one's working life. Other conditions for admission were based on the worker's civil status and the level of his family's resources. This latter criterion excluded many married working women. Aid was granted to the family, not to the individual. All aid was paid

19. Ville de Troyes, Reglement du Fonds de chômage applicable aux chômeurs totaux au 1 Janvier 1937, AMT 7F 86.
20. Valdour 1934, 183.

to the male breadwinner as head of household. He was not entitled to benefits for his wife, whether she was unemployed or not, nor for other dependents, except with proof that his resources would be insufficient to assure the subsistence of his family.[21] Since only men qualified, it was inevitable that married women were heavily underrepresented among the unemployed. Such a woman became an "unemployed worker" only when she was herself recognized as head of household. For this reason few married women textile workers addressed their needs to the local relief organizations. Instead they went out looking for work, no matter how precarious, to help the family economy.

Despite these difficulties in understanding the parameters of women's unemployment, we do know from official census reports in 1931 and 1936 that in the Aube a much higher proportion of women textile workers were unemployed—by comparison with men—the great majority of them former outworkers, described by the census as "isolées." According to government sources, between 1931 and 1936 about two and a half times as many women were unemployed as men.[22] However, here again the floating population of industrial homeworkers easily escaped the Inspection du travail. The archives of the Valton mill revealed that in 1930 production at the Usine St.-Joseph in Troyes included some 621 millworkers, a workforce supplemented by an outworking network of 1,400 workers in all. In 1931, alone one-third of this workforce was laid off, including all the women homeworkers.[23] It is clear that the flexibility of the outwork system, so characteristic of the garment industry in general, allowed millowners to suppress all homework.[24]

A closer profile of some aspects of unemployment in the Troyes knitted goods industry for 1932 can be reconstituted from individual case files in the records of the Departmental Unemployment Fund.[25] The records provide the

21. "Admission au chômage des conjoints chômeurs," Circulaire du Ministère du Travail et de la Prévoyance sociale to the prefects, August 25, 1933, AMT 7F 86.

22. Out of a total textile workforce in the Aube of 31,000 in 1931, 655 men and 2,319 women textile workers were unemployed and on relief. For 1936, the corresponding figures are 564 men and 1,857 women out of 27,230 workers. The drop of some 12 percent in the workforce in 1936 suggests a worker exodus from the department to look for work elsewhere (*Statistiques du recensement générale de la population,* 1931, 1936).

23. Boucraut and Boucraut 1986, 133.

24. See Salais et al. 1986 on the specificity of women garment workers as homeworkers in a dual manufacturing system in 1896 and the relation to the notion of *chômage* (58–63).

25. The records concern the suburbs of Pont Sainte-Marie, Saint-André-les-Vergers, and Saint-Julien-les-Villas. My sample of 101 workers from the knitted goods industry, 35 women and 66 men, was based on the unemployment rolls for these three suburbs in 1932. The fund was opened on January 1, 1932; by January 31 some 90 *chômeurs* were listed, and by the end of

occupation, sex, age and civil status of those who were full-time unemployed. In general, unemployment appeared to touch a larger number of knitters and bobbin winders than workers in other occupations. This fact can be explained by their importance in the initial stages of the production process, where any reduction in output would logically start. The sample of 101 workers (35 women and 66 men) included four couples in these occupations. But unemployment also hit all age groups. The range of ages in the sample ran from 18 to 77 for the men, and from 14 to 66 among the women. There was, nevertheless, a concentration of younger and older workers, those who could be considered among the least "productive."[26] Moreover, relief aid clearly targeted married men. Married women accepted for unemployment relief were rare exceptions and appeared only in couples with multiple dependents for whom some means test had been applied. Most aid to women went to widows and single women.

Still, the sample from the unemployment rolls does suggest that there was a larger percentage of women on unemployment relief in Troyes (36 percent) in relation to men, than in the nation generally (20 percent in February and 27 percent in August and September of 1932).[27] While it is difficult to draw clear conclusions from the disparate data contained in these individual case files, it is evident that women's unemployment followed a different pattern and was experienced differently from that of men.

Short-Time Working

By contrast, the importance of short-time working was well documented by the Inspection du travail. Millowners used a reduction in working hours as a way to regulate the labor market in relation to the decline in industrial production. Short time meant working fewer than forty-eight hours a week. After

---

March the number had increased to 240. Social workers had not always made complete entries on all cases, so much of the data does not offer comparison. All unemployed workers on the list had been laid off at the end of 1931 or in early 1932 and were struck from the relief rolls by the end of the year (benefits were only granted for two hundred days). It was impossible to reconstruct any pattern showing the length or frequency of job loss (ADA SC 2313 and ADA SC 2325).

26. This image of the "relatively old unemployed worker" was confirmed by the mayor of Troyes in his monthly report for November 1932, but also by the director of the employment office working with both the municipal and the departmental relief funds in a statement in *Le Petit Troyen*, January 21, 1936. The Letellier sample also found that, judging from wage levels, it was the "least productive" worker who was often laid off. Letellier et al. 1938–49, 2:57.

27. Letellier et al. 1938–49, 1:65.

a first wave of layoffs in 1931, manufacturers attempted to distribute the decline in work among the entire workforce by reducing work hours. Both the unions and the government approved this policy. The unions admitted that this system "was detrimental to workers, but in any case it was fairer and more humane than the brutal dismissal of hundreds of workers that had taken place at the Société Générale de Bonneterie," a large mill that manufactured knitting machines and knitted goods.[28] When there was a slight recovery, millowners preferred to increase the working hours of those workers already on the job than to rehire others. But the sudden economic downswing in 1934 raised the problem of relief, because short-time workers were only authorized to receive food, not money, under the current government regulations. Early in 1935 there was even talk in Troyes of creating a special fund for the partially unemployed.[29]

While nearly three-quarters of workers were employed for a forty-eight-hour week in 1932, the situation deteriorated considerably in 1934. By then, less than one-quarter of the workforce worked forty-eight hours, while the vast majority (76 percent) were reduced to forty hours or less.[30] The practice of short-time work was widespread in French textile and garment industries. In one study it was estimated that in 1932 short-time workers accounted for 78.4 percent of the French textile labor force.[31] In Romilly during this period workers were said to show up for work in the morning and wait for the mail carrier to come. If there were sufficient orders in the day's mail, they would work only to fill these orders, a practice soon known as "mail-order work." Under such circumstances, wages were often extremely low.[32] This example underlines the sharp fluctuations in production and the precariousness of reduced wages. Workers' testimony from this period underscored the sharing of work among family members that was provoked by the reduction in working hours: "We worked three or four days a week. Preference was given to single women rather than married women, because they felt that at least [married women] were covered by one wage."[33] Whether unemployed or housewives, married women could rarely qualify for relief, and they were therefore relegated by the crisis to marginal work in the informal sector.

28. *Aube Ouvrière,* November 1930.
29. AN F22 668.
30. The short-time work figures come from monthly reports by the Inspection du travail (AN SC 2311).
31. Letellier et al. 1938–49, 1:49.
32. Ricommard 1934, 180.
33. Testimony from M. Labourie, interview, 1987.

The overwhelming majority of textile workers in Troyes experienced the depression as short-time workers. Their vastly reduced working hours, combined with wage cuts, made them extremely vulnerable, and women workers even more so.

Union Reaction

Relief was organized at several levels. Both departmental and municipal unemployment funds, subsidized by the state, distributed benefits. Placement offices operated at the Bourse du Travail, serving as an additional service to unemployed workers. But aid also came from other groups, such as the Comité de secours en nature aux chômeurs, which was created at the outset of the crisis to distribute food to short-time workers. In 1934, as the depression suddenly deepened, this committee distributed relief to 450 people a day in Troyes.[34] Soup kitchens were organized for some 250 to 300 people in February 1932, and the town council hired fifty unemployed workers on public construction jobs during the same year. With the election of dissident communist René Plard as mayor of Troyes in March 1935, the municipal council voted to raise unemployment payments and to increase food aid. Conditions for admission to the rolls were also slightly relaxed.

Workers' organizations reacted rapidly as they saw the depression deepening. As early as May 1931, the CGT and the Catholic union, the Confédération française des travailleurs chrétiens (CFTC), constituted a joint action committee to combat the wage cuts. The CGTU, however, called for work stoppages, or "grèves sur le tas," and in Romilly the entire textile workforce went out on strike. While these movements mobilized relatively small numbers of workers, the unions clearly took the lead in formulating concrete demands, which were submitted to the local authorities. Thus, in February 1935 the committee of unemployed workers in the suburban community of St.-Julien-les-Villas, created jointly by the CGT and the CGTU, gave the municipal council a list of demands that included an increase in the daily allowance, the suppression of the family means test, equal benefits for women in relation to men, tax exemption during the crisis, suspension of rents for the unemployed, and finally, the suppression of employer dispensations for overtime with respect to the eight-hour day.[35]

---

34. AN F22 668.

35. Joint actions were undertaken between the CGT and the CGTU to prepare for reunification, and organizing unemployed workers by formulating and presenting their demands to the

The last grievance, concerning what the unions considered to be infringements against the eight-hour-day law of 1919, had been formulated by all the unions. In the unions' view, millowners were partly responsible for the disorganization of work. Before the crisis broke out, manufacturers had made abusive demands for overtime to circumvent the eight-hour-day law. Unions now sought ways to redistribute work and to absorb unemployment by limiting working hours. Getting the unemployed back to work would raise wage earners' purchasing power and combat low domestic consumption, a factor that the unions considered to be one cause of the depression. For the CGT, notably, one of the remedies for reviving the economy was the reduction of working hours, made possible through more productive technology. Stricter application of the eight-hour day was key to their program. When the Radical Chautemps government intervened by decree in January 1934, suspending all overtime credit hours for six months, the CGT warned militants to report any abuses of the decree. In the same spirit, when several millowners in Troyes reverted to shift work during a slight recovery in 1933, on the pretext of filling urgent orders, the unions protested vehemently. "For the past six months the textile industry has executed urgent orders, reinstated shift work, and used overtime. . . . We think that the time has come for employers to keep their promises, all the more so because they have been increasing their sale prices."[36]

Workers' loss of income can be explained by unemployment and short-time work, but it can also be imputed to successive wage cuts since 1927. In March 1931, millowners announced a first cut of 6 percent for male workers, and 8 percent for female workers. The prefect urged the employers' union to reconsider the measure against women workers, bringing the cut to 7 percent instead of 8 percent. Millowners agreed to this compromise, but in December 1931 they imposed a further reduction of 8 percent on all wages. It could be argued that this specific wage cut for women was smaller in absolute terms, since their wages were less than men's.[37] But it was the blatant discriminatory nature of such workplace practices against women that may have moved the

---

local government was part of their program. See the letter from the CGT-CGTU leaders to the prefect that proposed measures to improve aid to the unemployed, January 18, 1935, ADA SC 2312.

36. Manifesto addressed by the CGTU to textile workers in the Aube in June 1933, transmitted by the prefect to the Minister of the Interior, June 14, 1933 (ADA SC 4251).

37. Letellier et al. 1938–49, 2:102. This study provides the following average daily wage: 28.6 francs for men, and 18.9 francs for women. The wage differential against women was even more marked in the garment making industry, reaching 59 percent.

prefect to intervene. Apparently, employers saw no contradiction between a wage system based on the male breadwinner and their own recourse to an over-whelming majority of women workers. As we have seen with regard to unemployment benefits, the sexual politics of the depression privileged the family over its individuals members, and heads of households over married working women. Moreover, during this period family allowances were not a universal welfare measure. It was not until 1932 that the state extended public control over the *caisse d'allocations familiales* (family welfare benefits fund) and required all employers in business and commerce to join.[38] Unions had long argued in favor of government control and for the extension of benefits to all workers.

In August 1934, employers posted a further wage cut of 10 percent. They maintained that the cost of living had declined and that their own economic difficulties persisted. At this time workers' organizations reacted with one voice to defend their interests. They denounced in the press the ways in which employers had been cutting wages during unemployment through frequent rate changes in the production of certain articles. Thus, they argued, the official wage reduction of 25 percent since 1931 was in reality much greater, reaching rates of some 30 to 40 percent, depending on the mill.[39] According to the unions, millowners were finding other devious means of cutting costs: the application of new labor-intensive methods of work, the dismissal of workers who were subsequently rehired at lower rates, the suppression of bonuses for shift work, and successive rate reductions for novelty items in production.[40] Union activists attributed part of the problem to the intense competition among Troyes millowners: "If employers were to show proof that they were in an unfavorable situation with regard to international competition, they would probably cite the wage differences from one country to another. But the existing ferocious competition between millowners has been of their own making, using the possibilities for disorder in production that they acquired during the slump."[41] Union leaders were referring here to such industrial practices as shift work and scientific-management techniques that were being developed to increase productivity.[42]

38. Pedersen 1993, esp. chaps. 5 and 7.
39. In the October 1934 issue of *Aube Ouvrière,* the CGT gave precise examples of wage cuts in certain Troyes mills through this manipulation of tarifs.
40. *Aube Ouvrière,* April 1, 1934.
41. Ibid., October 1, 1934.
42. Manufacturers in Troyes sought to justify the third wage cut in August 1934 in a letter to the prefect that explained the difficulties specific to their industry. They stressed that the

Union unity effectively took place in the fall of 1934 when CGT and CGTU leaders created the Comité des chômeurs for both short-time textile workers and the full-time unemployed. Working together, the two unions had organized a meeting of the unemployed workers in January 1935 for the purpose of drafting a list of measures to increase employment and attenuate the effects of the crisis. The movement grew as part of a more general political mobilization against unemployment, wage cuts, and fascism, which is treated later in this chapter. By February 1934 a mass movement had begun in Troyes that defined itself in terms of class. The conditions under which unemployment and the depression evolved demonstrates how left-wing political parties in Troyes managed to channel worker discontent and to create unity at the base. However, in the process, political leaders had to overcome tensions among workers that had originated in the economic crisis itself, not the least of which was the differential effects of unemployment. Married women's right to work was the subject of a national political debate, behind which was a desire to limit women's waged work. We might ask how this issue was presented to women textile workers, and what basis it had in reality.

The Family Economy During the Depression

Working-class families' everyday experience of the depression touched men and women differently, first, in terms of subsistence, and second, on the level of job insecurity. The harsh reality of daily life was reflected in worker testimony covering these years and in the observations of social reformer Jacques Valdour, who worked in the Troyes mills just as the layoffs began. Valdour arrived in Troyes in August 1930 and found work as an ordinary laborer sweeping the workshops in a large mill. His first problem was finding housing: "I had to pound the pavement for a whole day to find a place to stay. The boardinghouses [*garnis*] are bursting and the furnished rooms are all occupied. . . . All the boarding houses are located in narrow streets, in old dark buildings with winding narrow wooden staircases."[43] The housing shortage signaled by Valdour, with families packed into rooms in the old town center, evokes the

---

"bitter competition unleashed by certain industrial practices like shift work" was a cause of economic trouble. The prefect had noted in the margins of the letter: "whose fault is this?" (ADA SC 2312). For the nineteenth century use of the argument in favor of a protected domestic market, see Heywood 1981.

43. Valdour 1934, 157.

poor housing and overcrowding at the turn of the century described in the census. Valdour observed that only workers lived in his building, three single women and several couples, only two of whom had children. He was struck by the number of irregular households among the working-class population—couples living together outside marriage—by the fact that couples had so few children, and by the "double day" put in by women millworkers.

Like many social inquirers of the nineteenth century, Valdour viewed factory life as morally unhealthy for young women workers. But he readily recognized the difficult life they led in August 1930. On the job, he questioned a married woman mender of fifty about the decline in the couple's income. "This woman earned at most twenty-five francs a day, basic wages plus a piece-work bonus. She earned more when she worked on silk. But with privation spreading, consumers were not buying silk stockings, and were turning to cotton instead. Her husband worked in another knitting mill, but only for one day and half a week."[44] Here the couple's reduced income was a consequence of her husband's short-time work, but it was also the result of her own re-duced wages brought about by the change in production. Even skilled workers such as this mender suffered a loss in income when they were shifted to work on ordinary knitted goods.

Valdour's observations concerning wages confirm the inferiority of women's wages in relation to men's: women's were 40 to 54 percent less. He estimated that a family of three needed 2,400 francs monthly income to live.[45] If we compare the daily wages reported by Valdour, and the daily unemployment allowance awarded to a head of household in 1932, we can appreciate to what extent workers suffered a loss of income. According to Valdour, a couple, com-posed of a knitter and a bonnetière could normally earn a minimum of 33 and 18 francs, respectively, or a total of 51 francs per day; the same couple unem-ployed would receive 11 francs a day, 7 francs for the head of household and 4 francs for his wife, whether she was unemployed or a housewife. Clearly, there had been a dramatic decline in income. In any case, the rules governing the unemployment fund stipulated that total benefits could not exceed half the wages earned on the last job, including family allowances.

It is likely that during the depression many unemployed knitters, whose wives continued to work, became fully conscious that a couple could not live on a women's low wages. Subsistence wages forced many women textile

44. Ibid., 188.
45. Ibid., 191.

workers to look for marginal outside work. Oral testimony underscored their resourcefulness in finding work while on short time. One bobbin winder related that during weeks when they stopped work two days a week in one mill, she would try to find extra hours on those days in other small mills.[46] Her husband was working short time, so the couple needed her pay. During these same years at the height of the depression, Suzanne Gallois had great difficulty in finding work.[47] As a union leader, she was virtually blacklisted by millowners and was forced to seek private domestic work.

In general the decline in family income forced many textile workers to look for work wherever they could. Working as an extra hand or as a replacement worker became as characteristic of men's work as it had always been for women. The depression did not significantly change the way some women worked—it only accentuated the discontinuities, making women's relation to their jobs more tenuous. But at no time was there any competition between men and women for jobs. Even during the economic crisis the sexual division of labor within the mills and workshops continued to operate, so that women were never put to work on the knitting machines. However, the reality of unemployment during the depression, the way it was lived and experienced by women in Troyes, bore little resemblance to the ways in which the legitimacy of married women's work was publicly debated at this time. Clearly, women textile workers had no choice but to work.

Women's Right to Work

During these depression years, the French government considered taking measures to limit married women's work, similar to those in neighboring Italy and Germany. Such proposals could be partially attributed to the action of various pressure groups supporting such policies. Catholic social organizations in particular multiplied their efforts in favor of returning married women to the home and family. Support for their position came from pronatalists and demographers who voiced their concern that the French birthrate be revived. By the 1930s other conservative groups had joined the campaign. Experts in home economics such as Eve Baudoin, argued that working outside the home was not conducive to a family role for a mother, who was idealized as "la

46. Testimony from Mme Chailloux, interview, 1983.
47. Testimony from Suzanne Gallois, interview, 1984.

femme gardienne du foyer."[48] Her arguments linked France's low fertility with women's waged work. But in her strategy Baudoin went one step further than most natalists by seeking to revalorize housework, to give it the professional status that she claimed many working-class men denied it.[49] In a similar effort Catholic social organizations offered home-economics training for working-class women and urged a maternal wage or special allocation for the mother who stayed home to look after her family. When such a measure was finally voted in on November 12, 1938, it appeared more as an element of family welfare policy than as an effort to limit women's work.

A counteroffensive on this issue was launched by radical and reformist feminist groups who supported women's right to work. The Ligue française du droit des femmes (LFDF) campaigned from 1933 against government measures that would limit women's advancement, particularly in public administration, where their jobs were threatened. The league pointed out that women were more frequently unemployed than men, since employers gave preference to men, and that statistics underestimated the numbers of women laid off. Cécile Brunschvicg, militant suffragist and leader of the Union française pour le suffrage des femmes (UFSF), denounced protective legislation as an insidious way of limiting women's right to work.[50]

Feminists found support for their positions at the CGT, which in 1933 adopted resolutions in favor of women's right to work. In Troyes, the CGT newspaper, *L'Aube Ouvrière,* addressed women workers through a special "Tribune Féminine" that gradually became a regular feature of the paper as the local unions worked toward unity. Several of these articles were reprinted from the national edition of the socialist *Le Peuple;* others were written by women authors affiliated with such feminist and women's rights organizations as the LFDF.

Four themes predominated, revealing the growing interest that unions showed toward issues concerning women. Class and gender were treated in ways that suggest that the union was experimenting with what line to take. The CGT, in contrast to the CGTU, had no model to offer working women. A

48. Eve Baudoin was the author of *La mère au travail et le retour au foyer,* published in Paris in 1931. Another champion of professionalizing housework, Paulette Bernège, was inspired by Taylor's ideas and sought to apply them to streamlining housework through the use of new domestic appliances. See Martin 1987, 89–106.

49. Baudoin 1931, 144.

50. See "La CGT et les revendications féministes," *Le Droit des Femmes,* June 1934. See also the discussion in Bard 1995, 313–26.

first major theme concerned the new 1932 law on family welfare benefits (*allocations familiales*). Most articles on this subject considered women workers in their capacity as housewives (*ménagères*), urging them to make good use of the law, to beware of its detractors, and to consider the worker's contribution as a "productive investment" that required women to become family finance managers.[51] As unemployment increased, some articles supported married women's return to the home, borrowing Paulette Bernège's arguments in favor of rationalizing housework. The union demand for the forty-hour week was proposed as a solution for women workers to get ahead on their household chores: "Think about all the things you would be able to do at home during those two free days. Make your home beautiful, do your washing, repair your clothes, give your children more of the time they have needed during your absence."[52] All these arguments presupposed an idealized domestic situation that women workers might have dreamed of, but that bore little relation to the double-breadwinner reality of working-class life.

Women millworkers' "double exploitation," or double day, formed a second closely related theme in *Aube Ouvrière*. Here the supporting arguments were more subtly presented, but often contradictory. It was recognized that women worked in factories out of necessity and that male wages were often insufficient to support the family. Moreover, women had the right to work, even if they would often be better off at home. "We respect freedom too much to argue that women should be excluded from the right to work in factories, even if they are not in competition with men; but wouldn't their independence be better safeguarded in their true role as mother at home?"[53] The contention that women were doubly exploited presented a double bind. On the positive side, it revealed union leaders' thinking about women's inferior wages and their defense of women's right to work. On the negative side, the argument anchored women in their first attribution as housewives and homemakers, their "true role." Viewed in this way, women's right to work became an "elastic" one that might be withdrawn according to economic circumstances.[54]

A third theme reflected the national and parliamentary debate on protective legislation regarding children and pregnant women working in factories. The debate had been revived within the context of shift work, a practice that

51. *Aube Ouvrière*, March 1931, January–February 1933.
52. Ibid., April 1, 1933.
53. Ibid., May 14, 1933.
54. Article signed Suzanne Ch., *Aube Ouvrière*, November 15, 1933.

unions in Troyes had denounced in vain. Articles in both *Aube Ouvrière* and *L'Ouvrier Textile,* the national union weekly, treated the issue of protective labor legislation in terms of the class struggle: "[W]orking women's suffering, bourgeois women's happiness," announced an article in the national textile union paper. Historically, such legislation had been a divisive issue for women workers, because it raised gender and class differences in ways that challenged their right to work. Advocates of protective legislation within the unions found ready allies among conservative pronatalist pressure groups and social welfare reformers.

Finally, the question of how to organize women workers was the object of several articles in the CGT press, since it was a politically important and timely issue for unions. The tone was at first reproachful: "[O]ur demand for 'equal pay for equal work' had little appeal up until now, due to our own indifference and inertia," wrote a woman militant in 1932.[55] Other authors attributed women workers' perceived indifference to collective action to their lack of political education and to their inexperience with union tradition, claiming that women felt indifferent "because women workers did not find the support they needed [in unions]— . . . union propaganda ignored them—[and] more especially because our women comrades themselves did not believe in the necessity of regrouping."[56] The message was clearly that working women had to be convinced of the need to turn to unions for support.

The CGT's propaganda efforts to reach out to women workers during this period seem condescending when compared to the appeals made by the CGTU. Given the slump in union membership in the early 1930s in Troyes, the CGTU renewed its efforts to recruit new members among women textile workers. But, as militant Suzanne Gallois affirmed, many workers of both sexes hesitated to join the union for fear of losing their jobs. In the columns of the *Dépêche de l'Aube,* union leaders tried to reverse the current. They showed a willingness to listen to men and women at work and to publish their daily struggles on the job. In a column titled "Voix des usines" (Millworkers' voices), workers' letters related complaints of employer control, foremen's bullying practices, and a variety of hidden wage cuts, often giving anonymous and direct expression to many women's grievances. One example concerned the practice of wage deductions called "pourcomptes," a practice that had been denounced in the 1900 strike as an injustice. Another complaint targeted a

55. Ibid.
56. *Aube Ouvrière,* July 1934.

harsh forewoman known as "casque d'or" or the "lieutenant in skirts" who worked at the Devanlay-Recoing mill. After the reunification of the CGT and the CGTU, the women's column, "Tribune Feminine," in the *Dépêche* was written by Suzanne Gallois.

Union propaganda directed at recruiting women ignored perhaps the biggest handicap for working-class women at that time: their perceived exclusion from the political sphere. One article that appeared in June 1936 in the *Dépêche de l'Aube,* titled "Les femmes et la politique," charged that men were in part responsible for women's reluctance to unionize and become involved in politics.[57] The author claimed that there were many preconceptions about, and prejudice against, women who were involved in politics, based on the assumption that this was not their proper place. Why didn't women attend political meetings, the author asked? Her answer to this question enumerated many of the gender norms attributed to women at that period: "No woman can claim to lead a balanced life, neither the woman who reduces her life to being a mother, the woman-ovary, nor the woman who is only a wife, the woman-sex, nor the one who is only 'coquette,' the decorative-woman, nor the woman-stomach, none of these one-dimensional characters, a kind of monster whose development has hypertrophied around one function at the expense of others. And how many men could be said to resemble women in this respect. . . . Male comrades, don't you think that you've kept your wife on the margins for too long? She isn't interested in politics? Whose fault is it?"

THE POPULAR FRONT IN TROYES

The election of François Mitterand to power as a Socialist president of France in 1981 revived interest in the Popular Front as a government, if only to connect and to legitimize the two experiences of the Left in power. The result was to strengthen the mythic quality of worker mobilization in June 1936 and to celebrate the Popular Front in a commemorative way that reclaimed a revolutionary precedent, but that also, as one historian has argued, weakened historical analysis of the events.[58] For Julian Jackson, however, the mythic quality of the event represents one of its strengths: "[T]he myth of the Popular Front was in an important sense its truth. It was lived as a myth, as a

57. Ersée [pseud.], "Les femmes et la politique," *La Dépêche de l'Aube,* June 6, 1936.
58. This problem has been suggested by Noiriel (1986, 153).

great revolutionary pageant, and what it said about itself is no less significant than what it achieved: its words were among its most important acts."[59]
The approach taken here is to examine both words and deeds, but also to
demonstrate the fragility and weakness of an alliance constructed among
divided political forces. It was, in fact, partly a defensive movement initially
mobilized in opposition to fascism, as Jackson has also emphasized. The success of the movement has to some extent masked the deep divisions within the
Left that had to be overcome in order to forge that alliance.

The victory of the Left in Troyes can be viewed as an integral part of the
national revolutionary pageant of mobilization against fascism and social inequality. But the significance of a local study like this one lies in looking within
the microcosm for explanations of, and links to, broader events at the national
level. From this analytical perspective, the Popular Front in Troyes confirms
and expands much of what is already known. Voters in the department of
the Aube overwhelming supported Popular Front candidates in May 1936,
with Radicals predominating among those elected. It was one of twenty-nine
departments throughout France in which all elected representatives supported
the Popular Front.[60]

However, the particularities of the popular movement in Troyes are here
evoked by a militant witness, Suzanne Gallois, whose testimony, together with
that of other actors, highlights the difficulties workers faced in transforming
social relations, both in the workplace and in the political sphere. These difficulties may be partly explained by the continued class antagonism noted
in the previous chapters. But even if the same social forces—millowners and
workers—faced off in an adversarial relationship once again, each group had
its own internal divisions and contradictions to overcome. We will examine
the stages in this process of mobilization, a process that depended on the construction of political unity, first at the level of the left-wing political parties,
then at the level of the unions. Leadership in this process came from the controversial and charismatic figure of René Plard, a dissident communist who
was elected both deputy and mayor of Troyes. Attempts to create a unified
movement of the Left could not have succeeded without him, but he also

59. Jackson 1988, xii.
60. See the maps of the May 1936 elections in Lefranc 1974, 539–41. The Popular Front was
in the majority in most of the north, the center, and the Midi (with the exception of the massif
Central) and found little or no support in the west, much of Alsace-Lorraine, and several departments in the east.

represented its central weakness. His support assured the success of the sit-in strikes of June 1936 in Troyes, which led to the collective bargaining agreement established in the knitted goods industry. But the particular problems that emerged concerning its application demonstrate that millowners in that town represented a formidable adversary.

Given the overwhelming feminization of the workforce by 1936—34.2 percent for France as a whole, 57 percent for the textile industry in the Aube—women workers had a numerically strong part to play in these events. In Troyes, women textile workers joined massively in the demonstrations, although they did not exercise any political responsibilities. As in the rest of France, in Troyes political and union leaders were in great majority male. This very fact raises the question of gender solidarity in the strikes and factory occupations, in the elaboration of specific grievances for women workers in the negotiations, and finally in the recruitment and unionization of women over the long term.

Images of the Popular Front have produced a paradigmatic picture of collective action and unity. Social reality was, in fact, much more complex. In an effort to reach some understanding of this complex situation, we will call on testimony from actors in these events. Workers' memory of the strikes in June 1936 were strongest among those who were primary actors. Because there were few women workers among the political activists, their experiences of the strikes were different from men's.[61] For men, the Popular Front was marked by divisions and rivalries among leaders, and by the difficulties in achieving social gains.

The Mobilization of the Troyes Working Class

Of the many factors that led to the historic Popular Front movement in Troyes, by far the most important were unemployment and the resultant economic hardship of the depression. The loss of income from work, demonstrated in the preceding section, constituted the reality of working-class life. Daily privations, the sharing of work, and the interdependence of family members when it came to relief benefits formed the daily experience of all workers' families. Left-wing political party leaders evoked this suffering in their appeals for unity in the struggle against fascism. Thus several leaders translated the theme of unemployment into political terms by associating fascism with capitalism at

61. For an analysis of the gender differences in the experience of these strikes, see Reynolds 1996, chap. 5.

the local level. This argument located the struggle against fascism in concrete economic terrain that was less abstract than the defense of republican democratic institutions, but nonetheless important. The latter argument took on greater importance later.

Antifascism thus became a strong mobilizing theme. In 1933 Pierre Brossolette, a local SFIO leader, declared in *Le Petit Troyen* that "the profound meaning of fascism is to crush the working class, to destroy its organizations, to silence political liberties."[62] But it was primarily René Plard who proposed mobilizing the Left's forces on this theme of antifascism. "More than the armed groups of De la Roque, fascism is identified with unemployment, wage cuts, humiliation in the mills, poverty maintained by the dominant class," he wrote in *Le Rappel de l'Aube* in January 1935. The political mobilization of the Left in the Aube also garnered strength from its opposition to the Troyes millowners, associated in the eyes of left-wing leaders with the organized fascism of extreme Right groups in the Aube. The antifascist meeting organized on February 8 in Troyes, in reaction to the events of February 6, 1934, in Paris, reworked the link between fascism and capitalism in an effort to build unity and appeal to the townspeople.

Several right-wing organizations were active in the Aube, groups ranging from the Action française and the Croix de feu, to the Jeunesses patriotes and Dorgères's peasant defense committees; several of these groups had overlapping membership. By far the largest of these groups were the Croix de feu, with some thirty-five hundred members in the department, and the Jeunesses patriotes. They were well organized, very mobile, and armed.[63] Soon they were exerting such pressure on political life in the town that antifascist vigilance committees, called *volontaires de la liberté*, were created in several neighborhoods for worker self-defense. These volunteer committees played a role in distributing information and in retaliating against right-wing incidents in the streets. Clashes with fascist groups typically occurred on Sundays as weekly newspapers were being hawked in the street. When René Plard became mayor of Troyes in May 1935, he immediately banned all public meetings of these

---

62. *Le Petit Troyen*, April 20, 1933. Pierre Brossolette, whose family came from the Aube, trained as a historian at the *école normale* before becoming a political journalist and a specialist on foreign policy for *Le Populaire*. He joined the SFIO in 1928 and became politically active in the Aube. At the outbreak of World War II he joined the Resistance and worked under de Gaulle as a liaison officer. He was arrested in January 1944 and died under torture without betraying his mission. See Baroin 1970.

63. Ibid., 100.

extreme Right groups in the town. The Right was forced to move its followers and political activity to the countryside, where it found a significant
constituency among peasant farmers.[64] But workers and militants on the left
believed that these fascist groups also had local support from industrialists
and shopkeepers. To what extent textile manufacturers in Troyes were implicated in the support of these extreme right-wing groups is a question that has
never been satisfactorily addressed in local histories. While police reports document the presence of millowners at private meetings of such groups, in which
rising anxiety was expressed over leftist attacks against traditional Catholic
values—"famille, patrie, réligion"—there is no convincing evidence of financial
support.[65] Yet because these relatively small groups were armed and could
mobilize larger numbers from neighboring departments—as they did for a
June 1935 meeting at the outskirts of Troyes—they were considered to pose a
real threat to the Popular Front government in town.[66] The leading speaker
at these rallies was André Mutter, a lawyer, who worked with the Dorgères
peasant defense committees, primarily in the western part of the Aube. In June
1936, Mutter became head of the right-wing Parti social français.

The traditional republican Right was represented by a group called l'Alliance démocratique, led by a millowner, Léon Boisseau, who had been elected
as one of the deputies from the Aube in 1932. These self-designated social
republicans favored the established order in the name of "democratic and
republican principles, hostile to any reactionary movement . . . against the
Revolution"; they also condemned state intervention in industrial capitalism.
Their opinions were expressed in the newspaper *La Tribune de L'Aube*. The
Radical newspaper *Le Petit Troyen* regularly attacked the *Tribune* for being
equivocal about its party's political alliances, particularly during the municipal
elections of May 1935.[67]

64. Couvreur 1973, 72–76; Jeannette Petitjean, "1935," *La Dépêche de l'Aube,* May 23, 1986;
ADA SC 4251.

65. Report from commissaire spécial in Troyes to prefect, May 20, 1933; and letter from the
Ligue des familles nombreuses to prefect, December 12, 1934, in ADA SC 4251. See also Baroin
1970, 100.

66. The meeting, organized by the Croix de feu and the Jeunesses patriotes, rallied some
twenty thousand people in Barberey. The *volontaires de la liberté* were posted as guards at roads
entering Troyes. See Couvreur 1973, 74. André Mutter later joined the Resistance, and at the end
of the war he was elected deputy from the Aube on a right-wing list. Baroin 1970, 431–32.

67. The Radical deputy Emile Brachard raised the issue at several electoral moments, notably
during the municipal elections of May 1935, at the time that the Tribune announced its support
for an "independent list." See his editorial in *Le Petit Troyen,* May 5, 6, 7, 1935.

The unifying theme of antifascism could not mask, however, the profound divisions among the three left-wing political parties in the Aube, and especially the political rivalries among their leaders. Since the 1920 split, the SFIO maintained a relatively small following in the Aube that centered around Mayor Emile Clévy at the Troyes town hall. In all, the Fédération socialiste in the department had only 350 carded members, and their local leaders maintained a constant public hostility toward the communists. By far the most important local socialist figure was Pierre Brossolette, who worked in Paris as a radio journalist, and joined the staff of *Le Populaire* in 1938.[68] The Radical Left possessed somewhat stronger support, thanks to the influence of native son Edouard Herriot, but its three thousand members came primarily from a rural base. In the 1932 elections, three Radical deputies were sent to the Chamber from the Aube. In 1929, the Communist Party (PCF) had been by far the largest urban-based political force on the left, with more than 3,000 members, including 2,140 in Troyes. They dominated the CGTU textile union and established several cells in the larger mills. Their influence also extended into cultural and leisure organizations, specifically two sports clubs and a marching band, and they were also active members of the workers' consumer cooperative the Laborieuse. Suddenly in 1929 their organization declined rapidly, as a result of the abandonment of their most influential leader, René Plard, and the arrest of several militants for antimilitarist propaganda. By June 1932 the police reported that the local PCF in Troyes was "inexistent or totally inoffensive" because of Plard's action, to the point that the remaining members were "incapable of fomenting a strike, demonstrating in the street, or mobilizing its few members."[69]

In fact, Plard's desertion deeply fractured the PCF in Troyes, and this internal dissension would be an important factor in the balance of power within the Popular Front in Troyes. It harmed the communist cause, sapped its membership, and created profound distrust among former comrades. Plard distanced himself from the positions of his party's leadership in 1930 and founded

68. "Pierre Brosselette (1903–1944) is a neglected political figure who died young in the Resistance. A collection of his press articles and radio broadcasts has been recently published, revealing his firm stand against fascism in the 1930s and a new, more strident voice as a resistant, calling upon the French to unite behind General de Gaulle. See *Pierre Brosselette, Résistance (1927–1943)*, Guillaume Piketty, comp. Paris: Odile Jacob, 2001.

69. Police files providing biographical data on the local militants portray the diversity of its local members: 33 men and 5 women, including fifteen textile workers, four railroad employees, a doctor, a retired primary school teacher, three manual laborers, two café owners, and so on. See ADA SC 4251.

a group, les Amis du Rappel, and a newspaper called *Le Rappel de l'Aube*.[70] From this new base he openly adopted the positions of Jacques Doriot in favor of unity of action against fascism. Doriot had voiced public criticism of the PCF line "class against class," adopted in 1927 under pressure from Moscow, and had urged forming an alliance with the socialists. Plard published articles by Doriot in the *Rappel de l'Aube*, thus giving him a wider constituency than his base in the working-class suburb of Saint-Denis. Doriot was still a man of the dissident Left until June 1936, despite his expulsion from the party in 1934.[71] Plard himself was excluded from the Troyes PCF in July 1930, and despite the personal intervention in his favor by national PCF leaders who came to plead his cause in Troyes, he was again excluded in May 1932. Plard gathered around him other ex-members of the PCF (those who had resigned or had been excluded), and some socialists. In 1932 Plard was elected deputy from Troyes, after having finally joined the Parti d'unité prolétarien (PUP), a party with ten deputies in the Chamber. While Plard's political behavior was extremely divisive, even contradictory, it needs to be understood in the context of an ideological crisis that affected many intellectuals of this period, intellectuals whose shifts of opinion often led to tragic consequences. This was not the case for Plard. In June 1935 he suddenly broke off all relations with Jacques Doriot, who had by then moved from the extreme Left toward the extreme Right. But Plard's political turnabout had by then severely damaged relations within the local PCF.

The existence of this fourth political force on the left, splitting from the PCF, was an original feature of the Popular Front in Troyes, the more so because of the presence of Plard as the predominant political leader. He had been elected deputy in the PUP in 1932 with more than 50 percent of the votes in Troyes, and he won reelection handily in May 1936; popular confidence was renewed in May 1935 when he was chosen mayor of Troyes. He was therefore one of the major artisans of the Popular Front in Troyes, and certainly its most popular leader. Plard worked to construct unity of action against fascism, but on a basis that would unify left-wing parties and restore the confidence of the working class in political organizations. As a first step he brought about a rapprochement between his group, les Amis du Rappel, and the socialists. This early, daring attempt at unity was later extended to include those in other left-wing parties who agreed to participate in his group's actions.

70. In 1932 the *Rappel de l'Aube* had a circulation of eight thousand copies, and his group Les Amis du Rappel numbered twenty-five hundred members in 1934 (Couvreur 1973, 25–27).
71. Soucy 1995, 211–12. See also Burrin 1986.

For communist organizations in the Aube, Plard's defection had disastrous consequences for party membership. Suzanne Gallois commented with bitterness on the extreme isolation of her party at this time: "[H]e damaged us considerably . . . we were reduced to 28 Communist Party members in Troyes." There was undoubtedly a generational effect at play here, since those who remained in the party were young and did not share the older members' admiration for Plard. Moreover, Plard publicly supported Doriot when on June 14, 1934, the latter came to a meeting in Troyes. This provocation resulted in a violent clash and exchange with local communist militants who attempted to disrupt the meeting. When commenting on the Popular Front victory in Troyes and Plard's election, Suzanne Gallois reflected on her complex and contradictory position: "[W]e were forced to work alongside him, and at that time I was the only woman political activist, so I was not going to be pushed around."[72] Her testimony stressed the passionate manner in which Plard's rupture with the PCF in Troyes had been experienced, and the real obstacles it posed to re-creating unity on the left. The very fact that she was a woman militant, the only prominent one in the political arena in Troyes, and her consciousness that politics was a male world, gave a gender dimension to the power relations of the period. Generally, women did not have political clout, because they did not even have political rights. But it can be argued that strongly committed women such as Suzanne Gallois exercised political roles through visible political action in ways that challenged the apparent "secure male monopoly." She was an actor to contend with in the political arena. It is important to stress that there were many women during the interwar years who had joined political parties and were actors without formal rights. And some were more visible than others.[73]

The fact that such important political cleavages existed between several prominent political leaders on the left, including union activists, implied a fragile and precarious unity of the Popular Front movement in Troyes from the outset. Perhaps for this very reason workers did not always place confidence in their leadership. Instead, they manifested their own profound discontent with

72. Testimony of Suzanne Gallois, interview, 1984.
73. Siân Reynolds (1996) has argued that among those women who were committed to political roles, their participation in politics did not depend on the vote. They were political actors during this interwar period: "The male monopoly of politics in France at this time was not secure. . . . It was being infiltrated, amended, influenced in a multitude of ways, some visible, like the appointing of women ministers, others less obvious but perfectly discoverable once one starts looking" (226). See also Bard 1995.

the millowners in conflicts that took place outside organized union and party activism. Between February 1934 and June 1936, short wildcat strikes erupted against wage cuts, against the hiring of scabs, and in protest against employers' attempts to increase productivity.[74] These spontaneous offensive strikes, often involving the demands of worker subgroups, such as the young rebrousseurs, suggest the deep popular aspirations for change and the store of energy that political leaders would attempt to draw upon. Popular mobilization proceeded by stages.

Building Support for Unity

To follow the various stages leading to unity on the left we need to turn back to the violent events of February 6, 1934, in Paris when right-wing and fascist leagues broke away from their demonstration and marched on the National Assembly. In the wake of these events, a demonstration in Troyes was organized at the Bourse du Travail on February 8, at the initiative of the socialists and Plard's group, les Amis du Rappel. The organizers sought to rally all republican political forces in the town. In fact, many of them did participate, with some eighteen hundred to two thousand people demonstrating their desire to establish unity in the struggle against fascism. The meeting's agenda was formulated in terms that evoked a sense of urgency and, simultaneously, a wide appeal:

> [T]he people of Troyes declare:
> —that they will oppose by all available means this banditry, they will bar the route to economic and financial groups and to fascist reactionaries. They will abandon the mills, the workshops, the offices, to respond to a call for worker mobilization.
> —in liaison with manual and intellectual workers the people decide a general strike of all trades for February 12 . . .
> —the people demand the dissolution of all fascist leagues, considering that the institution of fascism would bring about an increase in poverty and unemployment, the massive reduction of wages, the

74. *L'Aube Ouvrière*, July 1, 1934, reported that a referendum had been proposed by the director of the Devanlay-Recoing mills to his personnel on setting up an uninterrupted workday, that is, with only one half hour pause for lunch. The mill employed an overwhelming majority of women for whom this proposal was incompatible with their family responsibilities.

negation of all personal liberties; the people of Troyes clearly affirm that in the event of any counterrevolutionary action by the privileged bourgeoisie, the proletariat will take determined action in favor of a social revolution coming to power.[75]

The manifesto was drafted in terms that would rally the greatest number of supporters among the working class, with its populist references to "the people of Troyes" and "intellectual and manual workers." There was no effort to analyze the causes of fascism. Rather, the manifesto was a call to action, stressing the consequences that would result, linking the economic to the political, and declaring that the people were ready to carry out a "social revolution." By translating fascism into unemployment and wage cuts, by linking economic and political consequences, the unions and political parties sought to mobilize workers across trades and across the political spectrum on the left.

It is significant that there was no direct appeal to women, as citizens or as workers, in this manifesto. What meaning did the authors of this text intend to convey by their use of the word *peuple,* a term already freighted with positive republican values? Legislation granting women political rights had been shelved by the Radical government on the pretext that there was no urgency and no consensus even among women. But when appeals were made to women to join in political action, these appeals were often formulated in gender-neutral or universalist terms that were deemed inclusive. To be sure, there were few women political activists on the scene in Troyes during this period. There were four women among the few remaining members of the PCF in Troyes. All were wives of militants and known to the police, who monitored their public activities. Thus, when Suzanne Gallois bicycled out from Troyes to attend a meeting of one of the extreme Right groups in the countryside—and to counter their arguments publicly ("porter la contradiction")—her presence was reported by the police. Women's attendance at political meetings drew police attention as something exceptional, all the more so when women actually spoke in public.

A street demonstration of considerable strength followed the February 8 protest, rallying a crowd of between three thousand and five thousand people, according to the sources.[76] More important, however, were the meetings,

75. Couvreur 1973, 45.
76. Speakers at the meeting included representatives from the PCF, the SFIO, the Radical Party, the Jeunesses radicales, the CGT, the CGTU, and the Ligue des droits de l'homme. The

public demonstrations, and rallies that ensued. Once the dynamic toward unity of political action was created, worker mobilization gained momentum. Thus an action committee of all left-wing organizations called for a protest strike on Monday, February 12, at the same moment as the one organized by the CGT in Paris. For textile workers alone (knitting mills, spinning mills, and dyeworks combined), the police estimated that a total of 13.5 percent of the workforce (totaling some thirteen thousand workers) went out on strike.[77] Strike action varied in relation to the mill, but the highest proportion of strikers was to be found in the largest mills, such as Mauchauffée and André Gillier. The CFTC refused to participate, invoking their opposition to a politically motivated strike. The account in the socialist *L'Aube Ouvrière* swelled the numbers of those participating and stressed employers' threats of repression, aimed at discouraging strikers: "Despite the CFTC posters announcing its opposition to the strike, thus joining sides with the employers and the fascists, despite the millowners' announcements in the press that their mills would remain open, despite the threats like those at the Marot dyeworks, that any absent worker would be fired, more than ten thousand workers stopped work in the mills, offices, workshops, and stores of the town."[78] While the strike was far from the "indisputable success" of the parallel events in Paris (as Georges Lefranc has described it), the afternoon demonstration in Troyes was impressive. The CGT had appealed for discipline and calm.

Yet divisions continued to plague the building of a local political coalition. The socialists, the communists, and Plard's group signed a pact of unity and action against fascism on July 29, 1934, creating an overarching antifascist committee of vigilance. This committee spawned local action groups that politicized workers' neighborhoods, and by January 1935 it was renamed the Committee of the Popular Front. This group provided an active network for organizing antifascist meetings and disrupting those on the right. Yet each party presented its own list of electoral candidates for the initial round of voting, first for the municipal elections in May 1935, and then for the legislative elections in 1936. In the runoff election, the Left rallied behind a single candidate. In May 1936, the incumbent Radical deputy, Gentin, who was close

---

police estimated the number of demonstrators at three thousand, the organizers at five thousand. See ADA SC 4260; Couvreur 1973, 31–36.

77. AMT 2J 49. Couvreur offers higher strike figures: 60 percent among textile workers and metalworkers, 80 percent among construction workers, 75 percent at the PTT, and 50 percent among teachers. However, she does not cite her sources.

78. *L'Aube Ouvrière*, February 15, 1934.

to party leader Edouard Herriot, maintained his seat on a moderate program of defense of the Republic. René Plard was also reelected deputy, with 72.7 percent of the vote in the first and second cantons of Troyes, identifying himself with the national Popular Front program.[79] With his double mandate as deputy mayor, it was Plard who claimed to represent the values and interests of Popular Front democracy in Troyes. Although he performed with revolutionary spirit in his activities as mayor, he remained a singular and contradictory person.

At the union level, the political situation was also complex, and unification took place in stages. Labor unrest and demonstrations had erupted when millowners announced another wage cut in August 1934. When a strike broke out in Aix-en-Othe, a small production center near Troyes, activists from both the CGT and the CGTU contested the strike leadership. The national textile union intervened to create the basis for reunification by means of a union cartel. This structure served to coordinate the unions' action in defense of wages and employment. By progressively building support for unity through concrete action—for example, the twenty-four-hour strike on September 7, 1934, and the congress of unemployed workers in January 1935—reunification was finally achieved at the local level. Official union reunification took place in Troyes in December 1935. During this process, the Syndicat du textile drafted a *cahier de revendications* (set of demands) with the help of employed and unemployed workers that was submitted to the Chambre syndicale patronale in February 1936.

The Strike Movement of June 1936

The strikes of June 1936 undoubtedly constituted the most massive strike movement in French history. One contemporary characterized them as "a social explosion," conveying their immediacy and their scale.[80] However, in Troyes, the strikes in the textile industry clearly had a prehistory: they were an extension of the labor unrest that had erupted earlier in the year. Nine strikes had broken out between January and the end of April 1936 over issues of wages. All of them were spontaneous, not instigated by the unions, and most of them had been successfully resolved in favor of the workers. In the case of

79. Couvreur 1973, 83–95, and Baroin 1970, 201–13. The Left obtained 80 percent of the votes in the first canton of Troyes in the second round.

80. Lefranc 1966, 7. Lefranc traced the origin of this description to a historian and journalist, Lucien Romier, writing in *Le Figaro* on September 1, 1936.

the conflict at the Touron spinning mill, where there had not been a strike for ten years, workers successfully opposed the application of a rationalization plan imposed by new mill management. After a ten-day strike, men and women spinners obtained better working conditions, a guarantee of wage revisions, and recognition of the CGT as representing the workers. On May 1, 1936, most of the mills in Troyes remained closed as the strike movement reached 80 percent, in some cases 100 percent, of the workforce. The demonstration following the ritual May Day meeting at the Bourse du Travail rallied some five thousand people in the streets.[81]

The pace of events in June followed a similar pattern of spontaneous action. The first strikes in June broke out without union instigation. By June 6, the work stoppage affected thirty thousand textile workers in the Aube. The strike wave next spread to the metallurgy, and by the tenth, workers and employees in the print trade, the food industry, and department stores had also been affected. In most cases, the level of unionization was so low that the strike movement started outside the CGT. To some extent the union was taken by surprise, but union leaders acted quickly in an attempt to channel the movement and take control. As the strikes spread, the CGT convened workers at the Bourse du Travail to formulate their demands. Those demands were then drafted in a *cahier de revendications* that would serve to elaborate special grievances for negotiation by trade; union leaders subsequently redrafted them for submission to a general assembly of workers at the Bourse du Travail.

The originality of the June 1936 strikes in Troyes concerned the nature of the confrontation. In most of the knitting mills, the strikes generally persisted for several days at most, and the factory occupations often lasted only one full day.[82] This unusual situation can be explained in large part by the fact that millowners yielded immediately, when they realized that the political tide had turned against them. Perhaps they also imagined that the occupations could take a more vehement turn if they did not agree to negotiate. Some strikes in the textile industry lasted longer, accompanied by occupation of the workshops. As a general rule, between June 2, when the first strike broke out at the Bellot knitting mill, and June 9, when the first agreement was signed between the Chambre syndicale patronale and workers' organizations, the strike movement was disciplined, and work resumed. In fact, the majority of workers in the knitted goods industry returned to the mills on June 11, before Maurice

81. ADA SC 4252.
82. AMT 2J 49.

Thorez's famous call to terminate the strikes. The CGT condemned any continuing conflicts beyond the June 9 agreement and intervened to enforce respect of its wishes.

It is significant that sit-in strikes with occupation took place primarily in mills and workshops that were owned by employers who did not belong to the Chambre syndicale patronale. In these mills, working conditions were manifestly difficult. This was the case in the Devanlay-Recoing mill, where new methods to enforce work discipline and expand productivity were being applied. Moreover, the mill employed large numbers of women workers. Suzanne Gallois had organized a female workshop there in the early 1930s until the management fired her. At the Devanlay mill the occupation lasted five days, factory committees were formed, and delegates elected by workshop presented their demands. Similar action took place at the Jourdain spinning mill, where a strike erupted the same day that work resumed in the knitting mills. Men and women spinners demanded a collective bargaining agreement like those being negotiated in other textile mills, and they stayed out on strike with occupation of the mill until they obtained satisfaction, on July 15.

Another particularity of the June 1936 movement in Troyes, by comparison with France as a whole, was the fact that many of the women millworkers had already participated in collective action in the past. The tradition of workplace struggle had been part of their daily lives since the 1920s. However, divisions persisted between unionized and nonunionized workers, between women millworkers and homeworkers, and finally between those women who were willing to extend the conflict in the hope of an immediate wage increase and those who wanted to return to work.

To be sure, the phenomenon of contagion certainly played a role in the second phase of worker mobilization, as it did everywhere in France. The signing of the Matignon agreements on June 7 also had an impact. For unorganized workers in the spinning mills and dyeworks in Troyes, the scope of the national political movement allowed them to undertake collective action that would previously have seemed too risky; they wanted the collective bargaining agreements and union rights that had been promised by the government. Moreover, the character of the national strike movement favored a particular cross-gender solidarity, promoting male workers to extend their strike in order to obtain better wages for women co-workers even when they might have settled earlier.[83]

83. See Reynolds 1996, chap. 5, esp. 122–28.

The CGT's policy was to channel and control the movement as it evolved. Once the first spontaneous strikes had erupted, the union sent militants into the factories to organize, formulate demands, convene workers, and then submit their grievances to the Chambre syndicale patronale. After the joint agreement had been signed on June 9, the CGT undertook to ensure a disciplined return to work. Union leaders refused to condone subsequent spontaneous strikes, such as the one at the Gillier mills that broke out on June 12. Workers at this large mill were dissatisfied with the agreement and continued their occupation in the hope of a larger wage increase and an immediate collective bargaining agreement. Adrien Gennevois of the CGT ordered the mill evacuated, and work resumed the next day.[84] The union's watchword was, "Beware of agitators, don't stop work without permission from the union."[85]

The very fact that the strike movement in Troyes remained disciplined was noted by all observers. It can be argued that René Plard captured the moment, and through his action as mayor, he was able to influence the course of events. On June 6, Plard had posters placed in town warning the population against those who would create panic and disorder against the Popular Front government and the town leadership. In firm language, he asserted the legitimacy of the Left's victory: "The just aspirations of the working class must be satisfied. The working class is, moreover, the guardian and the guarantor of order. The mayor of Troyes has entire confidence in them."[86] Through his popularity and his electoral mandates, Plard played a dominant role in strengthening workers' positions and in resolving conflicts in their favor. To some extent he came to embody the Popular Front in Troyes. Throughout his mandate as mayor, he organized popular celebrations of the workers' victory and new versions of the Fêtes de la Bonneterie that would lend symbolic legitimacy to the working-class movement.

Workers' Experience of the Sit-in Strikes

Oral-history testimony and local press reports help to re-create the ways in which workers lived the strikes of June 1936. It is hardly surprising that those workers who were politically active, and considered themselves actors in the events, were the ones who had the strongest memory of this period as a

84. See declaration of Adrien Gennevoix, *Le Petit Troyen,* June 15, 1936.
85. Communique from the CGT, quoted in Couvreur 1973, III.
86. AMT 2J 49.

372   THE FABRIC OF GENDER

historic turning point. Even when interviewed many years later, they were able
to evoke their aspirations for transformative change. Suzanne Gallois confided her hopes during the factory occupations, and her disappointment in the
events that followed:

> The Popular Front, I was happy that these people occupied the mills.
> Ah! I was so happy! It didn't happen everywhere, but it happened at
> Devanlay and I was happy to see that, because for me as a militant
> syndicalist, this was workers' revenge against the single omnipotent
> fellow [employer], who was always present even through his under-
> lings [sous-chefs] who made life difficult for women workers. I saw . . .
> at that time an expanding labor movement, something I didn't see
> when Mitterand came to power [1981]. I was wrong, [but] I believed
> in the Popular Front because of the occupation of the mills.[87]

This reference to "revenge" against the employer conveyed the deep-seated
meaning many workers attributed to the factory occupations: their sense of
revenge felt justified by a legitimate reappropriation of the mill workshops
after the lockouts of the previous strikes. But Suzanne Gallois also expressed
the aspiration that the new Matignon agreement would transform relations
between millowners and workers: "I told myself that we were going to be
able to talk with our employers, that we were not going to be continually
treated like dogs . . . because, you know, when I started working in 1914, it
must be said, the employer was king. . . . And you can imagine that when I
saw the mills occupied, I said, now there's going to be a formidable opening,
and then the situation closed down." At the outset, such aspirations toward
change in work relations raised high expectations for the collaborative measures established in the collective bargaining agreement. For this reason the
difficulties that ensued in applying the agreement in the knitted goods industry dashed workers' hopes.

Some political actors in these events estimated that the unions did not go
far enough in their demands to employers. One militant, who did not take
part in the negotiations, expressed it this way: "When '36 came, the great
mistake we made was not to go further."[88] Both these reactions from militants seem overshadowed by the retrospective feeling that the Popular Front

87. Suzanne Gallois, interview, 1984.
88. Marcel Mathieu, interview, 1983.

movement had been a failure at the political and union level. For nonmilitants, the Popular Front had never raised such high hopes in the first place.

In fact, testimony from unorganized textile workers in Troyes raised the problem of worker solidarity. One such woman worker remembered an incident during the strike that prevented her from returning to work on June 11 as planned. A minor work stoppage had broken out without orders from the union. But in her mind it was the unions that controlled the movement for a strike whose objectives she could no longer even recall. "A stranger came ordering them to strike . . . everyone stopped working like sheep."[89] The hostility she expressed when faced with a situation she did not understand reminds us that worker solidarity even at this time cannot be assumed as a given. Women workers in small workshops had notably refused to join the strike movement.

Photographs from the period provide a powerful means of preserving the memory of the sit-in strikes. For Troyes, the period photograph most often reproduced portrays the occupation of the Devanlay-Recoing mill. The sit-in strike at this mill provoked unusual attention because of the large numbers of women workers who occupied the workshops over several days and drew up a list of their grievances.[90] Their list of demands included equal pay for equal work. In fact, the strike at Devanlay rendered women workers highly visible, popularizing their active, supportive role in the factory occupations. Accounts of this sit-in strike in *La Dépêche de l'Aube* called to mind previous bitter strikes that had taken place against the mill management, including the sequestering of the director in 1921. The newspaper took pains to underscore the reversal of Suzanne Gallois's situation: after having been laid off in a strike movement in 1933, she was now the one who returned the keys to the mill managers at the end of the occupation. To be sure, the descriptions of the occupation itself helped create a "Front Popu" myth in their evocation of workplace ambiance. The communist *Dépêche de l'Aube* recounted a celebratory mood: "Inside the mill, workers are getting unionized. Membership cards are filled out, while other workers are having fun. A jazz group plays for dancing couples; some are playing Ping-Pong in a corner; and the theater ensemble Groupe Octobre, carrying out its work of propaganda and education, makes two recreational appearances."[91] This account also underscored the propriety of sexual behavior

89. Mme Binet, interview, 1983. The incident is confirmed in the archives as a social fact. On the ambiguity of worker testimony on the June 1936 strikes, see Rhein 1977.

90. *La Dépêche de l'Aube*, June 6, 1936.

91. Ibid., June 13, 1936.

in a mill that had an overwhelmingly female workforce, noting that women workers did not occupy the mill at night. Thus the newspaper countered any suspicions of immorality that might have been leveled against striking women workers.[92] It was but a small detail, but one that mattered for the social identity of women textile workers in Troyes.

The Cultural Politics of the Popular Front

There has been much speculation and debate on the ways in which this brief experience of the Popular Front victory might have transformed working-class consciousness and identity and how the cultural policies of Léon Blum's government might have contributed. Julian Jackson maintains that the Popular Front was far more concerned with "the democratization of an existing traditional culture" than in creating an alternative one.[93] What mattered, in his view, was creating and reaching a popular audience with the political message of the moment. To these ends, intellectuals on the left, together with workers' organizations and the PCF, initiated a number of experimental theater groups and political films, many of them didactic in nature, that were directed at creating a new, even revolutionary consciousness. Such innovative cultural forms were a continuation of politics by other means, and their content was to some extent inspired by the Popular Front program. Three such elements are particularly important to our understanding of the political culture of the Left in Troyes during this period: first, performances by an agit-prop theater group among communist militants styled the "Groupe Octobre"; second, a series of political films inspired by the Popular Front that were shown at three popular cinemas in Troyes; and finally, renewed celebrations of the Fêtes de la Bonneterie, now revived for the circumstances. Each of these three cultural forms merits analysis.

The Groupe Octobre was an agit-prop amateur theater group launched by Jacques Prévert, a still relatively unknown Parisian poet and future screenwriter. Based on early Soviet-style propaganda performances for workers, the Groupe Octobre became the most celebrated activist theater group of the period and spawned several other militant groups of workers and artists by emulation. Since 1931 such groups had shared their texts and experiences through an

92. See Reynolds 1989.
93. Jackson 1988, chap. 4, esp. 126–28.

umbrella federation, the Fédération du théâtre ouvrier français (F.T.O.F.), created in 1931.[94] In Troyes, the Groupe Octobre was lead by young communist
militants who performed at popular festivals sponsored by the PCF in the
quartier bas, and notably during the sit-in strikes in the mills. Suzanne Gallois
was among the PCF militants who presented a skit called *The Tractor* in an
effort to mobilize peasants from the surrounding countryside to join with
workers in the alliance against fascism. Many of their performances included a
form of Greek chorus (*choeur parlé*) enunciating appropriate political slogans.
Such amateur plays or skits were drawn from current events to illustrate themes
of political propaganda: the relation between capitalism, war, and poverty;
pacifism; and the duplicity of the social-democratic press. But in fact, many
of these performances were not informed by clear political party directives.
Rather, they embodied a collective spirit of reaction to the polemical politics
of the times. For many workers, politics and class struggle were the order of the
day. From this perspective there was a clear continuity between the Groupe
Octobre street theater in Troyes and the political propaganda techniques
employed by Guesdist militant Etienne Pédron more than thirty years earlier.
Unfortunately, both forms of political theater have left little written trace.

By contrast, cinema was an entirely new medium for political education in
Troyes. In fact, most of the films produced between the advent of "talkies" in
1927 and the fall of the Third Republic were overwhelmingly oriented toward
entertainment and were predominately escapist in nature. Many were drawn
from the popular melodramas of boulevard theater, while others featured life
in French colonies.[95] Nevertheless, the few political films produced during the
Popular Front years have gained critical acclaim and provoked interest over
the years. There is no doubt that this brief innovative moment created new
icons of working-class culture that reached a wide public. Films by directors
Marcel Carné, Julien Duvivier, and Jean Renoir brought the world of the
working class to the popular screen, depicting everyday life in the industrial
suburbs with an almost documentary realism. These directors are notable

94. Several groups performed in the suburbs of Paris, among them les Blouses Bleues in
Bobigny. For the history of the Groupe Octobre under Jacques Prévert, see Buschbaum 1988,
36–42, and Fauré 1977.
95. For a typology of the films produced and shown during the 1930s, see Hayward 1993,
138–54. See also Andrew 1995, for a comprehensive analysis of films described by critics as
"poetic realism." Film critic and historian Jacques Siclier sees the mythic film characters of this
period, workers included, as representing the end of certain interwar illusions. For example, see
his review of *Le jour se lève* when it was shown on French television in 1970 (*Télérama,* April 24,
1970).

for their attempt to situate the working class in its own cultural environment. But the very absence of the workplace in most such films (factory life in itself was not entertaining) is striking. When the workers' world was represented, it was signified by authentic signs of work, that is, the tools and clothing of the trade. For the first time, working-class leisure emerged as a visible theme. Workers were presented through an ambient populism often evoked by public balls or scenes of dancing along the banks of the Marne to the sound of accordion music. The ubiquitous figure of Jean Gabin personified the quintessential worker *en casquette*, embodying many of the dreams and realities of workers' lives.

A number of important political and social themes were woven into the filmic narratives of the years 1935–36. By far the most significant was the dream of worker solidarity in the collective ownership of a business venture, much in the spirit of the consumer cooperative the Laborieuse in Troyes. Julien Duvivier's film *La belle equipe,* which opened in September 1936, starred Jean Gabin and Charles Vanel as two unemployed workers who win the lottery with two other friends, and set out to rebuild a leisure *guingette* along the Marne, an establishment symbolically named Chez Nous. Embedded in this dream is their desire to escape from their condition as workers.[96] However, the collective enterprise flounders on the individual fortunes and romantic attachments of its members. From this moment, the director endowed this controversial film with two possible endings: the first, a pessimistic, melodramatic one, in which Jean Gabin kills his associate in a dispute over a femme fatale; the second, an optimistic one, in which male worker solidarity and the collective dream triumph. The latter was favored by viewers in a Paris suburb after a preview screening of the film, but the two different versions continued to be shown. Contemporary reviewers criticized the ambiguity of the film's message about the workers' collective experiment, and later critics felt that its pessimism foreshadowed the failure of the Popular Front itself.[97] Textile workers in Troyes could easily have identified with many of the themes and values of

96. The national lottery had just been instituted in June 1933, in the midst of the depression, so that many workers who viewed the film must have shared vicariously in the celebration of those holding the winning ticket.

97. The dossier at the Bibliothèque du film cites several contemporary reviews, including one from *L'Humanité* that praised the first part of the scenario for its portrayal of the real difficulties of unemployed workers, but criticized the story's development, particularly the ambiguities of the cooperative's failure, interpreted by the communist critic as playing into the hands of the fascist Right, who immediately condemned any experiment with collectivism.

working-class life as represented on their local screen. *La belle equipe* was shown there during the last week of March 1937. Among the spectators present was Jacques Siclier, a historian of French cinema, who remembered much later having discovered and admired this great populist film (with its original tragic ending) along with the workers of his native Troyes.[98]

Popular Front politics also contributed to the revival of another popular cultural manifestation in Troyes, the Fêtes de la Bonneterie. By 1934, the purpose of this event was an overtly commercial one. The festival was organized to benefit the municipal fund for the large numbers of unemployed workers. The election of the queen—once chosen in a vote by her co-workers—now took place at the Bourse du Travail before an all male jury, who made their selection from among young women workers according to obvious beauty-contest criteria. Other queens elected by similar criteria in other cities and regions of France were brought to Troyes by train to be paraded about as an attraction for local business. To encourage popular consumption during the festival, shopkeepers distributed lottery tickets for every purchase costing more than ten francs, giving chances to win a Peugot automobile.[99] Clearly, for the consumer world of the 1930s, beauty queens had become the marketing agents of commodity culture.

From 1935 to 1938, René Plard, as the Popular Front mayor of Troyes, promoted a revised version of the festival. A new generation of young women had by then joined the mill workforce. The festival queens' election marked the historic victory of the Popular Front, and Plard constantly reminded the townspeople that their queen was a symbol of working-class unity. For the first time the crowning ceremony opened with the "Marseillaise," as if to demonstrate that the historic election of a socialist government had been incorporated within the republican tradition. In the festival rhetoric, the queen was metamorphosed into "la fille du peuple," a visible symbol of the new social and political order, legitimized by working-class unity under the Popular Front.[100]

Of course, maintaining continuity with the past was also important. Many speakers referred to the queen as representing those who created through their

98. Jacques Siclier, "Les lendemains qui ne chantaient pas" *L'Evènement du Jeudi*, October 14, 1993.x

99. *Le Petit Troyen*, September 6, 1934.

100. Martine Segalen (1982) finds a similar transformation of gender representations, in particular the queen's incarnation of working-class legitimacy in 1936, in the the rose queen of Nanterre.

work the riches of industrial Troyes. Rhetoric at the crowning ceremony in 1935 exhalted the work ethic: "[T]he labor of men, and in the context of our town, the labor of women, have both come to personify our working-class town."[101] And again in 1936: "The queen of the festival is the queen of Troyes labor."[102] But in the space of that one year, the Popular Front had come to power and the queen was no longer just a daughter of the Troyes working class, but rather "a daughter of the people of France." The Popular Front festival had created a new pageant from the old, and used the local symbol of a working-class queen to legitimize power. Once again the festival served its historic purpose of renewing social solidarity, and in this historic context Plard intended to integrate the working class into national politics.

Deputy Mayor Plard knew how to capitalize on these festivals to garner popular support for his policies. But he also had to contend with opposition both from within his own party and from right-wing groups. To critics in 1935 who accused him of offering "bread and circuses" to "his" working class, he replied that he sought to maintain Popular Front unity and to discourage partisan interests. At the crowning ceremony the following year, after a triumphant May Day celebration and sit-in strikes had forced the millowners to yield rapidly to worker demands, Plard praised the discipline workers had displayed during these events. He then handed the queen back to her employer, Pierre Mauchauffée, who would escort her through the town. As one journalist described the event: "[Here was] a symbolic vision of the modest woman worker taking the arm of her boss."[103] This gesture of rapprochement between capital and labor renewed one of the fundamental rhetorical strategies and illusions of the festival. In subsequent years, Plard as mayor sought to broaden the social base of these celebrations by subsidizing the festivities in working-class quarters of Troyes and in its outlying suburbs. The festival became an extension of the new August paid vacations, a legitimation of working-class leisure. We can perhaps measure the festival's success in terms of the number of activities that by the end of the 1930s mobilized the working class to celebrate leisure. Throughout the three festivals of the Popular Front, sports competitions and leisure activities replaced the corporative ceremonies organized by the Confrérie des bonnetiers during the festival's first decade. The festival

101. *Le Petit Troyen,* September 9, 1935.
102. Ibid., September 13, 1936.
103. André Seure, "Quand Troyes célébrait sa bonneterie dans la liesse populaire," *Almanach Est-Eclair,* 1990, 50.

had become, in fact, a celebration of leisure, rather than of work, and, along with leisure, a celebration of the right to consume.

The Collective Bargaining Agreement

If gendered meanings were everywhere present in the Fêtes de la Bonneterie, they were also prominently inscribed in the new collective bargaining agreement. It was the unions' task to present textile workers' collective interests and demands to the millowners and their representatives. Union leaders, emboldened by the union rights established in the Matignon agreements, did not necessarily reformulate strikers' concerns as voiced in the *cahiers de revendications*. They saw their role as establishing an institutional framework for future negotiation with employers. At stake in the process was recognition of the unions as legal representatives of the workers, a factor that millowners had been avoiding for years. The resulting contract included important guarantees, but it also left certain points open to subsequent interpretation. As a result, a number of worker grievances were laid aside or postponed in the effort to reach a general agreement. As one union leader present at the negotiations confided, "[W]e defined the trade."[104] While this was their purpose in theory, it proved difficult to fulfill in practice.

Any negotiated agreement is a product of compromise. Union leaders, acting in function of class interests, assumed an identity of interests between men and women workers. While they attempted to codify occupations in the trade within a general contract for the knitted goods industry as a whole, they failed to understand that their action limited women's work rights. The collective bargaining agreement consecrated existing gender relations and failed to correct unequal wages and women's lack of promotional mobility. While women textile workers had massively participated in the strikes, and many had been elected by their workshops as delegates to draft their grievances, their role had stopped there. None of the CGT women militants took part in the actual negotiations. It was male leaders who decided their fate.

What happened between the moment these demands were drafted and the time they were formulated for negotiation is difficult to understand, given the lack of sources.[105] Here we can only explore the steps in the negotiations.

104. Marcel Mathieu, interview, 1983. Mathieu was a leader of the Syndicat du textile CGT.
105. The archives located at the Bourse du Travail burned in 1963, and the personal archives of leading militants were either seized by Vichy authorities during the war or destroyed.

A first agreement signed on June 9 between the Chambre syndicale patronale and five textile unions reaffirmed the terms of the Matignon accords and put an end to the strikes and occupations. Millowners agreed to apply the government reforms, granting freedom of expression within the mills, the right to unionize, a forty-hour workweek, two weeks' paid vacation, and a general wage increase of 10 percent (Blum had demanded an average increase of 12 percent at Matignon).[106] More important, they agreed to negotiate a collective bargaining agreement.

In fact, employers agreed in June to negotiate a further, more detailed agreement that would cover the definition of job composition and hourly wage rates in the entire industry. But millowners were themselves divided at this time into two employers' associations. Only the traditional employers' union, the Chambre syndicale patronale, yielded rapidly when faced with the strikes and signed the agreement. While it represented the majority of millowners, the Chambre syndicale patronale was obviously weakened by division. Their members would later try to limit the extent of the agreement they had just signed and to delay application of the measures it stipulated. The second association, l'Union syndicale des industries de la maille et annexes (USIMA), grouped many of the employers of spinning mills and dyeworks who had never accepted unionization. They would fight strike action and occupations into the summer of 1936.

Over the course of the summer, discussions continued on the drafting of a collective work contract. According to the working-class press, negotiations were blocked over the question of wage scales, and discussions were suspended in mid-August. A first version of the collective bargaining agreement was signed on September 18; it would be modified by a rider on November 3. It is likely that, once again, wages were the point of contention between employers and unions.

The account given in *Aube Ouvrière* by Marcel Mathieu and Adrien Gennevois, negotiators for the CGT Syndicat du textile, stressed the issue of wages. Their goals, they said, were twofold. First, they had attempted to reach agreement on some kind of uniform wage scale for each occupation, based on similar work throughout the Troyes mills. This demand was an old one that had been formulated during the great strike of 1900. Second, they had struggled to raise "abnormally low wages" that affected primarily women's work.

106. AMT 2J 49 and *Le Petit Troyen,* June 10, 1936.

Both union leaders sought to justify their delegations' position and forestall any worker discontent that could degenerate into further strike action. Notably, they affirmed that "employers intended to impose women's wages at rates that we find unacceptable. . . . We find unacceptable, wages for bobbin winders at Fr 2.50 an hour like those now existing in certain mills."[107] They appealed for calm and discipline, reminding workers of the gains achieved since the Popular Front government had come to power.

The issue of "abnormally low wages" remains ambiguously posed. Were women's wages the only stumbling block, or were questions of skill at issue? Most likely women's wages served as a reference point in the public mind. According to George Lefranc's account, the Matignon accords stipulated "that the collective contract should fix minimum wages by region and by occupation," including "the necessary readjustment of abnormally low wages," for the purpose of "maintaining a normal relation between employee salaries and worker wages."[108] The goal was therefore to reach a minimum guaranteed wage and reduce the sizeable wage gaps between job categories.

It is important to state that women's wages in certain occupations in Troyes were not the lowest in the knitted goods industry. Some women workers in certain skilled occupations earned more than their knitter husbands, even though the women did piecework. Still others, such as the bobbin winders or those working on specialized tasks, earned poor wages. Union leaders were proud of the results they obtained in November 1936 for the latter categories of workers:

> Women workers, who for the most part had insignificant wages, will find their living standards improved. For just those working as "petites mains," that is, those unraveling threads, trimming stockings, sewing labels, etc., all those tasks generally given to older women workers, their wages can no longer be inferior to Fr 2.38 an hour, an increase of 40 to 50 percent of their former pay. The same holds true for those who were formerly called the pariahs of the textile industry, the dyers and spinners, whose starting wages will now be Fr 2.65 an hour for women and Fr 3.25 for men.[109]

107. *Aube Ouvrière*, August 1936.
108. Lefranc 1966, 152–53.
109. Article by Marcel Mathieu in *Aube Ouvrière*, November 1, 1936.

Union leaders' arguments were based on the significant wage increases that women workers would receive. Nevertheless, the agreement legitimized existing gender distinctions of skill in their definition of job composition and wage rates.

The major issue was, in fact, the relation between women's skills, unrecognized and undervalued, and their wages. The latter continued to correspond more to her status as a woman than to her place in production. For the unions, the issue was closing the wage gap by raising piece rates for women workers. During the negotiations this issue was treated as a simple retroactive adjustment of wages, rather than as fundamental gender inequality. Thus the collective bargaining agreement legitimized the existing sexual division of labor and maintained the real basis for wage discrimination. Under these circumstances, the principle of "equal pay for equal work" that had been initially formulated in the *cahiers de revendications,* remained an abstract formula that no one attempted to apply. A closer look at the ways in which men's and women's work were defined in the agreement makes these distinctions even clearer.

The text of the first collective bargaining agreement deserves a close reading. Its significance lies in the fact that it was intended to serve as a basis for future negotiations. It can be read as both a technical and a gender description of production jobs. First, the job content was codified by sex. Women's work was, as usual, sharply distinguished from men's. As a result, the definitions of job content and wages were entirely separate and gender specific. Each job in the production process was defined by sex, by the type of articles produced (stockings, socks, knitted fabric), by the gauge of the machine operated, or by the specific task executed; and on the basis of this analysis, an average piece-work rate and a minimum hourly wage was attributed.

Second, a comparative analysis of the occupations described demonstrates a striking difference in the gender representations of work. Customary work tasks for women were grouped together and classified on a scale from 1 to 8, ranging from the unskilled finishing tasks of *petites mains* to fine-gauge seaming on more difficult and delicate knitted fabric. In the effort to define more uniform job categories, skill distinctions were made to stand out ever more sharply. One job was identified simply as *travaux féminins* (women's work), characterized as unskilled, task-oriented, and manual. Without an understanding of the work process, it would have been difficult to distinguish a hierarchy of women's occupations, the nature of the task, and their place in production.

By contrast, the male occupations maintained a clearly defined hierarchy, established by function, the complexity of the machine operated, the gauge and the fabric. In October 1938 the proposals put forward by the CGT to establish a collective work contract at the national level corrected the worst errors in the definition of women's work through a more complete description of the difficulties involved in each women's job.

Third, few possibilities were acknowledged in the agreement for comparable work between men and women, possibilities that might have justified equal wages. One mixed-sex occupation did exist that gave women some technical-skill affinity with men. This occupation, one that involved operating a circular knitter, appeared to be gendered as both masculine and feminine. But in the collective bargaining agreement, a simple distinction was made: women were "knitter-minders" but not "knitter-operators," the assumption being that women could not intervene to fix the circular frames—a job on which a small number of women had been working since World War I. This distinction would lead to a wage loss for women of 20 percent.

Women's work as defined in the agreement did not allow leverage for raising the problem of gender equality. The issue appeared in the following terms: "[W]hen a woman does the same work as that generally attributed to a man, the piece rate is the same, although she could not claim the same earnings if her production is lower."[110] But this notion would remain a dead letter, because gendered definitions of men's and women's work precluded any competition. It seems evident from this text that union leaders had protected men's skills and jobs from any possible competition in the future. The skilled craft tradition, with its notion of male *métier,* had left a lasting imprint on the collective bargaining agreement.

Renewed Social Conflict

Georges Lefranc categorized the changes that intervened in the world of work in June 1936 as "the revolution through law." But were the legislated changes really revolutionary? The law did indeed require employers to recognize union rights on paper and accept wage arbitration, but their subsequent application turned out to be very problematic. Historians disagree about whether the

---

110. "La convention collective passée à Troyes le 18 Septembre 1936 entre les organisations patronales et ouvrières de l'Industrie de la Bonneterie et Industries annexes du Département de l'Aube," article 14, paragraph (d), p. 9, ADA SC 4336.

Matignon agreements forced employers to totally capitulate.[111] At the time, Blum obviously had the upper hand. But employers of large industry also had clear advantages by comparison with small business owners. In fact, in the summer of 1936 the Federation of Textile Employers, grouping thousands of small textile employers, withdrew from the national association, the Confédération générale du patronat français (CGPF).[112] Among these small employers, who felt a sudden loss of authority after the occupations of their factories, no doubt the massive strikes and the new measures by the Popular Front government raised fears of further concessions to come.

In Troyes a number of problems rapidly emerged concerning the application of the collective bargaining agreement. The principal employers' union, the Chambre syndicale patronale, which had agreed to an immediate settlement, soon prepared a counteroffensive. At issue was not only the application of the measures outlined in the agreement, but also their extension to all the knitting mills in the Aube. In fact, several employers who were not even affiliated with the two employers' unions refused to comply until October 1937, when an administrative decree made the collective contract mandatory for the entire department. A similar procedure was necessary to extend the same guarantees to homeworkers that their factory co-workers had received.

The application of the agreements presented several difficulties. Millowners delayed carrying out the restrictions on working hours as long as unemployment continued in the mills. Like all textile employers, they struggled against the limits placed on their prerogatives. More especially, they felt that the law imposing a forty-hour week lacked the flexibility necessary in their industry, with its seasonal periods of rush orders. Shorter working hours were a handicap in times when they had urgent orders to fill. In fact, in June 1937, work hours were lengthened to forty-five hours a week even though unemployment persisted. Another confrontation concerned the role within the mills of the new worker delegates, whose powers met with resistance from foremen and supervisors. The delegates found it difficult to bring conflicts before a management that was quite uninterested in applying the new rules. Millowners

111. Jackson (1988) points out that employers were not necessarily forced to capitulate at Matignon, but that they were willing to negotiate on certain points such as collective contracts, for which certain preliminary steps had already been taken in particular industries. Other issues, such as the forty-hour week and paid vacations, provoked their staunch opposition, and these issues Blum promised to institute with separate legislation that might allow for gradual introduction of the shorter workweek (264–68).

112. Ibid., 266.

frequently fired delegates, refused to negotiate wage increases, and laid off workers before the paid vacation period began. But the major issue that resurfaced time and time again during this period was wages. The 10 percent increase granted in June was rapidly absorbed by the steep rise in the cost of living in August 1936. The Syndicat du textile was determined to fight to make up what it considered to be an important loss of income. It argued that "the manufacturers who massively cut wages, who trimmed rates for certain articles, should not harbor any illusion that we are satisfied with the results obtained. Wages have been reduced by some 30 to 50 percent. We are far from what we are owed."[113] In fact, little by little the economic policies of the Popular Front led to the erosion of the increase in real wages.

A six-week strike with occupation at the Devanlay-Recoing mill in late 1936 illustrates some of the problems in applying the collective bargaining agreement. The strike was a major test case, and it involved a mill that employed some one thousand workers and that had a long history of ignoring workers' demands. The conflict broke out on November 18, 1936, over the interpretation of an article concerning wages in the collective contract. Both parties agreed to carry the dispute before the Chambre syndicale patronale, which gave a favorable opinion to the workers, and so work resumed. But on payday, workers realized that management had not abided by its agreement, and the entire workforce immediately went on strike. Management then fired a workshop delegate they considered a "provocateur marqué." Every effort at conciliation provided for by law failed, and the conflict intensified. On December 17, workers voted to uphold union action and support their delegate. Even the prefect reported to the Ministry of the Interior that the mill management had displayed "deplorable intransigence."[114] Mill managers then demanded the dismissal of three other worker delegates for their role in generalizing the strike movement. A general assembly of the personnel rejected their co-workers' dismissal, and in an effort to find a solution, the prefect proposed using the new arbitration law. The CGT accepted, putting pressure on the mill management to accept the principle. As the process began, the union abandoned its sit-in, and work resumed on January 11. But hostility between the two sides immediately defeated the arbitration process, particularly after managers accused the union lawyer, René Plard, of partisan practices in support of the workers.

---

113. *La Dépêche de l'Aube,* June 6, 1936.
114. Prefect of the Aube to minister of the interior, December 21, 1936, ADA SC 4334.

The prefect then turned to a superarbitrator, whose decision on February 5, 1937, was unfavorable to the workers' position on several counts.[115]

This conflict was exemplary in many ways. For millowners, it involved taking a firm stand against what they termed "the wind of revolution that agitated the workshops."[116] In fact, they had decided to test their own workers' resolution concerning the new measures stipulated in the collective contract. From this perspective, millowners launched a counteroffensive at the factory-floor level that was doubtless motivated by revenge against the humiliations of the past months. The mill management's offensive continued, through the use of various forms of harassment, until the outbreak of war.

During this prolonged conflict, workers at Devanlay demonstrated their confidence in the government through their tenacity, combativity, and solidarity. It was an offensive strike that mobilized some seven hundred to eight hundred workers at meetings (out of a workforce of one thousand). Moreover, it revealed exceptional worker solidarity with the delegates, who risked sanctions, and with the union leaders, who led the workers into the arbitration process. The attitude of the CGT was, in fact, conciliatory in its attempt to resolve the conflict within the new arbitration procedures established by the government. The CGT maintained this positive attitude until the famous pause initiated by Blum in the spring of 1937, followed by his resignation, a move that considerably weakened the Popular Front movement. In the fall of 1937, the union's former combativity reemerged in a new offensive against employers. But by then workers had begun to consider the relative failure of the strike at Devanlay as a cause for demobilization. In the textile industry there were seven strikes in 1937, but only three in 1938. Unemployment and hardship returned, and union membership declined significantly.

For textile workers in Troyes, the conflict at the Devanlay mills represented the real test of the collective bargaining agreement, and, more important, their defense of the Popular Front gains. By contrast, the one-day nationwide general strike that was called by the CGT on November 30, 1938, became the ultimate test of political wills at the national level. The CGT had decided to

115. According to the superarbitrator's decision, workers were responsible for striking without the legal eight days' notice; management could not require a strike indemnity because workers had lost their wages during the lengthy strike; the three delegates were held responsible and condemned to one month's suspension, and all sanctions against the mill management formulated by the CGT were refused. The arbitration procedure would be used to settle all future wage conflicts up until World War II (AMT 2J 49; Couvreur 1973, 120–26).

116. Mémoire de la Direction de Devanlay Recoing, quoted in Couvreur 1973, 123.

order the general strike as a protest against the Daladier government's decree laws, passed on November 12, 1938, that all but abolished the forty-hour week. While the CGT maintained that the strike movement would take place without demonstrations or factory occupation, as a symbolic protest, not a political movement, the government used all the repressive powers at its disposal— troop and police mobilization, threats and intimidation, requisition of rail- road engineers—to break the strike's potential momentum. Foreign-policy events weighed heavily at this juncture. Daladier had only just returned from negotiations with Hitler in Munich, and the tragic appeasement may have overdetermined the premier's reactions to the threat of a general strike. In Troyes, the strike failed miserably to mobilize workers: no absences were cited among public service employees, and in private industry, a bare 3 or 4 percent followed union orders.[117] Militants and strikers were summarily fired. Textile union leaders had regarded defense of the forty-hour week as essential because of continued unemployment and short-time work. In the textile industry nationwide, participation in the general strike was highest in the Nord (60–70 percent), and much lower in more isolated centers such as Reims, Belfort, Cholet, and Roanne (10–20 percent).[118] CGT union leaders in the Aube addressed their members on the following day, emphasizing all the media campaigns against the strike that had misrepresented its objectives, and the refusal of the CFTC to support it as well. Leaders urged textile workers to remain organized as a means to defend their rights. "The battle is not over; it has just begun," a local textile union leader proclaimed. "The union remains the bastion of future victories in the mills."[119]

While Blum remained in power, the Popular Front movement in Troyes remained united. But the fall of his government in June 1937 provoked a sharp reaction from both René Plard and local leaders of the SFIO. Plard called upon workers to protest in the streets, and in the *Rappel de l'Aube* he announced that Blum's government had been "assassinated" and that "vengeance" should fol- low.[120] At the SFIO congress in Marseilles, Pierre Brosselette, socialist leader from Troyes, expressed in passionate terms his disappointment at Blum's resig- nation: "[O]ur faith in the Party came above all from the fact that we thought

117. *Le Petit Troyen*, December 1, 1938.
118. Bourdé 1977, 207, 330. Bourdé's sources included the CGT, *Le Peuple*, and *La Vie Ouvrière*.
119. Jules Fèvre, "Dans le textile," *Aube Ouvrière*, December 1938.
120. *Le Rappel de l'Aube*, June 30, 1936.

it was not a party *like the others,* that its leader was not a man *like the others,* and that it could not fall *like the others.*" Blum replied that his government's legitimacy, while strengthened by "unprecedented popular will," was indeed a government relying on legality like the others.[121] Local Radical leaders rallied behind the Chautemps government, firm in their belief that the Popular Front was not yet defunct.

Our analysis of the Popular Front in Troyes has revealed the deep social and political cleavages within the town that can to some extent be generalized to French society as a whole during the 1930s. In this sense, Troyes can be considered a microcosm of the social polarization identified by Marc Bloch in his reflections on the Popular Front experience in *Strange Defeat*. It seems important in the case of Troyes, however, to stress the considerable political will that was exercised by actors on the left on three levels: first, to overcome political rivalries within the local Popular Front coalition; second, to combat local fascist groups who, while not numerically strong, were armed and supported by important groups of peasants, shopkeepers, and local manufacturers; and finally, to confront the antagonism of millowners after the Matignon agreements had partially eroded their power. In this highly dramatic context, René Plard assumed leadership in Troyes and played the essential role in uniting all political forces behind the Popular Front movement. He alone, and by his early initiative, was able to create a mass movement of solidarity. His dissident position in relation to the PCF was the basis for a timely overture to socialists for their collaboration in building a common front. The failure of the PCF to take this step before June 1934 was determined by Moscow's reluctance to change their tactics until then.[122] Only after the International's shift to antifascism and promoting unity at the base would communists in Troyes join the movement to unify left-wing groups. While Plard had initially questioned the party line by supporting Doriot, Suzanne Gallois had not. Both Plard's and Gallois's political actions were symptomatic of the strengths and weaknesses of the PCF during these tortured years. On the one hand, the communists' strength had been in creating a disciplined organization, in giving expression to worker discontent, and in opening their ranks to women while taking up their cause for political rights. On the other hand, the weakness shown by the PCF was to follow the political line dictated by the International

121. Jackson 1988, 274. Emphases are in the source cited by Jackson.
122. For the bigger picture, see Jackson 1988, 32–33; Eley 2002, 263–64.

and its representatives in France. Sooner or later, local communists would have to make their own decisions as the preparations for war again forced Moscow to change its strategic stance.

The gains instituted by the Popular Front for the working class in Troyes were insecure. The renewed conflict over wages and power inside the Devan-lay mill during the 1938 strike was symbolic of the Popular Front's decline. By then, millowners were aggressively undermining the transformative changes in work relations enacted by the Blum government. As the old adversarial relationship between millowners and millworkers resurfaced, more polarized than before, it resulted in what Stanley Hoffman has so astutely termed "a stalemate society."[123] For all textile workers, the wage gains of the Matignon agreement were wiped out by persistent unemployment and the rising cost of living. For women workers, the wage increases that were intended to close the wage gap between them and their male co-workers did not fundamentally alter their status. In fact, women's gains during the strike movement were negligible in relation to their impressive militancy. The collective bargaining agreement actually codified the status quo, thereby limiting women's chances for skill recognition and upward mobility. For this reason, the principle of "equal pay for equal work," formulated by many women workers during the strikes, remained an empty principle.

As Suzanne Gallois so aptly commented, the historic window of oppor-tunity for change, opened by Blum's victory and the sit-in strikes of June 1936, quickly closed. The reform measures provided by Popular Front legisla-tion were applied in the mills only in cases in which men and women workers fought to maintain them. For those union militants who did fight, they became once again targets of layoffs and repression. The period closed on tension and conflict between the political forces in the coalition. The difficult years that followed, leading to the "strange defeat" of June 1940, forced many political leaders to choose between collaboration with or resistance to the German occupation and the Vichy government. For many of the actors on the left, the choice was clear: René Plard, Pierre Brosselette, and Suzanne Gallois refused to collaborate. Plard helped organize the evacuation of civilians and the wounded from Troyes when the Germans invaded in June 1940, and then he resigned his office as mayor, taking refuge in the countryside.[124] Pierre

123. Hoffman 1963.
124. Still mayor of Troyes in 1940, Plard was present to help organize a sudden evacuation of the town on the night of June 13–14. His absence when the Germans invaded the city on the

Brosselette joined the Resistance, was arrested, and died under torture.[125] After the PCF was outlawed in 1939, Suzanne Gallois resigned from the CGT and left to join a communist-led armed resistance group in southwestern France.

Following the occupation and the war, Troyes millowners would call on rationalization and new scientific work methods in order to compete on the national and international market. These new work methods massively transformed the production process, and the resulting modernization of knitted goods production would require new infrastructure and intensive retraining of the workforce. By then, a new generation of men and women textile workers would enter the mills.

---

fourteenth was never clearly explained. Already ill, he resigned several weeks later for health reasons and left to hide in the countryside. He died in Nevers in 1946 (Beury 1980, 148).

125. Baroin 1970, 394–95.

CONCLUSION

At his Riom trial by the Vichy government in February 1942, Léon Blum defended the social reforms of the Popular Front against accusations of his "weakness in the face of revolutionary unrest."[1] In his testimony he affirmed that "far from creating divisions and disunity, [these reforms] had given workers a greater stake in the society in which they lived, created in them a love for the Republic, and a loyalty to France."[2] The significance of these contested reforms appears with dramatic urgency when viewed within the extended time frame of the present study. The extension of substantive social rights in France had been long overdue. In this regard, France had lagged noticeably behind both Britain and Germany. From this longer perspective, our analysis of the world of industrial work and production in Troyes provides an important insight into the unevenness of social justice in France, and into the complex ways it was often thwarted. We have attempted to view the struggles of Troyes textile workers within the larger framework of the process of democratization during the long Third Republic and to demonstrate the halting and incremental nature of social change. Our narrative has described advances and retreats, rather than a steady linear progression; it has emphasized the complexity, even the contradictions, in the evolution of gender and labor relations over time.

1. This phrase resumes the third count of indictment against Blum. See the trial records in Blum 1943, 126.
2. Joel Colton's (1966) paraphrase of the trial records in his biography of Léon Blum (413). See also Blum 1943, 150.

However, looking back over the sixty years since the early socialist movements of the 1880s, certain patterns of change in working-class culture in Troyes do emerge. Early in that period, despite the existence of universal male suffrage, instituted by the Second Republic in 1848, social justice had not yet been achieved by the ballot, and women were still disenfranchised citizens. The groundswell of socialist activism and labor protest at the turn of the century had challenged the Third Republic to create a "social republic," one that would be more egalitarian and confer greater respect for workers' and women's rights. To these ends, socialist militants, inspired by the goals of the revolutionary general strike, had defied authority at every level—in the mills, the town, and the state—to promote their alternative to the present parliamentary regime. For such militants, the government was a class-based bourgeois republic that effectively marginalized workers. To underscore the material base of the regime's power and influence, several dissident socialist leaders caricatured the Third Republic as the "Assiette au Beurre"—a parliamentary system that enriched politicians on fat sinecures.[3] Workers opposed this republic of self-interest to their vision of a truly "Social Republic" in which all would have a fair share through the redistribution of social and political power.

Three decades of labor militancy culminated in Troyes when textile workers mobilized behind the local leaders of the Popular Front movement, democratically elected to pursue many of the social reforms that they had long demanded. The fact that these reforms were then promulgated into law represented the promise of revolutionary change without revolution: the legitimization of workers' demands for greater social equality through elections, the parliamentary system, and a common program of action. The sheer power of the Popular Front strikes throughout France dramatically demonstrated the workers' will to remain a political force for change within the Third Republic. However brief, the sit-in strikes constituted a visible reversal of power within the mills in favor of workers' rights and signaled the potential transformation of labor relations within industry nationwide. The workers' mobilization in favor of the Blum government also provided the ultimate defense against fascism, which compromised the future of the Republic itself.

3. The metaphor evokes unmerited political jobs and easy soft money during a period of Third Republic politics that favored compromise (see Dixmier and Dixmier 1974, 9). The expression was used widely by Emile Pouget. A cartoon appeared in *Le Père Peinard* on March 28, 1897, that portrayed the clergy, judges, and bourgeois parliamentarians eating out of the same plate, while workers were sitting at the foot of the table in front of a barrel of mashed potatoes. Etienne Pédron also used it in his speeches at Guesdist meetings. See Chapter 1.

In our analysis of this long struggle for effective social and gender equality in Troyes, five major themes have emerged. The first theme reevaluates the standard linear narrative of French industrialization by emphasizing different dynamics of change and challenging the commonly accepted chronology. Our analysis of the knitted goods industry in Troyes has revealed a process of technological and industrial transformation that was relatively late, partial, and nonlinear. Throughout the Third Republic, production continued to rely not only on urban mills, but also on small domestic or artisan workshops in the suburbs and countryside. For this reason, many of the customary generalizations about nineteenth- and twentieth-century industrialization seem quite inapplicable to the case of Troyes. There was no clear transition from domestic manufacture to highly mechanized mills, from artisan workshops to larger-scale industrial ones, and finally from the production of basic goods to luxury ones, before returning to more standardized production. Technological changes in the 1880s did lead to a certain concentration of the labor force in larger urban mills as intensive mechanization peaked in 1900. But technological innovation was uneven and piecemeal. Many different types of machinery coexisted, resulting in overlapping stages of development. This "unfinished" pattern of industrialization is probably more typical of the textile and garment industry in general than that of other industries. In the system of production practiced in Troyes, the most powerful economic logic related not to technological change, but to the transformation of the labor force: the increasing employment of low-waged female labor for many of the garment-making tasks, and the reliance on a residual culture of production that transferred skills from one generation to the next. Indeed, one of the distinctive features of industrialization in Troyes was the overwhelming feminization of the labor force over the course of this long period, a feature that has continued to the present. Urban industrialization never eliminated the outwork system of industrial homework. In the process, women's work became progressively fragmented and deskilled.

Within such a system, workers' demands for a living wage often yielded meager gains as laboring men and women struggled against overall instability of income and employment throughout the Third Republic. It is therefore not surprising that life expectancy remained so low for millworkers well into the early 1920s, and notably for young women. Low wages, crowded housing, and tuberculosis all took a toll on workers' lives. Such social facts represent an important way of measuring the level of exploitation and the lack of material change. Some workers found escape and relative autonomy in small-scale traditional forms of outworking that coexisted alongside the large, modern mill. Many male artisans, such as Emile Caillot, dreamed of continuing to work at home with their families rather than sending their children into the mills. For this reason, and because of the low capital cost to millowners, outworking of this kind persisted well into the early twentieth century. But by the 1930s this ancillary form of production had virtually disappeared, and with it, the workers' dream of relative autonomy and potential social mobility.

Second, our study has underlined the salient feature of labor relations in Troyes: the aggressive behavior of millowners and the confrontational nature of their relations with workers. We have seen the millowners' continuing success in circumventing the application of social-reform laws specifying workers' rights. The recognition of unions; the arbitration of labor disputes; the reduction of working hours, notably for women; and later, the eight-hour day—all such measures were contravened with impunity by the millowners, since the government refused to intervene, except to repress worker revolts. In this sense the dynamics of change in Troyes prior to 1914 were rooted, not in political legislation, but in the social relations between millworkers and millowners. Arguably, it was only after World War I that national events and government decisions came to weigh more heavily on labor relations and industrial policies. Throughout the Third Republic, the dialectical relationship between these principal actors was played out both in the mills and in the associative life of town society itself. Periods of intense productive work, collaboration, and joint celebrations of the trade at the Fêtes de la Bonneterie alternated with disruptive strikes and protests.

Millowners' virtual monopoly over the local labor market locked workers into a situation of industrial conflict, in which the worst abuse of employers' authority resulted in lockouts. Employers organized production around the defense of their authority within the mills and the preservation of their political power and influence in the town. Many of them practiced a form of paternalism that was based, in their view, on the reciprocal ties binding workers and employers. For this reason they rejected the very notion of class conflict and refused to recognize the unions. In times of contention, the owners sought to circumvent the unions and break worker solidarity. After the strike of 1921, economic modernization lagged as millowners redirected production to dispersed rural workshops, where nonunionized workers, primarily women, accepted lower wages. Simultaneously, the owners instituted new forms of discipline and work organization to increase productivity, measures that were virtually imposed in the mills without negotiation. The millowners' aggressive strategies forced workers to contest arbitrary changes in the work process and wage rates by either going out on strike or by changing jobs. The high turnover rate can be construed as a system of self-defense for obtaining better wages. After World War I, the chronic shortage of skilled labor sometimes allowed for better wages, but even limited gains could quickly dissolve. Workers' experience during the 1930s depression years and the Popular Front is just one example, as wage cuts were followed by new benefits under the Blum government, which were then rapidly eroded by rising prices and localized struggles. In these renewed conflicts, union militants were blacklisted, as millowners launched a counteroffensive to crush the unions. In this context, class consciousness among workers was shaped by the omnipresence of several generations of family manufacturers whose lives intersected with their own.

Third, this study has explored the development of worker resistance to millowner strategies through the formation of a counterculture of opposition. To be sure, the industrial working class, initially drawn from domestic manufacture in the countryside and from urban artisan workshops, had diverse ideological and social roots. The organization of production frequently divided workers against themselves, as production regularly shifted between homeworkers and millworkers, and between urban and rural workshops. Nevertheless, the experience of class conflict opened the real prospect for worker solidarity against the employers. Several socialist groups attempted to organize textile workers in Troyes. Local Guesdist leaders had proposed seizing power through the ballot by forming a disciplined political party that might win elections first locally, and then at the national level. Their organizing helped introduce Marxian socialism into the Champagne region thanks notably to several exceptional male leaders. But ultimately, the Guesdists failed to garner sufficient votes at the polls. Revolutionary syndicalists criticized such electoral strategies, arguing that they would only strengthen parliamentary socialism within a bourgeois regime. Instead, they militated in favor of workers founding their own democratic institutions of solidarity. To this end, they established labor unions, workers' consumer cooperatives, and other institutions of solidarity such as the Bourse du Travail. Many of these initiatives had deeper roots in mutualist societies from earlier in the nineteenth century. But the new associations would be long lived and survive the infighting that had characterized socialist politics well into the twentieth century, empowering workers with a sense of autonomy.

A fourth theme has been the role of consumption as a central component in working-class counterculture. During the early Third Republic, workers had been only marginal consumers, constrained by long working hours and low wages, and their consumer practices had lagged noticeably behind that of other social groups. Social distinctions in clothing began at the factory gate. It was obvious to textile workers in Troyes that the quality, luxury clothing they produced in the mills was intended for other social classes. In fact, mill-owners were long reluctant to market clothing explicitly for the masses and to shift production to more standardized goods. When the Third Republic finally authorized the formation of labor unions in 1884, workers in Troyes linked the right to work to the right to consume, by founding their own coopera-tive store at the same time as they created the first textile union. In this way, they took charge of their material existence and effectively practiced a form of social entrepreneurship that sustained their everyday lives. The consumer cooperative the Laborieuse was designed to market goods for the satisfaction of needs, not for the production of profit. It was conceived as an alternative to commercial capitalism that could transform economic relations in society through more egalitarian practices: the collective ownership and management of the store by its members, the setting of fair prices, and the sharing of profits, all measures that would ensure cooperative ideals. The Laborieuse defied the wage-earning system by its no-credit rule, and it even offered fash-ionable clothing to women workers at affordable prices. Consumer coopera-tion of this kind not only represented an effective means of social integration for workers into French society, as Maurice Halbwachs had suggested, but it also provided a substantial measure of social change in workers' lives through the new products and services it offered them. As the cooperative grew in membership, it expanded its activities beyond the provisioning of consumer commodities to the creation of such services as a credit union, a mutualist pharmacy, and a lending library and reading room. By the late 1920s it was also providing the organized leisure activities for workers' families that are associated with modern consumer culture. Both in spirit and organization, the cooperative was a utopian venture that succeeded for nearly fifty years in sus-taining a viable community of consumption.

Our study has also underscored the growing significance of material goods in workers' search for greater social and economic equality. Socialist workers' organizations had commonly argued that capitalist consumer society would weaken class consciousness and worker activism by stimulating individual

desires. Jules Guesde, and Marxist socialists in general, feared that cooperatives would direct workers away from collective action to nonpolitical goals.
But the present study has challenged this view of consumer cooperation. Far
from being a source of worker alienation, the cooperative store offered economic solidarity to those who had often lacked adequate means of participating in a consumer society, and it reinforced class identity. In Pouget and
Pataud's revolutionary utopian society, the primordial goal was to ensure the
satisfaction of needs and desires by establishing worker control over the production and distribution of goods. Once the production of necessities had
been secured, even luxury trades could keep operating in a modified form. In
these authors' imaginary scheme, production and consumption could operate
in more equitable ways to guarantee material well-being. For their part, managers of the Laborieuse in Troyes satisfied workers' needs consonant with their
class; they provisioned affordable clothing, goods that shaped worker identity
in a deliberate way. Men more than women found ready-to-wear clothing to
fit their budget, while women selectively appropriated fashion and customized
their clothing through their own skills and individual tastes.

Several factors, then, influenced workers' consumer behavior during these
years. Before 1914, the availability and display of some forms of ready-made
clothing and novelty fashion revived the desire to consume on the part of both
men and women workers. This desire was constrained by lack of disposable
income and by customary thrift, thus conforming to a pattern of consumption that was consistent with working-class culture. Workers felt pulled in two
directions: they felt constrained to purchase within their existing pattern of
consumption and also forced to transform it by acquiring goods with new and
different social meanings.[4] Class consciousness for many strengthened their
desire to retain visible cultural markers of worker identity.

It was not until the interwar years that the consumer market expanded,
offering broader social access to more democratic dress than had been available
earlier. The fall of export prices by the 1930s forced many Troyes millowners
to shift production away from luxury goods and toward more standardized
clothing for the popular domestic market. A surge in the democratization of
demand coincided with new standards of public dress in the street. But the
transition to more egalitarian consumer patterns would remain a long, slow

---

4. Anthropologist Grant McCracken has identified this type of consumer behavior as the
"Diderot effect," with reference to the philosopher's famous essay "Regrets for My Old Dressing Gown." See McCracken 1988, chap. 8.

process with modest gains. Many of the advances were interrupted by the depression and by the wage cuts and unemployment that ensued, restraining workers' purchasing power. Overall, however, workers in the late Third Republic enjoyed a wider variety of clothing that offered greater social mobility than before. Only after World War II, and the rebirth in France of a national economy and marketplace, would a modern, more socially unified consumer society come into being.

Finally, this study has stressed the central significance of gender for our understanding of working-class culture in Troyes. Gender distinctions were embedded in the organization of the knitted goods industry, from its origins in domestic manufacture to its expansion in the modern mill. Gender permeated the trade—in segregated work spaces, in occupations that defined a strict sexual division of labor, and even in the symbolic representations of the trade in the Fêtes de la Bonneterie. Trade organization traditionally stressed the complementarity of gender tasks, which attributed the more productive knitting frame to men, while women were assigned to less productive finishing tasks. But by the early twentieth century, women's work had been partially mechanized so that the woman worker, or bonnetière, could claim a skilled *métier* alongside men. Textile and garment making flourished in Troyes during the economic expansion of the Belle Epoque, and in the process, it consecrated female employment in these trades.

But as this study has shown, the gendered meanings of *bonnetière* evolved substantially during the interwar years, shifting from designating the independent wage earner and skilled worker embodied in the festival queen of 1909, to describing the common "factory girl" of the 1930s. By then, women represented 58 percent of the labor force in the industry, and the term had come to connote an unskilled, low-waged female worker. The social status of women marked by this previous skill distinction had sharply declined.

The fabric of gender and class solidarity was present in workplace and community throughout these years in Troyes. Women were recognized as vital members of the working-class community: as millworkers alongside their husbands and children, as homeworkers, skilled seamers, family breadwinners, and even strikers. Despite their lack of political rights, working women commonly joined the ranks of protests and collective action. Yet problems of gender and sexual difference remained strong, arising in part out of the growing feminization of the labor force, an evolution that could potentially afford women greater responsibility in the workplace and in the family. At issue for women was an increase in wages to reflect a valorization of their skills, and union recognition of their specific needs. At the turn of the century, union leaders had formally supported equal wages for equal work, but they had taken little action to put this slogan into practice with respect to women. In fact, union practice concerning women's work was frequently in contradiction with the union's own goals. Working women's sense of solidarity was further weakened by male leaders' failure to recognize women as a potential force within the labor movement and by sectarian rivalries that split the socialists in 1920. Union recruitment of women began in earnest only after World War I, when their participation in the workforce came largely to outnumber that of men. Yet contradictions in union policies appeared, as national union newspapers attempted to address women workers' concerns, while local union leaders at the base focused increasingly on factional politics. Negotiations for the collective bargaining agreement of 1936 that codified skill definitions in the trade largely accepted the deskilling of women's occupations, in exchange for higher wages across the trade. The few women militants in the Communist Party and the CGTU during the interwar years in Troyes struggled to maintain their voice in an overwhelmingly masculine world.

Women militants' experience at work had taught them ways of accommodation and resistance similar to those of men. Yet the lack of recognition for workingwomen's political action, and their continued exclusion from suffrage, suggest that competing political aspirations and ambitions between men and women militants may well explain why certain male leaders refused to share power in Troyes during these difficult years. Moreover, women's specific concerns were not adequately addressed by the polemical political language of the times. Even earlier in the twentieth century, the utopian society imagined by Pouget and Pataud was essentially a male-run community, strongly resembling the contemporary political world of 1900. After the revolution, they argued, women would no longer be restricted to Proudhon's "brutal" regime of "housewife or harlot." A woman would be free to "remain a woman—to work or not, to become a mother or not." There was in this text, to be sure, a certain nod to growing feminist demands. But the ambiguity of the notion of freedom to "remain a woman" once again raises the question of who within this historical context was defining *woman*.[5] Feminists were competing with socialists on these very grounds during this period. Their debates centered

5. Pouget and Pataud 1995, 173.

on the same issues of femininity and the promotion of change for women in society.

This study has cast worker resistance to the particular pattern of industrialization and labor management in Troyes within the larger framework of political power and culture under the Third Republic. It has stressed workers' demands for a redistribution of power toward more egalitarian ends, down to relations in the workplace. Perhaps the greatest challenge to textile manufacturers in Troyes and to their social order was made during the sit-in strikes of June 1936. Workers' disciplined occupation of the mills appeared so frightening to millowners that they agreed to negotiate almost immediately. "But as Blum pointed out at the Riom trial, it was precisely 'this tranquility, this sort of majesty' which inspired such terror in the bourgeoisie. Were the workers intending to take over the factories themselves?"[6] We can only speculate on whether millowners in Troyes feared that this might actually happen. Certainly the lived experience of these events shook the certainties of employer authority, and created the historic possibility of a different, negotiated path to industrial relations that would forcefully incorporate labor unions as social partners in the collective bargaining process. This was, indeed, an important legacy of the Matignon agreements.

With the fall of the Third Republic in June 1940 and the German occupation, the window of opportunity of the Popular Front virtually disappeared. The postwar era would bring a renewed national economy, a surge in industrial modernization through Marshall Plan aid, and a resurgence of the labor movement in its wake. A dramatically different world from the one we have described would emerge within the context of a European economy, bringing with it the challenges of global industrial capitalism, which had a notable impact on the textile industry. Starting in 1958, the Troyes textile industry would face not only competition from within the new Common Market, but also, through decolonization, the loss of a protected colonial market. Progress in textile technology would bring imported American nylon fiber and expensive, electronically operated knitting machines. Even Taylorized methods to increase productivity, introduced in the postwar years, could not keep pace with the need for more semiskilled women garment workers. The continuity with the past was striking: by 1976 women workers represented 77.5 percent of

---

6. Jackson 1988, 86. See also Blum 1943, 57, and his comment that the law instituting collective bargaining agreements modified employers' authority: "The divine right of employers is dead" (153).

the knitting industry labor force in the Troyes region.[7] By the end of the twentieth century, the textile town of Troyes had been caught in a slow, seemingly inevitable industrial crisis. However, the fact that a growing number of factory-outlet stores had put Troyes back on the map as a commercial center, while local production had declined, only emphasized the contradictions of global industrial capitalism and the paradoxical possibility of a future industrial renewal.

7. For an analysis of the post-1945 years, see Vanier 1993, 69–88.

BIBLIOGRAPHY

PRIMARY SOURCES

Archives Nationales, Paris (AN)

Series C: National Assembly
7318 and 7321 Enquête sur la situation de l'industrie textile (1902–4)
Series F7: Police
12497 Activité socialiste dans le département (1900–1914)
12767 Enquêtes économiques et sociales, dossiers sur l'industrie textile (1901–10)
13819 (1905–8); 13820 (1909–13) Congrès national du textile
13880 (1909–10); 13910 (1919–20); 13911 (1920) Grèves travailleurs du textile
Series F22: Syndicats et grèves
177 (1920); 181–83 (1921–23); 197 (1929); 206 (1930); 214 (1931); 218 (1932); 221 (1933); 225 (1934); 229 (1935) Grèves dans l'Aube
418 (1922–26); 419 (1930–36) Journée de huit heures, textiles
438 Travail des femmes et des enfants, législation, enquêtes (1886–1930)
463 Travail des femmes et des enfants, commissions départementales du travail (1898–1922) Aube
668–75 Situation du marché du travail dans les départements: Tableaux envoyés par les préfets (1931–37)

Archives départementales de l'Aube, Troyes (ADA)

Series J: Archives privées
90 103 Etablissements Vitoux, Relevés des salaires (1922–23)
39 1119 Etablissements Mauchauffée, Renseignements clients: Registre 1891–1910
Series M: Administration
132 Listes électorales, élections municipales, Troyes (1900)
791 Syndicats patronaux et ouvriers (1876–1901)
792 Syndicats effectifs (1893–1907)
1273 Crise Boulangiste—1er Mai 1890
2281–82 Travail des enfants et des adultes dans les usines et manufactures (1833–1888)
2291–92 Différends entre patrons et ouvriers: Salaires, chômages, grèves (1848–1893)

2293 Salaires, chômages, grèves

2345 Syndicats et sociétés coopératives (1891–1907)

2346 Chambres syndicales

2352 Syndicats professionnels et Sociétés coopératives (1894–1900)

Série continue (SC)

330 Fêtes du Premier Mai et manifestations (1906–13)

337 Grèves, coalitions (1897–1900), Congrès ouvriers (1897–1900)

338 Socialisme-syndicalisme-anarchisme (1889–1900)

340 Parti ouvrier français

353 Manifestations du Premier Mai (1892–1901)

365 Anarchistes . . .

385 Cabinet: Affaires diverses, conférences, socialistes, anarchistes (1908–14)

408 Guerre de 1914–1918: Surveillance des établissements travaillant pour la défense nationale

416 (1912–13); 417–18 (1900); 419 (1901–7); 421 (1907–9) Grèves

667 Travail des femmes et enfants dans l'industrie (1902–5)

704 Société de secours mutuels des bonnetiers (1884–1897)

819 Grèves, rapports mensuels (1913–14)

922 Syndicats professionnels, statistiques (1907–13)

1204 Chômage: Situation dans l'Aube, rapports de police et de sous préfets (1899–1900)

1230 Statistiques des coopératives (1921–23)

1232–33 Vie chère, rapports de police (1926–27)

1288–89 Syndicats professionnels patronaux et ouvriers

1325 Syndicats professionnels, révision générale (1921)

2307 Fonds départmantal de chômage

2310 Chômage: Renseignements 1932

2311 Chômage, affaires diverses de 1933 à 1940

2312 Chômage, affaires diverses de 1934 à 1935

2313 Fonds départemental de chômage, dossiers de chômeurs antérieurs à 1933

2314 Fonds départemental de chômage, fonctionnement en 1934, listes nominatifs avec allocations

2315 Chômage divers

2316 Fonds de chômage de Troyes, antérieurs à 1936

2325 Fonds départemental de travail, dossiers de chômeurs antérieurs à 1933

2332 La loi du 23 Avril 1919 sur la journée de huit heures

2335 Travail, divers, contraventions à la législation du travail (1911–22, 1929–32)

2462 Inspection du travail (1920–39)

2469 Manifestations du 1er Mai dans l'Aube: Surveillance policière des réunions et manifestations publiques (1923–25)

4251 Surveillance des manifestations et réunions politiques et syndicales dans l'Aube (1926–42)

4252 Manifestations de 1936

4260 Emeutes Fevrier 1934

4334 Conflits du travail 1936–1939, application de la convention collective, grève Devanlay-Recoing

4336 Conventions collectives (1936–37)

8598 Société Mutuelle des Coopérateurs de la Laborieuse de Troyes et de Sainte-Savine

20685 Groupement départemental des Coopératives de consommation

21102 Dépôts de statuts des Docks de l'Aube et de la Société "la Laborieuse"

Series 3Q: Enregistrement

Tables des successions

8213 1866–1870

8214 1869–1872

8218 1878–1880

8219 1879–1883

8222 1886–1891

8226 1897–1899

14378 1924–27

Table des mutations après décès

9399	9460	11389
9401	9463	11390
9402	9466	11392
9406	9419	
	9506	
9422		

Série 2E: Notarial Records, Troyes

2E/6	466 Maître Rousselet	2E/3	762 Maître Laty
2E/8	291 Maître Payen	2E/3	767 Maître Laty
2E/8	357 Maître Huez	2E/4	498 Maître Pargny
2E/10	1581 Maître Voix	2E/3	838 Maître Champeaux
2E/4	541 Maître Pargny	2E/4	571 Maître Pignon
2E/11	473 Maître Bompard	2E/3	390 Maître Huez
2E/7	615 Maître Pignerol	2E/4	570 Maître Vignon

Série H

H dépôt 387/1662   Nécrologie générale 1902–14

H dépôt 387/1663   Nécrologie générale 1914–25

H dépôt 387/1664   Nécrologie générale 1925–36

1033 W 63 Actes déposés au greffe de la Justice de Paix au 2e canton de Troyes (1935)

Archives municipales de Troyes (AMT)

Series F: Population, économie sociale, statistique

1F 58–60 Listes nominatives recensement de 1906

1F 69 Listes nominatives recensement de 1926

2F 46 Exposition universelle à Paris, rapports des délégués, bonneterie (1889)

2F 47 Exposition universelle à Paris, rapports des délégués (1900)

2F 70 Statistique industrielle (1808–1813, 1826, 1856–1906)

4F 129 Commission paritaire/Indice du coût de la vie (1922–32)

4F 530 *Report of an Enquiry by the Board of Trade into Working Class Rents, Housing, and Retail Prices together with the Rates of Wages in the Principal Industrial Towns of France.* 1909. London: H.M.S.O.

7F 1 Durée du travail dans les manufactures (1824–1884)

7F 4 Travail des femmes dans les manufactures (1882)
7F 32–42 Syndicats professionnels
7F 57 Office départemental de placement (1916–35)
7F 76 Livrets ouvriers (1809–1906)
7F 78 Congrès ouvriers (1879–1912)
7F 83 Caisse municipale de chômage (1921–39)
7F 84 Rapports de chômage (1927–1933)
7F 86 Chômage (1937–38)
7F 92 Grèves dans la bonneterie (1878–1933)
Series J: Police, Hygiène publique, Justice
1J 154 Première Fête de la Bonneterie (1909)
1J 155 Fêtes de la Bonneterie (1925–26)
1J 156 Fêtes de la Bonneterie (1935)
1J 157–58 Fêtes de la Bonneterie (1936); 159 (1937); 160 (1938)
2J 34 Manifestations politiques (1906–30)
2J 41 Réunions syndicats, meetings politiques (1930–35)
2J 46 Confédération générale du travail unitaire, documents (1926–29)
2J 47 Grèves dans les usines de Troyes (1891–1900); 2J 48(1901–20); 2J 49 (1921–37)
Series R: Instruction publique, science, lettres
1R 33 Ecole des fabriques (1852–1882)
1R 198 Ateliers-écoles (1929–39)
1R 257 Ecole française de bonneterie (1889–1937)
1R 289 Enseignement secondaire des jeunes filles, programme des cours (1881)
Series 1K: Elections
1K308 Elections au Conseil des prud'hommes (1905–8)
1K309 Elections au Conseil des prud'hommes (1910)
1K311 Elections au Conseil des prud'hommes (1913)
1K314 Elections au Conseil des prud'hommes (1921)
1K319 Elections au Conseil des prud'hommes (1932–34)
1K320 Elections au Conseils des prud'hommes (1935)

Archives du Musée de la Bonneterie, Troyes

Les réglements de la Confrérerie des bonnetiers de la ville de Troyes (1862)
Les statuts de la Société de secours mutuels des bonnetiers (1881)
Les statuts du Syndicat troyen de la bonneterie (1886)
Les statuts de la Laborieuse, société coopérative de consommation (1886)
Les statuts de l'Oeuvre des Cercles catholiques d'ouvriers (1887)
La Chambre syndicale des fabricants de bonneterie. 1921. *Après la Grève (26 Septembre–7 Novembre 1921)*. Troyes: Imprimerie Henri Riez

Archives du Conseil des prud'hommes, Palais de Justice, Troyes

Trade court cases concerning knitted goods industry from 1900 to 1939

Archives privées

Chambre de commerce de Troyes, Chambre syndicale des fabricants de bonneterie et des industries s'y attachant. *Registre de procès-verbaux,* 7 Janvier 1921 au 5 Février 1926.

Groupe de l'Aube, Union française pour le suffrage des femmes, Cahier de comptes rendus de réunions, 1913–1915.

Les Coopérateurs de Champagne, Château Thierry, Aisne

NEWSPAPERS AND OTHER PERIODICALS

L'Aube Ouvrière (1928–40).
La Défense des Travailleurs de l'Aube (1900–1920).
La Dépêche de l'Aube (1920–39, 1976–95).
La Dépêche Troyenne (February 27–October 16, 1900).
La Maille Moderne (January–December 1928).
Le Moniteur de la Maille (January 1930).
L'Ouvrière (1924, 1926–27).
L'Ouvrière Textile (1903–14, 1919–22, 1924–35).
Le Père Peinard (1892–93, 1897, 1900).
Le Petit Troyen (1881–1939).
Le Rappel de l'Aube (1932–36).
Le Reveil des Travailleurs de l'Aube (1892–1901).
Le Socialiste Troyen (1893).

LIBRARIES AND MUSEUMS WITH COLLECTIONS OF POSTCARDS, SALES CATALOGS, AND ADVERTISEMENTS

Bibliothèque Forney, Paris.
Bibliothèque historique de la Ville de Paris.
Musée de la bonneterie, Troyes.

BOOKS AND ARTICLES BY CONTEMPORARIES

Almanach de la Coopération socialiste illustré pour 1910. 1910. Paris: L'Emancipatrice.
d'Avenel, Georges. 1902. "Le mécanisme de la vie moderne." 4e série. L'habillement féminin, la publicité, le théâtre, le prêt populaire. Paris: A. Colin.
Babeau, Albert. 1874. "La population de Troyes au XVIIIe siècle." *Annuaire de l'Aube.*
Ballot, Charles. 1923. *L'introduction du machinisme dans l'industrie française.* Lille-Paris.
Balzac, Honoré de. 1966. *Le deputé d'Arcis.* 1854. Reprint, Paris: Seuil.
Baudoin, Eve. 1931. *La mère au travail et le retour au foyer.* Paris: Bloud et Gay.
Bloch, Marc. 1968. *Strange Defeat.* 1940. Reprint, New York: Norton.
Blum, Léon. 1943. *Léon Blum Before His Judges.* London: Routledge.
Bonneff, Léon, and Maurice Bonneff. 1908. *La vie tragique des travailleurs.* Paris: J. Rouff.
Bourse des Coopératives Socialistes de France. 1907. *Compte rendu, 6e Congrés National tenu à Troyes, March 31–April 2, 1907.* Paris: Bourse des Coopératives Socialistes de France.

Bouvier, Jeanne. 1983. *Mes mémoires: Une syndicaliste féministe, 1876–1935.* 1936. Reprint, Paris: Maspero.

Chaptal, Jean-Antoine. 1819. *De l'industrie française.* Vol. 2. Paris.

Compère-Morel, A. 1913. *Encylopédie socialiste, syndicale et coopérative de l'Internationale ouvrière.* Vol. 2., *Les fédérations socialistes.* Paris: Librairie Aristide Quillet.

———. 1937. *Jules Guesde: Le socialisme fait homme, 1845–1922.* Paris: Librairie Aristide Quillet.

Delbet, E. 1983. *Manoeuvre agriculteur de la Champagne Pouilleuse (Marne).* Les ouvriers des deux mondes. Première série. 1856. Reprint, Paris: A l'Enseigne de l'Arbre Verdoyant Editeur.

Delpech, Henry. 1938. *Recherches sur le niveau de vie et les habitudes de consommation.* Paris.

"Les douze vertus de la coopération." 1894. In *Almanach de la coopération française.* Paris.

Felkin, William. 1867. *A History of Machine-Wrought Hosiery and Lace Manufactures.* London: Longmans, Green and Company..

Franklin, Alfred. 1906. *Dictionnaire historique des arts et métiers et professions exercés dans Paris depuis le treizième siècle.* Paris: Burt Franklin.

Gaumont, Jean. 1924. *Histoire générale de la coopération en France.* 2 vols. Paris: Fédération Nationale des Coopératives de Consommation.

Ghesquière, Henri. 1898. *La femme et le socialisme.* Lille.

Gonnard, R. 1906. *La femme dans l'industrie.* Paris: Armand Colin.

Gréau, Aîné. 1850. "Statistique de l'arrondissment industriel de la ville de Troyes pour l'année 1846." *Annuaire de l'Aube,* 1–28.

———. 1851. "Notice sur les meilleurs moyens de combiner les travaux de l'agriculture avec ceux de l'industrie manufacturière." *Annuaire de l'Aube,* 13–16.

Guérin, Daniel. 1997. *Front Populaire, révolution manquée, témoignage militant.* 1963. Reprint, Paris: Actes Sud.

Guérin, Urbain. 1896. *Fileur en peigné et régleur de métier de la Manufacture du Val-des-Bois (Marne).* Les ouvriers des deux mondes. Deuxième série, no. 83. Paris: Librairie de Firmin-Didot.

Guerrier, Maurice. 1912. *Le salaire de la femme.* Paris: Imprimerie Jardin.

Guesde, Jules. 1894. *Le problème et la solution: Les huit heures à la Chambre.* Paris.

Halbwachs, Maurice. 1913. *La classe ouvrière et les niveaux de vie.* Paris: Librairie Félix Alcan.

———. 1933. *L'évolution des besoins dans les classes ouvrières.* Paris: Félix Alcan.

———. 1939. "Genre de vie." *Revue d'économie politique* 53.

Hauser, Henri, and Henri Hitier, eds. 1917. "La bonneterie de coton." In *Enquête sur la production française et la concurrence étrangère—Industries textiles.* Vol. 2. Paris.

Jamerey, E. 1900. "Mémoire et monographie, Commune de Maizières-la-Grande Paroisse, Département de l'Aube, Grande et petite industrie (bonneterie)— Exposition universelle de 1900." Groupe XVI-Classe 103. Manuscript.

Jouenne, Alice. 1911. *La femme et la coopération.* Paris: Bourse des Coopératives Socialistes.

Lacoste, Andrée Bibolet. 1998. "Elèves de l'école de la rue Hennequin et du 'Quartier-bas' Troyes (1930–1932)." *Les Cahiers Aubois d'Histoire de l'Education* 14 (April).

Lafargue, Paul. 1883. *Le droit à la paresse*. Paris. Translated as *The Right to Be Lazy*. Trans. Charles Kerr. Chicago: Charles Kerr, 1907.

———. 1904. *La question de la femme*. Paris.

Lagoguey, Lucien. 1918. "Essai statistique sur la dépopulation des campagnes auboises." In Mémoires de la Société Académique de l'Aube, 131–309.

Lamotte, F., ed. 1924. *L'Aube*. Special issue of *Illustration économique et financière*, March 22, 1924.

Lavergue, Bernard. 1923. *Les coopératives de consommation en France*. Paris: Armand Colin.

Michelet, Jules. 1973. *The People*. 1845. Reprint, Urbana: University of Illinois Press.

———. 1987. *Tableau de la France*. 1833. Reprint, Paris: Editions Olivier Orban.

Mortier, Auguste. 1891. *Le tricot et l'industrie de la bonneterie*. Troyes: Léopold Lacroix.

———. 1902. *La bonneterie à l'Exposition Universelle de 1900*. Troyes.

Pédron, Etienne. 1906. *Chansons socialistes*. Paris: La Librairie du Parti.

Pelloutier, Fernand, and Maurice Pelloutier. 1975. *La vie ouvrière en France*. 1900. Reprint, Paris: Maspero.

Picard, M., Docteur. 1873. "Mémoire sur la topographie médicale de Troyes et de ses environs en 1786." In *Mémoires de la Société Academique d'Agriculture, des Sciences, Arts et Belles-Lettres du département de l'Aube*. Vol 10, 151–203. Troyes: Dufour-Bouquot.

Poisson, Ernest. 1921. "Le mouvement coopératif, 1914–1919." In *Annuaire de la FNCC pour 1920*. Paris.

———. 1934. *Comment j'ai vécu les malheurs de la Banque des coopératives de France*. Rouen.

Pouget, Emile, and Emile Pataud. 1995. *Comment nous ferons la révolution*. 1909. Reprint, Paris: Editions Syllepse.

Prévot, A. 1931. *Fontaine-les-Grès*. Troyes.

Ricommard, Julien. 1934. *La bonneterie à Troyes et dans le département de l'Aube: Origines, évolution, caractères actuels*. Paris: Hachette.

Simmel, George. 1957. "Fashion." 1904. *American Journal of Sociology* 62, no. 6:541–58.

Simon, Jules. 1861. *L'ouvrière*. Paris: Hachette.

Tarlé, Evgenii. 1910. *L'industrie dans les campagnes en France à la fin de l'ancien régime*. Paris: Edouard Cornély, Editeur.

deToytot, Ernest. 1887. *Gantier de Grenoble (Isère)*. Les ouvriers des deux mondes. Deuxième série, no. 55. Paris: Librairie Firmin-Didot.

Truquin, Norbert. 1977. *Mémoires d'un prolétaire à travers la révolution*. 1888. Reprint, Paris: Maspero.

Ude, Georges. n.d. [c. 1927]. *Etude générale de la bonneterie, le vade-mecum du bonnetier*. Paris: L'Edition Textile.

Valdour, Jacques. 1924. *La méthode concrète en science sociale*. Giard et Rousseau Editeurs.

———. 1934. *Le flot montant du socialisme: Ouvriers de Lyon et de Troyes, observations vécues*. Paris: Nouvelles Editions Latines.

Veblen, Thorsten. 1970. *Théorie de la classe de loisir*. Paris: Gallimard.

———. 1994. *The Theory of the Leisure Class*. 1899. Reprint, London: Penguin.

Vernier, J. J. 1909. *Cahier de doléances du baillage de Troyes*. Troyes: Imprimerie Noirel.

Verville, E. P. 1909. *En souvenir de la première grande Fête de la Bonneterie Troyenne*. Troyes.

GOVERNMENT SOURCES

Chambre des Députés. 1906. *Procès-verbaux de la Commission chargée de procéder à une enquête sur l'état de l'industrie textile et la condition des ouvriers tisseurs.* Vol. 5. Paris: Imprimerie de la Chambre des Députés.

Résultats statistiques du recensement général de la population. 1896, 1901, 1906, 1911, 1921, 1926, 1931, 1936. Paris: Imprimerie Nationale.

ORAL SOURCES

All interviews were by the author and took place in Troyes, with a tape recording and transcript, unless otherwise indicated. Names of interviewees, with the exception of those of Suzanne Gallois and Marcel Mathieu, were chosen randomly from the Paris telephone book to ensure anonymity.

Mme Aubron (b. 1908), *raccoutreuse* (mender). August 24, 1982.

Mme Binet (b. 1909), *raccoutreuse* (mender). August 4, 1983.

Mme Chailloux (b. 1915), *bobineuse* (bobbin winder). October 21, 1983.

M. Desvignes (b. 1911), *mécanicien-monteur* (mechanic-assembler). October 8, 1985.

Mme Esnault (b. 1909), *bobineuse* (bobbin winder). August 17, 1986.

Mme Fournet (b. 1906), *remmailleuse* (looper). August 17, 1986.

Mme Suzanne Gallois (b. 1898), *ourleuse/couseuse* (seamer), union militant. May 14 and 24, 1984; June 8, 1985.

Mme Gayet (b. 1904), *bobineuse* (bobbin winder). February 12, 1986.

Mme Henon (b. 1893), *employée* (white-collar worker). January 22, 1981. Tape recording.

M. Laborie (b. 1906), *bonnetier* (knitter). May 18, 1987.

Mme Laborie (b. 1909), *bobineuse* (bobbin winder). May 18, 1987.

M. Marcel Mathieu (b. 1900), *bonnetier* (knitter), union militant. October 7, 1983. Jaulges (Yonne). Tape recording.

SELECTED SECONDARY SOURCES

Accampo, Elinor. 1989. *Industrialization, Family Life, and Class Relations: Saint-Chamond, 1815–1914.* Berkeley and Los Angeles: University of California Press.

Accampo, Elinor, et al. 1995. *Gender and the Politics of Social Reform in France, 1870–1914.* Baltimore: Johns Hopkins Press.

Amar, Micheline, comp. 1999. *Le piège de la parité: Arguments pour un débat.* Paris: Hachette.

Antoine, Patrick. 1975. *L'Aube de 1918 à 1923.* Troyes.

Aron, Raymond. 1970. "Avez-vous lu Veblen?" Preface to *Théorie de la classe de loisir,* by Thorsten Veblen. Paris: Gallimard.

Auslander, Leora. 1993. "Perceptions of Beauty and the Problem of Consciousness: Parisian Furniture Makers." In *Rethinking Labor History,* ed. Lenard Berlanstein, 149–81. Urbana: University of Illinois Press.

———. 1996a. "The Gendering of Consumer Practices in Nineteenth-Century France." In *The Sex of Things: Gender and Consumption in Historical Perspective,* ed.

Victoria de Grazia and Ellen Furlough. Berkeley and Los Angeles: University of California.

———. 1996b. *Taste and Power: Furnishing Modern France*. Berkeley and Los Angeles: University of California Press.

Auzias, Claire, and Annik Houel. 1982. *La grève des ovalistes, Lyon, Juin–Juillet 1869*. Paris: Payot.

Barbet, Denis. 1991. "Retour sur la loi de 1884: La production des frontières entre du syndical et du politique." *Genèses* 3 (March): 3–50.

Bard, Christine. 1995. *Les filles de Marianne: Histoire des féminismes, 1914–1940*. Paris: Fayard.

———. 1996. "A la recherche des diversités féministes dans le Dictionnaire." In *La part des militants,* ed. M. Dreyfus, Claude Pelletier, and Nathalie Viet-Depaule. Paris: Editions de l'Atelier.

———. 1998. *Les garçonnes, modes et fantasmes des années folles*. Paris: Flammarion.

Baroin, Michel. 1970. *Les Aubois et la politique sous les IIIe et IVe Républiques*. Paris: ESPER.

Baron, Ava. 1991. "Gender and Labor History: Learning from the Past, Looking to the Future." In *Work Engendered,* ed. Ava Baron, 1–46. Ithaca: Cornell University Press.

Barret P., and J.-N. Gurgand. 1980. *Ils voyageaient la France: Vie et traditions des Compagnons du Tour de France au XIXe siècle*. Paris: Hachette.

Baudelot, Christian, and Roger Establet. 1994. *Maurice Halbwachs: Consommation et société*. Paris: Presses Universitaires de France.

Beale, Marjory. 1999. *The Modernist Enterprise*. Stanford: Stanford University Press.

Bedin, Michel. 1975. "La presse ouvrière auboise, 1919–1922." Memoire de maîtrise, University of Dijon.

———. 1977. "Le socialisme dans l'Aube: Des origines à la création de la S.F.I.O." 2 vols. Mémoire de DEA, Université de Dijon, Octobre.

Berger, John. 1980. "The Suit and the Photograph." In *About Looking*. London: Writers and Readers Publishing Cooperative.

Bergeron, Louis. 1978. *Les capitalistes en France (1780–1914)*. Paris: Gallimard.

Bérisé, Claude. 1993. *La mémoire de Troyes: Cartes postales anciennes.*Troyes: Maison du Boulanger.

———. 1999. *La mémoire de Troyes II*. Troyes: Maison du Boulanger.

Berlanstein, Lenard. 1984. *The Working People of Paris, 1871–1914*. Baltimore: Johns Hopkins Press.

———. 1992. "The Distinctiveness of the Nineteenth-Century French Labor Movement." *Journal of Modern History* 64:660–85.

———, ed. 1993. *Rethinking Labor History: Essays on Discourse and Class Analysis*. Urbana: University of Illinois Press.

Berstein, Serge. 1988. *La France des années 30*. Paris: Armand Colin.

Beury, André. 1980. *1940 dans l'Aube*. Troyes: Imprimeries Paton.

Bibliothèque Forney. 1992. *Rayon lingerie, un siècle de publicité*. Exh. cat. Paris.

———. 1999. *De Bébé Cadum à la Mamie Nova: Un siècle de publicité*. Exh. cat. Paris.

Bibolet, Françoise. 1997. "Statuts de la Confrérie des bonnetiers de Troyes." In *Les Fêtes de la Bonneterie*. Exh. cat. Paris: Ministère de la Culture.

Bigorne, Didier. 1992. "Mouvement ouvrier et fêtes dans les Ardennes (1885–1936)."

In *Fêtes et politique en Champagne à travers les siècles,* ed. Sylvette Guilbert. Nancy: Presses Universitaires de Nancy.

Borzeix, Anni, and Margaret Maruani. 1982. *Le temps des chemises.* Paris: Syros.

Bonnell, Victoria, and Lynn Hunt, eds. 1999. *Beyond the Cultural Turn.* Berkeley and Los Angeles: University of California Press.

Boorstin, Daniel. 1973. *The Americans: The Democratic Experience.* New York: Random House.

Boucraut, Louis, and Marie-Madeleine Boucraut. 1985. *Antoine Quinquarlet, industriel Troyen (1813–1897).* Troyes: Imprimerie La Renaissance.

———. 1986. *Pierre Valton et ses fils (1892–1940).* Troyes: Imprimerie La Renaissance.

———. 1987. *Les fils de Valton (1940–1970).* Troyes: Imprimerie La Renaissance.

Boulard, Fernand, et al. 1987. *Matériaux pour l'histoire religieuse du peuple français, XIXe–XXe siècles.* Vol. 2. Paris: FNSP, EHESS, CNRS Editions.

Bourdé, Guy. 1977. *La défaite du Front Populaire.* Paris: Maspero.

Boyer, Robert. 1991. "Le particularisme français revisité: La crise des années trente à la lumière des recherches récentes." *Paradoxes français de la crise des années 1930. Le Mouvement Social* 154 (January–March): 3–40.

Braudel, Fernand. 1981. *The Structures of Everyday Life.* New York: Harper and Row.

Braverman, Harry. 1974. *Labor and Monopoly Capital.* New York: Monthly Review Press.

Brewer, John, Neil McKendrick, and J. J. Plumb. 1982. *The Birth of a Consumer Society.* Bloomington: Indiana University Press.

Burdy, Jean Pierre, et al. 1987. "Rôles, travaux et métiers de femmes dans une ville industrielle: St Etienne, 1900–1950." *Le Mouvement Social* 140 (July–September): 27–53.

Burns, Michael. 1992. *Dreyfus: A Family Affair.* New York: Harper.

Burrin, Philippe. 1986. *La dérive fasciste: Doriot, Déat, Bergery, 1933–1945.* Paris: Seuil.

Buchsbaum, Jonathan. 1988. *Cinéma Engagé: Film in the Popular Front.* Urbana: University of Illinois.

Canning, Kathleen. 1992. "Gender and the Politics of Class Formation: Rethinking German Labor History." *American Historical Review* 97 (June): 736–68.

———. 1996. *Languages of Labor and Gender: Female Factory Work in Germany, 1850–1914.* Ithaca: Cornell University Press.

Caron, François. 1981. *Histoire économique de la France XIXème–XXème siècles.* Paris: Armand Colin.

Cauzard, Daniel, Jean Perret, and Yves Ronin. 1989. *Images de marques, marques d'images.* Paris: Ramsay.

Cazals, Rémy. 1978. *Avec les ouvriers de Mazamet dans la grève et l'action quotidienne, 1904–1914.* Paris: Maspero.

———. 1983. *Les révolutions industrielles à Mazamet, 1750–1900.* Paris: Maspero.

Chabert, Alexandre. 1960. *Les salaires dans l'industrie française (les textiles).* Paris: Armand Colin.

Chaplain, Jean Michel. 1984. *La chambre des tisseurs, Louviers: Cité drapière.* Seyssel: Champ Vallon.

Chapman, Stanley. 2003. "The Hosiery Industry, 1780–1914." In *The Cambridge History of Western Textiles*, ed. David Jenkins. Vol. 2. Cambridge: Cambridge University Press.

Chartier, Roger, et al. 1998. *La ville des temps modernes*. Histoire de la France Urbaine, vol. 3. Paris: Le Seuil.

Chassagne, Serge. 1979. "La diffusion rurale de l'industrie cotonnière en France (1750–1850)." *Revue du Nord* 240 (January–March).

———. 1991. *Le coton et ses patrons, 1760–1840*. Paris: Editions de l'Ecole des Hautes Etudes en Sciences Sociales.

Chenut, Helen. 1987. "La constructruction sociale des métiers masculins et féminins dans la bonneterie troyenne, 1900–1939." Final research report, GEDISST-CNRS, Paris.

———. 1988. "Les bonnetières troyennes: Formation d'une culture ouvrière féminine." Thèse de troisième cycle, University of Paris 7.

———. 1996a. "Analyse d'un auto-portrait: Suzanne Gallois, militante syndicaliste de l'Aube." *Clio* 3:182–90.

———. 1996b. "The Gendering of Skill as Historical Process: The Case of French Knitters in Industrial Troyes, 1880–1939." In *Gender and Class in Modern Europe*, ed. Laura Frader and Sonya Rose, 77–107. Ithaca: Cornell University Press.

———. 1996c. "Troyes, capitale de la bonneterie: La ville comme vitrine." In *La révolution des aiguilles: Habiller les français et les américains, 19e–20e siècles*, 63–75. Paris: Editions de l'Ecole des Hautes Etudes en Sciences Sociales.

———. 1997a. "Les Fêtes de la Bonneterie à Troyes de 1909 à 1938: Fête corporative, fête industrielle et fête populaire." In *Les Fêtes de la Bonneterie*. Exh. cat. Paris: Ministry of Culture.

———. 1997b. "Produire et consommer: Discours et pratiques de classes sur la consommation au début du siècle." *La Vie en Champagne* 10 (April): 31–46.

———. 1998. "Identités de classe et de genre: Le cas de quatre syndicalistes français, 1920–1970." In *L'histoire sans les femmes est-elle possible?* ed. Anne-Marie Sohn et al., 35–51. Paris: Editions Perrin.

Chessel, Marie-Emmanuelle. 1998. *La publicité: Naissance d'une profession, 1900–1940*. Paris: CNRS Editions.

Cholvy, Gerard, and Yves-Marie Hilaire. 1986. *Histoire religieuse de la France contemporaine, 1880–1930*. Paris: Privat.

Clark, Anna. 1995. *The Struggle for the Breeches: Gender and the Making of the British Working Class*. Berkeley and Los Angeles: University of California Press.

Claverie-Rospide, Xavier. 1995. "Les Buxtorf: Une famille du négoce." *La Vie en Champagne*, no. 1 (January–March): 25–32.

Clause, Georges. 1987. "Le patronat Rémois sous le Second Empire." In *Travail et travailleurs dans l'industrie textile*, ed. Jean-Claude Rabier, 9–27. Paris: CNRS-GRECO 55.

Cockburn, Cynthia. 1983. *Brothers: Male Dominance and Technological Change*. London: Pluto Press.

Coffin, Judith. 1996a. "Consumption, Production, and Gender: The Sewing Machine in Nineteenth Century France." In *Gender and Class in Modern Europe*, ed. Laura Frader and Sonya Rose, 111–41. Ithaca: Cornell University Press.

———. 1996b. *The Politics of Women's Work: The Paris Garment Trades, 1750–1915*. Princeton: Princeton University Press.

——. 1999. "A 'Standard' of Living? European Perspectives on Class and Consumption in the Early Twentieth Century." *International Labor and Working-Class History* 55 (Spring): 6–26.

Cohen, Lizabeth. 1999. "Encountering Mass Culture at the Grassroots: The Experience of Chicago Workers in the 1920's." In *Consumer Society in American History: A Reader,* ed. Lawrence Glickman. Ithaca: Cornell University Press.

——. 2003. *A Consumers' Republic: The Politics of Mass Consumption in Postwar America.* New York: Knopf.

Confédération générale du travail. 1978. *Affiches et luttes syndicales de la CGT.* Paris: Editions du Chêne.

Colomes, André. 1943. *Les ouvriers du textile dans la Champagne Troyenne, 1730–1852.* Paris: Editions Domat-Montchrestien.

Colton, Joel. 1966. *Léon Blum, Humanist in Politics.* New York: Knopf.

Corradin, Irène, and Jacqueline Martin, eds. 1999. *Les femmes sujets d'histoire.* Toulouse: Presses Universitaires du Mirail.

Corbin, Alain. 1998. *Le monde retrouvé de Louis François Pinagot.* Paris: Flammarion.

Corbin, Alain, Noelle Gérôme, and Danielle Tartakovsky. 1994. *Les usages politiques des fêtes aux XIXe–XXe siècles.* Paris: Publications de la Sorbonne.

Cosson, Armand. 1987. "Innovations technologiques et mutation des entreprises: La bonneterie cévenole au XXième siècle." In *Travail et travailleurs dans l'industrie textile,* ed. Jean-Claude Rabier, 39–73. Paris: CNRS-GRECO 55.

Cottereau, Alain. 1980. "Vie quotidienne et résistance ouvrière à Paris en 1870." In *Le sublime ou le travailleur comme il est en 1870 et ce qu'il peut être,* by Denis Poulot. Paris: Maspero.

——. 1986. "The Distinctiveness of Working-Class Cultures in France, 1848–1900." In *Working-Class Formation,* ed. Ira Katznelson and Aristide Zolberg, 111–54. Princeton: Princeton University Press.

Couvreur, Liliane. 1973. "Le Front Populaire à Troyes, 1934–1937." Mémoire de maîtrise, University of Reims.

Cross, Gary. 1989. *A Quest for Time: The Reduction of Work in Britain and France, 1840–1940.* Berkeley and Los Angeles: University of California Press.

——. 1993a. *Time and Money: The Making of Consumer Culture.* New York: Routledge.

——. 1993b. "Time, Money, and Labor History's Encounter with Consumer Culture." *International Labor and Working-Class History* 43 (Spring): 2–17.

Crubellier, Maurice, ed. 1975. *Histoire de la Champagne.* Toulouse: Privat.

Darbot, Jean. 1980a. "Industrialisation à domicile: Les métiers à bonneterie dans les foyers troyens." *Culture technique* 3 (September): 205–10.

——. 1980b. *La Trinité, première manufacture de bas au métier de Troyes.* Troyes: CNDP de Troyes.

——. 1984. "Le progrès technique à Troyes, centre de bonneterie au XIXe siècle." In Mémoires de la Société Académique de l'Aube.

——. 1989. *Les constructeurs aubois: 400e anniversaire du métier à tricoter.* Exh. cat. Troyes: Musée de la Bonneterie.

Daumas, Jean-Claude. 1995. "La photographie de l'usine-modèle: Blin et Blin, Elbeuf, 1888." In *Archives sensibles: Images et objets du monde industriel et ouvrier,* 21–37. Cachan: Editions de l'ENS.

Dauphin, Cecile, et al. 1986. "Culture et pouvoir des femmes: Essai d'historiographie." *Les Annales* 2 (March–April): 271–93.

Daric, Jean. 1947. *L'activité professionnelle des femmes en France*. Paris: I.N.E.D.

Debouzy, Marianne. 1988. "Permanence du paternalisme?" *Le Mouvement Social* 144 (July–September): 3–16.

Debrosse, Juliette. 1994. "La mode populaire citadine à travers les catalogues et les prospectus des magasins et bazars (1880–1914)." Mémoire de maîtrise, Université de Paris IV Sorbonne.

de Grazia, Victoria. 1989. "The Arts of Purchase: How American Publicity Subverted the European Poster, 1920–1940." In *Remaking History,* ed. Barbara Kruger and Phil Mariani, 221–57. Seattle: Bay Press.

———. 1993. "Beyond Time and Money." *International Labor and Working-Class History* 43 (Spring): 24–30.

de Grazia, Victoria, with Ellen Furlough. 1996. *The Sex of Things: Gender and Consumption in Historical Perspective*. Berkeley and Los Angeles: University of California Press.

Deudon, Catherine. 2003. *Un mouvement à soi, 1970–2001*. Paris: Syllepse.

Dixmier, Elisabeth, and Michel Dixmier. 1974. *L'Assiette au beurre*. Paris: Maspero.

Downs, Laura Lee. 1995. *Manufacturing Inequality: Gender Division in the French and British Metalworking Industries, 1914–1939*. Ithaca: Cornell University Press.

———. 2002. *Children of the Promised Land*. Durham: Duke University Press.

Dubesset, Mathilde, and Michelle Zancarini-Fournel. 1988. "Parcours de femmes, réalités et représentations: St. Etienne, 1880–1950." Doctoral thesis, University Lumière Lyon II.

Dubesset, Mathilde, et al. 1992. "The Female Munition Workers of the Seine." In *The French Home Front, 1914–1918*, ed. Patrick Fridenson, 183–218. Oxford: Berg.

Dreyfus, Michel. 1995. *Histoire de la CGT*. Paris: Editions Complexe.

Eley, Geoff. 2002. *Forging Democracy*. Oxford: Oxford University Press.

Eley, Geoff, and Keith Nield. 2000. "Farewell to the Working Class?" *ILWCH* 57 (Spring): 1–30.

Enstad, Nan. 1999. *Ladies of Leisure, Girls of Adventure*. New York: Columbia University Press.

Fairchilds, Cissie. 1993. "The Production and Marketing of Populuxe Goods in Eighteenth-Century Paris." In *Consumption and the World of Goods,* ed. John Brewer and Roy Porter, 228–48. New York: Routledge.

Faraut, François. 1987. *Histoire de la Belle Jardinière*. Paris: Editions Belin.

Fassin, Eric. 1999. "The Purloined Gender: American Feminism in a French Mirror." *French Historical Studies* 22 (Winter): 111–61.

Faure, Alain. 1978. *Paris-Carême Prenant*. Paris: Buchet-Chastel.

Fauré, Michel. 1977. *Le Groupe Octobre*. Paris: Christian Bourgois.

Favier, Hubert. 1963. *Tableau économique du département de l'Aube*. Paris: Armand Colin.

Fohlen, Claude. 1956. *L'industrie textile au temps du Second Empire*. Paris: Plon.

Fougeyrolas, Dominique. 1998. "Travail domestique et salariat." In *Le partage du travail,* ed. H. Defalvard and D. Guienne. Paris.

Fourcaut, Annie. 1982. *Femmes à l'usine en France dans l'entre-deux-guerres*. Paris: Maspero.

Frader, Laura. 1996a. "Engendering Work and Wages: The French Labor Movement and the Family Wage." In *Gender and Class in Modern Europe,* ed. Laura Frader and Sonya Rose, 142–64. Ithaca: Cornell University Press.

———. 1996b. "Social Citizens Without Citizenship: Working-Class Women and Social Policy in Interwar France." *Social Politics* 3:111–34.

———. 2003. "Labor History After the Gender Turn: Transatlantic Cross Currents and Research Agendas." *ILWCH* 63 (Spring): 21–31.

———.1998. "Women and French Unions: Historical Perspectives on the Current Crisis of Representation." In *A Century of Organized Labor in France,* ed. Herrick Chapman et al., 145–66. New York: St. Martin's Press.

Frader, Laura, and Sonya Rose, eds. 1996. *Gender and Class in Modern Europe,* Ithaca: Cornell University Press.

Fraisse, Geneviève. 1996. *La différence des sexes*. Paris: Presses Universitaires de France.

Freifeld, Mary. 1986. "Technological Change and the 'Self-Acting Mule': A Study of Skill and the Sexual Division of Labor." *Social History* 11 (October): 319–43.

Friedman, Gerald. 1997. "Revolutionary Unions and French Labor: The Rebels Behind the Cause, or Why Did Revolutionary Syndicalism Fail?" *French Historical Studies* 20 (Spring): 155–81.

Furlough, Ellen. 1991. *Consumer Cooperation in France: The Politics of Consumption, 1834–1930*. Ithaca: Cornell University Press.

———. 1993. "Selling the American Way in Interwar France: Prix Uniques and the Salons des Arts Ménagers." *Journal of Social History* 26 (Spring): 491–519.

Geertz, Clifford. 1973. *The Interpretation of Cultures: Selected Essays*. New York: Basic Books..

Ginzburg, Carlo. 1980. "Signes, traces, pistes: Racines d'un paradigme de l'indice." *Le Debat,* November.

Glickman, Lawrence B. 1997. *A Living Wage: American Workers and the Making of Consumer Society*. Ithaca: Cornell University Press.

Godelier, Maurice. 1980. "Work and Its Representations: A Research Proposal." *History Workshop* 10.

Goldberg, Harvey. 1962. *The Life of Jean Jaurès*. Madison: University of Wisconsin Press.

Green, Nancy. 1997. *Ready to Wear, Ready to Work: A Century of Industry and Immigrants in Paris and New York*. Durham: Duke University Press.

Guilbert, Madeleine. 1966a. *Les femmes et l'organisation syndicale avant 1914*. Paris: Editions du Centre National de la Recherche Scientifique.

———. 1966b. *Les fonctions des femmes dans l'industrie*. Paris: Mouton.

———. 1968. "La présence des femmes dans les professions et ses incidences sur l'action syndicale avant 1914." *Le Mouvement Social* 63:125–41.

Guillaumin, Colette. 1992. *Sexe, race et pratique du pouvoir*. Paris: Editions Côté-femmes.

Guillaume-Grimaud, Geneviève. 1986. *Le cinéma du Front Populaire*. Paris: Editions Lherminier.

Gullickson, Gay. 1986. *Spinners and Weavers of Auffray*. Cambridge: Cambridge University Press.

Hafter, Daryl, ed. 1995. *European Women and Preindustrial Craft*. Bloomington: Indiana University Press.

Hall, Stuart. 1994. "Cultural Studies: Two Paradigms." In *Culture/Power/History,* ed. Nicholas Dirks, Geoff Eley, and Sherry Ortner, 520–38. Princeton: Princeton University Press.

Hanagan, Michael. 1980. *The Logic of Solidarity: Artisans and Industrial Workers in Three French Towns, 1871–1914.* Urbana: University of Illinois Press.

Hanson, Paul. 1988. "The 'Vie Chère' Riots of 1911: Traditional Protests in Modern Garb." *Journal of Social History* 21 (Spring): 463–81.

Hartmann, Heidi. 1976. "Capitalism, Patriarchy, and Job Segregation by Sex." *Signs* 1.

Harvey, John. 1995. *Men in Black.* London: Reaktion Books.

Hayward, Susan. 1993. *French National Cinema.* London: Routledge.

Heywood, Colin. 1976. "The Rural Hosiery Industry of the Lower Champagne Region, 1750–1850." *Textile History* 7:90–111.

———. 1981. "The Launching of an 'Infant Industry'? The Cotton Industry of Troyes Under Protectionism, 1793–1860." *Journal of European Economic History* 10 (Fall): 553–81.

———. 1990. "The Revolutionary Tradition in Troyes, 1789–1848." *Journal of Historical Geography* 16, no. 1:108–20.

———. 1994. "Cotton Hosiery in Troyes c. 1860–1914: A Case Study in French Industrialisation." *Textile History* 25:167–84.

———. 1998. "Mobilizing the Workers in Fin-de-Siècle France: The Parti Ouvrier in Troyes." *French History* 12:172–94.

Hilden, Patricia. 1984. "Class and Gender: Conflicting Components of Women's Behaviour in the Textile Mills of Lille, Roubaix, and Tourcoing, 1880–1914." *Historical Journal* 27:361–85.

———. 1986. *Working Women and Socialist Politics in France, 1880–1914.* Oxford: Oxford University Press.

———. 1987. "Rewriting the History of Socialism: Working Women and the Parti Ouvrier Français." *European History Quarterly* 17:285–306.

Hoffmann, Stanley, et al. 1963. "Paradoxes of the French Political Community." In *In Search of France.* Cambridge: Harvard University Press.

Horn, Jeff. *The Paths Not Taken.* Forthcoming.

Hufton, Olwen. 1975. "Women and the Family Economy in Eighteenth Century France." *French Historical Studies* 9 (Spring): 1–22.

Humbert, Jean-Louis. 1994. "Sainte-Savine, faubourg bonnetier de Troyes (1870–1914)." DEA thesis (Histoire et Civilisations), Ecole des hautes etudes en sciences sociales, Paris.

———. 1995. *Les établissements de bonneterie à Troyes (1870–1914).* Troyes: Centre Départemental de Documentation Pédagogique de L'Aube.

———. 1996. "Les établissements de bonneterie à Troyes (1870–1914): Un patrimoine industriel à sauvegarder." *La Vie en Champagne,* April.

Hunt, Lynn. 1978. *Revolution and Urban Politics in Provincial France, Troyes, and Reims, 1786–1790.* Stanford: Stanford University Press.

———, ed. 1989. *The New Cultural History.* Berkeley and Los Angeles: University of California Press.

Imbert, Françoise, and Danièle Combes. 1978. "Travail féminin: Production et reproduction." Analyse du processus d'extension du salariat féminin. Rapport de recherche, Centre de sociologie urbaine, March.

Jackson, Julian. 1985. *The Politics of Depression in France, 1932–1936*. Cambridge: Cambridge University Press.

———. 1988. *The Popular Front in France, Defending Democracy, 1934–38*. Cambridge: Cambridge University Press.

Johnson, Christopher. 1974. *Utopian Communism in France: Cabet and the Icarians, 1839–1851*. Ithaca, Cornell University Press.

———. 1979. "Patterns of Proletarianization: Parisian Tailors and Lodève Woolen Weavers." In *Consciousness and Class Experience in Nineteenth Century Europe*, ed. John Merriman. New York: Holmes and Meier.

Jonas, Raymond. 1994. *Industry and Politics in Rural France*. Ithaca: Cornell University Press.

Judt, Tony. 1986. *Marxism and the French Left*. Oxford: Clarendon.

Julliard, Jacques. 1988. *Autonomie ouvrière: Etudes sur le syndicalisme d'action directe*. Paris: Gallimard.

Kaplan, Steven, and Cynthia Koepp, eds. 1986. *Work in France: Representations, Meaning, Organization, and Practice*. Ithaca: Cornell University Press.

Katznelson, Ira, and Aristide Zolberg, eds. 1986. *Working-Class Formation: Nineteenth Century Patterns in Western Europe and the United States*. Princeton: Princeton University Press.

Kergoat, Danièle. 1978. "Ouvriers = ouvrières?" *Critiques de l'Economie Politique* 5 (October–December): 65–97.

———. 1982. *Les ouvrières*. Paris: Editions Le Sycomore.

———. 1984. "Masculin/féminin: Division sexuelle du travail et qualification." In "Qualifications," *Cadres* (c.f.d.t.), no. 313, July, 26–29.

———. 1984b. "Plaidoyer pour une sociologie de rapports sociaux: De l'anaylse critique des catégories dominantes à la mise en place d'une nouvelle conceptualisation." In *Le sexe du travail*. Grenoble: Presses Universitaires de Grenoble.

Klejman, Laurence, and Florence Rochefort. 1989. *L'égalité en marche*. Paris: Editions des Femmes.

Kuisel, Richard. 1981. *Capitalism and the State in Modern France*. New York: Cambridge University Press.

Labriffe, Charles. 1945. *L'apprentissage dans l'industrie textile*. Paris: Les Editions de l'Industrie Textile.

Landes, David. 1964. "French Business and the Businessman: A Social and Cultural Analysis." In *Modern France*, ed. Edward Mead Earle. New York: Russell.

Lazzarotti, Raymond. 1971. "Les difficultés d'une activité industrielle liée aux aléas de la conjoncture économique dans une situation urbaine évolutive donnée: L'exemple de la Bonneterie Troyenne." Faculté d'Angers, November.

Lefranc, Georges. 1966. *Juin 36: L'explosion sociale du Front Populaire*. Paris: Julliard.

———. 1974. *Histoire du Front Populaire*. Paris: Payot.

Lequin, Yves. 1976. "La formation du prolétariat industriel dans la région lyonnaise au XIXe siècle: Approches méthodologiques et premier résultats." *Le Mouvement Social* 97 (October–December): 121–37.

———. 1992. "Le métier." In *Les lieux de mémoire*, ed. Pierre Nora. Vol. 3, *Les France*, 376–429. Paris: Gallimard.

Letellier, Gabrielle, et al. 1938–49. *Enquête sur le chômage*. 3 vols. Paris: Sirey.

Levi, Giovanni. 1996. "Comportements, ressources, procès: Avant la 'révolution' de la consommation." In *Jeux d'échelles: La micro-analyse de l'expérience,* ed. Jacques Revel, 187–207. Paris: Gallimard/Le Seuil.

Lévy-Leboyer, Maurice. 1979. "Le patronat français, 1912–1973." In *Le patronat de la seconde industrialisation.* Cahier du mouvement social, no. 4, 137–88. Paris: Les Editions Ouvrières.

———. 1985. "Le patronat français a-t-il échappé à la loi des trois générations?" *Le Mouvement Social* 132 (July–September): 3–7.

Lévy-Leboyer, Maurice, and François Bourguignon. 1990. *The French Economy in the Nineteenth Century: An Essay in Econometric Analysis.* New York: Cambridge University Press.

Lhomme, Jean. 1968. "Le pouvoir d'achat de l'ouvrier français au cours d'un siècle: 1840–1940." *Le Mouvement Social* 63:41–69.

Lipovetsky, Gilles. 1994. *The Empire of Fashion: Dressing Modern Democracy.* Princeton: Princeton University Press.

Liu, Tessie. 1994. *The Weaver's Knot: The Contradictions of Class Struggle and Family Solidarity in Western France, 1750–1914.* Ithaca: Cornell University Press.

———. 1996. "What Price a Weaver's Dignity? Gender Inequality and the Survival of Home-Based Production in Industrial France." In *Gender and Class in Modern Europe,* ed. Laura Frader and Sonya Rose, 57–76. Ithaca: Cornell University Press.

Lown, Judy. 1988. "'Père plutôt que maître': Le paternalisme à l'usine dans l'industrie de la soie à Halstead au xIxe." *Le Mouvement Social* 144 (July–September): 51–70.

McCracken, Grant. 1988. *Culture and Consumption.* Bloomington: Indiana University Press.

Maitron, Jean. 1976. *Dictionnaire biographique du mouvement ouvrier français.* 41 vols. Paris: Les Editions Ouvrières.

Marglin, Stephen. 1973. "Origines et fonctions de la parcellisation des tâches: A quoi servent les patrons?" In *Critique de la division du travail,* ed. André Gorz, 43–89. Paris: Seuil.

MARHO, the Radical Historians Organization. 1983. *Visions of History.* New York: Pantheon.

Marx, Karl. 1974. *Capital.* Vol. 1. London: L. Wishart.

Mathieu, Nicole, ed. 1985. *L'arraisonnement des femmes: Essais en anthropologie des sexes.* Paris: Cahiers de l'Homme, EHESS.

Martin, Martine. 1987. "Menagère: Une profession? Les dilemmes de l'entre-deux-guerres." *Le Mouvement Social* 140 (July–September).

Marty, Laurent. 1982. *Chanter pour survivre.* Lille: Fédération Léo Lagrange.

Maza, Sara. 1989. "The Rose-Girl of Salency: Representations of Virtue in Pre-revolutionary France." *Eighteenth Century Studies* (Spring): 395–413.

Mendels, Franklin. 1972. "Proto-industrialisation: The First Phase of the Process of Industrialization." *Journal of Economic History* 32:241–61.

Milkman, Ruth. 1979. "Le travail des femmes et la crise économique: Quelques leçons tirées de la grande crise." *La Revue d'en Face* 5 (March): 7–15.

———. 1987. *Gender at Work.* Urbana: University of Illinois Press.

Mitchell, Barbara. 1990. "French Syndicalism: An Experiment in Practical Anarchism." In *Revolutionary Syndicalism: An International Perspective,* 25–43. Aldershot: Scolar Press.

Morlot, Jean. 1986. *Les Aubois et l'éducation populaire, 1866–1940.* Bar-sur-Aube: Imprimerie Némont.

Moss, Bernard. 1976. *The Origins of the French Labor Movement: The Socialism of Skilled Workers, 1830–1914.* Berkeley and Los Angeles: University of California Press.

Mossuz-Lavau, Janine, ed. 1998. *Femmes/hommes, pour la parité.* Paris: Presses de Sciences Politiques.

Mottez, Bernard. 1966. *Systèmes de salaire et politiques patronales.* Paris: C.N.R.S.

Mouriaux, René. 1998. "Strategies and Events: The 'Form' of the CGT from 1936 to 1968." In *A Century of Organized Labor in France,* ed. Herrick Chapman et al., 25–33. New York: St. Martin's Press.

Moutet, Aimée. "Les origines du système de Taylor en France: Le point de vue patronal (1907–1914)." *Le Mouvement Social* 93 (October–December 1975): 15–49.

Musée de la publicité. 1988. *Doré-Doré: L'empreinte DD, 1819–1988.* Exh. cat. Bibliothèque Forney. Paris.

Nivelle, R. 1975. "L'entreprise de bonneterie à Troyes dans les années 1840: Essaie de définition." Diplôme d'études supérieures, Dijon.

Noble, Emile. 1951. *Le métier Cotton.* Paris: Editions La Maille.

Noiriel, Gérard. 1986. *Les ouvriers dans la société française.* Paris: Seuil.

Offen, Karen. 1982. "Depopulation, Nationalism, and Feminism in Fin-de-Siècle France, 1920–1950." *American Historical Review* 89, no. 3:283–98.

Oudart, Jocelyn. 1975. "La bonneterie dans l'Aube." Ministère du Travail, Direction régionale du travail et de la main-d'oeuvre, Echelon régional de l'emploi, Chalons-sur-Marne, December 31.

Ozouf, Mona. 1976. *La fête révolutionnaire, 1789–1799.* Paris: Gallimard.

Parker, Rozsika. 1984. *The Subversive Stitch.* London: Routledge.

Parr, Joy. 1988. "Disaggregating the Sexual Division of Labor: A Transatlantic Case." *Comparative Studies in Society and History* 30 (July): 511–33.

——. 1990. *The Gender of Breadwinners.* Toronto, University of Toronto Press.

Partington, Angela. 1993. "Popular Fashion and Working-Class Affluence." In *Chic Thrills: A Fashion Reader,* ed. Juliet Ash and Elizabeth Wilson, 145–61. Berkeley and Los Angeles: University of California Press.

Pedersen, Susan. 1993. *Family, Dependence, and the Origins of the Welfare State: Britain and France, 1914–1945.* Cambridge: Cambridge University Press.

Pellegrin, Nicole. 1994. *Modes en noir.* Exh. cat., Musée Sainte-Croix of Poitiers, December 14, 1994 to March 5, 1995.

——. 1989. *Les vêtements de la liberté.* Aix-en-Provence: Editions Alinéa.

Perdriset, Françoise. 1980. "Recherches sur le vocabulaire de la Bonneterie." Thèse de doctorat de 3e cycle en linguistique. University of Paris.

Perlmutter, David. 1994. "Visual Historical Methods: Problems, Prospects, Applications." *Historical Methods* 27:167–81.

Perrot, Michelle. 1974. *Les ouvriers en grève, 1871–1890.* 2 vols. Paris: Mouton. Translated as *Workers on Strike, 1871–1890.* Trans. Chris Turner. 1 vol. New Haven, Yale University Press, 1987.

——. 1978a. "De la nourrice à l'employée: Travaux de femmes dans la France du XIXe siècle." *Le Mouvement Social* 105:3–10.

——. 1978b. "Le témoignage de Lucie Baud." *Le Mouvement Social* 105:139–46.

——. 1986. "On the Formation of the French Working-Class." In *Working-Class Formation: Nineteenth Century Patterns in Western Europe and the United States*, ed. Ira Katznelson and Aristide Zolberg, 71–110. Princeton: Princeton University Press.

——. 1987. "Qu'est-ce qu'un métier de femme?" *Le Mouvement Social* 140:3–8.

——. 1998. *Les femmes ou les silences de l'histoire*. Paris: Flammarion.

Perrot, Philippe. 1981. *Les dessus et les dessous de la bourgeoisie. Une histoire du vêtement au XIXe siècle*. Paris: Librairie Fayard.

Petit, F. et al. 1985. *Au fils du temps*. Paris: Editions Laffont.

Peudon, Jean-Louis. 1962. "La vie ouvrière à Troyes de 1815 à 1848." Diplôme d'études supérieures d'histoire, Troyes. Microfiche.

Phillips, Ann, and Barbara Taylor. 1980. "Sex and Skill: Notes Towards a Feminist Economics." *Feminist Review* 6:79–88.

Pickering, Paul. 1986. "Class Without Words: Symbolic Communication in the Chartist Movement." *Past and Present* 112:144–62.

Planté, Christine, Michelle Riot-Sarcey, and Eleni Varikas. 1988. *Le genre de l'histoire*. Cahiers du GRIF, no. 37/38. Paris: Editions Tierce.

Poisat, Jacques. 1982a. *Les origines de la bonneterie en France et dans le Roannais*. Roanne: Groupe de Recherches Archéologiques et Historiques du Roannais.

——. 1982b. "Les qualifications ouvrières dans l'industrie de la bonneterie à Roanne." Thèse de doctorat de 3e cycle en sciences économiques, University of Lyon II.

Prost, Antoine. 1964. *La CGT à l'époque du Front Populaire, 1934–1939*. Paris: Armand Colin.

Rabier, Jean-Claude. 1987. *Travail et travailleurs dans l'industrie textile*. Paris: CNRS-GRECO 55.

Rancière, Jacques. 1981. *La nuit des prolétaires*. Paris: Fayard.

——. 1986. "The Myth of the Artisan: Critical Reflections on a Category of Social History." In *Work in France: Representations, Meaning, Organization, and Practice*, ed. Steven Kaplan and Cynthia Koepp, 317–34. Ithaca: Cornell University Press.

Rancière, Jacques, and Pierre Vaudray. 1975. "L'ouvrier, sa femme et les machines." *Les Révoltes Logiques* 1.

Reddy, William. 1976. "Decoding Wage Demands: The Tariff in the Linen Mills of Armentières (1889–1904)." September. Mimeo.

——. 1977. "The Textile Trade and the Language of the Crowd at Rouen, 1752–1871." *Past and Present* 74:62–89.

——. 1984. *The Rise of Market Culture: The Textile Trade and French Society*. Cambridge: Cambridge University Press.

——. 1986. "The Moral Sense of Farce: The Patois Literature of Lille Factory Laborers, 1848–70." In *Work in France: Representations, Meaning, Organization, and Practice*, ed. Steven Kaplan and Cynthia Koepp, 364–94. Ithaca: Cornell University Press.

Reid, Donald. 1991. *Paris Sewers and Sewermen: Realities and Representations*. Cambridge: Harvard University Press.

——. 1992. "Metaphor and Management: The Paternal in *Germinal* and *Travail*." *French Historical Studies* 17 (Fall): 979–1000.

——. 1993. "Reflections on Labor History and Language." In *Rethinking Labor History,* ed. Lenard Berlanstein, 39–54. Urbana: University of Illinois Press.

Reynolds, Siân. 1984. "Allemane avant l'allemanisme: Jeunesse d'un militant (1843–1880)." *Le Mouvement Social* (January): 3–28.

——. 1989. "Women, Men, and the 1936 Strikes in France." In *The French and Spanish Popular Fronts: Comparative Perspectives,* ed. Martin Alexander and Helen Graham. Cambridge: Cambridge University Press.

——. 1996. *France Between the Wars: Gender and Politics.* London: Routledge.

Rhein, Catherine. 1977. "Jeunes femmes au travail dans le Paris de l'entre-deux-guerres." Doctorat de 3e cycle, Université de Paris 7.

Riot-Sarcey, Michèle. 1998. *Le réel de l'utopie.* Paris: Albin Michel.

Riot-Sarcey, Michèle, et al. 2002. *Dictionnaire des utopies.* Paris: Larousse.

Rioux, Jean Pierre. 1971. *La révolution industrielle, 1780–1880.* Paris: Seuil.

Robert, Hélène. 1980. "Le machinisme et le travail féminin au XIXe siècle." Thèse de doctorat de 3e cycle, University of Paris 1.

Roberts, Mary Louise. 1993. "Samson and Delilah Revisited: The Politics of Women's Fashions in 1920s France." *American Historical Review* 98 (June): 657–84.

——. 1994. *Civilization Without Sexes: Reconstructing Gender in Postwar France, 1917–1927.* Chicago: University of Chicago Press.

——. 1998. "Review Essay: Gender, Consumption, and Commodity Culture." *American Historical Review* 103 (June): 817–44.

Roberts, Penny. 1996. *A City in Conflict: Troyes During the French Wars of Religion.* Manchester: Manchester University Press.

Roche, Daniel. 1987. *The People of Paris.* London: Berg.

——. 1994. *The Culture of Clothing: Dress and Fashion in the Ancien Regime.* Cambridge: Cambridge University Press.

——. 1997. *Histoire des choses banales: Naissance de la consommation dans les sociétés traditionnelles (XVIIe–XIXe siècles).* Paris: Fayard.

Roche, Michel. 1985. *La vie dans l'Aube pendant la guerre de 1914–1918.* Troyes: C.D.D.P.

Rochefort, Florence. 1998. "A propos de la libre-disposition du salaire de la femme mariée: Les ambiguités d'une loi (1907)" *Clio* 7:177–90.

Rodriguez, Michel. 1990. *Le 1er Mai.* Paris: Gallimard.

Rogerat, Chantal. 1995. "Femmes et syndicalistes, assimilation ou intégration? La dynamique du compromis." In *La liberté du travail,* ed. Pierre Cours-Salies, 165–82. Paris: Editions Syllepse.

Rose, Sonya. 1987. "Gender Segregation in the Transition to the Factory: The English Hosiery Industry, 1850–1910." *Feminist Studies* 13:163–84.

——. 1992. *Limited Livelihoods: Gender and Class in Nineteenth Century England.* Berkeley and Los Angeles: University of California Press.

——. 1997. "Class Formation and the Quintessential Worker." In *Reworking Class,* ed. John Hall, 133–66. Ithaca: Cornell University Press.

Rossel, André. 1977. *Le premier 1er Mai.* Paris: Editions de la Courtille.

Royer, Jean-Michel, ed. 1978. *Le livre d'or de l'Assiette au beurre.* Vol. 2, *1906–1912.* Paris: Jean-Claude Simoen.

Rule, John. 1987. "The Property of Skill in the Period of Manufacture." In *The Historical Meanings of Work,* ed. Patrick Joyce. Cambridge: Cambridge University Press.

Sabel, Charles, and Jonathan Zeitlin. 1985. "Historical Alternatives to Mass Production: Politics, Markets, and Technology in Nineteeth Century Industrialisation." *Past and Present* 108 (August): 133–76.

———, eds. 1997. *World of Possibilities: Flexibility and Mass Production in Western Industrialization*. Cambridge: Cambridge University Press.

Salais, Robert, et al. 1986. *L'invention du chômage*. Paris: Presses Universitaires de France.

Samuels, Raphael. 1994. "The Eye of History." In *Theatres of Memory*. London: Verso.

Sauvy, Alfred, ed. 1965–75. *Histoire économique et sociale de la France entre les deux guerres*. 4 vols. Paris: Fayard.

Schama, Simon. 1988. *An Embarrassment of Riches*. Berkeley and Los Angeles: University of California Press.

Scholliers, Peter. 1999. "The Social-Democratic World of Consumption: The Path-Breaking Case of the Ghent Cooperative Vooruit Prior to 1914." *International Labor and Working-Class History* 55 (Spring): 71–91.

Schwartz, Vanessa. 2001. "Walter Benjamin for Historians." *American Historical Review* 106 (December): 1721–43.

Schwartz, Yves. 1979. "Pratiques paternalistes et travail industriel à Mulhouse aux XIXe siècle." *Technologies, Idéologies, Pratiques* (October): 9–77.

Scott, Joan. 1974. *The Glassworkers of Carmaux*. Cambridge: Harvard University Press.

———. 1988. *Gender and the Politics of History*. New York: Columbia University Press.

———. 1999. "Some More Reflections on Gender and Politics." In *Gender and the Politics of History*, 199–222. 2d ed. New York: Columbia University Press.

Segalen, Martine. 1982. "Du village à la ville: La Fête de la Rosière à Nanterre." *Ethnologie Française* (April–June): 185–94.

Sewell, William. 1980. *Work and Revolution in France: The Language of Labor from the Old Regime to 1848*. Cambridge: Cambridge University Press.

———. 1986a. "Artisans, Factory Workers, and the Formation of the French Working Class, 1789–1848." In *Working-Class Formation: Nineteenth Century Patterns in Western Europe and the United States,* ed. Ira Katznelson and Aristide Zolberg. Princeton: Princeton University Press.

———. 1986b. "Visions of Labor: Illustrations of the Mechanical Arts Before, in, and After Diderot's *Encyclopédie*." In *Work in France: Representations, Meaning, Organization, and Practice,* ed. Steven Kaplan and Cynthia Koepp, 258–86. Ithaca: Cornell University Press.

———. 1999. "The Concept(s) of Culture." In *Beyond the Cultural Turn,* ed. Victoria Bonnell and Lynn Hunt, 35–61. Berkeley and Los Angeles: University of California Press.

Smith, Bonnie G. 1981. *Ladies of the Leisure Class*. Princeton: Princeton University Press.

Soucy, Robert. 1995. *French Fascism: The Second Wave, 1933–1939*. New Haven: Yale University Press.

Sowerwine, Charles. 1982. *Sisters or Citizens? Women and Socialism in France Since 1876*. Cambridge: Cambridge University Press.

Stearns, Peter. 1971. *Revolutionary Syndicalism and French Labor: A Cause Without Rebels*. New Brunswick: Rutgers University Press.

———. 1997. "Stages of Consumerism: Recent Work on the Issues of Periodization." *Journal of Modern History* 69:102–17.

Steedman, Carolyn. 1987. *Landscape for a Good Woman*. New Brunswick: Rutgers University Press.

Stewart, Mary Lynn. 1989. *Women, Work, and the French State: Labour Protection and Social Patriarchy, 1879–1919*. Kingston: McGill-Queen's University Press.

Stuart, Robert. 1992. *Marxism at Work: Ideology, Class, and French Socialism During the Third Republic*. Cambridge: Cambridge University Press.

———. 1996. "'Calm, with a Grave and Serious Temperament, Rather Male': French Marxism, Gender, and Feminism, 1882–1905." *International Review of Social History* 41:57–82.

———. 1997a. "Gendered Labour in the Ideological Discourse of French Marxism: The Parti Ouvrier Français, 1882–1905." *Gender and History* 9 (April): 107–29.

———. 1997b. "Whores and Angels: Women and the Family in the Discourse of French Marxism, 1882–1905." *European History Quarterly* 3 (July): 339–69.

Tabet, Paola. 1979. "Les mains, les outils, les armes." *L'Homme* 19 (July–December): 5–62.

———. 1985. "Fertilité naturelle, reproduction forcée." In *L'arraisonnement des femmes: Essais en anthropologie des sexes*, ed. Nicole Mathieu. Paris: Cahiers de l'Homme, EHESS.

Thébaud, Françoise. 1986. *La femme au temps de la guerre de 14*. Paris: Stock.

———. 1998. *Ecrire l'histoire des femmes*. Fontenay/SaintCloud: ENS Editions.

Thibert, Marguerite. 1933. "Crise économique et travail féminin." *Revue International du Travail* 27 (April): 465–93 and (May): 647–57.

Thompson, Edward P. 1968. *The Making of the English Working Class*. London: Penguin.

———. 1967. "Time, Work Discipline, and Industrial Capitalism." *Past and Present* 38 (December): 56–97.

Thompson, Paul. 1983. *The Nature of Work*. London: Macmillan.

Tiersten, Lisa. 2001. *Marianne in the Market: Envisioning Consumer Society in Fin-de-Siècle France*. Berkeley and Los Angeles: University of California Press.

Trempé, Rolande. 1976. "Pour une meilleure connaissance de la classe ouvrière. L'utilisation des archives d'entreprise: Le fichier du personnel." In *Mélanges d'histoire sociale offert à Jean Maîtron*. Paris: Les Editions Ouvrières.

Turner, Patricia R. 1999. "Hostile Participants? Working-Class Militancy, Associational Life, and the 'Distinctiveness' of the Prewar French Labor Movement." *Journal of Modern History* 71 (March): 28–51.

Vallerant, Jacques. 1982. "Savoirs-faire et identité sociale." *Ethnologie Française* 12 (April): 223–28.

Vanier, Martin. 1993. *Maille et bonneterie auboises, 1505–1989*. Reims: Editions ORCCA.

Varikas, Eleni. 1988. "L'approche biographique dans l'histoire des femmes." In *Les Cahiers du GRIF*, 41–56. Paris: Editions Tierce.

———. 2005. *Du sexe au genre: Territoire du politique*. Paris: Presses Universitaires de France.

Verley, Patrick. 1997. *La révolution industrielle*. Paris: Gallimard.

Walton, Whitney. 1992. *France at the Crystal Palace: Bourgeois Taste and Artisan Manufacture in the Nineteenth Century*. Berkeley and Los Angeles: University of California Press.

Weitz, Eric. 1996. "The Heroic Man and the Ever-Changing Woman: Gender and Politics in European Communism, 1917–1950." In *Gender and Class in Modern*

Europe, ed. Laura Frader and Sonya Rose, 311–52. Ithaca: Cornell University Press.

Wells, F. A. 1935. *The British Hosiery Trade.* London: George Allen and Unwin.

Willard, Claude. 1965. *Les Guesdistes.* Paris: Editions Sociales.

——. 1991. *Jules Guesde: L'apôtre et la loi.* Paris: Editions Ouvrières.

Williams, Raymond. 1977. *Marxism and Literature.* Oxford: Oxford University Press.

——. 1980. "Advertising: The Magic System." In *Problems in Materialism and Culture,* 170–95. London: Verso.

Williams, Rosalind. 1982. *Dream Worlds: Mass Consumption in Late Nineteenth-Century France.* Berkeley and Los Angeles: University of California Press.

Wolnikow, Serge. 1996. *Le Front Populaire en France.* Paris: Editions Complexe.

Zerner, Sylvie. 1987. "De la couture aux presses: L'emploi féminin entre les deux guerres." *Le Mouvement Social* 140 (July–September): 9–25.

Zeyons, Serge. 1997. *Sorties d'usines en cartes postales.* Paris: Editions Ouvrières.

Zylberberg-Hocquard, Marie-Hélène. 1978. *Féminisme et syndicalisme en France.* Paris: Editions Anthropos.

——. 1981. *Femmes et feminisme dans le mouvement ouvrier.* Paris: Editions ouvrieres.

INDEX